The Colonial Comedy

Imperialism in the French Realist Novel

JENNIFER YEE

OXFORD
UNIVERSITY PRESS

OXFORD
UNIVERSITY PRESS

Great Clarendon Street, Oxford, OX2 6DP,
United Kingdom

Oxford University Press is a department of the University of Oxford.
It furthers the University's objective of excellence in research, scholarship,
and education by publishing worldwide. Oxford is a registered trade mark of
Oxford University Press in the UK and in certain other countries

© Jennifer Yee 2016

The moral rights of the author have been asserted

First Edition published in 2016

Impression: 2

Published in the United States of America by Oxford University Press
198 Madison Avenue, New York, NY 10016, United States of America

British Library Cataloguing in Publication Data
Data available

Library of Congress Control Number: 2015957416

ISBN 978–0–19–872263–2

Printed in Great Britain by
Clays Ltd, St Ives plc

Acknowledgements

The Colonial Comedy has been long in gestation, which has made it possible for me to get feedback on some of my ideas as they emerged through presentations at seminars and conferences. I am grateful to colleagues at the University of Southern California and the University of Cambridge for inviting me to share my work in research seminars (in 2010 and 2011), and to the organizers of the Cambridge graduate conference who invited me to give a keynote paper way back in 2008. Parts of my work in progress were presented at the annual conferences of the Society of Dix-Neuviémistes in Birmingham (2011), Limerick (2012), and Sheffield (2014), the Société internationale d'étude des littératures de l'ère coloniale (SIELEC) in Montpellier (2010), the Society of Francophone Postcolonial Studies in London (2012), and the Nineteenth-Century French Studies conference in Princeton (2015). I am grateful for comments and discussion of papers by Andrew Counter, Jean-François Durand, Tim Farrant, Anne Green, Robert Lethbridge, Francesco Manzini, Bernard Mouralis, Panivong Norindr, Mary Orr, Christopher Prendergast, Jean-Marie Seillan, the late regretted Jean Sévry, Timothy Unwin, and Nicholas White, among others. And I owe special thanks for advice and feedback on various chapters as they were written, to Gabi Duigu, Jane Hiddleston, Timothy Unwin, and Danny Yee, though naturally any errors are my own.

My thanks are also due to the staff of the Taylorian Library, the Bodleian Library, the Bibliothèque de l'Institut, and the Institut des Textes et Manuscrits Modernes (ITEM) for their cheerful help and patience with my odd demands. Also to my student Wanrug Suwanwattana for some invaluable last-minute library assistance. And to Julie Rrap, for her inspiring rethink of Manet's *Olympia*, which has been my desktop while I was working on this book and which she has very kindly given me permission to use as its cover.

I am extremely grateful to the Leverhulme Trust for a one-year research fellowship during which the majority of the work was done. The project was also made possible by sabbatical leave accorded by the University of Oxford and Christ Church, and by my husband's calm presence and sensible attitude to the sharing of childcare and housework: I am thankful for all of these.

Acknowledgements

The Colonial Convent has been long in gestation, which has made it possible for me to get feedback on some of my ideas as they emerged through presentations at seminars and conferences. I am grateful to colleagues at the University of Southern California and the University of Cambridge for inviting me to share my work in research seminars (in 2010 and 2011), and to the organizers of the Cambridge graduate conference who invited me to give a keynote paper way back in 2008. Parts of my work in progress were presented at the annual conferences of the Society of Dix-Neuviémistes in Birmingham (2011), Limerick (2012), and Sheffield (2013), the Société internationale d'étude des littératures de l'ère coloniale (SIELEC) in Montpellier (2010), the Society of Francophone Postcolonial Studies in London (2012), and the Nineteenth-Century French Studies conference in Princeton (2013). I am grateful for comments and discussion of papers by Andrew Counter, Jean-François Durand, Tim Farrant, Anne Green, Robert Lethbridge, Francesco Manzini, Bernard Mouralis, Panivong Norindr, Mary Orr, Christopher Prendergast, Jean-Marie Seillan, the late regretted Jean Sévry, Timothy Unwin, and Nicholas White, among others. And I owe special thanks for advice and feedback on various chapters as they were written, to Gabi Drigu, Jane Hiddleston, Timothy Unwin, and Danny Yee, though naturally any errors are my own.

My thanks are also due to the staff of the Taylorian Library, the Bodleian Library, the Bibliothèque de l'Institut, and the Institut des Textes et Manuscrits Modernes (ITEM) for their cheerful help and patience with my odd demands. Also to my student Warang Suwanwattana for some invaluable last-minute library assistance. And to Julie Reap for her inspiring rethink of Manet's Olympia, which has been my desktop while I was working on this book and which she has very kindly given me permission to use as its cover.

I am extremely grateful to the Leverhulme Trust for a one-year research fellowship during which the majority of the work was done. The project was also made possible by sabbatical leave accorded by the University of Oxford and Christ Church, and by my husband's calm presence and sensible attitude to the sharing of childcare and housework. I am thankful for all of these.

Contents

Introduction

FRENCH COLONIALISM AND THE
NINETEENTH CENTURY

From a French perspective, the nineteenth century began with what seemed to be the ending of an imperial age: the sale of Louisiana by Napoleon in 1803, and the loss of France's most profitable colony, Saint-Domingue (Haiti) in 1804. Despite the conquest of Algeria in the 1830s and 1840s, colonial ideology did not take on a central role in French popular culture until the last decades of the century, under the Third Republic.[1] This goes some way to explaining the apparent absence of colonial issues in the French realist novel, the dominant literary form of the century. There are far fewer direct fictional accounts of the colonial encounter in French than can be found in British literature of the period, and there is no major realist novel set in the French colonies. All of which makes it understandable that there have been no major studies of the relationship between the French realist novel and colonialism. Considerable critical attention has been paid to Orientalism or exoticism, but less to colonialism or imperialism per se, especially in relation to Realism.

It would however be a mistake to see nineteenth-century French culture as entirely divorced from imperialism until the 1880s. Such a view depends on the idea that there is a clear-cut separation of French imperialism into two periods, the 'Old' Empire of the *ancien régime* and the 'New' Empire, mainly built up under the Third Republic. The heyday of French literary Realism falls into what was once considered the gap between the two empires. Now while it is true that French imperialism in the period lacked a pervasive and coherent ideology, in fact its presence in French culture is felt in multiple ways. France still had some of the remains of its earlier colonial empire, albeit much reduced; French culture was marked by the loss of other colonies; Napoleon's abortive Egyptian invasion of 1798 had a disproportionate influence on the century as a whole; French colonies in the West Indies depended on slave labour until 1848; and of course the *prise d'Alger* in 1830, and the ongoing conquest of Algeria in the 1840s, initiated—almost behind the backs of the general public—the era of modern imperial conquest. The last two decades of the century saw the consolidation and geographical expansion of this imperialism, and as will become clear there are strong grounds

---

[1] According to Raoul Girardet colonial culture played a significant role in French popular culture only from the 1880s, with a peak in the 1930s (see *L'Idée coloniale en France de 1871 à 1962* (Paris: La Table ronde, 1972)).

for understanding much of the prose fiction of the earlier period, too, in relation to imperialism.

The influence of France's overseas territories was felt in domains as varied as scientific advances, popular fashions, architecture, colonial foodstuffs, and travel writing. They also offered penal colonies to which the losers in France's political upheavals were sent, and career prospects for younger sons, disinherited aristocrats, and adventurers of all kinds. Still, there was no coherent imperialist discourse in France comparable to the mid-century consensus in Britain. As Edward Said puts it, 'empire had a less secure identity and presence in French culture' than the British empire did in contemporary British culture.[2] This does *not*, however, mean that responses to France's colonial enterprises, its economic imperialism, and the long inheritance of its slave-trading past, are absent from the nineteenth-century French novel. It *does* mean that such responses are often oblique or discordant, that they do not refer to something that can be taken for granted, and that there is no consensual culture of empire.

In a now classic study, Fredric Jameson suggested that we take the Berlin Conference of 1884 as the 'emblematic' point at which the new imperialist world-system was codified; this choice of date allows him to link it seamlessly to his discussion of the birth of Modernism. And yet he explicitly takes imperialism to mean 'the imperialist dynamic of capitalism proper, and not the wars of conquest of the various ancient empires'.[3] I follow him in considering that it is far more urgent now to focus on imperialism, including economic imperialism, rather than on colonialism per se. Unlike Jameson, however, I would argue that one of the results of this broader angle of definition is that imperialism must be seen as playing an important role much earlier in the century. It is necessary now to define what I mean by 'colonialism' and 'imperialism', a task that is more problematic than one might think, although in practice the terms are often used interchangeably in literary studies.

In the French context the term 'imperialism' refers most obviously to the Bonapartist First or Second Empires, and as Robert Young points out it was used by the British as a derogatory reference to the French Second Empire under Napoleon III.[4] Since then, 'imperialism' has been used by Marxist-inspired critics, following Lenin, to refer to an international system of production and consumption,

---

[2] Edward Said, *Culture and Imperialism* (London: Chatto and Windus, 1993), p. 74; he later adds that 'the French imperial consciousness is intermittent until the late nineteenth century, the actuality too impinged on by England, too lagging in system, profit, extent' (p. 91).

[3] 'Modernism and Imperialism', in *Nationalism, Colonialism and Literature: A Field Day Pamphlet*, 14 (Derry: Field Day Theatre Co., 1988), pp. 5–23 (p. 6, p. 8). For a discussion of Said and Jameson's adoption of different dates for the origin of modern imperialism, see Laura Chrisman, *Postcolonial Contraventions: Cultural Readings of Race, Imperialism and Transnationalism* (Manchester: Manchester University Press, 2003), p. 54.

[4] Robert Young, *Postcolonialism: An Historical Introduction* (Oxford: Blackwell, 2001) p. 29. Young distinguishes between 'imperialism' and 'colonialism' by emphasizing central governmental control in the former, and settlement founded by individual communities or trading companies in the latter; 'imperialism' is ideologically driven, 'colonialism' more pragmatic. In the case of French expansion after around 1880, however, only 'imperialism' would seem to apply if we adopt this definition. Once it did get up and running, French imperialism was relatively systematic, and its operations tended to be more centralized than those of British imperialism (see ibid., p. 16 and p. 18).

or capitalist colonialism, as distinct from colonialism in a pre-capitalist phase. As such, it can usefully be related to the emergence of a new global system, or 'capitalism's accelerated penetration of the non-capitalist zones'.[5] The present study will examine not only colonialism (taken to mean direct political control and/or settlement of a foreign territory) but also imperialism in the broad sense, which is taken to include the extension of influence by economic or political means.[6] Such imperialism is often 'proto-colonialist' (for example private financial interests preparing the way for outright political intervention), which I use as a pendant to a term that has entered general usage, 'neocolonialist' (control exercised through economic or otherwise indirect means by ex-colonial powers). Any account of European imperialism that focused exclusively on settler colonies would be in danger of lulling the twenty-first-century reader into a false sense that these concerns belong to the past, whereas neocolonialism, or the continuation of colonial dependency through indirect means, generally economic, is on the contrary very much with us today.[7] Moreover, if studies of the nineteenth-century French novel have tended to suggest that it largely ignored imperialism, it is because the latter was too narrowly defined. Critics influenced by Fredric Jameson have argued that 'the crucial issue is less the lack of mimetic depiction of imperial atrocity in terms of novelistic content than whether European realism could ever intellectually grasp the totality of capitalist social relations without intellectually addressing imperialism in both its domestic and geographically distant manifestations.'[8] The idea of a novelistic blind spot must however be nuanced: imperialism is in fact reflected in the nineteenth-century novel, though not always in direct focus.

French literature of the period prior to the 1880s is marked by imperialism as well as by colonialism proper, and in particular by the proto-colonialist expansion of trading networks, as well as the legacy of the slave trade. Imperialism in this sense will also lead us to include the 'question d'Orient' or 'Eastern Question', in other words the dilemma faced by European statecraft throughout the long nineteenth century: how to divide up the territories of the declining Ottoman empire without triggering a war between the Great Powers of Europe.[9] I shall nevertheless sometimes use only one of the terms 'colonial' or 'imperial' as a shorthand where both would apply, and indeed the borderline between the two is not always clear-cut.[10]

---

[5] Benita Parry, *Postcolonial Studies: A Materialist Critique* (London/New York: Routledge, 2004), p. 108; see also Ania Loomba, *Colonialism/Postcolonialism* (London/New York: Routledge, 2005 [1998]), pp. 10–11; Chrisman, *Postcolonial Contraventions*, p. 52.

[6] It is to avoid the ambiguity of the term 'imperial' in the French context, and not only for the sake of alliteration, that the title of this book refers to the 'Colonial Comedy' rather than the 'Imperial Comedy'.

[7] On neocolonialism see Young, *Postcolonialism*, p. 42, pp. 44–56, and on the introduction of the term by the Ghanaian leader Kwame Nkrumah in 1965, p. 46.

[8] Joe Cleary, 'Realism after Modernism and the Literary World-System', in *Modern Language Quarterly*, Prologue to the special issue 'Peripheral Realisms', 73:3 (2012), 255–68 (p. 259).

[9] The Eastern Question, in the form of frustrated Serbian nationalism, was of course to provide the trigger for the First World War. See *Turkey: A Modern History*, Erik J. Zürcher (London/NY: I.B. Tauris, 1993), p. 40.

[10] Although I shall be using the term 'imperialism' rather than 'globalization', it is useful to keep in mind recent discussions of a 'global approach to literary history', for example by Christie McDonald and Susan Rubin Suleiman, who call for '[t]he sense of a globe that is interconnected, of cultural

Back in 1993 Edward Said remarked that 'the extraordinary formal and ideological dependence of the great French and English realist novels on the facts of empire
has [...] never been studied from a general theoretical standpoint'.[11] In fact, since
the publication of his paradigm-shifting *Orientalism* in 1978, there have been
many studies examining colonialism in the Victorian novel,[12] or slavery (and to a
lesser extent colonialism) in British Romantic literature.[13] The critical field is not
as rich when we turn to colonialism in nineteenth-century French literature,
though there have been signs of new interest.[14] Early approaches to colonial discourse, in the aftermath of decolonization, tended to be limited to a critique of
'images of empire' that judged literary depictions either by the degree of explicit
anticolonial sentiment that they expressed or by their documentary 'truth' value.[15]
The ideologically motivated, thematic, and descriptive approach taken by the early
studies of colonial discourse tended to sideline issues of form and genre. More
recently, Benita Parry, while calling for a materialist approach to postcolonial theory, nevertheless regrets the fact that criticism pays 'scant attention to the asym-
metrical relationships between the social and the literary, shows little suspicion
about the craft of representation and is largely confined to the observation of tropological transpositions.'[16] Laura Chrisman, in a similar vein, argues that there is
an unfortunate tendency to read imperial discourses in a reductive way; she calls
for 'a shift away from a focus on "images/allegories/tropes" of Others to an analysis
of narrative structures and processes, attending to the diverse, overdetermined, and
contradictory formal dynamics and ideological codes which produce certain forms
of Othering but which are not reducible to it'.[17] According to Eli Park Sorenson,

differences within and beyond the nation' (*French Global: A New Approach to Literary History* (New
York: Columbia University Press, 2010), Introduction, p. x).

[11] *Culture and Imperialism*, p. 40.

[12] See for example work by Patrick Brantlinger (notably *Rule of Darkness: British Literature and
Imperialism, 1830–1914* (Ithaca, NY: Cornell University Press, 1988)), and Susan Meyer (*Imperialism
at Home: Race and Victorian Women's Fiction* (Ithaca, NY: Cornell University Press, 1996)).

[13] See for example Michael J. Franklin, ed., *Romantic Representations of British India* (London:
Routledge, 2006); Tim Fulford and Peter J. Kitson, eds, *Romanticism and Colonialism: Writing and
Empire, 1780–1830* (Cambridge, Cambridge University Press, 1998); Nigel Leask, *British Romantic
Writers and the East: Anxieties of Empire* (Cambridge: Cambridge University Press, 1992); and Saree
Makdisi, *Romantic Imperialism: Universal Empire and the Culture of Modernity* (Cambridge: Cambridge
University Press, 1998).

[14] See for example Pratima Prasad, *Colonialism, Race, and the French Romantic Imagination*
(London/New York: Routledge, 2009) and Geoffrey Baker, *Realism's Empire: Empiricism and
Enchantment in the Nineteenth-Century Novel* (Columbus, OH: Ohio State University Press, 2009).
Further references will be given as this study progresses.

[15] The 1950s–70s saw publications of this kind that gave useful, if rather descriptive, overviews of
the terrain. In France such studies did not always foreground colonialism per se, for example the
important contributions by Léon-François Hoffmann (*Le Nègre romantique* (Paris: Payot, 1973)) and
Pierre Citron ('Le Rêve asiatique de Balzac', *L'Année balzacienne* (1968), 303–36). More specifically
focused on colonialism was a study by Martine Astier Loutfi, which remains invaluable: *Littérature et
colonialisme: l'expansion coloniale vue dans la littérature romanesque française 1871–1914* (Paris/La
Haye: Mouton, 1971). Colonial literature was also studied by critics of the colonial era, with a clearly
pro-colonial agenda; some of these works will be referred to later.

[16] Parry, *Postcolonial Studies*, p. 109.

[17] Laura Chrisman, 'The Imperial Unconscious? Representations of Imperial Discourse', *Critical
Quarterly*, 32: 3 (1990), 38–58 (p. 40).

postcolonial studies is now beginning to 'return to a focus on literariness and literary form', though he discusses in some detail the resistance to this approach within what is sometimes a prescriptive and dogmatic discipline.[18] *The Colonial Comedy* aims to situate the realist novel in the context of France's varied imperial engagements, ongoing and abortive, but also to renew our understanding of the permutations of the genre itself.

COLONIALISM AND THE RISE OF THE NOVEL

Before postcolonial theory made its mark, accounts of the birth of the modern novel tended to explain it by invoking the rise of capitalism or of the middle classes, which entailed the growth of individualism and the reading public.[19] The role played by extra-European expansionism was relatively peripheral in such accounts because capitalism was treated in a narrow national frame. Since then, however, the emergence of the novel has been linked to the rise of nationalism, and indeed to the moment when national identity came to be defined in terms of race.[20] Postcolonial critics, following Said, have claimed that imperialism itself is integral to the origins of the novel. Said himself memorably asserted that 'the novel, as a cultural artefact of bourgeois society, and imperialism are unthinkable without each other' and 'imperialism and the novel fortified each other to such a degree that it is impossible, I would argue, to read one without in some way dealing with the other'.[21]

Narrower approaches to the early English novel distinguished it from the 'romance'—which tends to be set 'in a remote and exotic location'—precisely because it is set in a place familiar to the author and reader[22] (in French, of course, the word *roman* covers both 'romance' and 'novel', incorporating these generic tensions). And yet these same accounts often see the modern English novel as originating with Daniel Defoe's *Robinson Crusoe* (1719) despite the fact that its geographical setting seemed (back in the 1980s) 'like the wrong locus—the

---

[18] Eli Park Sorenson, *Postcolonial Studies and the Literary: Theory, Interpretation and the Novel* (Basingstoke/New York: Palgrave Macmillan, 2010), pp. x–xi, pp. 4–5.

[19] See for example Ian Watt, *The Rise of the Novel: Studies in Defoe, Richardson and Fielding* (London: Pimlico, 2000 [1957]); F.W.J. Hemmings, *The Age of Realism* (Penguin, 1974), p. 16. For Fredric Jameson it is Realism (rather than the novel more generally) that is inseparable from the rise of capitalism (*The Ideologies of Theory* (London: Verso, 2008), p. 422).

[20] See Benedict Anderson (*Imagined Communities: Reflections on the Origin and Spread of Nationalism* (London/New York: Verso, 1991 [1983]). Laura Doyle claims that race is not simply a metaphor for class difference in the novel, but its conceptual basis: the rise of the English-language novel is inseparable from the new 'racialized' conception of history that emerged from 1640 onwards in England, a conception in which the superiority of whiteness is grounded in a capacity for freedom and mastery (*Freedom's Empire: Race and the Rise of the Novel in Atlantic Modernity, 1640–1940* (Durham/London: Duke University Press, 2008)).

[21] *Culture and Imperialism*, p. 84.

[22] Lennard J. Davis, *Factual Fictions: the Origins of the English Novel* (New York: Columbia University Press, 1983), p. 40. He sees the English novel as emerging more or less in a vacuum 'relatively unaffected by continental influence and interchanges', p. 43.

exquisitely wrong place—to begin a consideration of the origins of the novel'.[23]
F.W.J. Hemmings also considered *Robinson Crusoe* to be 'the fountainhead of the
English realist novel', which was about metropolitan capitalism and the growth of
middle-class aspirations; and this despite the fact that he saw a contemporary metropolitan setting as 'one basic requirement of a realist novel'. Following Ian Watt's
lead, Hemmings managed this sleight of hand by emphasizing that *Robinson Crusoe*
'bears only a superficial resemblance to the traditional travel-yarn, since it is not
out of desire for adventure but in the hope of a fat profit that Crusoe takes ship',
and by seeing it instead as 'an extended metaphor translating the situation of the
lower middle classes at the start of their slow rise to prominence'.[24] It seems a little
hasty to dismiss the 'foreignness' of *Robinson Crusoe* as mere metaphor (and I shall
discuss the relative limitations of metaphorical readings below). I am not, however,
dismissing the view that the rise of the modern novel is a response to capitalism
and the emergence of the middle classes. Said argues that '[t]he colonial territories
are realms of possibility, and they have always been associated with the realist
novel. *Robinson Crusoe* is virtually unthinkable without the colonizing mission.'[25]
One can, however, turn this the other way: the colonial territory is unthinkable
without metropolitan capitalism, and the distant setting of Defoe's exotic island
does not remove the novel from the world-system.

    Defoe's island is the stage for a meeting of two time schemes: the stasis of an
apparently timeless past encounters the forward movement of modernity, which is
understood in terms of striving and accumulation. In contrast, the realist writing
of the following century tends to situate modernity in the changing landscapes and
cityscapes of metropolitan industrialization. And yet both cases reflect Europe's
self-definition in terms of its own modernity and movement, and a view of history
in which non-European cultures are relegated to the past in what Johannes Fabian
has called a 'denial of coevalness'.[26] *Robinson Crusoe* marks the realist novel, from
the outset, as addressing capitalism in its global implications as a new world-system
that produces combined and uneven development.[27] Later exotic and colonial
novels take as their subject the point of meeting between cultures, the very point
at which a non-industrial culture becomes part of the new system of unequal capitalist modernity. Writers enamoured of the exotic project of maintaining cultural
difference bemoan the arrival in the colonies of industrial culture and European
bourgeois pretention, as embodied in manufactured objects imported from

---

[23] Davis, *Factual Fictions*, p. 155. He sees the geographical setting of *Robinson Crusoe* as a mere
accident.

[24] Hemmings, *The Age of Realism*, pp. 15–16. See also Watt, *Rise of the Novel*, p. 67.

[25] Said, *Culture and Imperialism*, p. 75; see also p. 82, p. 84.

[26] Johannes Fabian, *Time and the Other: How Anthropology makes its Object* (New York: Columbia
University Press, 2002 [1983]). For Europe's self-definition as modernity, see also Thierry Hentsch,
L'Orient imaginaire: La vision politique occidentale de l'Est méditerranéen (Paris: Éditions de minuit,
1988).

[27] Recent work on world literature (or world-literature, as they prefer to call it) by the WReC
collective calls for a focus on the cultural repercussions of Trotsky's formulation of combined and
uneven development. See WReC, Warwick Research Collective, *Combined and Uneven Development:
Towards a New Theory of World-Literature* (Liverpool: Liverpool University Press, 2015). The full effect
of this 'worlding' is truly felt only from the long nineteenth century onwards (see p. 15).

Europe. Symmetrically, in metropolitan culture itself, the tension between pre-industrial culture and the industrialized metropolis is pinpointed through metonymy in the form of objects or goods that are imported from the colonies.[28] Modernity defines itself in relation to this encounter, that is, the simultaneous presence of capitalism and non-capitalist social structures.

Said, in linking the novel to the rise of European imperialism, set a trend towards ideological condemnation that takes as its target less the novel as a whole than the form it took in the nineteenth century. As Parry puts it, Said saw 'overseas empire as engraved in the very entrails of the nineteenth- and early twentieth-century realist novel *form*', and she quotes his assertion that 'conventional narrative is...central to imperialism's appropriative and dominative attitudes. Narrative itself is the representation of power, and its teleology is associated with the global role of the West.'[29] There is a certain danger here that 'narrative' might be seen as a purely Western phenomenon, which would of course be a preposterous assertion; what is meant is more specifically the narrative traditions of the nineteenth-century novel, and it is precisely those traditions with which the present study will engage. (I shall return to the contrast of nineteenth-century 'conventional narrative' with modernist form in the conclusion of this volume.)

Following Said's *Orientalism*, and in the same year as *Culture and Imperialism*, Firdous Azim spelt out that the 'birth of the novel' coincides 'with the European colonial project': its focus on one central subject makes it 'concerned with the construction of a universal and homogeneous subject' whose very existence depends on 'the annihilation of other subject-positions'. This view of the novel as hegemonic and monological arises from the idea that 'the realistic school' gives its readers 'the easy narrative of growth that capitalist ideology would have liked to provide for its subjects'.[30] This demonization of the realist novel has had reinforcement from recent attempts to defend eighteenth-century literature from accusations of proto-imperialist ideology. Srinivas Aravamudan, notably, has argued that Enlightenment Orientalism is less to blame than the nineteenth-century 'domestic realism' that followed it: only the latter is guilty of racism and '"Saidian" Orientalism'. In Aravamudan's lively account of the rise of the novel, nationalist 'domestic realism' does 'battle with various kinds of romance', among them tales of the long ago and the faraway. Rather more reductively, in order to stress the diversity and internal ambiguities of eighteenth-century Orientalism, he projects a monolithic vision of 'a nineteenth-century imperial machine and its neocolonial successors' in which 'images and ideas of the Orient' were easily 'functionalized as part of a homogeneous discourse with a singular politics'.[31] *The Colonial Comedy* argues that in the case of the French nineteenth-century realist novel this idea of a

---

[28] Here, and throughout this study, I shall be using the terms 'metropolis' and 'metropolitan' to refer to European countries' geographical basis in Europe itself, in contrast to their colonial territories, not to indicate the contrast of urban space and countryside.

[29] Parry, *Postcolonial Studies*, p. 116.

[30] Firdous Azim, *The Colonial Rise of the Novel* (London/New York: Routledge, 1993), p. 30, p. 27.

[31] Srinivas Aravamudan, *Enlightenment Orientalism: Resisting the Rise of the Novel* (Chicago: Chicago University Press, 2011), p. 3, p. 6, p. 10.

'homogeneous discourse' is particularly hard to defend. Aravamudan does, in fact, go on to ask whether it might be possible to develop a 'theory of realism [...] founded on the pursuit of dissimilitudes rather than the recognition of same-ness?'[32] And there is much food for thought in his arguments. Notably, the idea of a generic battle between the oriental tale and the metropolitan novel is a fruitful one. I would however argue that the battle waged by the new 'domestic realism' often seeks less to overcome than to *incorporate* other genres. They are incorporated as examples of bad writing and bad reading, but also as examples of bad Orientalism, as we shall see in Chapter 4.

One of the aims of the present study is to show that French novels in the realist mode did *not*, in general, presuppose a straightforward narrative of economic and technical progress or of easy and desirable colonial expansion, although such narra-tives are indeed apparent in some works. Said himself introduces a note of caution when he says that 'most of the great nineteenth-century realistic novelists are less assertive about colonial rule and possessions'.[33] *The Colonial Comedy* examines the hesitations, as well as the assumptions, of the realist novel. Moreover, French Realism is in fact remarkable for its sidelining of imperialism rather than for its close relation-ship with it. In Dorian Bell's striking terms, in relation to the 'cartographic precision' of Balzac's *Comédie humaine* the colonial space is like a 'phantom limb'.[34] French imperialism is apparent in what might be called its *present absence*, rather than through direct portrayal within the 'domestic realist' novel. What *The Colonial Comedy* pro-poses to study are sub-texts, spaces offstage, objects imported from the colonies, mar-ginalized immigrants, and racial perspectives imported from colonial anthropology. Despite the relative marginality of imperialism, the French realist novel does return, again and again, to the encounter between capitalist and pre-capitalist societies, and close reading of colonial sub-texts can contribute to the 'worlding' of even those canonical texts that seem to present the narrowest geographical range.[35]

WHAT DO WE MEAN BY 'REALISM'?

The elusive nature of the colonial subtext in the realist novel can to a large extent be explained by the constraints of the realist mode itself, so it is necessary to explain what that mode is. The term 'Realism' generated intense debates in mid-nineteenth-century France, and has continued to do so. Recently arguments have been made for a return to Realism, or rather for an acknowledgement that Realisms of various kinds never ceased to play an important role in literatures of contestation.[36] Even setting aside philosophical Realism, however, definitions of

---

[32] *Enlightenment Orientalism*, p. 21.   [33] *Culture and Imperialism*, p. 76.
[34] Dorian Bell, 'Balzac's Algeria: Realism and the Colonial', *Nineteenth-Century French Studies*, 40:1–2 (2011–12), 35–56 (p. 35).
[35] WReC gives the name 'world-literature' to literature that registers the human experience of capitalist modernity (*Combined and Uneven Development*).
[36] Claims concerning a 'new realist turn' are articulated in a very useful overview article by Jed Esty and Colleen Lye ('Peripheral Realisms Now', *Modern Language Quarterly*, 73:3 (2012), 269–88 (p. 276)). Their argument, however, concerns

literary Realism are so problematic that only pity for my reader has prevented me from putting the word in scare quotes throughout this volume. Literary Realism could be understood, at one extreme, as an (impossible) aspiration or philosophical position, that is, the belief that one can represent 'the real' directly and in a transparent way through writing. At the other extreme Realism could be seen as a common trait of any writing, which must necessarily reflect the real to some extent, except insofar as it tends towards the non-figurative qualities of music. Between these two extremes, the realist mode might be understood as writing that gives a certain priority to mimesis or the referential function. A literary-historical approach would lead us to see Realism in much narrower terms, as a specific sub-genre of the novel, flourishing in France in the nineteenth century, which has its roots in English writing of the previous century. Although *The Colonial Comedy* focuses on that period, what I am calling the realist *mode* is something that is both more diffuse and more long-lasting. It can usefully be identified not through a philosophical definition, but more pragmatically through a series of recurrent characteristics—not all of which are present at all times in a given work—of which I shall give a rapid overview now.

One of the driving forces behind the realist mode is the rejection of idealism in favour of materialism: it emphasizes materialist causality and foregrounds everyday, material human needs such as food, shelter, clothing, and social standing, as well as the money that is necessary to acquire them. Linked to this materialism is Realism's serious treatment of 'low' or everyday subjects, sometimes including the harsher, even sordid, aspects of human existence. In addition, the realist mode often aims for a holistic vision in which character is defined by a closely related, determining milieu. Character and milieu belong to a larger social whole, and they are charged with embodying a typical individual or part of that whole. This sometimes leads to a focus on characters as 'types', or to a tendency to prefer mediocre or banal characters rather than outstanding individuals or unique experience. The emphasis on material needs and on a defining milieu means that the realist mode makes great use of metonymy, the trope that conveys meaning by association, which I shall come back to in more detail. Realism also aims to give the *impression* that it reflects the real world (an aim that led Maupassant to suggest realist writers should be called Illusionists[37]): it strives for an effect of verisimilitude, often relying on linguistic markers of familiarity to reassure the reader that the fictive world is a recognizable one; and it tends to focus on contemporary or near-contemporary events and on social, economic, or technological changes that are specific to the period. Linked to this is a tendency towards a conservative use of style, in an attempt to convey an impression of transparency and thus the illusion of a directly mimetic relation to the outside world.

---

primarily the use of Realism in recent global fiction rather than in the nineteenth-century novel. I shall return to this issue in the Conclusion.

[37] Guy de Maupassant, 'Le Roman', Preface to *Pierre et Jean*, in *Romans*, ed. by Louis Forestier (Paris: Gallimard 'Pléiade', 1987) p. 709. Future references to Maupassant's novels, given in parentheses in the text, will be to this edition.

Adopting this broad and pragmatic approach to literary 'Realism' means that 'Naturalism' can be considered as a further development within the realist mode. Naturalism introduces some important innovations, but none that need prevent it from falling into the overall category of Realism as broadly sketched out above. These innovations include the privileging of impersonal forces over individual voli- tion; insistence on the use of direct observation (the famous *documents humains*); and a more pronounced claim to base the novel in specialist, often scientific, knowledge.[38] Many of the traits I have listed are also, of course, to be found in literature written long before and after the heyday of the realist novel, which falls, roughly speaking, between 1830 and 1890.

To this list of characteristics I wish to add another, perhaps more surprising, trait of the realist mode, which is the dualism of its epistemological stance. The realist narrative takes the reader into a specific social milieu, and its narrator—even when this narrator is near-invisible, as is frequently the case after 1856—is implicitly in possession of specialist knowledge that is shared with the reader. The author, above all, must be convincingly knowledgeable, becoming 'l'écrivain-qui-doit-savoir-de- quoi-il-parle'.[39] This implicit possession of knowledge is underlined by the fact that realist narratives often incorporate professional terminology such as that of journalism or the natural sciences. The fiction is predicated on the possession of specialist information about the real (about recent innovations in the technology of the printing press, say, or the workings of mines). And yet at the same time the realist mode *explores* the adequacy of human representations of the real. This explo- ration is at times positive and assertive, but it is often sceptical, and it is based on a conception of representation and knowledge as ongoing processes rather than fixed and immutable givens. Characters call on different, and sometimes incom- patible, theories to explain their experiences; they try to produce or interpret let- ters, poems, paintings, journalism, and family trees; they struggle with contracts that represent their situation in particular ways. In this sense mimesis may indeed be understood as a dynamic process of cognition and discovery.[40] Realism is far from precluding self-reflexivity: in fact, writers working in the realist mode fre- quently incorporate reflection on the referential function itself. Mimesis, under- stood as imitation or representation of the world, cannot simply be seen as 'a system striving for maximal semantic unity and stability'.[41] Many writers using the realist mode, who give high priority to mimesis, *also* incorporate anxieties about

---

[38] There have of course been some very persuasive arguments emphasizing the break between the Realism of the 1830s–1870s and Naturalism. Georg Lukács saw Naturalism as more concerned with the spectacular, surface side of everyday life (*Studies in European Realism*, trans. by Edith Bone (London: The Merlin Press, 1989 [1950], and 'Narrate or Describe' [1936] in *Writer and Critic*, trans. by Arthur Kahn (London: Merlin Press, 1978), pp. 110–48. David Baguley emphasizes its new pessi- mism or 'entropic' tendency (*Naturalist Fiction: The Entropic Vision* (Cambridge: Cambridge University Press, 1990)). These arguments tend to use a narrower conception of Realism as a genre or movement rather than as a general mode, which is my approach here.

[39] Philippe Hamon, 'Le savoir dans le texte', *Revue des Sciences humaines*, 4 (1975), 489–99 (p. 490).

[40] This argument, made by Ricœur, is discussed by Christopher Prendergast in *The Order of Mimesis: Balzac, Stendhal, Nerval, Flaubert* (Cambridge: Cambridge University Press, 1986), p. 22.

[41] Prendergast, *Order of Mimesis*, p. 13.

the possibility of semantic stability, foregrounding the referential or poetic functions and thus, as Christopher Prendergast puts it, encountering the experience of the 'limit' (of representation).[42] Jameson has even argued recently for a redefinition of Realism that would include its own self-questioning nature: 'We may even wonder whether the most useful "definition" of realism may not lie in the capacity of a text to raise the issue of realism as such within its own structure, no matter what answer it decides to give. In that case, we might call realist any literary work which raises the question of realism, whether to problematize it or to attempt to reinvent it: realism would then name any narrative that is organized [...] around the very interrogation of realism and the realistic itself.'[43] This view of Realism as a form of epistemological enquiry[44] will be developed in Chapter 4, and we shall explore its implications for postcolonialism in the Conclusion.

Several elements in the list of characteristics I have given in themselves suggest that the representation of colonialism might pose a problem for Realism. The realist novel's reliance on the recognizable, the predictable, and the familiar in order to sustain the effect of verisimilitude is such that some 'definitions' of the realist novel actually stipulate its contemporary *metropolitan* subject matter. The unfamiliarity of distant lands to the intended readership is inherently problematic. Verisimilitude, as Nicholas Harrison puts it, 'can be said to serve a regulatory function that makes "realism" narrower than the "real": this is why fact is stranger than (realist) fiction'.[45] In addition, the need for the possession of specialist knowledge by the writer (or at least the convincing appearance of this knowledge) makes the portrayal of a distant setting, and foreign characters, considerable problems in their own right.[46] And the holistic vision of a milieu that has a determining relation to individual behaviour is challenged if a novel set in the colonies focuses on characters who are foreign in that setting; even foreign objects imported into the metropolis carry something of the separateness of their original milieu. As a result colonial settings and characters, and to a lesser extent objects, present a *generic* challenge. A narrative that focuses on them runs the risk of slipping out of the realist mode and into exoticism.

ROMANTIC EXOTICISM AND REALIST COLONIALISM?

Extra-European encounters within the novel are, as we have seen, part of the story Europe tells itself about the meeting of modernity with pre-industrial 'immobile' time. It is a recurrent critical truism to distinguish between exotic and colonial

---

[42] *Order of Mimesis*, p. 15.

[43] Fredric Jameson, 'Antinomies of the Realism–Modernism Debate', *Modern Language Quarterly*, Afterword to the special issue 'Peripheral Realisms', 73:3 (2012), 475–85 (pp. 478–9).

[44] The term is used by Timothy Unwin in *Textes réfléchissants: réalisme et réflexivité au dix-neuvième siècle* (Bern: Peter Lang, 2000), p. 6.

[45] Nicholas Narrison, *Postcolonial Criticism: History, Theory and the Work of Fiction* (Cambridge: Polity, 2003), p. 24.

[46] This problem of specialist knowledge is raised by Paul Bonnetain, trying to write a Naturalist novel set in what was then called Indochina. See the preface to his novel *L'Opium* (1886) reprinted by Frédéric Da Silva in 'Pour un naturalisme exotique: *L'Opium* et sa préface inédite', *Les Cahiers naturalistes*, 85 (Special issue on Paul Bonnetain) (2011), 67–75 (pp. 72–3).

narratives of this meeting. According to this view, the former frame the non-European world in a positive light as a refuge for values that are excluded from modernity—mystery, enchantment, colour, sensuality, and passion—whereas the latter are grounded in reality and informed by a more or less overt pro-colonialist agenda.

This neat separation is not new: writers and critics of French 'littérature coloniale' (1880s–1930s) were eager to police the boundary between the exotic and the colonial. These critics engaged in a territorial war to stake out the 'seriousness' of colonial literature by attempting to align it with Realism and Naturalism and against exoticism, which was seen as inherently Romantic. In 1911 the latter was still a threat to be warded off: 'Passé certaines latitudes le vieux romantisme reconquiert sur nous tout son prestige déchu.'[47] Today's postcolonial critics tend to agree, some arguing that *any* Orientalism—and one might imagine any exoticism—indicates a Romantic stance, and that 'realistic Orientalism' is an oxymoron.[48] The terms used are sometimes slightly modified however, with 'imperialist exoticism' replacing the older 'littérature coloniale' and 'exoticizing exoticism' replacing 'exoticism' *tout court*.[49]

More importantly for our present purposes, the long-defended distinction between exoticism and colonialism is seen as being mapped over the boundary between Romanticism and Realism, and is thus situated on the front line of the old battle between idealism and materialism. Indeed, Jean-Marie Seillan explains the relative marginalization of colonial themes in the late nineteenth century by the fact that naturalist writers, rejecting any potential association with Romanticism, abandoned exotic subjects to the Decadents and Symbolists with their anti-realist approach.[50]

A hasty acceptance of this neat separation would however lead to a misunderstanding of the relationship between Realism and exoticism. Indeed, the idea that these categories are watertight has been questioned, for example in an excellent critical overview by Jean-Marc Moura.[51] I wish to suggest instead a form of coexistence, for which one can take as a model the fantastic tale of the 1830s and

[47] Louis Cario and Charles Régismanset, *L'Exotisme: la littérature coloniale* (Paris: Mercure de France, 1911), p. 283. Pierre Jourda, in the 1930s, also identifies the first stage of French exoticism with Romanticism. The second stage is that of the Realists, the third stage (dealt with very briefly) the Parnassiens and the fourth that of contemporary Naturalism, which 'transporte à la colonie les méthodes naturalistes: le livre colonial devient objectif et documentaire; l'observation exacte l'emporte sur l'analyse sentimentale. La littérature coloniale [...] peindra la colonie telle qu'elle est et non plus telle qu'on la rêve' (*L'Exotisme dans la littérature française depuis Chateaubriand: t. 2, du romantisme à 1939* (Paris: Presses Universitaires de France/Slatkine Reprints, 1970 [written 1939 but published for the first time in 1956]), p. 222).
[48] Mohammed Sharafuddin, *Islam and Romantic Orientalism: Literary Encounters with the Orient* (London: Tauris, 1994), p. 49; p. xviii.
[49] Chris Bongie, *Exotic Memories: Literature, Colonialism, and the Fin de Siècle* (Redwood, CA: Stanford University Press, 1991), pp. 16–17.
[50] Jean-Marie Seillan, *Aux sources du roman colonial: L'Afrique à la fin du XIXe siècle* (Paris: Karthala, 2006), p. 7. In an article on Zola, Seillan also argues that 'quant à la méthode d'enquête naturaliste, elle excluait l'exotisme' ('L'Afrique utopique de *Fécondité*', *Les Cahiers naturalistes*, 75 (2001), 183–202 (p. 183)).
[51] Jean-Marc Moura, 'Littérature coloniale et exotisme: examen d'une opposition de la théorie littéraire coloniale' in *Regards sur les littératures coloniales, t. 1, Afrique francophone: découvertes*, ed. by Jean-François Durand (Paris: L'Harmattan, 2000), 21–39.

1880s, which is a clear counterpart to exotic literature. Both the fantastic and the exotic reintroduce realms of possibility that seem closed to a narrowly rationalist world-view, but whereas the fantastic situates them in the supernatural, exoticism situates them in terms of geographical distance. As Tzvetan Todorov has argued, the fantastic tale incorporates tension between genres into its very being, since it focuses on the encounter of realist verisimilitude with elements that break the comforting illusion of familiarity: the protagonist and reader alike hesitate between two incompatible interpretative modes.[52] The same kind of incorporated generic tension, I argue, marks the realist/exoticist distinction too. These apparently incompatible modes are in fact often used by the same writers, sometimes in different works, but also within one novel or story, so that the unresolved tension— the uneasy relationship between the Romantic/exotic on the one hand, and the realist/colonial on the other—becomes a subject in its own right. Exoticism is one of Realism's 'antinomies', incorporated, as Jameson has recently argued, as an antagonistic presence within the realist mode.[53] It is used in order to challenge the assumptions of realist verisimilitude and familiarity, but it is frequently deployed in this way *by practitioners of Realism*: it is one of the ways in which Realism questions itself.

READING THE COLONIES INTO THE METROPOLIS: SOME CONCEPTUAL TOOLS

In most of the canonical French narrative fiction that is the focus of *The Colonial Comedy* the colonies, at first sight, are striking by their absence. In a period when the novel was more than ever concerned with the particularities of space and place, its engagement with the emerging world-system seems marginal. Balzac himself declared the centrality of the Paris–Provinces axis to his vast project,[54] so it is not surprising that critical approaches to realist fiction have focused on geographical awareness in these terms.[55]

Now of course, if the colonies *were* entirely absent from the realist novel that would be a remarkable fact in itself. Postcolonial theorists have followed Said in adopting Pierre Macherey's stance that what a text chooses *not* to say is often as important as what it *does* say.[56] This fits within a broader critical tendency towards

[52] Tzvetan Todorov, *Introduction à la littérature fantastique* (Paris: Seuil, 1970).

[53] Fredric Jameson, *The Antinomies of Realism* (London: Verso, 2013).

[54] 'Mon ouvrage a sa géographie comme il a sa généalogie et ses familles, ses lieux et ses choses' declared Balzac; he is referring specifically to that 'antithèse sociale', 'Paris et la province' (*Avant-propos*, in *La Comédie humaine*, ed. by Pierre-Georges Castex, 12 vols (Paris: Gallimard 'Pléiade', 1976–81), I, pp. 18–19). References to Balzac's *Comédie humaine*, hereafter included in parentheses after quotations, are to this edition.

[55] On the provinces see notably Nicole Mozet, *La Ville de province dans l'œuvre de Balzac. L'espace romanesque: fantasme et idéologie* (Paris: SEDES, 1982) and Andrew Watts, *Preserving the Provinces: Small Town and Countryside in the Work of Honoré de Balzac* (Oxford: Peter Lang, 2007). On Paris, see among others Christopher Prendergast, *Paris and the Nineteenth Century* (Oxford: Blackwell, 1995 [1992]).

[56] For Pierre Macherey, it is what the work does not spell out that it uncovers: 'ce silence lui donne aussi son existence' (*Pour une théorie de la production littéraire* (Paris: François Maspero, 1974 [1966]),

symptomatic or suspicious readings of texts, that is, an interpretive method that takes into account what a text represses as well as—or perhaps even more than— what it does explicitly say. In the present case, however, the absence or repression of the colonies is only relative. For in fact colonial spaces and identities *are* explicitly evoked, but as something that is absent because it is elsewhere: imperialism happens offstage. For example, Balzac's works are full of references to European colonies and to the slave trade. To see Paris as 'largely divorced [...] from the imperial apparatus of which Balzac makes it an integral part' is nothing less than a critical blind spot, as Geoffrey Baker has argued in an invaluable recent study.[57] Certain postcolonial critics, such as Chrisman, have indeed argued for the importance of studying 'metropolitan imperialism': that is, the presence of imperialism within the metropolis itself. Such an analysis, she says, will need to 'disaggregate "the metropolis" itself, differentiating its subject-productions from those of settler colonials, and incorporate the analysis of economic and administrative processes— capitalism, government and bureaucracy—in the materials of metropolitan culture'.[58]

In order to approach this space from the metropolitan heartland of the French nineteenth century we need a series of analytical tools, sketched out below, which will serve us throughout *The Colonial Comedy*.

'Offstage' Spaces in the Novel

Since the main narrative of most French realist fiction is set in the metropolis, the colonial comedy is largely played out in the wings, in extra-narrative or 'offstage' space. It is attached to the main narrative by what Said calls 'geographical notation[s]'.[59] These take various forms: embedded narratives about colonial events (which can be called metadiegetic or 'au second degré', that is, events recounted within the main narrative by a 'diegetic' narrator[60]); imported or fake exotic objects, or colonial merchandise, that point metonymically to geographically distant spaces; exotic ekphrasis, that is, the verbal portrayal of visual images of the colonies; immigrants and returning colonists or soldiers from colonial armies within the metropolitan space; and the wholesale importation of metaphors derived from slavery, imperialism, or racial difference. The marginal nature of these geographical notations suggests a collective disavowal—the emerging world-system

p. 103 (see also pp. 102–10). Said claims that '[i]n reading a text, one must open it out both to what went into it and to what its author excluded' (*Culture and Imperialism*, p. 79; see also p. 60). For a treatment of absence as a trope, and a breakdown of different kinds of absence, see Philippe Hamon, *Texte et idéologie* (Paris: Presses Universitaires de France, 1984), pp. 11–19.

[57] Baker, *Realism's Empire*, p. 71.

[58] Laura Chrisman, 'Rethinking the Imperial Metropolis of Heart of Darkness', in *Conrad at the Millennium: Modernism, Postmodernism, Postcolonialism*, ed. by Gail Fincham, Atti De Lange, and Wieslaw Krajka (Boulder: Social Science Monographs, 2001), pp. 399–426 (p. 423).

[59] *Culture and Imperialism*, p. 69.

[60] Gérard Genette, *Figures III* (Paris: Seuil, 1972), pp. 238–9; *Figures II* (Paris, Seuil: 1969), p. 202. These embedded accounts can be quite minimal, for example brief reports on colonial events in the course of a conversation. On minimal embedded narratives, see Mieke Bal, *Narratology: Introduction to the Theory of Narrative* (Toronto: University of Toronto Press, 2009 [1985]), p. 60.

is visible, as it were, out of the corner of one's eye while the main focus is on the central drama of metropolitan bourgeois identity—but at the same time the unpalatable truths of slavery, or the administrative manipulation and individual venality behind colonial ventures, *are* written into the fabric of the central, and centralizing, novelistic genre.

Space offstage in the novel remains largely under-theorized, but my study has been guided by some suggestive leads. For example, the term 'heterotopias' was coined by Michel Foucault to refer to spaces that are distinct from utopias or dystopias because they are real geographical places that exist within 'l'institution même de la société'. They are 'des sortes de contre-emplacements, sortes d'utopies effectivement réalisées'. Foucault was thinking primarily of metropolitan spaces such as the madhouse and the prison, but he cites colonial space as another such heterotopia. He also points out that heterotopias are usually linked to 'des découpages du temps' or 'hétérochronies'.[61] The concrete separation in geographical space corresponds to an implicit temporal discontinuity.

This temporal disjunction, implicit in the relation between metropolitan and colonial space, brings us back to the combined and uneven development of the new world-system. In literary works, it can be understood not only via Foucault's heterotopias, but also through Mikhail Bakhtin's concept of 'chronotopes'. The narrow spatial focus of realist narrative corresponds to Bakhtin's *everyday chronotope*, while tales set in a wider geography deploy what he calls the *adventure chronotope*. As well as being spatially distinct, he argues, these chronotopes generally have different narrative speeds and temporal frameworks—the term 'chronotope' itself serves to remind us of the imbrication of space and time.[62] The evocation of offstage spaces in embedded narratives within a metropolitan setting yokes together Bakhtin's adventure and everyday chronotopes in a relationship that is often uneasy.

Colonial heterotopias are frequently reminiscent of Bakhtin's view of the pastoral as an 'idyllic model for [...] restoring folkloric time' with its 'immanent unity'.[63] For nineteenth-century Realism, heterotopias present a distinct advantage over true utopias, or even distant historical periods, in that they do have some claim to actual existence. So the utopian and pastoral imagination often takes refuge in extra-European space, and increasingly in the space made available to European fantasy through imperialism. In the early nineteenth century the pastoral imagination produces a new subgenre, the novel of the frontier or *roman pionnier*.[64] This subgenre focuses on the violence, and the seemingly limitless opportunities for adventure, of the American frontier; it had a long-lasting

---

[61] Michel Foucault, 'Des espaces autres' [lecture 1967, published 1984] in *Dits et Écrits*, ed. by Daniel Defert and François Ewald, 4 vols (Paris: Gallimard, 1994), IV, pp. 752–62 (p. 755, p. 759).

[62] Mikhail Bakhtin, 'Forms of Time and of the Chronotope in the Novel' [1937–38], in *The Dialogic Imagination: Four Essays*, ed. by Michael Holquist, trans. by Caryl Emerson and Michael Holquist (Austin: University of Texas Press, 1981), pp. 84–258.

[63] *Dialogic Imagination*, p. 224, p. 225.

[64] According to Hoffmann the *roman pionnier* emerges at the beginning of the nineteenth century as a belated successor to *Robinson Crusoe* (*Le Nègre romantique*, p. 140), though I suspect its arrival in France could be more precisely dated to the late 1820s.

influence on French literature, notably through translations of James Fenimore Cooper's novels.[65] Though America will not be the subject of much discussion in *The Colonial Comedy*, it does play a role as a major 'realm of possibility'. Antebellum America is associated not only with adventure, but also with slavery, and we shall see in Chapter 2 that this form of heterotopia allows what I call 'sinister pastoral': that is, the nostalgia for a real or fantasized past as master of slaves in a rule-free libertarian idyll.

Of course, one might be tempted to dismiss the role played by extra-European spaces in the novel as simply a matter of narrative convenience. Excessively promising or authoritative characters can be removed from the main narrative space so that the plot can occur in the remaining narrative vacuum.[66] Franco Moretti, in a sideswipe at Said, suggests that in *Mansfield Park* Sir Thomas Bertram leaves for Antigua simply because 'Austen needs him out of the way'. Along the same lines, Moretti suggests the colonies function as a form of narrative magic, a 'mythic geography' from which to derive a *'pecunia ex machina'*, that is, a narrative source of fortunes that do not need to be explained.[67] And Raymond Williams had already suggested that the colonies were used as a facile narrative sleight of hand: 'characters whose destinies could not be worked out within the system as given were simply put on the boat'.[68]

In fact Williams saw the colonial subplot as a way of avoiding the real issues of class conflict within metropolitan society, since a colonial twist in the story implied that 'there could be no general solution to the social problems of the time; there could be only individual solutions, the rescue by legacy or emigration'.[69] Jameson however argued that the blind spot is not so much class-conflict within the metropolis, as the worldwide nature of the emerging economic system itself. The nineteenth-century novel tends to relegate the portrayal of non-European peoples to 'non-canonical adventure literature', which he sees as 'a strategy of representational containment' whose effects include the inadequate representation of 'the new imperial world-system': the invisibility of 'the colonized other' who is an essential component of the new world-order leads to a 'spatial disjunction' that 'has as

---

[65] The American novelist James Fenimore Cooper (1789–1851) began writing fiction in the 1820s; he was (and is) most famous for the Leatherstocking series that recounts the adventures, in the American wilderness of the eighteenth century, of a hardy woodsman and his Native American allies. Fenimore Cooper lived in Paris between 1826 and 1828, and returned at the moment of the July Revolution to support the Republic; his most famous novel was translated into French in 1828 as *Le Dernier des Mohicans*. His novels were widely read in France, though perhaps mostly by children. His influence on Balzac is well documented.

[66] For example, a particularly promising young man is a casualty of Abd-el-Kader's resistance to the occupying forces in Algeria in Balzac's *Le Député d'Arcis* (VIII: 743); this leaves the narrative free to take a satirical course. In *La Femme de trente ans* Balzac has Abel d'Aiglemont die in Algeria 'devant Constantine' or, in an earlier version, in Paris and at a different date, depending on the shifting needs of the internal chronology of the *Comédie humaine* (II: 1202). Vautrin evokes the colonial dead-end as a powerful alternative history, reminding us that Napoleon was nearly sent away to the colonies before revealing his potential (III: 141). Said discusses some of the many narrative uses of the colonies in *Culture and Imperialism*, p. 75.

[67] Franco Moretti, *Atlas of the European Novel 1800–1900* (London: Verso, 1998 [1997]), pp. 26–7.

[68] Raymond Williams, *The Long Revolution* (London: Chatto and Windus, 1961), pp. 66–7.

[69] *The Long Revolution*, p. 67.

its immediate consequence the inability to grasp the way the system functions as a whole.'[70]

This blind spot of the new world-system, as reflected by the nineteenth-century metropolitan novel's near silence in relation to the colonies, is not, however, absolute, and it is a little hasty to reduce the colonial space to the function of mere narrative 'magic'. Characters who return from heterotopic space offstage are frequently contaminated by the violence inherent in the experience of the slave trade or colonialism. Close reading suggests that it is necessary to nuance Moretti's view that the geography of colonial romances is a single, one-dimensional line with no bifurcations, a journey whose only obstacles are dangerous animals or natives, and whose objects are to find a clean, fairy tale treasure, or to recuperate a 'Lost European' in an innocent story of self defence.[71] The spatial logic of colonialism in the novel is neither one-dimensional nor harmless.

Colonial Metaphor and Colonial Metonymy

As well as offstage, extra-narrative spaces, the colonies are a source of metaphors that are imported to describe metropolitan phenomena. Slavery and racial difference are for example used metaphorically to describe the dominance of one gender over another, or class difference within Europe. Settler colonialism and military expansion are sometimes used as metaphors for European internal politics, or for individual psychology. Foucault calls this use of extra-metropolitan space a heterotopia of the mirror, in which the colonial space offers an idealized or a negative version of the metropolitan space.[72]

This use of colonialism or slavery as metaphor risks reducing the real lived experience of non-European peoples to the status of mere analogy. Grace Moore observes that 'nineteenth-century male writers [...] have been complicit in aligning white women with slaves' and 'race has been adopted as a metaphor to explore gender issues' particularly in the domestic novel.[73] Chrisman argues that using the issue of slavery as an allegory rather than treating it in its own right effectively instrumentalizes it, subsuming it within metropolitan discourse.[74] That something else happens alongside this instrumentalization is however suggested by Susan Meyer. While a careless equivalence between gender or class domination and imperialism risks emptying out the specificity of slavery and race, Meyer argues that 'the full signification of the vehicle of metaphor remain[s] present at the margins of our consciousness as we perceive metaphors', so that the 'yoking of the two terms [...]

[70] 'Modernism and Imperialism', pp. 10–11. Martin Green also discusses this inhibition or prohibition felt by 'literary' writers in relation to colonial themes, which are instead dealt with in the 'non-serious' genre of the adventure novel (*Dreams of Adventure, Deeds of Empire* (London: Routledge, 1980), p. 63 and p. 65).

[71] *Atlas of the European Novel*, p. 58, pp. 60–2.

[72] 'Des espaces autres', p. 756. This mirroring of European society is the primary function of much eighteenth-century exoticism, notably Montesquieu's *Lettres persanes* of 1721.

[73] Grace Moore, 'Colonialism in Victorian Fiction: Recent Studies', *Dickens Studies Annual: Essays on Victorian Fiction*, 37, (2006) 251–86 (p. 272).

[74] Chrisman, 'The Imperial Unconscious'.

produces some suggestion in the text of the exploited or vulnerable situation of the people of the race invoked'. Part of the energy of metaphor comes from a marginal awareness of 'what remains dissonant' between its two terms, and one result is that 'the fuller existence of the "dark races" used as the vehicle of the metaphor has a way of pushing back into each novel, of making its presence felt'.[75] Parry, however, takes issue with Meyer's claim that the use of race or slavery as metaphors is 'justified on the grounds that such tropological transference opens the door to the way the history of British colonialism finds its way into the fictions'. For her, such metaphors reveal cognitive blind spots rather than insights.[76]

This debate over the effects of colonial metaphors is, it seems to me, itself skirting around a blind spot, though this time it is literary-critical rather than ideological. Alongside metaphor we need to analyse *metonymy* as a trope by which the colonial territories enter the metropolitan novel. Like metaphor, metonymy opens a side door through which colonialism enters metropolitan fiction; and it is, in some ways, a more open trope than metaphor, despite the leap of analogy on which the latter is based. In metaphor, the vehicle (for example, slavery) points towards one main tenor (for example, the condition of women in nineteenth-century France). Metonymy, in contrast, generates meaning through association, so that it can operate in more than one direction at a time. And the densely productive, almost overflowing presence of metonymy in the nineteenth-century realist text is perhaps the most important means by which it incorporates the realities of the wider world into the metropolitan sphere.

As is well known, one of the most striking stylistic traits of nineteenth-century realist writing is the detailed description of settings and inanimate objects. Balzac himself declared that his description of humanity in terms of social species, in contrast to a naturalist's approach to animal species, would necessarily examine 'les hommes, les femmes et les choses'; the inclusion of objects is essential, he argues, because they give us the 'représentation matérielle' of human thought (I: 9). In turn, it is impossible to understand the realist novel without taking into account the role of the material object. Indeed, as Harry Levin reminds us, 'realism' etymologically evokes 'thing-ism', since 'real' derives from the Latin 'res'.[77] Realist 'things' convey meaning not as symbols for an invisible, inner world, but predominantly through metonymy. Indeed, one of the most important theoretical distinctions between literary Realism and Romanticism or Symbolism comes to us from Roman Jakobson, for whom the mainstay of realist fiction is a characteristic emphasis on non-essential details, and the priority given to contiguity, in other words metonymy or synecdoche.[78]

---

[75] Meyer, *Imperialism at Home*, pp. 22–3.   [76] Parry, *Postcolonial Studies*, pp. 110–11.

[77] Harry Levin, *The Gates of Horn: A Study of Five French Realists* (Oxford: Oxford University Press, 1963), pp. 33–4.

[78] Roman Jakobson, *Language in Literature*, ed. by Krystyna Pomorska and Stephen Rudy (Cambridge, MA: Harvard University Press, 1987), p. 111. This is part of his influential article on 'Two Aspects of Language and Two Types of Aphasic Disturbances' [1956]. Jakobson does not distinguish between metonymy, which signifies by association, and synecdoche, in which the part stands for the whole or vice versa.

Colonial objects have attracted critical attention recently, as part of a new interest in material culture inspired by Cultural Studies, neatly evoked by Bill Brown's coining of the term 'Thing Theory'.[79] Elaine Freedgood invokes Macherey's emphasis on the splitting within the novel by which objects point to 'the play of history beyond its edges, encroaching on those edges'. She adopts a 'strong, literalizing, or materializing, metonymic reading' rather than the standard weak one in which the object simply tells us something about the subject/character. Placing the object back in its material context reinstates it within multiple meanings. It has, she argues, a 'subversive ability to disrupt meaning, to be endlessly vagrant and open ended' and at times 'recuperate[s] historical links that are anything but random'.[80] Metonymy is at work not only via objects and setting, of course, but at times also in the relation between different characters. Marginalized, secondary figures of the immigrant thus open up the metropolitan narrative to multiple meanings via historical and geographical chains of association. In a vivid commentary on such an opening, the artwork by Julie Rrap which figures on the cover of this volume[81] startles the viewer's gaze into recognizing the disruptive signifying potential of the black maid as a secondary figure. This form of metonymy will be discussed in Chapter 5.

It is through sheer density of description that writing in the realist mode most compellingly brings in history in the broadest sense. And it is the same density of the novel's apparently overburdened surface that makes the introduction of gaps, incompletion, and implausibility more striking. *The Colonial Comedy* will examine both metaphors imported from colonial contexts (notably the over-arching metaphor of racial difference standing for class difference, in Chapter 6) and metonymy, which brings colonialism in by the side door.

Internal Strain in Realist Verisimilitude: the *effet d'exotisme*

Colonial metonymy not only brings in historical links with extra-metropolitan realities; it introduces a strain into the very functioning of the realist text. Metonymy, the central trope of Realism, is often understood by reference to contiguity (derived from the Latin *contiguus*, 'touching'). This reference to contiguity itself introduces a metaphor where *spatial* proximity stands for *conceptual* proximity, or association.[82] When we think about metonymic association, we tend to imagine it via this spatial metaphor. This works very well for classic cases of

---

[79] Bill Brown, 'Thing Theory', *Critical Inquiry*, 28:1 (2001). For applications of this to colonial material objects see Catherine Hall and Sonya O. Rose, eds. *At Home with the Empire: Metropolitan Culture and the Imperial World* (Cambridge: Cambridge University Press, 2006); Elaine Freedgood, *The Ideas in Things: Fugitive Meaning in the Victorian Novel* (Chicago: University of Chicago Press, 2006); and Susan Hiner, *Accessories to Modernity: Fashion and the Feminine in Nineteenth-Century France* (Philadelphia, PA: University of Pennsylvania Press, 2010).

[80] *The Ideas in Things*, p. 3, p. 12, pp. 15–16.

[81] Julie Rrap, *Untitled (after Manet's 'Olympia')*, 2002. Vutek print; solvent pigment inks on canvas. Courtesy of the artist and Roslyn Oxley9 Gallery, Sydney.

[82] For a useful attempt to break down the very varied types of metonymic relation, and a critique of the vague metaphorical basis of the term 'contiguity' that is so often our starting point when thinking about metonymy, see Hugh Bredin, 'Metonymy', *Poetics Today*, 5:1 (1984), 45–58.

metonymy, in which an object tells us about something else that is physically close to it (Mme Vauquer's slovenly woollen petticoat, showing beneath her skirt, sums her up, just as her whole person provides a key to understanding her boarding house, in the opening chapter of *Le Père Goriot*). But conceptual and spatial contiguity no longer work so smoothly together in the case of colonial objects in a metropolitan context. Exoticism and colonialism introduce a hiatus between the 'here' and the 'there'.

Of course, French Realism plays endlessly on the contrast of urban centre and provincial periphery, but this distance is conceived as concrete and relative. It is very far from the gap or hiatus that separates the fictional metropolis from its colonies.[83] Such a distance seems inherently embarrassing for the realist mode, which evacuates the vast openings of colonial space but at the same time reinscribes them *within* the strict limitations of the metropolitan frame through detached metonymical fragments. This might be seen as a process of taming or containment; but colonial and exotic fragments nevertheless retain the awkwardness resulting from the rupture of contiguity that they represent. Colonial metonymy is an uneasy presence in the claustrophobic, narrowly determined world of metropolitan Realism; and this awkwardness is often exploited deliberately by writers in order to broaden, and question, the limitations of the realist mode.

Barthes has argued that realist metonymy seeks to establish an impression of verisimilitude partly through the *effet de réel*: objects whose function in the novel is simply to signal the fictional world's reality, its familiarity.[84] And yet, alongside the famous *effet de réel*, a surprising number of realist novels also use an *effet d'exotisme*, introducing objects that have almost exactly the opposite effect, since what is emphasized is foreignness and unfamiliarity. Whereas the *effet de réel* confirms the mimetic contract, the *effet d'exotisme* suggests a rupture with that contract. In addition, the *effet de réel* seems to block 'meaning', in the sense that objects appear to exist only for themselves, while in contrast the exotic object seems to suggest meaning far beyond itself. Oriental objects are the most frequent examples of this *effet d'exotisme* within the metropolitan novel, and indeed Orientalism poses a particularly acute set of problems for Realism. Victor Hugo's preface to *Les Orientales* in 1829 already laid out a manifesto for a certain use of the 'Orient' as an anti-figurative space, a usage later taken up by the 'Art for art's sake' movement. As a figuration of the non-figurative the (middle-eastern) Orient was particularly attractive because of the association of Islam with nonrepresentational, decorative art.[85] Oscar Wilde argued that the history of the decorative arts 'is the record of the struggle between Orientalism, with its frank rejection of imitation, its love of artistic convention, its dislike of the actual representation of any object in Nature,

---

[83] Moretti suggests that this difference, in Austen's novels, is an opposition between absolute, ontological distance and concrete, relative distance (*Atlas of the European Novel*, p. 22).

[84] Roland Barthes, 'L'effet de réel' [1968] in *Œuvres complètes*, ed. by Éric Marty, 3 vols (Paris: Seuil, 1993) II, 479–90.

[85] This argument is developed by Emily A. Haddad in *Orientalist Poetics: The Islamic Middle East in Nineteenth-Century English and French Poetry* (Aldershot: Ashgate, 2002).

and our own imitative spirit'. Orientalism is thus one way of escaping what he calls 'the prison-house of realism'.[86]

So exotic, and *a fortiori* oriental, objects are associated with a rejection of the referential function. In its introduction of strangeness into the realist aesthetic, Aravamudan suggests that exoticism anticipates Bertolt Brecht's defamiliarization or alienation-effect (*Verfremdungseffekt*), though often with a politically conservative purpose.[87] Of course, vaguely 'exotic' signifiers do differ from specifically 'colonial' signifiers. Lawrence Schehr points out that Flaubert's *Salammbô* 'produces' the world it describes rather than appearing to offer itself as a mere reflection of a pre-existing reality.[88] When a novel invokes not ancient Carthage but the contemporary colonies, however, it does point to a precise geographical and political referent. Even so, at the same time it introduces a hiatus—a spatial gap—in which persists an *effet d'exotisme*, or alienation-effect.

The *effet d'exotisme* is arguably more apparent in French literature than across the Channel, where empire and racial tropes had a certain 'everydayness' or 'taken-for-grantedness'.[89] In France, for most of the nineteenth century, colonial expansion was not taken for granted, and it is often flagged up by the realist novel as problematic in one way or another. Realist writers frequently employ exotic objects or names as a means of showing our grasp on reality to be less than straightforward. The first three chapters of *The Colonial Comedy* will look more closely at the duality of the exotic object and its relation to metropolitan experience.

A LITERATURE OF DOUBT: HESITATIONS OVER COLONIALISM

In the wake of Said's *Orientalism*, postcolonial criticism has tended to argue for the complicity of literature in the ideology of imperialism. Critics since 1978 have however sought to nuance the idea of a homogenous Western discourse, taking into account the 'discursive ambivalences and ideological uncertainties'[90] of Western culture and of the European novel. Said himself later called for a 'contrapuntal' reading of cultural history, one that would reflect an awareness 'both of the metropolitan history that is narrated and of those other histories against which

[86] 'The Decay of Lying' [1891] in *De Profundis and Other Writings* (London: Penguin, 1987), pp. 57–87 (p. 70, p. 72). In the visual arts pictorial Orientalism of the nineteenth century has sometimes been seen as a form of Realism, but Linda Nochlin makes a convincing case against this view ('The Imaginary Orient' in *The Politics of Vision: Essays on Nineteenth-Century Art and Society* (Thames & Hudson, 1991 [1989]), pp. 33–59, particularly pages 33–7).

[87] Srinivas Aravamudan, 'Response: Exoticism beyond Cosmopolitanism?', *Eighteenth-Century Fiction*, 25:1 (2012), 227–42 (p. 230). Despite this conservatism, he does see exoticism, at least of the eighteenth century, as 'a poetics of the object' that is not just about acquisition but 'a dynamic process of making and framing'.

[88] Lawrence Schehr, '*Salammbô* as the Novel of Alterity', *Nineteenth-Century French Studies*, 17:3–4 (1989), 326–41.

[89] Hall and Rose, *At Home with the Empire*, Introduction, p. 23.

[90] See Ali Behdad, *Belated Travelers: Orientalism in the Age of Colonial Dissolution* (Cork: Cork University Press, 1994), p. 14.

(and together with which) the dominating discourse acts'.[91] But even in 1993 he tended to read texts such as Jane Austen's *Mansfield Park* as ideologically unified and unambiguously affirmative of empire.[92] Such a reading is, according to Chrisman, a 'consequence of his progressive view of social and cultural history' in which narrative structure does not admit of formal and ideological divisibility until the advent of modernism, and even then only of ironic, not oppositional, 'awareness of imperialism's political limitations'.[93] She argues that we need 'a model of cultural representation that permits of more internal ideological contradiction and contestation than Said allows'. This would enable us to read colonial-era texts 'as containing, potentially, both oppositional and affirmative relations to empire'.[94] As Patrick Brantlinger points out, before we hasten to define the nineteenth-century novel as the 'creature of imperializing nationalisms rather than of anti-imperialistic nationalisms' we must remember that novels 'carry multiple, contradictory ideological values'.[95]

An interpretative model that allows for the presence of contradictory values is certainly necessary in the case of French literature during the politically tumultuous nineteenth century. For much of the century, French literature foregrounded doubts or at least a certain pathos about the colonial project. Pronouncements from the last decades of the century on the 'mission civilisatrice' and the energizing nature of the colonial experience should not lead us to ignore the presence of a long-standing and peculiarly French downbeat tone concerning the colonies. The high seriousness of Kipling's 'white man's burden' is a far cry from Flaubert's entry, in the *Dictionnaire des idées reçues* where he had begun to collect stereotypes taken from popular discourse: 'COLONIES (nos): S'attrister quand on en parle.'[96] French ambivalence towards colonial expansion does not, of course, reduce the impact of that expansion on populations that were the subject of expropriation, appropriation, and near-genocidal violence.[97] And it is possible that a long-standing familiarity with doubt was to delay France's acceptance of the end of its colonial empire in the twentieth century. But French colonial culture of the period from 1830 until at least the 1880s does not share the sense of certainty that characterized imperialism in British Victorian colonial culture. The heyday of the realist and naturalist

---

[91] *Culture and Imperialism*, p. 59.

[92] Other critics have however seen Said as too willing to defend Austen's ethics in *Mansfield Park* (see notably Cora Kaplan, 'Imagining empire: history, fantasy and literature,' in *At Home with the Empire*, ed. Hall and Rose, pp. 191–211).

[93] *Postcolonial Contraventions*, pp. 53–4.   [94] *Postcolonial Contraventions*, p. 67.

[95] Patrick Brantlinger, 'Nations and Novels: Disraeli, George Eliot, and Orientalism', *Victorian Studies: A Journal of the Humanities, Arts and Sciences*, 35:3 (1992), 255–75 (p. 261). He draws on Bakhtin to argue that the nature of the novel is to include disparate voices and thus a 'utopian internationalist dimension'.

[96] The *Dictionnaire des idées reçues* is reproduced in *Bouvard et Pécuchet*, ed. by Jacques Suffel (Paris: GF-Flammarion, 1966), pp. 333–78 (see p. 342).

[97] Some historians working in the field of genocide studies have argued recently that France's military campaigns and use of systematic violence against civilians in Algeria amount to attempts at genocide. See William Gallois, 'Genocide in nineteenth-century Algeria', *Journal of Genocide Research*, 15:1 (2013) 591–610.

novel corresponds to a period of doubt, hesitation, and fluctuation in France's colonial policy and culture.

Classic studies of French colonial ideology and of colonial literature, along with a more recent study of anticolonial attitudes by Claude Liauzu, all emphasize a division into a period of doubt and apprehension, followed by a new glorification of imperialism.[98] Death, or physical and moral destruction, dominate the novels that deal with the colonies in this first period: this reflects the wave of anticolonial feeling that inspired opposition to Jules Ferry's colonial policies; it is particularly strong in literature concerning Sub-Saharan Africa.[99] Liauzu's study of anticolonialism concentrates on political writing, and he asserts that there is no equivalent anticolonial tendency in *art*.[100] This appears to hold true of the literature of the period, albeit with a significant nuance: although there is indeed little truly *anticolonial* literature in the nineteenth century, France produced what could be called a *literature of colonial doubt*. Even in the closing decades of the century, when the *parti colonial* tried to give France a systematic and coherent imperial policy and a colonial ideology did begin to emerge, it was often fraught with disagreement. Colonialism inspired doubt, cynicism, and indifference as well as ambition and enthusiasm. This can be partly explained if one understands French imperialism since the eighteenth century as being less a story of concrete economic gain than one of political rivalry, mainly with Britain; to which can be added attempts to consolidate French national identity and to distract public attention from metropolitan affairs.[101] Although Lenin saw imperialism as the highest stage of capitalism, one could instead understand French imperialism as the 'highest stage of nationalism'.[102]

French literature of the nineteenth century thus incorporates a certain hesitation concerning colonialism. In realist writing, as I have suggested, this is accompanied by another kind of doubt, one that could more properly be called epistemological. In order to understand this literature of colonial doubt, it will be necessary to distance ourselves from views of Realism as naïve and reductive on the one hand, and ideologically concomitant with imperialism on the other. Postcolonial theory does not always offer us a sure guide in doing this. One of the (many) ways Said attempted to define Orientalism as a discourse was to see it as a form of 'radical realism' through which an aspect of the Orient is fixed with a word

---

[98] See Claude Liauzu, *Histoire de l'anticolonialisme en France, du XVIe siècle à nos jours* (Paris: Armand Colin, 2007), chapter 2, as well as the studies already mentioned by Girardet and Astier Loutfi.

[99] Astier Loutfi, pp. 39–40. Jean-Marie Seillan argues that it was for generic reasons that the colonial 'adventure' novel tended to offer an image of a hostile, uninhabitable Africa (in contrast to travel writing that often sought to make the opposite argument), and that it slipped into anticolonialism almost accidentally ('Littératures coloniales et contraintes génériques', *Les Cahiers de la SIELEC*, 6 (2010), 28–50 (pp. 37–43)).

[100] Liauzu, p. 87.

[101] See Henri Brunschwig for the argument that France's colonies were in fact of relatively little importance to her economy (*Mythes et réalités de l'impérialisme colonial français, 1871–1915* (Paris: Armand Colin, 1960)); see also Jennifer Sessions, *By Sword and Plough: France and the Conquest of Algeria* (Ithaca: Cornell University Press, 2011), p. 10.

[102] William Gallois, *Zola: the History of Capitalism* (Bern: Peter Lang, 2000), p. 127.

or a phrase 'which is then considered either to have acquired, or more simply be, reality'.[103] Homi K. Bhabha, whose work appears to offer a means of accounting for the ambiguities of colonial discourse by discussing its 'aporia, ambivalence, [and] indeterminacy' nevertheless excludes realist literature from this suggestive ensemble. In his formulation, as in Said's, Realism is the dominant mode of colonialism: 'Colonial power produces the colonized as a social reality which is at once an "other" and yet entirely knowable and visible' and colonialism 'employs a system of representation, a regime of truth, that is structurally similar to realism'.[104]

In contrast with this idea of a Realism that reifies its object to such an extent that it effectively produces it, recent approaches from outside postcolonial theory have sought to move away from the critical tendency to reiterate 'the complicity of realism with repressive ideological discourses': such approaches offer on the whole 'a negative critique unable to account for the pleasures of a text or acknowledge a text's capacity to generate its own forms of knowledge'.[105] This is not only a response to postcolonialism, but reflects wariness concerning earlier approaches to literary Realism that too often adopted simplistically 'realist' and positivist attitudes themselves; such approaches, as Nicole Mozet puts it, 'ont plaqué sur les textes littéraires leur rêve d'une transparence absolue des êtres et des choses'.[106] Rather than seeing Realism as stuck in pursuit of an impossible transparency, or gaining all its energy from epistemological naïvety accompanied by ideological conservatism, it is more useful to understand Realism in terms of a dialectic. Thus Baker, for example, sees Realism as including its own 'counternarrative that unfolds simultaneously': 'realist authors regularly amplify their texts' own claims to empiricism and secularism while simultaneously—and often explicitly and self-consciously—troubling those very claims.'[107] This dialectic movement between absolute empirical knowledge and possession of the Other, and a parodying of such assertions, will be the basis for my study of 'Critical Orientalism' in Chapter 4.

If realist writing constructs the Other, it also comments on the institution of imperialism in ways that incorporate doubt and hesitation. Exotic motifs are one device employed by realist narratives to interrogate the boundaries of what is known. The magic skin in Balzac's *La Peau de chagrin* (1831), and the Chinese ghost in Theodore Fontane's naturalist novel *Effi Briest* (1896), are striking examples of the foregrounding, within the realist mode, of elements that challenge the epistemological foundations of that very mode. Twentieth-century critics may at times have dismissed these elements as flaws in the novels, mere left-overs from the Gothic, but that simply reveals their own adherence to a rigidly 'secular criticism'.[108] The realist novelists themselves, on the contrary, frequently include space for the unknown or the unknowable. The colonial comedy is introduced in a

---

[103] *Orientalism*, p. 72.

[104] Homi K. Bhabha, *The Location of Culture* (London/New York: Routledge, 1994), p. 173, pp. 70–1.

[105] Pam Morris, *Realism* (London/New York: Routledge 'New Critical Idiom', 2003), p. 138.

[106] Nicole Mozet, 'Yvetot vaut Constantinople. Littérature et géographie en France au XIXème siècle', *Romantisme*, 12:35 (1982), 91–114 (p. 113).

[107] Baker, *Realism's Empire*, p. 16, p. 206. On this dialectic approach see also Marshall Brown, 'The Logic of Realism: A Hegelian Approach', *Publications of the Modern Language Association of America*, 96:2 (1981) 224–41.

[108] Baker, *Realism's Empire*, pp. 182–3.

highly self-conscious way, through the uneasy incorporation of these generically challenging elements, but also through parody or irony; it is associated with fake objects, imposture, fraudulent activities, failed writing, or misguided reading. This is not a mere hangover from Romanticism, but a deliberate strategy through which Realism addresses its own epistemological unease. Far from constructing the Other thanks to an all-conquering Western knowledge-machine, the realist novel includes a reflection on the *difficulties* of knowing the Other. This in turn becomes a stereotype in its own right, as we shall see in the Conclusion; but it is a stereotype that troubles overly simplistic views of European culture as monolithically sure of itself.

BALZAC, FLAUBERT, ZOLA: COLONIAL PROJECTS

The colonies, as we have seen, posed a generic problem for Realism, since the realist mode tended to establish verisimilitude largely by calling on the reader's familiarity with certain settings and types. It is perhaps not surprising, then, that although some of the central writers of the realist canon entertained the idea of writing realist fiction that would actually be set in the colonies, they never fully accomplished it.

Around 1830 Balzac planned an oriental tale to be called *La Mauresque*.[109] About two years later a planned volume of *Fantaisies* was to include *Voyage à Java*; *Une Passion dans le désert*; *L'Amour dans le harem*; and *Un Despote: La Femme en Asie*.[110] The *Catalogue de 1845*, which includes works Balzac had not yet completed, mentions, under the title 'Les Français en Égypte' in the *Scènes de la vie militaire*, a series of episodes including *Le Prophète* and *Le Pacha*, along with one that was already written, *Une passion dans le désert*. Among the other *Scènes de la vie militaire* planned were volumes called *L'Émir* and *Le Corsaire algérien*.[111] These projects suggest a much wider geographical range for the *Comédie humaine*—and potentially a response to France's ongoing aggressive action in North Africa as well as its nostalgia for the Napoleonic campaign in Egypt—but few of them came to fruition. Balzac's finished works that are actually set in areas of extra-European imperialist expansion—*Une passion dans le désert* and the *Voyage de Paris à Java*—are few indeed. Balzac is also one of the rare French writers of the nineteenth century to have published no fully-fledged travel narrative.[112] And yet in his

---

[109] Also spelt *La Moresse* or *La Mauresse*. This is mentioned in the album 'Pensées, sujets, fragmens [*sic*]', Lov. A 182, fol. 2, in Balzac, *Œuvres complètes*, 28 Vols (Paris: Guy Le Prat/Club de l'honnête homme, 1956–63) p. 659. The tale 'Le Succube' in the *Cent contes drolatiques* (written 1832–3), which recounts the trial of a 'Morisque' from 'Mauritanie', is probably the only completed version of this project.

[110] Folios 22, 24 and 53 in 'Pensées, sujets, fragmens [*sic*]', p. 675, p. 677, p. 696. *L'Amour dans le harem* (or *au harem*; or *dans le sérail*) seems to have become *La Fille aux yeux d'or*. On these projects, see the discussion by Citron 'Le Rêve asiatique', pp. 317–18.

[111] *Catalogue de 1845*, I: cxxv.

[112] For a discussion of this exception, see Aude Déruelle, '"L'Égypte, c'est tout sables": Balzac et le récit de voyage', in *Voyager en France au temps du romantisme: poétique, esthétique, idéologie* ed. by Alain Guyot and Chantal Massot (Grenoble: ELLUG, 2003), 325–41. See also C.W. Thompson, *French Romantic Travel Writing: Chateaubriand to Nerval* (Oxford: Oxford University Press, 2012), p. 1.

published works the European colonial territories appear again and again, if one looks for offstage spaces and colonial metonymy.[113]

Whereas Fernand Baldensperger in the 1920s saw Balzac's Orientalism and his Realism in terms of conflict (a conflict in which the Orient elbows the 'réel' into second place),[114] Pierre Citron sees the two as less incompatible. For him, Balzac gave up on producing a fully-fledged oriental volume, but instead injected Orientalism into the *Comédie* as a whole.[115] Balzac, as we shall see, employs Orientalism as a foil to Realism, in order to introduce conflict within the world-view of the *Comédie humaine*. That is not to say that his attitude was anticolonial.[116] Indeed, Honoré de Balzac the man was firmly in favour of France's conquest of Algeria, and at least one colonial administrator was later to declare Balzac a 'Voyant' who saw in the conquest of Algiers the possibility of an enduring colony in Africa, was unhesitatingly in favour of colonization, and planned a series of 'Scènes algériennes'.[117] But—as is ever the case with Balzac—his novels offer a far more complex and ambivalent view of socio-historic processes, including colonialism, than his own opinions would seem to allow. Colonial realities nevertheless remain marginal in the projects that Balzac did bring to fruition. Dorian Bell, whose recent article on Balzac's Algeria is an invaluable contribution to the field, sees this marginalization of Algeria as resulting from the fact that the class distinctions that were so dear to Balzac were blurred in the military context of the colonies. In addition, the 'determinate relation' of milieu and character so integral to his project in *La Comédie humaine* made the incorporation of colonial or exotic elements a challenge to Realism's generic boundaries.[118]

---

[113] Aimé Dupuy wrote an article on 'Balzac colonial' in 1950 (*Revue d'histoire littéraire de la France*, 50:3 (1950), 257–79) that lists the main 'colonial' episodes mentioned in the *Comédie humaine*.

[114] The Orient 'tient dans sa prodigieuse fantaisie une place qui, chez cet apparent réaliste, me semble avoir précédé le réel et contraint celui-ci de s'accommoder avec ce devancier.' Fernand Baldensperger, *L'Appel de la Fiction Orientale chez Honoré de Balzac* 'The Zaharoff Lecture' (Oxford: Clarendon Press, 1927), p. 4.

[115] 'Le Rêve asiatique', p. 318. See also Éric Bordas, 'L'Orient balzacien ou l'impossible narratif d'un possible romanesque—l'exemple de "La Fille aux yeux d'or"', *Studi francesi*, 122 (1997), 322–30 (p. 330).

[116] Although I shall at times ask how *writers* situated themselves in relation to the issues of slavery, conquest, and colonial expansion, *The Colonial Comedy* is more concerned with the question of how the *novel* deals with these issues. In some cases the views of the man (for all the key French realist writers are men), at least as expressed in journalism, differ significantly from the image that is developed in his fiction. This discrepancy is relevant in the case of Balzac, but perhaps most striking in that of Maupassant, who was explicitly critical of colonial procedures in his journalism.

[117] Dupuy, 'Balzac colonial', pp. 271–3. Dupuy, oddly, argues for Balzac's pro-colonial stance by citing examples that do not reflect an entirely positive view of colonization. Following the conquest of Algiers Balzac did however express approbation in letters (e.g. to Victor Ratier, 21 July 1830, *Correspondance*, ed. by Roger Pierrot, 5 vols (Paris: Garnier, 1960–9) I, p. 463) and in his journalism ('Lettre II' (9 October 1830) and 'Lettre XII' (18 January 1831) in 'Lettres sur Paris', *Le Voleur*, *Œuvres diverses*, ed. by Pierre-Georges Castex, 2 vols (Paris: Gallimard, 'Pléiade', 1990–6), II: 878–9; 944). At the height of the Algerian conquest Balzac boasts to Mme Hanska of France's imperial glory, present and future (*Lettres à Madame Hanska*, ed. by Roger Pierrot, 2 vols (Paris: Robert Laffont, 1990), II, 26 February 1845, p. 28 and 24 December 1846, p. 479. Balzac did clearly have some sympathy with anticolonial sentiments when the colonizing power was not France (e.g. *La Femme de trente ans*, II: 1195), and his pro-colonialism arises partly from his fear of British expansionism.

[118] 'Balzac's Algeria', p. 41, p. 44, p. 47, p. 52.

A considerable proportion of Flaubert's completed works is of course 'oriental', but far from contemporary, being set in ancient Carthage, fourth-century Egypt, and the Holy Land at the time of Christ. The extent to which these works can be considered 'realist' is an interesting question, but one that would deserve a book in its own right. Between 1859 and 1877, episodically, Flaubert also entertained the project of writing a comic novel set in the modern Orient, to be called *Harel-Bey*. 'Le grand roman social à écrire' he noted, 'doit représenter la lutte ou plutôt la fusion de la barbarie et de la civilisation. La scène doit se passer au désert et à Paris, en Orient et en Occident. [...] le héros principal devrait être un barbare qui se civilise près d'un civilisé qui se barbarise.'[119] The Goncourt brothers' journal also recounts Flaubert talking of this project to write about 'l'Orient en habit noir', a novel to be based on a series of antithèses with scenes in Paris alternating with scenes in Constantinople or on the Nile.[120] The 'habit noir' is the uniform of realist verisimilitude, a far cry from the exotic jewels of *Salammbô*. Flaubert's plans never materialized, but colonial modernity surfaces repeatedly, if somewhat elliptically, in his metropolitan novels, which is where we shall look for it in this volume.[121] It has been claimed that the 'Orient'—in fact North Africa—was the fountainhead of his inspiration even for his most metropolitan works.[122] Certainly it was from Constantinople in 1850 that he wrote of his project to work on the story of 'Anubis', 'la femme qui veut se faire baiser par le Dieu', one of the sources of *Salammbô*; he expressed anxiety that it was too closely linked to another project, this time for a provincial novel about a

[119] See *Carnets de travail*, 2 fol. 5v (dating from 1859–60) in *Œuvres complètes*, ed. by Claudine Gothot-Mersch, 3 vols to date (Paris: Gallimard 'Pléiade', 2001–13), III, p. 1047 (further references to the three volumes of the *Œuvres complètes* that have so far appeared in the Pléiade edition will be given within the text). See also Pierre-Marc de Biasi, *Gustave Flaubert: Une manière spéciale de vivre* (Paris: Grasset, 2009), p. 329; Marie-Jeanne Durry, *Flaubert et ses projets inédits* (Paris: Nizet, 1950) pp. 104–8; Anne Green, 'Flaubert's myth of civilisation and the Orient', in *Romantic Geographies*, ed. by Colin Smethurst (Glasgow: University of Glasgow French and German Publications, 1996), pp. 215–25. Maxime du Camp claims that Flaubert's novel, planned as early as 1849–51, was to take place 'sur les territoires à opium'; it was to be '*le Roman comique en Orient*' (emphasis in original; *Souvenirs littéraires* [1892], ed. by Daniel Oster (Paris: Aubier, 1994) p. 331). The project of a modern oriental novel is also evoked in Flaubert's letters to Jules Duplan (17 March 1867 and 14 March 1868), *Correspondance*, ed. by Jean Bruneau and Yvan Leclerc, 5 vols (Paris: Gallimard 'Pléiade', 1973–2007) III, p. 615, p. 735; and to Edma Roger des Genettes (10 November 1877) V, p. 324. Flaubert also wrote to his friend Ernest Feydeau encouraging him to write a 'grandissime roman sur l'Algérie'; 'Il y a plus à faire sur ce pays que Walter Scott n'a fait sur l'Écosse' (20 September 1860, *Correspondance*, III, p. 116).
[120] See Edmond and Jules de Goncourt, *Journal*, ed. by Robert Ricattte and Robert Kopp, 3 vols (Paris: Robert Laffont, 1989), I, p. 793 (29 March 1862).
[121] The presence of the colonies within Flaubert's metropolitan fiction has been discussed, though with more emphasis on Orientalism than on colonialism per se, for example by Lisa Lowe (*Critical Terrrains: French and British Orientalisms* (Ithaca/London: Cornell University Press, 1991)), Anne Green, 'Flaubert: Paris, Elsewhere', *Romance Studies*, 22 (1993), 7–15, and Jennifer Yee, 'Undermining Exoticism: Flaubert's use of antithesis in *L'Éducation sentimentale*', in *Dix-Neuf*, 15:1 (2011), 26–36.
[122] According to Du Camp's much-repeated account, it was in Egypt that Flaubert found inspiration for Emma Bovary (*Souvenirs littéraires*, p. 314). Later, the colonial writer Louis Bertrand, who had his own agenda, claimed that Flaubert's inspiration and literary energy, from 1850 onwards, had its sources in Africa (*Gustave Flaubert* (Paris: Mercure de France, 1912), chapter 'L'Orient et l'Afrique dans l'œuvre de Flaubert', pp. 49–94).

woman who dies 'vierge et mystique', which was one of the sources of *Madame Bovary* as well as of 'Un cœur simple'.[123]

Zola was clearly less attracted by travel and distant lands than were Balzac and Flaubert. Colonial themes were present in his early works *Madeleine Férat* and *Thérèse Raquin*, but they largely go underground in the Rougon-Macquart. They are to be found there in the form of embedded narratives and imported metaphors of racial difference.[124] They return in his later *roman à thèse*, *Fécondité* (1899), one of the 'Quatre Évangiles' series.[125] The ending of *Fécondité* strikes a note of colonial triumphalism that reflects an ideology that was only just emerging at the time. Indeed, Martin Steins credits Zola with being among the first to reject the overall attitude of anticolonialism among French writers.[126] Seillan argues that Zola shared the general pessimistic view of the colonies when he began to write *Fécondité*, seeing them as 'porteuses de mort'; the novel's utopian finale centring around the regenerative powers of the colonies was added very late in the writing of the novel, and with little basis in real knowledge of France's colonial situation in Sudan.[127] Zola had initially planned to have one of the young sons of the family die in a colonial war, which would have been more in keeping with the pessimistic attitude that was current at the time.[128] In any case, the colonial episode in *Fécondité* remains resolutely offstage, which is where imperialism is also to be found in the Rougon-Macquart series—even in *L'Argent*, where it plays an important role.[129]

From the 1880s onwards the growing 'littérature coloniale' movement applied many of the techniques of Zola's naturalist novel directly to France's colonial experience. Unlike the mainstream, metropolitan realist tradition, this new literature tended to take an overtly political stance in favour of colonialism in general, and more specifically of settler colonization. Here the techniques of Realism, in its naturalist variant, are identified much more clearly with the domination of extra-European lands and peoples. And yet even these novels, and even after the beginnings of a more pervasive colonial ideology in the last decades of the century, leave considerable space for doubt and anxiety.

[123] Letter to Louis Bouilhet (14 November 1850), *Correspondance*, I, p. 708.

[124] Susan Harrow gives a brief survey of some of the irruptions of colonialism into the Rougon-Macquart series in a footnote beginning 'What evidence is there for a postcolonial Zola?' (*Zola, The Body Modern: Pressures and Prospects of Representation* (Oxford: Legenda, 2010), p. 37 n. 26). References to the Rougon-Macquart series, given in parentheses, will be to *Les Rougon-Macquart: Histoire naturelle et sociale d'une famille sous le second empire*, ed. by Armand Lanoux and Henri Mitterand, 5 vols (Paris: Gallimard 'Pléiade', 1960–7).

[125] The final volume of the Quatre Évangiles series, *Justice*, was unfinished at Zola's death in 1902. According to Carmen Mayer-Robin, Zola's plan for *Justice* reveals an anti-imperialism that contrasts emphatically with the paean to colonial expansion that he included in *Fécondité* not many years earlier ('*Justice*, Zola's Global Utopian Gospel', *Nineteenth-Century French Studies*, 36:1–2 (2007), 135–49 (p. 136)).

[126] Martin Steins, 'Zola colonialiste', *Revue des Langues vivantes*, 41:1 (1975), 15–30.

[127] Jean-Marie Seillan, 'L'Afrique utopique de *Fécondité*', *Les Cahiers naturalistes*, 75 (2001), 183–202 (p. 184). See also David Baguley, Fécondité *d'Émile Zola: roman à thèse, évangile, mythe* (Toronto: University of Toronto Press, 1973), p. 98, p. 226.

[128] Martin Steins, 'L'épisode africain de *Fécondité*', *Les Cahiers naturalistes*, 48 (1974), 164–81 (p. 169).

[129] For an invaluable discussion of the minimal nature of Zola's response to French colonialism, see Jean-Marie Seillan, 'Zola et le fait colonial', *Cahiers naturalistes* 88 (2014), 13–26 and Corinne Saminadayar-Perrin, 'D'impossibles nouveaux mondes: Zola, *L'Argent* / *Fécondité*', *Cahiers naturalistes* 88 (2014), 27–44.

As we have seen, the representation of colonial issues in the realist novel created a sense of unease that was partly a question of genre; there was a tendency for novels that incorporated such issues to slip towards exoticism or the 'lower' genre of the adventure novel. Nevertheless, realist novelists often made use of colonial or exotic elements precisely in order to harness this unease, which echoed the geographical disjunction between metropolitan capitalism and its increasingly global reach. The short story form, meanwhile, seemed to welcome the exotic challenge to the very foundation of the novel's dominant mode of verisimilitude. This might help to explain why 'serious' writers who did seek to deal directly with extra-European lands or colonial spaces often avoided the novel in favour of short accounts, tales, vignettes, or snapshots. These range from fantastic oriental tales earlier in the period to the new, impressionistic 'littérature instantanée comme la photographie' of travel writing in the last decades of the century.[130] Their settings are often in the Middle East, India, or China, and they thrive on these 'remote and fabulous lands'.[131] These shorter forms lent themselves to a polemical use of exoticism *against* Realism—a self-aware exoticism that situates itself as a derivative, textually inspired tradition, in an implicit rupture with the mimetic contract. It is perhaps no surprise, then, that Balzac's oriental works took the form of long 'tales' instead of the novels he had planned.

Within the metropolitan novel itself, the colonial territories often become visible when one looks at the relation of text to subtext, or framing story to embedded story. The colonial comedy is to be found via these narrative doublings, as well as within the implicit framing that is evoked by fraudulent representation of many kinds. Indeed, as we shall see, fraudulence and ironic framing are recurrent features of Realism's approach to colonialism. Nineteenth-century Realism does engage with the colonial, extra-metropolitan nature of the emerging world-system, albeit indirectly. In doing so, at times it perpetuates stereotypes; at others it attempts to question them. The *idée reçue*—and the ironic framing of the *idée reçue*—will reappear throughout *The Colonial Comedy*.

---

[130] Paul Bonnetain, *Au Tonkin*, ed. by Frédéric Da Silva (Paris: L'Harmattan, 2010 [1884]), p. 73.
[131] Moretti, *Atlas of the European Novel*, pp. 55–7.

1

Imported Objects

Although the term 'Realism' came to the fore in debates during the 1850s, the beginnings of the realist novel are usually traced to the 1830s, which corresponds precisely with the opening of France's modern colonial period and the beginnings of the conquest of Algeria. It has been common literary-historical practice to police the boundaries between literary Realism on the one hand, and Orientalism or exoticism on the other, but such a separation is in fact deliberately explored by many writers. Balzac initiated his great realist works with a metropolitan novel haunted by Orientalism, *La Peau de chagrin*, the first of his novels to be signed with his own name and in many ways the doorway by which one enters the vast social world of *La Comédie humaine*.[1] Flaubert's 1869 *L'Éducation sentimentale* was written shortly *before* the rise of 'la littérature coloniale',[2] but it may offer us a hint of what such a literature could have become in his hands: in 1862, on completing *Salammbô*, Flaubert hesitated between his great Parisian novel and another project, which would have been a novel about 'l'Orient moderne'.[3] The most obvious Balzacian intertext for *L'Éducation sentimentale* is of course *Le Père Goriot*, but reading it alongside *La Peau de chagrin* instead can help us to understand how metropolitan Realism imports material objects from the broader world, and deliberately uses them to question the conventions of the realist mode even as those conventions are being established.[4]

THE DUALISM OF THE IMPORTED OBJECT

In the realist novel, the material object plays a central role through metonymy, often a multi-directional metonymy that points outward to the wider world and pins the novel to geographical and historical contexts through what Edward Said

---

[1] On *La Peau de chagrin* as the 'cellule-mère' of the *Comédie humaine,* see Albert Béguin, *Balzac lu et relu* (Paris: Seuil, 1965), p. 203.

[2] French 'littérature coloniale' is generally understood as dating to the period 1880s–1930s, though traces of it can be seen as early as the 1860s; in his acute awareness of France's North African colonies, Flaubert is ahead of his time.

[3] Goncourt, *Journal*, 1, p. 793 (29 March 1862). It was in March 1862 that Flaubert began a period of more than two years' reflection before beginning to write *L'Éducation sentimentale* (see Flaubert, *L'Éducation sentimentale: les scénarios*, ed. by Tony Williams (Paris: José Corti, 1992), Preface, p. 9). For more details of this project to write 'le *Roman comique en Orient*', see Durry, pp. 103–8.

[4] Page references, included in parentheses after quotations, are to *L'Éducation sentimentale*, ed. by Claudine Gothot-Mersch (Paris: GF-Flammarion, 1985).

calls 'geographical notations'.[5] The material objects that concern us here, imported into Europe from territories newly open to its political and economic expansion, have, by definition, a metonymic function that is at least *double*: they operate within their present context as consumer objects circulating in the metropolis, and at the same time as geographical notations pointing towards their original context. Through their function as geographical notations, imported objects give rise to an *effet d'exotisme*: standing for an absent 'elsewhere', they themselves come to signify foreignness and absence. Their exoticism appears to transcend the everyday banal world, but at the same time they belong within the inescapable realist context of money and work. This fundamental dualism of the realist exotic object can be linked to what Baudrillard calls the double meaning of 'les objets singuliers, baroques, folkloriques, exotiques, anciens'.[6] Their presence in the metropolitan or 'domestic realist' novel points in two metonymic directions simultaneously, thus indicating the radical unevenness that is integral to modernity.[7]

As we saw in the introduction, Moretti claims the colonies function primarily as a 'magic' source of money in the nineteenth-century English novel.[8] In the French realist novel, too, the imported object serves as a 'magic' sublimation of money; but it acts simultaneously *as a reminder that such sublimation is impossible*. Like the Freudian fetish object, the exotic object within the realist mode reinstates what it appears to deny. Moreover, the *effet d'exotisme* presents several problems to the realist mode. It introduces a rupture in the spatial contiguity that usually supports realist metonymy. And it has an antithetical relation to Barthes' *effet de réel*, which supports the impression of verisimilitude, often through evoking the familiar. In contrast, exotic or colonial imported objects focus on the unfamiliar (the *unheim-lich*), and thus appear to be undermining the very basis of the realist signifying mode. For the postcolonial critic Bhabha, culture is simultaneously *heimlich* and *unheimlich*, but 'mimetic narratives' are definitely on the *heimlich* side (along with 'disciplinary generalizations' and 'coherence').[9] Realist writing cannot however be reduced to the mimetic function alone, and it very often deliberately seeks to incorporate the *unheimlich* along with the mimetic, and disturbance within its coherence.

POLEMICAL USES OF THE EXOTIC AND FANTASTIC WITHIN REALISM

Within realist narratives, exotic objects sometimes serve to indicate banal literary stereotypes, and are thus a means of attacking Romanticism. This polemical use is however already present in a certain disillusioned Romanticism from the 1830s onwards. Realism in fact follows late Romanticism in employing exoticism as a self-conscious trope, and the exotic object provides a means of reflecting on the

[5] *Culture and Imperialism*, p. 69.
[6] Jean Baudrillard, *Le Système des objets* (Paris: Gallimard, 1968), p. 103.
[7] On unevenness as constitutive of the world-system of modernity, see WReC, ch. 1.
[8] *Atlas of the European Novel*, p. 27.   [9] *Location of Culture*, pp. 136–7.

problematic nature of the mimetic function itself. Firdous Azim suggests a similar function for the Gothic, which 'subverts and challenges the presuppositions of the realistic school, disturbing the easy narrative of growth that capitalist ideology would have liked to provide for its subjects'.[10] In the 1830s, when the realist novel is taking shape, the Gothic and fantastic modes develop alongside it. Indeed, the very nature of the fantastic arguably depends on the establishment of a convincing, recognizable contemporary context; take away the realism, and we would be in the domain of the 'marvellous'.[11] So the fantastic writing of the 1830s can be seen as a late-Romantic phenomenon that, far from being antithetical to realism, is part of its birth-throes. Indeed, the newest writing of the 1830s–1850s is arguably best characterized by its focus on questioning its own relation to the real. The debates around the term 'Realism' assumed such importance in French culture around the mid century precisely because of the emphasis on the real adopted by Romanticism, which meant that 'the conception of reality had become increasingly problematic'.[12]

Like the fantastic, exoticism allowed the realist narrative to test its preconditions from within. Balzac's Orientalism is not, as is sometimes suggested, self-indulgent wish-fulfilment, inconsistency, or weakness;[13] in fact he uses it to test the realist stance of his writing. After the 1830s the exotic object often entirely replaces the fantastic as a refuge for enchantment: the parrot of Flaubert's *Un cœur simple*, for example, comes from the Americas via a black servant, and its role as an exotic object is to provide an empty shell in which Félicité can invest the fantastic, or transcendence of everyday banality.

We shall begin, then, with an object that is both fantastic and quintessentially Oriental: the 'talisman' or wild ass's skin of Balzac's *Peau de chagrin* (1831).[14] This Skin is not subject to the laws of age and damage, but it exists within the emphatically materialist, familiar world of Balzac's contemporary Paris. In the antiquarian's shop on the *quai Voltaire* where the reader, and the at first nameless protagonist, initially see it, the Skin gleams mysteriously when everything else is plunged into shadows. Marked by what purports to be the Seal of Solomon, it appears to

---

[10] *Colonial Rise of the Novel*, p. 27. Along similar lines, Makdisi sees Romantic literature more generally as 'a privileged site for the exploration of alternatives to modernization, or the celebration of anti-modern exoticism' (*Romantic Imperialism*, p. 8).

[11] It is of course the influential, though perhaps a little too neat, definition of the fantastic developed by Todorov, that hinges on a distinction between the 'fantastic' (which has a realist context) and the 'marvellous' (which does not) (see his *Introduction à la littérature fantastique*).

[12] Brown, 'The Logic of Realism', p. 227.

[13] Mid-twentieth-century critics tended to look down on Balzac's Orientalism. Raymond Schwab sees Balzac's Orient as merely magical or fabulous, 'un fabuleux de Fortunatus. [...] Orient de talismans et de pierreries, de libertés sans fond et de facultés à double fond' (*La Renaissance orientale* (Paris: Payot, 1950), p. 371. It is seen as colourful *bric-à-brac* by Béguin in *Balzac lu et relu*, p. 83. Samuel Silvestre de Sacy sees Balzac's use of fantastic and exotic elements as a way of escaping his own doctrine that there should be interdependence between the human animal and his or her milieu ('Balzac et le mythe de l'aventurier', *Mercure de France* (1 January 1950), 115–28 (p. 120)).

[14] 'Le Talisman' is the title of the first of three books into which *La Peau de chagrin* is divided. It is also the title of a novel by Walter Scott (1825, translated into French the same year) in which the mysterious talisman comes from the Sultan Saladin himself. A 'chagrin' is an onager, or oriental ass, whose skin is supposed to have mysterious properties.

offer fabulous wealth, narrative potential, and meaning, in contrast to the constitutional hypocrisies of nineteenth-century Paris.[15]

Balzac uses the qualifier 'Oriental', at the most basic level, to evoke something that exceeds the everyday norms of metropolitan reality (the orgiastic dinner in book two of *La Peau de chagrin*, for example, is 'une féerie digne d'un conte oriental', X: 107). More specifically, the Oriental object stands for a world that miraculously escapes the grinding regime of Western capitalism and work. There is a fault-line between the realm of fortune and fulfilment and the demystified, secular world, and it is situated between East and West. An idealist lover would clothe his mistress in 'un moelleux tissu d'Orient' (X: 60), but is more often reduced to possessing her in squalor. The luxurious oriental décor of *La Fille aux yeux d'or* (1835) also offers a haven from the pitiless Parisian world in which individual energy must be spent working to earn money (the only means to sexual and social fulfilment), a world vividly described at the outset of the tale.[16] The implicit evocation of the *Arabian Nights* in these references suggests a fairy tale promise that it is possible to bypass the need for work in order to acquire money; this is precisely the premise of magical objects in many fantastic and marvellous stories, of which Fortunatus's eternally replenished purse is the archetype.[17]

In *La Peau de chagrin*, the mysterious object that purports to offer a fortune without work is the eponymous Skin. If its supposed magical properties are to be believed, it could in theory grant any wish at all, but the protagonist Raphaël de Valentin seeks to use it primarily in pursuit of material goals. The Skin thus shares some of the narrative characteristics of the motif of a fortune inherited from distant colonial lands: both could, on the surface, be described by Moretti's neat phrase '*pecunia ex machina*'. And alongside the Skin Balzac does in fact deploy the narrative device of the colonial fortune, not once but twice. Each of the wishes apparently granted by the supernatural Skin is realized in a way that could also have a naturalistic explanation, and most strikingly Raphaël's wish for a miraculous fortune sees him inheriting from an Irish uncle who died in Calcutta leaving a fortune with the Compagnie des Indes (described by one humorous commentator as 'une fortune *incalcuttable*', X: 208). Pauline, the devoted maiden who loves him, comes just as suddenly into a fortune when her father returns with his own fortune from 'les Indes'[18] (X: 140; 163; 228–9; 232).

[15] On Balzac's Orient as 'un espace idéologique à partir duquel se pense la réalité parisienne au lendemain immédiat de 1830', see Pierre Laforgue's excellent *1830: romantisme et histoire* (Paris: Eurédit, 2001), pp. 243–4.

[16] In another portrayal of the world of work, in his 'Traité de la vie élégante', Balzac shows that different material objects come to stand as 'des signes matériels du plus ou du moins de repos qu'un homme pouvait prendre', that is, of the extent to which he was exempt from the requirements of labour. The need for these material signs of status became more acute after the Revolution, when social standing was no longer defined simply by inheritance (XII: 218).

[17] Fortunatus, the hero of a popular tale dating from the fifteenth or sixteenth century, possessed a magic purse that was always full.

[18] Probably also India rather than the West Indies, given that he seems to have reached them overland from Siberia after the defeat of the Napoleonic army in Russia. On Balzac's tendency to use the term 'Indes' without distinguishing between the West Indies and India, see Citron, 'Le Rêve asiatique', p. 306.

This double evocation of distant India, where France maintained a narrow imperial stake in the form of its *comptoirs*, has a parallel in the choice of an Indian language, Sanskrit, for the mysterious text that appears on the Skin, and in the
antiquarian's acquisition of it from a 'bramine' or 'brachmane' (X: 88; 204). However,
when Balzac decided to include the original of the inscription for the 1838 edition
(in earlier editions only the French had been given), he opted to change its language
from Sanskrit to Arabic. He failed to make the necessary changes to the overall text
of the novel, so that an embarrassing inconsistency persists; but the half-completed
shift from Sanskrit to Arabic is in itself revelatory. The initial choice of Sanskrit
reflects the important role of that ancient Indian language as part of a Romantic
quest for meaning (the first translations of the *Upanishads*, from Sanskrit into Latin,
had been published by Anquetil-Duperron in 1801–02, and Herder and Schlegel
saw the study of Sanskrit and ancient India as the means to understand the origins of
language and humanity itself). However, by the time Balzac began to write the story
in the second half of 1830, India may have seemed less important. France had lost its
Indian colonies and retained only a few trading posts, whereas the conquest of
Algeria, about which he was enthusiastic, had just begun in June–July of that very
year. Moreover, France was in thrall to a new daydream of oriental imperialism
bequeathed by the brief Napoleonic expedition to Egypt: the final volume of the
twenty-three-volume *Description de l'Égypte* initiated by Napoleon had appeared
only in 1828, and the 'question d'Orient' held out tantalizing possibilities concerning the future of the weakened Ottoman empire, with all its resonance of the *Arabian
Nights*.[19] So, while the East—in a broad sense stretching from the Mediterranean to
India—seemed a land of inexhaustible potential, the focus of French attention was
shifting closer to home, to lands where Arabic was spoken rather than to those whose
mysterious insights were written in Sanskrit.

Despite this shift towards a more contemporary focus, even the 'naturalistic'
sources of fortune in *La Peau de chagrin* are touched by the improbability of the
East. Not only does Raphaël not benefit from his Oriental fortune, his family *lost*
its fortune when 'Le gouvernement révolutionnaire n'a pas voulu admettre [leurs]
créances dans la liquidation qu'il a faite de la compagnie des Indes' (III: 99). There
is something not only improbable but ghostlike about the Indian inheritances of
Pauline and Raphaël, which ties in with the nostalgic melancholy of Raphaël's
(various) lost family fortunes and lost mother: his friend Émile jestingly sums up
his air of failed inheritance by playing on his surname to call him 'le descendant de
l'empereur *Valens* [...] héritier légitime de l'empire d'Orient. Si nous laissons
trôner Mahmoud à Constantinople, c'est par pure bonne volonté, et faute d'argent
ou de soldats' (X: 99).

However implausible, the colonial explanations given for Raphaël and Pauline's
sudden inheritances appear to offer a materialist '*pecunia ex machina*'. The supernatural
Skin itself does not, however, offer a fortune without any strings attached: an allegory

---

[19] Balzac discussed the shifts of power resulting from the weakness of the Ottoman empire at some
length in 'La France et l'étranger', *Chronique de Paris*, 24 February–24 July 1836 (in *Œuvres complètes*,
28 vols (Paris: Guy Le Prat/Club de l'honnête homme, 1963), vol. 27, 311–436).

for the finite nature of human energy, it—and its owner's life—shrinks with every wish. In the Balzacian world where energy, or capital, exists in a tight balance of input and output, the Orient (or, in other novels, the Americas) appears to offer an exception, but this proves illusory. In *La Peau de chagrin* the offer of a 'free' fortune relies either on the fantastic wealth of the *Arabian Nights* or on a colonial inheritance; this is part of the tension between supernatural and materialist explanations that gives the novel its productive energy. But within a world inescapably dominated by the contemporary metropolitan reality of money, neither a naturalistic-colonial fortune nor a magical fortune can provide a viable solution. The Oriental Skin serves as a test case for Realism in other ways too, since the limits of empirical knowledge are exposed when scientists and doctors are unable to explain its fabrication or combat its effects. The inexplicable Oriental object—inherently unfamiliar, in rupture with contiguity, and not subject to the laws of materialism—tests the boundaries of the new realist project. And yet it is most emphatically tied to the real world, through the contexts of capitalism and—less obviously—imperialism.

CAPITALISM: THE OBJECT WITHIN A SYSTEM OF EXCHANGE

As well as being a metaphor or an allegory for life, Balzac's Skin also works as metonymy. The recent fashion for studies of collections has led some to forget the obvious, namely that the Skin is acquired not in a museum but in a shop and that therefore, by implication, it circulates as an object within a system of exchange.[20] Paradoxically, it defies materialist rules and suggests an archaic, pre-capitalist economy, while at the same time standing for materialism and appearing to offer the luxury without which Raphaël cannot conceive of life or love. In Balzac's hands the double metonymy of the exotic object allows it to yoke together the system of exchange and monetary value on the one hand, and the illusory promise of a transcendence of this system: it asserts and disavows at the same time.

The pinning of the Oriental object to the harsh regime of money occurs first of all through the emphatically metropolitan context. Instead of a heroic Napoleonic adventurer in the Orient, we have an anonymous individual entering a Parisian shop (in Théophile Gautier's half-serious parody of the scene, 'Pied de momie' (1840), Balzac's suicidal 'jeune homme' becomes a nonchalant *flâneur*/consumer).[21] The irony of a mysterious Oriental object being on sale in a Parisian shop has later echoes in Flaubert's 1869 *L'Éducation sentimentale* where mass-produced plaster

[20] The grounding of *La Peau de chagrin*'s Orientalism in a shop, like the fact that the initial scene of the novel takes place in a gambling hall, makes it clear that we are in a world in which money (and by extension) energy, circulates; this is in sharp contrast to the immobile oriental interior of *La Fille aux yeux d'or* (see Éric Bordas, 'L'Orient balzacien', p. 327 n. 20; p. 328).

[21] Gautier's short story, a fine example of Romantic irony, links the banal metropolitan context of financial exchange to the ultimate pre-capitalist world of Ancient Egypt (Théophile Gautier, 'Le Pied de momie', in *Contes fantastiques* (Paris: José Corti, 1986 [1962]), pp. 149–63.

negroes and oriental-style pottery are for sale.[22] The Skin itself is not literally paid
for with money, but Raphaël accepts a contract in which he pays with his life;
the references to Mephistopheles and the diabolical pact are frequent enough to
remind us of the Faustian antecedents of such a transaction, though in this secular
context there is no mention of his immortal soul. The opening scene of the novel
saw him lay down his last gold coin (a Napoleon, worth about 20 francs) in a
gambling house in the Palais Royal: that coin is a synecdoche for his life, and its
loss is proleptic of his fatal transaction in the antiquarian's shop. In the opening
scene of *L'Éducation sentimentale* too, the young protagonist Frédéric hands over
his last gold coin to the ragged singer of an Oriental song on the boat where he has
just fallen in love, in a furtive act of homage to his idol (though the sacrifice is
bathetic since his mother's servant is to meet him to take him home after the boat
trip). With this last gold coin both men hand over their life energy in exchange for
an obscure Oriental object of desire, Raphaël in the tragic mode, and Frédéric in
the mode of bathos and parody. The protagonist-narrator of Gautier's parody
exchanges not one, but five gold coins for the perfect object of Oriental fetishism,
that is, the mummified foot of an Egyptian princess.[23] So a monetary transaction
is, implicitly at least, at the heart of the matter, and as Raphaël leaves the shop to
pursue his postponed suicide, he unthinkingly puts the Skin in his pocket (X:
89)—the same pocket in which he had previously heard a few stray 'sous' 'retentir
d'une manière véritablement fantastique' when he thought he had nothing left at
all (X: 66) and from which he had taken his last gold coin not long before. In this
realist world everything can be bought, even the Renaissance painting of Christ by
Raphaël's namesake, which Balzac's shopkeeper says that he covered in gold coins.
Nor should one consider the links between Orientalism and the commercial to be
fortuitous: as Jeanne Bem puts it, 'en français, dans *Orient* il y a *or*'.[24]

That the Skin operates as a financial fetish, sublimating the power of money,
naturally does not prevent it evoking another kind of phallic object altogether.
Thanks to Raphaël's own dirty joke the metaphor by which it is an allegory for life
and human desire can be unpacked to make it also that other skin that normally
grows with desire rather than shrinking (X: 204), and whose shrinkage causes the
despair of beautiful women (X: 258). Peter Brooks argues that Balzac's Skin is a
figuration of desire, but that desire is 'inherently unsatisfied and unsatisfiable'.[25] In
other words, it is possible to read this tale as a parable of impotence in a world
where sexual and monetary energy are finite, and once spent are spent. The poetics

---

[22] Christophe Ippolito makes the comparison: 'Arnoux's store recalls that of Magus in *La Peau de
chagrin*', though he appears to be conflating Élie Magus (who appears notably in *Le Cousin Pons*) with
the unnamed antiquarian of *La Peau de chagrin*. See *Narrative Memory in Flaubert's Works* (New York/
Oxford: Peter Lang, 2001), p. 118.

[23] Gautier explicitly states that the transaction undertaken in the Parisian *bric-à-brac* shop is bind-
ing not only in the material, but also in the spiritual world ('Le Pied de momie', p. 158). Gautier's
Parisian shopkeeper is very much like the antiquarian of *La Peau de chagrin* (with his Jewish air and
vice-like hands), but even older, and certainly more humorously diabolical (p. 153).

[24] Jeanne Bem, 'L'Orient ironique de Flaubert', in *Le Texte traversé* (Paris: Champion, 1991),
pp. 131–41 (p. 135).

[25] *Reading for the Plot*, p. 55.

of impotence that arise from this parallel are as crucial to Flaubert's writing as they are to Balzac's.

In *L'Éducation sentimentale*, Frédéric Moreau remains in thrall to the Romantic ideal of the exotic as transcendence, but this allegiance is repeatedly satirized, specifically through the linkage of the exotic with capitalism and colonialism. While his childhood friend Deslauriers dreams of wealth 'comme moyen de puissance sur les hommes', Frédéric 'se meublait un palais à la Moresque, pour vivre couché sur des divans de cachemire, au murmure d'un jet d'eau, servi par des pages nègres' (104). Unlike Raphaël he *expects* an inheritance from his uncle; when anticipating, and later spending it, he focuses on accessory and ornamental *things*, exotic material objects that stand for the transcendence of everyday modern life. Frédéric's exotic impulses are inseparable from commodity fetishism in that they are tied to a sublimation of money. He purchases three earthenware plates 'décorées d'arabesques jaunes, à reflets métalliques'; Deslauriers says that if it were him, he would buy 'de l'argenterie', revealing 'par cet amour du cossu, l'homme de mince origine'. Here the orientalist impulse is associated with Frédéric's bourgeois status, whereas Deslauriers is attracted to immediately apparent commercial value; but ironically, the plates are worth 'cent écus la pièce' (500 francs) and their metallic sheen reminds us that they too incarnate bourgeois value (168). The exotic commodity fetish is thus simultaneously a *denial* of the central role of money and the sign of its covert *reinscription*. At another stage of Frédéric's daydreams, expecting to inherit the wealth of the banker M. Dambreuse through marriage to his widow, he plans the changes he will make in the house: a private art gallery,[26] perhaps, and 'il y avait moyen, peut-être, d'organiser en bas une salle de bains turcs. Quant au bureau de M. Dambreuse, pièce déplaisante, à quoi pouvait-elle servir?' (456). So exoticism offers a sublimation of metropolitan commercial realities, replacing the solid values of *l'argent* or *l'argenterie* with arabesques, and the drab workplace with a Turkish bathroom. The office where money was procured through financial manipulation is to be erased from the daydream house, plumbing permitting.

Walter Benjamin situates the historical separation of the private space of dwelling from the place of work at exactly this time, during the reign of Louis-Philippe when '[t]he private individual [...] needs the domestic interior to sustain him in his illusions' and it must be kept separate from the office. This new private individual is most clearly in evidence in the form of the collector who—like Frédéric imagining his inheritance of the banker's domain—has the task of 'divesting things of their commodity character by taking possession of them'. The exotic object, in particular, serves the collector's purpose because it evokes 'a world that is not just distant and long gone but also better [...] in which things are freed from the drudgery of being useful'. Benjamin also quotes letters from Paris in the 1840s that describe the fashionable 'dreamy and, if possible, oriental interior': 'Everyone here

---

[26] According to Rémy G. Saisselin, *L'Éducation sentimentale* shows us how 'the arts in bourgeois society came to be the pretext of [...] a life divorced from work'. See *Bricabracomania: The Bourgeois and the Bibelot* (London: Thames & Hudson, 1985), p. 29.

dreams of instant fortune; everyone aims to have, at one stroke, what in peaceful and industrious times would cost a lifetime of effort. The creations of the poets are full of sudden metamorphoses in domestic existence; they all rave about marquises and princesses, about the prodigies of the *Thousand and One Nights*. It is an opium trance that has overspread the whole population, and industry is more to blame for this than poetry.'[27]

Flaubert's novel self-consciously shows us the exotic object in its dual function, reiterating the very banality it appears to transcend. Jeanne Bem, following Marx, stresses the sublimation of money in circulation so that gold is replaced by increasingly abstract symbols of value.[28] The social aspirations of that peasant's daughter, Emma Bovary, are also invested in her fetishization of commodities that stand for money, rather than in money itself, which is only manipulated directly by the capitalist Dambreuse or the trader Lheureux. In Marxist terms, the fetishization of commodities sublimates what is essentially the production of labour; the exotic object, like the fantastic object, simply exaggerates what is already fantastic and transcendent in the commodity in general.[29] The stance of the orientalizing collector both denies the centrality of money and covertly reinstates it; like Freud's sexual fetishist, he or she has simultaneously retained and given up a belief in his or her missing object.[30] It is important, however, to note that we are deliberately reminded of this sublimation. Balzac's fantastic oriental Skin is ironically held up as escaping normal processes of production ('[l]'industrie du Levant a des secrets qui lui sont réellement particuliers', X: 83). Flaubert's exotic objects remind us more directly of the processes of manufacture and transaction (Arnoux's exotic pottery; the bungled paintwork on the plaster statues in the Alhambra dance hall).[31]

THE OBJECT IN COLONIAL CONTEXT

In *La Peau de chagrin*, as we have seen, the distinction between orientalist and colonial geographical notations is situated along the same fault-lines as the tension between the fantastic and realist modes: of the two possible explanations for Raphaël

[27] Walter Benjamin, 'Paris, Capital of the Nineteenth Century' (1939), in *The Arcades Project*, trans. by Howard Eiland and Kevin McLaughlin (Cambridge, MA: Belknap Press, 2003 [1999]), p. 19; quoting Gutzkow (*Briefe aus Paris*, 1842), p. 214.

[28] Jeanne Bem, *Clefs pour l'Éducation sentimentale* (Tübingen/Paris: Gunter Narr/Jean-Michel Place, 1981), p. 78.

[29] Marx emphasizes the 'fantastic' nature of the commodity, which can best be understood by analogy with 'the misty realm of religion' where human products appear to be 'endowed with a life of their own' and human labour is sublimated as a 'relation between things' (*Capital*, trans. by Ben Fowkes, 3 vols (London: Penguin, 1990 [1976]) vol. 1, pp. 165–6).

[30] Sigmund Freud, 'Fetishism' (1927), in *On Sexuality*, trans. by James Strachey, ed. by Angela Richards (London: Penguin 1977), p. 353.

[31] It seems a little reductive, then—given that both Balzac and Flaubert expose this sublimation for what it is—to say along with Edward Said that in their novels 'the consolidation of authority includes, indeed is built into the very fabric of, both private property and marriage, institutions that are only rarely challenged', *Culture and Imperialism*, pp. 91–2.

and Pauline's sudden fortunes, one is supernatural, fantastic, and Romantic-Orientalist, while the other is materialist, realist, and colonial. This contrast of Romantic Orientalism and Realist colonialism is also used to deliberately ironic effect by Flaubert in the 1869 *L'Éducation sentimentale*.

From the 1850s onwards, Flaubert's Orientalism is self-consciously 'belated'. He himself had been attracted in his youth to a Byronic, that is primarily Turkish Orient, but during his travels in 1849–51 he 'discovered' a new, grittier exoticism in North Africa.[32] *Madame Bovary* and *L'Éducation sentimentale* parody the older Turkish Orientalism; and they juxtapose it with explicitly colonial references.[33] This introduces another layer to the polemical effect of the imported object: not only is the exotic referent a challenge to the realist mode (as we have seen), but exoticism itself is challenged by the (new) colonial context. To do this without resorting to authorial intervention, Flaubert uses an 'echoing' technique, where a brief mention early in the book is picked up and transformed later on, most notably in the famous references to the brothel that begin and end *L'Éducation sentimentale* (arguably Flaubert's most tightly structured novel). In the second chapter, Frédéric and Deslauriers stroll past a 'maison basse' (65); in the final chapter of the novel, they reminisce about the abortive visit paid by their youthful selves to this establishment 'au bord de l'eau' (bordello) run by a woman called 'de son vrai nom Zoraïde Turc' who may be, as many believe, 'une musulmane, une Turque', an episode they now judge to have been the high point of their lives precisely because the sexual encounter they had planned did not take place (509–10). The pseudo-Turkish brothel reduces to a dodgy advertising ploy the spectre of the Romantic Orient made popular by Byron and Hugo; it is the space in which the two friends had hoped to reach a climactic transcendence of the everyday. The failure of this exotico-sexual aspiration is a structuring device that frames the entire novel, *including* any potential transcendence contained in Frédéric's unfulfilled love for Mme Arnoux. And a whole series of false exotic signifiers appear throughout the novel.

At Frédéric's first meeting with Mme Arnoux, in the opening scene of the novel, he perceives her through an aura of misleading exoticism. He imagines her to be Creole or Andalusian, whereas she is from Chartres; the boat on which they meet suggests the context of an exotic voyage, whereas it is taking him back to his mother's provincial house. The scene includes surprising reminders of Flaubert's own travels in Egypt and his earlier exotic novel, *Salammbô*.[34] It has attracted considerable

---

[32] On the contrast of the Byronic, Turkish Orient with the 'Orient' of the desert and North Africa, which he prefers, see his letters to Louis Bouilhet, 14 November 1850 (*Correspondance* I: 709) and to Louise Colet, 27 March 1853 (II: p. 283). Flaubert does not however reject the Byronic Orient as being false (see letter to Ernest Chesneau, 27 September 1868 (III: 807)).

[33] This is explored in more detail in my article 'Undermining Exoticism: Flaubert's use of antithesis in *L'Éducation sentimentale*', *Dix-Neuf*, 15:1 (2011), 26–36.

[34] The influence of Flaubert's Egyptian travels on his metropolitan writing is discussed by Adrianne Tooke ('Flaubert's travel writings', in *The Cambridge Companion to Flaubert*, ed. by Timothy Unwin (Cambridge: Cambridge University Press, 2004), pp. 51–66 (p. 64)). See also Jennifer Yee, '"Like an apparition": Oriental Ghosting in Flaubert's *Éducation sentimentale*', *French Studies*, 67:3 (2013), 340–54.

critical attention,[35] and I shall return to it, to look more specifically at Mme Arnoux's black maidservant, in Chapter 5. Here I wish to concentrate instead on the second meeting of Frédéric and Marie Arnoux, when he is at last invited to the Arnoux's home. The scene has been the object of much less analysis, but it too is key to an understanding of how Mme Arnoux herself is constructed by Frédéric's gaze as an Oriental object that transcends the everyday and yet, at the same time, is bathetically pinned down to colonial and capitalist contexts.

Entering the Arnoux apartment, Frédéric literally stumbles over the eclectic exotic objects that it contains, signs of M. Arnoux's social and artistic pretentions.[36] When the object of Frédéric's affections does at last appear, she is near invisible apart from one dramatic detail:

> Arnoux rentra; et, par l'autre portière, Mme Arnoux parut. Comme elle se trouvait enveloppée d'ombre, il ne distingua d'abord que sa tête. Elle avait une robe de velours noir et, dans les cheveux, une longue bourse algérienne en filet de soie rouge qui, s'entortillant à son peigne, lui tombait sur l'épaule gauche. (95)

As in her much-discussed 'apparition' on the boat, Frédéric is fixated by Mme Arnoux's clothing and intimate objects *in lieu* of her body.[37] Her dark clothing has been understood as suggestive of chastity, which neglects the fact that it gives even more emphasis to the brilliant red colour of the detail.[38] Here, as Claude Duchet says of Emma Bovary, female clothes 'au lieu de se dissoudre dans la chair [...] prennent leur autonomie à l'égard du corps'.[39] Strangely, the 'longue bourse algérienne en filet de soie rouge' has received little critical elucidation in the English-speaking world, perhaps partly because the main translations of the novel

---

[35] On Orientalism in Flaubert's metropolitan works, see in particular Lisa Lowe's 'Nationalism and Exoticism: Nineteenth-Century Others in Flaubert's *Salammbô* and *L'Education sentimentale*', in *Macropolitics of Nineteenth-Century Literature: Nationalism, Exoticism, Imperialism*, ed. Jonathan Arac and Harriet Ritvo (Philadelphia, PA: University of Pennsylvania Press, 1991), pp. 213–42; Giovanni Bonaccorso, *L'Oriente nella narrativa di Gustave Flaubert*, 2 vols (Messina: Edizioni Dott. Antonino Sfameni, 1979–81); Anne Green, 'Flaubert: Paris, Elsewhere', *Romance Studies*, 22 (1993), 7–15.

[36] The Arnoux's antichambre is 'décorée à la chinoise, avait une lanterne peinte au plafond, et des bambous dans les coins'; Frédéric stumbles over 'une peau de tigre' and counter-intuitively finds their home 'un endroit paisible, honnête et familier tout ensemble' (95)—which underlines the dishonesty and unfamiliarity of the exotic masquerade.

[37] See for example Maureen Jameson, 'Métonymie et trahison dans *L'Education sentimentale*', *Nineteenth-Century French Studies*, 19:4 (1991), 566–82; and Françoise Grauby, 'Corps privé et vêtement public: Les Jeux et les enjeux du costume féminin dans *L'Education sentimentale* de Flaubert', *New Zealand Journal of French Studies*, 18:1 (1997), 5–19.

[38] Dark clothing emphasizes Mme Arnoux's sexual non-availability according to R.J. Sherrington (*Three Novels by Flaubert: A Study of Techniques* (Oxford: Clarendon Press, 1970), pp. 275–6 and p. 278); Michel Raimond ('Le Corps féminin dans *L'Éducation sentimentale*', in *Flaubert, la femme, la ville*, ed. by Marie-Claire Bancquart (Paris: Presses Universitaires de France, 1983), 23–31 (p. 28)); and Milad Doueihi ('Flaubert's Costumes', *Modern Language Notes*, 101:5 (1986), 1086–9). Evelyne Woestelandt instead points out the double function of nineteenth-century female dress, the 'double jeu d'incitation et de refus', where details play a role of particular importance ('Système de la mode dans *L'Éducation sentimentale*', *The French Review*, 58:2 (1984), 244–54 (p. 245)).

[39] Claude Duchet, 'Romans et objets. L'exemple de *Madame Bovary*', *Europe* (1969), 172–201 (p. 175). Duchet excludes clothing from his definition of the Flaubertian object, but he makes an exception for items of clothing that do not simply blend in.

all elide the word 'bourse'.[40] Returning to the 'bourse' of the original French allows us to see the curious headdress as a striking example of the multiple metonymy of the imported object, fitting as it does into two very different paradigms: Algeria on the one hand; and the purse or money on the other. It also initiates a third paradigm, which can be understood as a sublimation of both colonialism and commerce: that of the red ornament worn in the hair. For Flaubert red is, according to Bem—who does mention the passage—'la couleur de l'Orient'.[41] The red Algerian purse, detached from its background, imprints itself on Frédéric's retina. After dinner, 'Il regardait attentivement les effilés de sa coiffure, caressant par le bout son épaule nue; et il n'en détachait pas ses yeux, il enfonçait son âme dans la blancheur de cette chair féminine' (98). That these 'effilés' belong to the Algerian net purse, and that this fixation is intended to highlight the gap between Frédéric's subjective urge towards transcendence and the objective materialization of his obsession in a simple purse, is suggested by Flaubert's repetition of the word 'filet' in a draft of the scene where he added in the margin 'Tout le temps qu'elle lui parla il regarda son filet—intensité—abîme entre l'objectif et le subjectif' (N.A.F.17600.163).

Mme Arnoux's 'longue bourse algérienne' also gives us a pun. A 'bourse' is a purse, standing metonymically for money; it is also a metaphor for the testicles.[42] The provocatively coloured 'longue bourse' is thus an opportune object for fetishist fixation. And of course this suggestive fetish-ornament also stands metonymically for the world of money and commerce, associating the chaste Marie Arnoux with commercial sexuality almost from the outset. Early plans of the novel saw Mme Arnoux becoming Frédéric's mistress in deed as well as in spirit, and the final version has retained, constantly present but invisible to Frédéric, hints at her potential availability.[43] But why does this object also point to Algeria?

Lisa Lowe's discussion of the oriental motif in *L'Éducation sentimentale* sees it as signifying only the emptiness of Orientalism itself as a discourse, and thus standing

[40] They give, variously: a 'long Algerian cap' (translation by D.F. Hannigan, for H.S. Nichols, 1898); a 'long Algerian headdress' (by Anthony Goldsmith, for Everyman's Library, 1941; and by Robert Baldick, 1964, revised by Geoffrey Wall, for Penguin Classics, 2004); a 'long Algerian red silk net' (by Douglas Parmée, for Oxford World's Classics, 1989); and a 'long Algerian snood in red silk net' (by Adrianne Tooke, for Wordsworth Editions, 2003).

[41] 'L'Orient ironique', p. 134; see also p. 137, p. 138. Bonaccorso also suggests parallels between Mme Arnoux in this scene and Flaubert's famous encounter with the Egyptian Kuchouk-Hanem (*L'Oriente*, pp. 191–2).

[42] This double meaning is reminiscent of a similar connotation in the red 'glands' of the awning on the boat, under which Frédéric first saw her. Charles Bernheimer points out the double meaning of the word 'glands', though only in relation to Flaubert's encounter with Kuchouk-Hanem (*Figures of Ill Repute: Representing Prostitution in Nineteenth-Century France* (Durham/London: Duke University Press, 1997 [1989], pp. 138–9).

[43] In the *Éducation sentimentale* of 1845, the love affair between Henry and Mme Renaud is far from being platonic. Here too we find a hanging ornament with a sensually caressing tassel and sexually suggestive shape. When Madame Renaud appears dressed for her dinner party, 'elle avait passé dans les dents du peigne une petite chaîne d'or qui se cachait dans sa chevelure comme un serpent et dont le gland qui en terminait un des bouts lui retombait sur l'oreille'. The use of a gold ornament points towards the 1869 purse, but here there is no colonial referent. *Œuvres de jeunesse*, ed. by Claudine Gothot-Mersch and Guy Sagnes (Paris: Gallimard, 2001), p. 854.

for incompletion.[44] While I agree that this is true of the *effet d'exotisme* and the Orient in general, an Algerian reference, in the context of 1840s Paris, is much more specific. Neferti Tadiar sees the details of the novel as 'not imaginary ornaments but material goods obtained from the colonies' whose 'integration into the domestic economy and incorporation into the modern subject's imaginary [...] is a central operation of the fantasy of imperialism'.[45] Flaubert is however commenting on, rather than simply participating in, the fantasy of imperialism. Indeed, like Barthes a century later,[46] he is exposing exoticism's central function as being the denial of history, and shows us, behind the vague Orient of fantasy, colonial Algeria: the exotic is brought out of the realm of the imaginary and into the world of *bêtise* and money. The juxtaposition of exotic daydream and colonial reality appears notably through delayed antithesis. Before inheriting his uncle's money, Frédéric daydreams of exotic adventure: 'il voulait se faire trappeur en Amérique, servir un pacha en Orient, s'embarquer comme matelot; et il exhalait sa mélancolie dans de longues lettres à Deslauriers' (146). In a direct reprise of this derivative list, with its echoes of Fenimore Cooper and Byron, we learn at the end of the novel that Deslauriers has actually lived out a version of Frédéric's fantasy: 'il avait été, ensuite, chef de colonisation en Algérie, secrétaire d'un pacha, gérant d'un journal, courtier d'annonces, pour être finalement employé au contentieux dans une compagnie industrielle' (506). The list structure used in both passages gives us a typically Flaubertian pseudo-inventory whose effect is to remove any sense of order or prioritization of one term over another. The second list is a degraded version of the first, which has occurred hundreds of pages, and some twenty-five years, earlier. Frédéric's daydream has become a sordid reality for Deslauriers; the vague exotic space (America, the Orient) has become specifically colonial Algeria; one does not simply 'serve' a pacha, one becomes, in the banal modern world of the colonial comedy, his secretary.[47] The terms are both precise and ill-defined—what exactly is a 'chef de colonisation en Algérie'?—suggesting a series of ill-assorted positions, vaguely corrupt, financially and socially precarious; and of course, in typical Flaubertian style, moving from a rhetorical flourish at the beginning to a desperately banal end-point.

Frédéric's orientalist daydreams are outdated in the 1840s, when the novel is set, and Flaubert's colonial references indicate this. The period 1840–7 saw the most intense and decisive campaigns of the French conquest of Algeria, which aroused new interest in the French press and general public, where the conquest allowed patriotism to regain some of the prestige it had lost following the revolutions of

---

[44] 'Nationalism and Exoticism', pp. 231–2.

[45] Neferti Xina M. Tadiar, 'The Dream-Work of Modernity: The Sentimental Education of Imperial France', *boundary 2*, 22:1 (1995), 143–83 (p. 173). Tadiar, working from the English translation, misses the multiple connotations of the 'longue bourse'.

[46] Roland Barthes, *Mythologies* [1957], in *Œuvres complètes*, ed. by Éric Marty, 3 vols (Paris: Seuil, 1993) vol. 1, p. 664.

[47] On the vague and serial nature of people's professions in *L'Éducation sentimentale*, see Alain Raitt, 'La Décomposition des personnages dans *L'Éducation sentimentale*', in *Flaubert: la dimension du texte*, ed. P.M. Wetherill (Manchester: Manchester University Press, 1982), pp. 157–74.

1789 and 1830 and the Napoleonic defeat.[48] As a result, Benjamin points out, the Parisian exhibition salons were 'full of oriental scenes calculated to arouse enthusiasm for Algiers'.[49] Such décor, like Marie Arnoux's fashionable Algerian headdress,[50] is part of an embryonic colonial ideology to which Flaubert, like Benjamin, carefully calls our attention: the Arnoux's dinner guests include two fictitious artists, Jules Burrieu, 'qui commençait à populariser par ses dessins les guerres d'Algérie', and 'l'inventeur du paysage oriental, le fameux Dittmer' (83).

We should be wary of dismissing such references, in the hands of a master of social observation such as Flaubert, as 'mere' period detail. As we know, one of the structuring principles of *L'Éducation sentimentale* is the divorce of individual experience from political events, which have no apparent relationship to individual volition or consciousness. Flaubert was writing a new sort of historical novel, in which attempts to reach a historical overview are deliberately frustrated.[51] Just as Flaubert gives us deliberately fragmentary glimpses of events leading up to the revolution of 1848, so too he introduces elliptical links between the metropolis and the broader context of France's new colonial expansion. The two are of course linked, since the conquest of Algeria had been initiated (by the Bourbon monarchy in 1830) and continued (by the Orleanist monarchy that succeeded it in that same year) in order to distract public attention from internal affairs. As a result, French imperialism in North Africa is a subterranean presence in the metropolitan politics of the novel. Defending the 'Arabes', as Frédéric does at one of Mme Dambreuse's evening receptions, is part of a provocative attack on the government and the King (305). His bourgeois audience does not take this at all seriously, fortunately for Frédéric, but the defence of the Arab cause is clearly associated with criticism of Louis-Philippe's government, and in one of the drafts there is an even clearer link between the 'Arab' cause and that of the working classes, since Frédéric 'défendit' 'les Arabes' and 'les prolétaires'.[52] In a less abstract allusion, when Frédéric and Rosanette go to the races, 'tous les regards se tournaient vers le célèbre Algérien Bou-Maza, qui se tenait impassible, entre deux officiers d'état-major' (266). Bou-Maza, one of the leaders of the Algerian resistance, had been made prisoner in April 1847. In an early draft version, he is described in a term resonant of Montesquieu as 'un Persan', suggesting he was to have had a function as outsider observing the cross-section of Parisian classes at the races.[53] The surrender of the

[48] Charles-André Julien, *Histoire de l'Algérie contemporaine*, vol. 1, *La Conquête et les débuts de la colonisation (1827–1871)* (Paris: Presses Universitaires de France, 1964), p. 173.

[49] Benjamin, quoting Gutzkow's letters of 1842 (*Arcades Project*, p. 215).

[50] In 1846 Flaubert mentions in a letter to Louise Colet that 'des bourses algériennes' were fashionable worn in the hair two years earlier (13 October 1846, *Correspondance*, I, pp. 386–7). See also Woestelandt, 'Système de la mode', p. 247, p. 250. On the widespread circulation of everyday consumer objects that served a propaganda purpose in relation to the ongoing conquest, see Sessions, p. 130.

[51] Bem follows Sartre in calling Flaubert's treatment of history 'non informative et même désinformative' (*Clefs*, p. 80).

[52] N.A.F.17605/191V°. Deslauriers, at the examination in which he fails his Law thesis, also gives a (very general) defence of the 'oppressed' races, with whom he clearly identifies (165).

[53] N.A.F.17605.13, crossed out. Since Montesquieu, the Persian has represented the epitome of the foreigner whose gaze reveals a new way of seeing the Parisian world. The same draft also makes

more famous Abd el-Kader, in December of the same year, is not explicitly mentioned in the novel, but arguably it is obliquely present. The bankrupt M. Arnoux is described by Pellerin as being on the point of embarking at Le Havre with 'toute sa smala', that is, his family (483). The word 'smala' indicates the tents of an Arab chieftain, and the term was specifically associated with the mobile military headquarters of Abd el-Kader. Just as Abd el-Kader loses his capital (Mascara) and then his 'smala'—seized by Louis-Philippe's son, the duc d'Aumale, in May 1843—so Arnoux is progressively defeated in his 'ownership' of social, financial, and artistic capital.[54] Louis-Philippe had commissioned an immense painting of the dramatic capture of the 'smala' from Horace Vernet, whose spectacular brand of Orientalism highlighted the epic qualities of the combats, and neatly linked them to members of the royal family, while adopting the new realist emphasis on precisely observed detail.[55] The hyperbolic association of Arnoux's bankruptcy with the defeat of Abd el-Kader, whom Flaubert admired,[56] holds up his pretentions to ironic deflation. From the outset Arnoux is associated with the exotic *bric-à-brac* of a poseur, which aligns him and his wife not only with the defeated Algerians, but also with the Algerianist propaganda of the doomed July Monarchy. Later, the bankrupt Arnoux family's personal belongings are sold off at auction on 1 December 1851, and that night sees the beginning of the coup d'état of Louis-Napoléon Bonaparte. This marks the final end to the Second Republic, but also to the bourgeois monarchy and the bourgeois Arnoux. In earlier drafts of the auction scene Frédéric's bitterness and disenchantment were to have coincided with him seeing for sale a painting

explicit the division of Parisian society into different strata. But the verso of the same page moves away from treating Bou-Maza as a generalized 'Persian' outsider-observer, giving instead a more detailed description with specific North-African touches, so that the illustrious prisoner is 'vêtu d'un haik noué autour des tempes/front par une cord[e] en poil de ch[ameau]' (N.A.F.17605.13V°). In his documentation preparing the novel, Flaubert noted under the heading 'Été de 1847': 'Le 12 avril: Bou Maza se rend au colonel Saint-Arnaud et est amené à Paris' (see Ms. 226, fols 129–132, in *L'Éducation sentimentale*, Appendice (Paris: Club de l'honnête homme, 1971) p. 446). Balzac, too, saw Bou-Maza, and was struck by the 'dégoût profond pour l'Europe' he saw reflected on the face of this 'sauvage d'Afrique', more terrifying than a vampire (*Lettres à Madame Hanska*, vol. 2, pp. 640–1 (25 July 1847)).

[54] The *Petit Robert* gives as a second, derived meaning of *smala*, 'Famille ou suite nombreuse qui vit aux côtés de quelqu'un, qui l'accompagne partout' and offers Daudet's use in 1872 as the first example; the *Trésor de la langue française* gives an example of this analogical use from 1861. Even in its analogical sense, the term is still closely associated with Abd el-Kader. In his notes documenting the historical background, Flaubert wrote, under the heading '1848': 'Le 1er janvier, on annonce aux Parisiens la prise d'Abd-el-Kader [*sic*]' (see Ms. 226, fols 129–32, in *L'Éducation sentimentale*, Appendice (Paris: Club de l'honnête homme, 1971), p. 448). Abd el-Kader's *smala*, or mobile capital city, may have included 30,000 people (Julien, *Histoire de l'Algérie*, p. 183, p. 194).

[55] Horace Vernet, *Prise de la smalah d'Abd-El-Kader à Taguin, 16 mai 1843* (1844, Musée national du château de Versailles). It was the talk of the Salon of 1845, and would have been seen by Flaubert then or in 1847 when he visited Versailles. On the propaganda value of this painting, and Vernet's Algerian paintings in the Versailles galleries more generally, see Sessions, pp. 96–124, particularly p. 112.

[56] Flaubert saw Abd el-Kader as an 'homme-idée' capable of raising up all of the Orient in revolt (letter of 26 September 1853, *Correspondance*, II: 442) and wished such an 'emetic' on Europe (letter of 21 September 1853, II: 435). However, he also enjoyed the ridiculous pretentions of a man, encountered on his oriental travels, who had written a tragedy called 'Abd el-Kader' (see Du Camp, *Souvenirs littéraires*, p. 307).

of 'un zouave caressant un enfant à la porte d'un café.—une bonne famille' which is likened to a 'tableau de Greuze'.[57] This kitsch piece of colonial propaganda, which echoes the much grander Vernet 'smala' scene, exposes both Arnoux's exotic pose and his role as family man: in both aspects he is a fake and a failure. Frédéric, devoid of aesthetic awareness or critical distance, simply responds to the primitive emotional appeal of the painting, suddenly thinking of establishing a family of his own with Louise Roque.

Parallels between the conquest of Algeria and the pacification of the Parisian masses in 1848 can also be read between the lines as the political unrest increases in Part III of the novel. In an (ineffectual) attempt to stem the rising tide of unrest, the forces of order bring in key figures whose names were associated with decisive military action in Algeria. In February 1848, Bugeaud, Governor-General of Algeria, was appointed commander of the Paris military garrison (355). Bugeaud had been the main leader of the French army in Algeria during the crucial period of active conquest (1840–7), and his radical innovations in military strategy involved the use of extreme violence against civilian populations, a violence that he then attempted to apply to the Parisian workers. The newly-tested colonial techniques included the use of *razzia* to destroy livestock and crops, and the infamous *enfumades* that killed whole tribes trapped in caves; one remembers the starkly shocking description of the treatment of defeated republicans locked up in the 'caveau' of the Tuileries, where M. Roque shoots a blond adolescent in the head because he was begging for bread (410–12).[58] Frédéric and Hussonnet, following the revolutionary masses into the Tuileries, see that the portraits of the Marshals are intact, 'sauf celui de Bugeaud percé au ventre' (359). Just as his image is symbolically castrated, so Marshal Bugeaud's Algerian-style repression is made ineffectual by the King's hesitations. In June 1848 the Second Republic called on other generals fresh from Algeria to act as conservative saviours, notably Cavaignac ('L'ordre était rétabli. Plus rien à craindre. "Cavaignac nous a sauvés!"' (415)), and Changarnier ('Dieu merci, Cangarnier…Espérons que Changarnier…Oh! rien à craindre tant que Changarnier…' (440)). M. Dambreuse's fatal illness is triggered by the downfall

---

[57] Scenario X, fol. 59. Repeated in scenario XLII, fol. 61 and scenario XLIII, fol. 62 (Williams, ed., p. 188, p. 315, p. 318). The zouaves, 'mauvais garçons de France rehabilités par l'habit militaire' were part of a new 'imagerie populaire' of Algeria according to Daniel Rivet, *Le Maghreb à l'épreuve, de la colonisation* (Paris: Hachette, 2002), p. 133.

[58] See Claude Liauzu on the use of African generals in suppressing popular uprisings in Paris and on Bugeaud's hatred of 'les rouges' (*Histoire de l'anticolonialisme en France, du XVIe siècle à nos jours* (Paris: Armand Colin, 2007), p. 60). One of the effects of the conquest of Algeria was the development of a new culture of violence in the army, so that for 'veterans of North Africa, it became ever more difficult to draw distinctions between foreign and domestic "savages"' (Antony Thrall Sullivan, *Thomas-Robert Bugeaud, France and Algeria, 1784–1849: Politics, Power, and the Good Society* (Hamden, CT: Archon Books, 1983), p. 13). Bugeaud, who approved the *enfumades* and extreme colonial violence, was a social conservative who expressed hatred of the revolutionaries of 1848, but died before he could publish a 'Traité de la guerre des rues' that even his friends found too extreme (Julien, *Histoire de l'Algérie*, pp. 165–7). 'Razzia' was the most popular loan-word in French in the 1830s, according to William Gallois ('Genocide', p. 72). See also William Gallois, *A History of Violence in the Early Algerian Colony* (Basingstoke: Palgrave Macmillan, 2013); and Sessions, *By Sword and Plough*, pp. 312–13.

of Changarnier, who has come to stand for the *parti de l'ordre*.[59] One might recall Pierre Bourdieu's analysis of *L'Éducation sentimentale*, which relies on the organizational principle of antithesis summed up in the contrast between Dambreuse and Arnoux (conservative established bourgeoisie versus ambitious liberal petite-bourgeoisie).[60] Over this antithesis it is possible to map another, that of Bugeaud/Cavaignac/Changarnier and the *forces de l'ordre* on the one hand, and Abd el-Kader/Bou Maza, revolutionary workers or Arab resistance, on the other.[61]

This sub-text of the Algerian war suggests one of the ways in which the novel brings the vague, Romantic oriental signifier into the realm of colonial politics. Some critics have gone so far as to talk about Flaubert's 'convictions anti-coloniales' and 'haine de l'impérialisme occidental'.[62] He did indeed express sympathy for the Arabs,[63] but his attitude is more clearly one of scepticism, and in his novels he strives to avoid adopting an overt political stance of any kind.[64] It is in fragments of reported conversations and the novel's dialogic inclusion of well-worn rhetoric that 'la question d'Orient restait pendante' (330)[65]—and also, as we have seen, in apparently inert objects. M. Dambreuse's strategic purchase, during the revolution, of Pellerin's painting showing 'la République, ou le Progrès, ou la Civilisation, sous la figure de Jésus-Christ conduisant une locomotive, laquelle traversait une forêt vierge' (370) allows us a marvellously farcical glimpse at the liberal party's doctrine of progress, and along with it what was to become France's 'mission civilisatrice' in the colonies:

[59] 'La révocation du général Changarnier avait ému extrêmement le capitaliste. Le soir même, il fut pris d'une grande chaleur dans la poitrine' (452). Changarnier was later exiled (1851–9), but by 1867 Flaubert was once again rigid with indignation against him and his ilk, describing him to George Sand as representative of 'les gens d'ordre' and their 'haine que l'on porte au Bédouin, à l'Hérétique, au Philosophe, au solitaire, au poète', a hatred in which fear plays an important part (12 June 1867, *Correspondance*, III, pp. 653–4).

[60] Pierre Bourdieu, *Les Règles de l'art: Genèse et structure du champ littéraire* (Paris: Seuil, 1992).

[61] Julien emphasizes the decisive roles played in the struggle for Algeria by Bugeaud and Abd el-Kader, 'opposant deux volontés égales' (Bugeaud considered the war as a duel between Abd el-Kader and himself), as well as Bugeaud's 'hostilité irréductible aux revendications sociales' in Paris after the June days in 1848 (*Histoire de l'Algérie*, p. 164, p. 179).

[62] Pierre-Marc de Biasi, *Gustave Flaubert: Une manière spéciale de vivre* (Paris: Grasset, 2009), p. 245: 'ces convictions anticolonialistes, tout à fait exceptionnelles à cette époque, ne feront chez Flaubert que se renforcer jusqu'à la fin de sa vie, et il les transmettra le moment venu à son fils spirituel, Guy de Maupassant.' Flaubert, he reiterates, 'était anticolonialiste et condamne la présence française au Maghreb' (p. 489). On his cynicism about French colonialism in Algeria, see also Mme A. Besson, 'Le Séjour de Flaubert en Algérie', *Amis de Flaubert* (1968), 4–52 (p. 17, pp. 32–3).

[63] See for example his letter of 13 August 1846 (*Correspondance*, I, pp. 300–1).

[64] On his cynical 'réaction d'artiste', see Gisèle Séginger, 'La Tunisie dans l'imaginaire politique de Flaubert', *Nineteenth-Century French Studies* 32:1–2 (2003–2004), 41–57 (p. 45). By the 1860s, at any rate, his attitude to colonialism seems to have become one of sardonic detachment: one can guess, between the lines of an entry in the Goncourts' journal, that he felt little enthusiasm when Taine pronounced 'La colonisation des pays sauvages et la découverte des grandes vérités, voilà l'avenir' at one of the 'dîners Magny' (23 May 1864, vol. 1, p. 1073). He appears to have evolved from an earlier identification with the 'barbarian' and the oriental towards a more cynical stance in which the Orient itself is subject to materialism and mediocrity (see Anne Green, 'Flaubert's Myth').

[65] This complaint is one item in a list that summarizes Deslauriers's bleak vision of the political situation. In the immediate context the question seemed urgent because of France's dissatisfaction with the resolution of the war between its protégée Egypt and Turkey.

in an earlier version, Flaubert had added, of the locomotive, '—Les sauvages la regardent passer'.[66]

I shall now return—as the novel itself does—to Mme Arnoux's Algerian head-dress, which reappears from time to time like an after-image. Long after that first dinner at her apartment, she again wears black at a dinner party at the Dambreuse house, 'et comme le premier jour où il avait dîné chez elle, [elle portait] quelque chose de rouge dans les cheveux, une branche de fuchsia entortillée à son chignon' (417). The object of his desire has imprinted itself on Frédéric's mind in a blurred after-image: the phallic 'longue bourse' is disavowed; so too are the vulgar colonial and financial metonymies; all that is left is the apparently innocent colour red, here edulcorated into mere flowers.[67] In a further sublimation, he imagines the daughter they might have had, with a red ribbon in her hair (436). These later apparitions of the red hair-ornament repress its financial, sexual, and colonial links, tracing the process by which Frédéric's desire is sublimated into banality.

The red purse also initiates a well-furnished series of objects that stand for money, a paradigm that brings together the apparent opposites of Marie Arnoux and Rosanette, the bourgeois housewife and the courtesan, shared love interests of Arnoux and Frédéric. Frédéric suggests that Pellerin paint a portrait of Rosanette, thus giving rise to the novel's most developed example of exotic ekphrasis.[68] Pellerin initially contemplates dressing his model 'avec un burnous oriental?' but decides the *burnous* would be vulgar, perhaps because it is so topical in the 1840s: the garment is specifically Berber, rather than vaguely 'oriental'. Rosanette herself has no such qualms, wearing a *burnous* to the races on her outing with Frédéric (265).[69] For his portrait, Pellerin opts to dress her as a Venetian beauty instead. Venice being the first frontier of the Orient for the Romantics, this neatly sublimates the initial reference to a piece of clothing specific to North Africa. Pellerin focuses at length on the accessories for the portrait, which are to include 'un coffret de vieil ivoire un peu jaune dégorgeant des sequins d'or; quelques-uns même, tombés par terre çà et là, formeraient une suite d'éclaboussures brillantes' (207–08). When Frédéric does eventually see the portrait, for which he does not wish to pay, exhibited in a shop window as belonging to him, the clothing and accessories are much reduced: Rosanette is 'vue de face, les seins découverts, les cheveux dénoués, et tenant dans ses mains une bourse de velours rouge' while a peacock stands behind her (299). So the North African *burnous*, sublimated as Venetian costume,

---

[66] Scenario XXX, fol. 44 (Williams, ed., pp. 274–5).

[67] Pierre Danger observes that among the colours associated with Mme Arnoux are des 'pointes de rouge, rares mais remarquables, comme le signe d'une violence contenue', and he mentions the 'filet de soie rouge' in her hair, but he concentrates on brown or black (*Sensations et objets dans le roman de Flaubert* (Paris: Armand Colin, 1973), p. 140).

[68] Exotic ekphrasis is the 'description d'une œuvre d'art étrangère, réelle ou imaginaire, telle qu'elle apparaît dans une œuvre de fiction. Dans l'ekphrasis, ce morceau détachable, peut s'ébaucher une réflexion de l'écrivain sur son propre art.' (Jean-Marc Moura, *La Littérature des lointains: histoire de l'exotisme européen au XXe siècle* (Paris: Champion, 1998), pp. 172–3).

[69] In the scenarios of the race scene, as early as scenario I, she is repeatedly described as dressed 'en burnous <*de cachemire*>' (I, fol. 89 (10), Williams, ed., p. 48), which suggests that Flaubert, in his desire to give her all the vulgarity of mixed exotic accoutrements, was himself confusing the geographical origins of popular fashion items.

has finally morphed into an Ingresque peacock, while the many accessories, cas-
kets, and gold coins are condensed into a—surely not coincidental—red purse.[70]
Mme Arnoux's Algerian red silk purse is thus replaced by a simulacrum, a painted
purse resonant of geographically vague Romantic Orientalism. The portrait does of
course end up in Frédéric's possession (334), and is standing in his apartment,
half-hidden and passed off as an old Italian painting, when Mme Arnoux comes to
see him in 1867, carrying a 'petit portefeuille grenat couvert de palmes d'or' of
which she says, 'Je l'ai brodé à votre intention, tout exprès.' It contains the sum he
'lent' to her husband in an attempt to prevent the latter's bankruptcy decades earlier (500–01). So the promise of sexual availability, contained all along in the red
purse, surfaces once again in the final meeting of Frédéric and his elusive object of
desire.[71] Through Oriental synecdoches, Frédéric had attempted to place Mme
Arnoux within a Romantic model of sublime exoticism, but metonymy forcibly
reminds us of their commercial and colonial contexts.

CONSUMER OBJECTS, FRAGMENTARY VISION, AND THE QUEST FOR THE ORIENTAL ABSOLUTE

Balzac famously asserted that humanity can only be portrayed if one takes into
account the material objects with which it surrounds itself ('Avant-propos' I: 9),
but it is Flaubert who brings the novel into the industrial era, focusing on 'l'avène-
ment de l'objet manufacturé, multiple et mobile'; with *L'Éducation sentimentale*,
the novel enters 'l'âge du Kitsch—pacotille, anti-art, poncif, tape-à-l'œil'.[72] Balzac's
Skin and Gautier's 'pied de momie' are unique and irreplaceable; as Pierre Laforgue
puts it, this is because they still possess that particular quality of the Romantic
symbol, which is to be 'réfractaire à tout ce qui pourrait compromettre son
intégrité'. Balzac's Oriental Skin comes from 'la contrée du sens' whereas Paris
in 1830 is struck by meaninglessness.[73] Of course Balzac's objects, too, circulate in
the contemporary Parisian world of work and money, and, as we shall see in
Chapter 3, they are not *always* authentic or unique. In Flaubert's metropolitan
fiction, in any case, exotic objects are plural, reproducible, and come with a

---

[70] We are reminded of the embarrassing portrait and its purse at the Dambreuse dinner, when
M. Roque asks if Pellerin is the creator of a 'tableau très remarquable'; 'cela représente une dame dans
un costume...ma foi! un peu...léger, avec une bourse et un paon derrière' (419). The association
of the peacock with Ingres's Orient is due to the peacock fan held by his famous 'Grande Odalisque'
of 1814, which drew on the Venetian painters Titian and Giorgione.

[71] Balzac's 1832 tale, 'La Bourse', is an interesting reflection of the fashion for personally embroi-
dered purses as gifts; more importantly, the tale hinges on the final revelation of the purse's true significance, which is to demonstrate the moral integrity and financial probity of the beloved embroiderer
after a week's doubt; Mme Arnoux's purse, after a twenty-year absence, is much more ambivalent. On
the dangers and delights of a Freudian reading of the final 'bourse' offered to Frédéric by Mme Arnoux
see Diana Knight, 'Object Choices: Taste and Fetishism in Flaubert's *L'Éducation sentimentale*' in
French Literature, Thought and Culture in the Nineteenth Century, ed. by Brian Rigby (London:
Macmillan, 1993), 198–217 (p. 205).

[72] Duchet, 'Romans et objets', p. 175, p. 176.

[73] Laforgue, *1830*, p. 248, pp. 250–1.

price tag. Like the antique, the exotic object may appear to proclaim its singularity, but in the brave new industrialized world this is in fact a lie.[74]

In a paradox underlined by Flaubert, the nineteenth-century bourgeois was able to assert his or her individual identity because of the increased availability of mass-produced objects. The two polychrome statues of 'nègres' that Louise Roque asks Frédéric to purchase for her from Arnoux's shop are a reification of nostalgia for a non-existent past era of privilege based on slave-ownership (164, 321)—a bourgeois daydream shared by Frédéric himself (104, as mentioned above). More importantly, she wants them not because they are unique but precisely because she has already seen them at the Préfecture de Troyes (321), and she aspires to assert her individualism through imitation.[75] The exotic object is now industrially produced, part of a series, and reflects its owner's aspiration to a position within a relative scale of wealth.

In *Madame Bovary*, too, everything is part of a series: Emma's love for Rodolphe necessarily uses the same worn-out language that earlier mistresses have used; her letters form part of a collection of indistinguishable mementoes kept in a mass-produced biscuit box; Emma herself has two lovers, not one. So too, the shopkeeper Lheureux begins his temptation of Emma with not one Algerian scarf, but three:

'Je n'ai besoin de rien', dit-elle.

Alors M. Lheureux exhiba délicatement trois écharpes algériennes, plusieurs paquets d'aiguilles anglaises, une paire de pantoufles en paille, et, enfin, quatre coquetiers en coco, ciselés à jour par des forçats. [...] De temps à autre, comme pour en chasser la poussière, il donnait un coup d'ongle sur la soie des écharpes, dépliées dans toute leur longueur; et elles frémissaient avec un bruit léger, en faisant, à la lumière verdâtre du crépuscule, scintiller, comme de petites étoiles, les paillettes d'or de leur tissu.

'Combien coûtent-elles ?

— Une misère, répondit-il, une misère; mais rien ne presse; quand vous voudrez; nous ne sommes pas des Juifs!' (III: 240–1)

Here a shopkeeper tempts Emma to pawn her life, like Raphaël before her, by entering into a pact where the most immediate acquisition is an oriental object that sparkles in a dimly lit room; but that object is no longer unique, it is part of a series. Needless to say, although Emma at first refrains from buying the scarves, when Léon leaves Yonville she buys the finest of them. Performing her own exotic masquerade, she ties it around her waist over her dressing-gown, and thus dressed she lies on her sofa like an odalisque (III: 259).

That Emma's first major temptation towards financial excess involves three Algerian scarves might not immediately betray a link with the dinner scene at

---

[74] Flaubert's *Dictionnaire des idées reçues* tells us: 'Antiquité et tout ce qui s'y rapporte.—Poncif, embêtant. Antiquités: (les)—Sont toujours de fabrication moderne.' The singularity and authenticity of the antique object was already challenged by Gautier's ironic incipit to 'Pied de momie', where the cobwebs are the most authentically old things in the antique shop.

[75] In an earlier version she was to have desired them because she saw them in the house of Mme Dambreuse (Scenario XXIX, fol. 43, in Williams, ed., p. 268)—this would prove challenging to the chronology of events, but it underlines the mimetic relationship between the four women in Frédéric's life.

which Mme Arnoux wears a 'bourse algérienne' in her hair. And yet in the plans for this scene, the shopkeeper (at this stage called L'heureux) tempted Emma with slightly different goods: 'bourse algérienne, petits cachemires. il vient tâter le terrain'.[76] And the 'bourse algérienne' was intended to reappear later on, in Emma's hair at the *Comices agricoles* scene (fols 21 and 22), and earlier, at a dinner she herself gives (fol. 19).[77] Writing *Madame Bovary* with the memory of his North-African travels still fresh in his mind, Flaubert introduced an Algerian motif linked to the key scenes of temptation that mark Emma's financial and sexual 'falls'. He then thought better of most of these motifs, but they return in force in his later metropolitan novel.

The rapacious Lheureux has a Balzacian precursor in the petty-bourgeois speculator who 'étend les mains sur l'Orient, y prend les châles dédaignés par les Turcs et les Russes; va récolter jusque dans les Indes' in *La Fille aux yeux d'or* (V: 1045). The motif of Oriental plenty and imperialist rapacity would later appear in more overtly imperialist mode in a display in the department store of Zola's *Au Bonheur des dames*—'La Turquie, l'Arabie, la Perse, les Indes étaient là. On avait vidé les palais, dévalisé les mosquées et les bazars' (III: 471)—in what Gallois aptly calls an 'Orientalist capitalist narrative'.[78] The degenerate Orient is ransacked to provide a new version of the fantastic, that is, to serve the sublimation of money by Western commodity culture, which exchanges credit for the 'paillettes d'or' of Emma's Algerian scarves. It is again not one, but several cashmere scarves, displayed in shop windows, that inspire Frédéric's oriental fantasies of Mme Arnoux: he gazes at 'les cachemires, les dentelles et les pendeloques de pierreries, en les imaginant drapés autour de ses reins, cousues à son corsage, faisant des feux dans sa chevelure noire' (119). These key accessories make it possible to imagine the chaste housewife in the guise of an odalisque. In her fascinating work on the cashmere shawl in the nineteenth century, Susan Hiner teases out its association with colonial conquest— both the earlier Egyptian campaign and the Algerian conquest of the 1830s–1840s.[79] In Frédéric's fantasy the cashmere shawls are in the plural, and repeatability is the key to his degraded Orientalism; indeed, the gleam of fire in her dark hair is yet another echo of the red headdress. (No doubt it is coincidental that the cashmere shawl, like Balzac's Skin, focuses consumerist desire on the mysterious by-products of an Oriental goat.) The downward trajectory of the oriental shawl after what may be its first appearance in the overdetermined striped shawl that Frédéric saved from the river when he first saw Mme Arnoux is complete, and its mystical eroticism completely degraded, when Frédéric sees the procuress Mlle Vatnaz with 'une écharpe orientale autour des reins' (437). In Flaubert's metropolitan texts, then, the oriental shawl stands in lieu of a woman's sex in a classic fetishist substitution

[76] See Bibliothèque municipale de Rouen, Plans, MS gg 9. fol. 22 (http://www.bovary.fr/).

[77] Rodolphe was also to have been an ex-officer still tanned from the colonial wars: 'officier de spahis brun', 'hâlé' (Plans, MS gg 9. fol. 1). These colonial elements in the manuscripts are mentioned by Mireille Naturel, 'Proust et Flaubert: réalité coloniale et phantasmes d'Orient', *Bulletin Marcel Proust*, 49 (1999), 55–69.

[78] *Zola*, p. 138.

[79] Hiner, *Accessories to Modernity*, pp. 80–1; and 'Lust for luxe: "Cashmere Fever" in Nineteenth-Century France', *The Journal for Early Modern Cultural Studies*, 5:1 (2005), 76–98 (p. 77).

focused on that ambivalent erotic zone, *les reins*; it is at the same time an object of consumption whose repeatability suggests the exchangeable nature of the women who are the objects of desire.[80] It is Arnoux's purchase of not one, but two cashmere shawls—one for his wife, and one for his mistress—that reveals to the former the existence of the latter, and leads her to confront him with his adultery. So despite its costly nature and suggestion of ultimate luxury, the imported oriental object lends itself to repetition and substitution in a way that leads directly to its own devaluation.[81] Its fantasized 'original' value as unique object is most evident in that quintessential oriental shawl, the *zaïmph* of Flaubert's Carthaginian novel *Salammbô*, which appears to be an 'exemplary fetish object' that 'restores the semblance of distinct wholes, confers on its possessors the illusion of self-identity, recenters an otherwise fragmented textual economy';[82] and yet the *zaïmph*'s status is undermined in other ways, notably by the disappointment its possession causes the heroine. In *Un cœur simple*, Félicité's parrot Loulou also seems a unique exotic object, and he is certainly not part of a manufactured series; but he fits within a pattern of multiple substitutions. He replaces the lost objects of Félicité's love (her fiancé; her nephew; her mistress's daughter) and also the lost objects of empty political and religious promises (Félicité purchases an image of the Holy Ghost that resembles Loulou, and substitutes it for an old royalist propaganda image of the then heir to the throne, the future Charles X, dating from the Restoration).[83]

In a further sign of the iterability of the oriental signifier in *L'Éducation sentimentale*, a beggar singing an oriental song on the boat seems to sum up Frédéric's transcendent experience of love at first sight, but Arnoux recognizes the singer as 'un ancien modèle' (52): what appears to be a unique Romantic experience is from the outset owned by Arnoux; and of course a model is by definition that which is copied. Later, in the context of the fake plaster exoticism of the Alhambra public dance-house, Delmas/Delmar sings 'Le Frère de l'Albanaise', reminding Frédéric of the words 'que chantait l'homme en haillons, entre les tambours du bateau' (125). So the apparently unique Romantic song, associated with the uniquely authentic first moment of love, is echoed by an actor whose very name is modified at will. And that actor himself replaces Arnoux, and precedes Frédéric, in bedding the courtesan who replaces Mme Arnoux.

---

[80] Hiner sees the cashmere shawl as a signifier of marital status (*Accessories*, p. 89) but also emphasizes its erotic associations with the harem. On the oriental associations of the first shawl seen on the boat, see my article 'Like an apparition'.

[81] The eventual decline of the prestige of the cashmere shawl was an inevitable side-effect of the successful introduction of mass-production in Europe. See Hiner, *Accessories*, p. 90, p. 103.

[82] Elizabeth Louise Constable, 'Critical Departures: *Salammbô*'s Orientalism', *Modern Language Notes*, 111:4 (1996), 625–46 (p. 637). Schehr, meanwhile, sees the *zaïmph* as standing in for 'the entirety of the text of alterity' itself ('*Salammbô* as the Novel of Alterity', p. 338).

[83] Gustave Flaubert, *Trois contes*, ed. by Pierre-Marc de Biasi (Paris: GF-Flammarion, 1986), p. 73 (further references to this edition will be given in parentheses in the text). Félicité's humble bedroom contains so many objects that it 'tenait tout à la fois d'une chapelle et d'un bazar' in which urges to transcendence via the exotic or the sacred are all reduced to banality; among these objects is a 'bénitier en noix de coco' which, like the implausible coconut eggcups sold by Lheureux, is wonderfully suggestive of cheap exoticism (p. 72).

Yet another recurrent oriental accessory is reminiscent of Mme Arnoux's Algerian purse. Rosanette, dressed somewhat against her wishes in an oriental style, wears a necklace of *piastres* (324); and the seedy Mlle Vatnaz, in fancy dress, wears *piastres* on her forehead (176). This use of *piastres* as a fancy-dress accessory had entered French popular culture from the headdresses of certain North African tribes, in particular the Ouled Naïl women; Flaubert had seen them worn by dancing prostitutes during his travels.[84] Coin jewellery is absent from Frédéric's daydreams of Mme Arnoux in the accoutrement of the vaguely Turkish Romantic harem ('D'autres fois, il la rêvait en pantalon de soie jaune, sur les coussins d'un harem', 120), just as they are absent from Ingres's idealized odalisques, who wore headscarves or pearls, but no coins, in their hair. Reality, on the other hand, produces specifically colonial masquerade in the form of Vatnaz with 'un mouchoir algérien sur la tête, beaucoup de piastres sur le front, de l'antimoine au bord des yeux' (176; she is not even graced with an elegant 'foulard', but only a small and functional 'mouchoir').[85] Like Mme Arnoux's Algerian purse, the *piastres* remind us of colonial and commercial realities—and of the financial value of sexuality. The *piastres* and the purse link sacred and profane love, undermining the apparent opposition between Mme Arnoux and Rosanette.[86] At the same time, they point to the dualism of the exotic signifier in the realist novel: exoticism stands for transcendence of everyday banality, but exotic objects have come to signify the debasement of that transcendence through infinite repetition, commercialization, and connections with the new colonial regime.

The imported object is a key example of what Naomi Schor calls realism's '*anxious detailism*' (her italics), through which the prosaic object at the basis of the realist narrative had to be endowed with meaning: 'Implicitly, realism in its formative stages had as its mission to demonstrate that the neo-classical opposition of particularity and the Sublime is not insuperable.' Realist narratives, she argues, thus seek to make the detail sacred, and any 'dispersion of attention caused by synecdochic proliferation will be offset by the absorption of the details in an overarching whole'.[87] While this idea of realist detail as an anxious striving for a sublime whole is compelling, I would stress that a certain amount of ongoing anxiety hinders the absorption of the detail, or synecdochic fragment, into a coherent totality. We have seen that imported objects are devalued by being plural and reproducible; they are also fragmentary, that is, they appear as part of a *bricolage* of exotic motifs from different origins. Balzac and Flaubert use this fragmentation to very different effect. The apparent chaos of the shop in *La Peau de chagrin* assembles

---

[84] 1 December 1849, *Correspondance*, I, p. 541.

[85] The *piastres* theme that concisely links money and Algeria seems to have been a relatively tardy introduction; in scenarios XIX, fol.19 and XX, fol.17, Mlle Vatnaz was to have been disguised as a 'Bohémienne', though in scenario VIII, fol. 18, the character, still called by her earlier name 'Mlle Matnas', was to have been disguised 'en Égyptienne' (Williams, ed., p. 222, p. 229, p. 151).

[86] D.A. Williams stresses the ambiguous nature of the central opposition between Marie Arnoux and Rosanette, the saintly and the profane, and suggests that Mme Arnoux's image is exposed to degradation through metonymic transfer ('Sacred and Profane in "L'Éducation sentimentale"', *The Modern Language Review*, 73:4 (1978), 786–98 (p. 795)).

[87] *Reading in Detail*, p. 176, p. 182.

exotic objects from very disparate geographical contexts. Here Balzac uses the fragment as a synecdochic shortcut pointing towards a totalizing vision of world history, that would include 'toutes les œuvres humaines et divines', and '[t]ous les pays de la terre'. Most famously: 'C'était une espèce de fumier philosophique auquel rien ne manquait, ni le calumet du sauvage, ni la pantoufle vert et or du sérail, ni le yatagan du Maure, ni l'idole des Tartares' (X: 69). However, all is 'confusion', things seem 'interrompus', 'inachevés'; 'rien de complet ne s'offrait à l'âme' (X: 70–2). Only poetic vision can make sense of these incomplete signifiers (X: 72) through a sort of 'extase' (X: 70). In Balzac's antique shop, the exotic object's fragmentary nature provides the material from which the individual subjectivity can leap to the Romantic Sublime; it is the rupture of contiguity, the removal of an object from its aesthetic context, that, by allowing such a leap, leads to the 'absorptive quality of the exotic image'.[88]

This leap of poetic vision that makes it possible to reach a totalizing vision is precisely what is removed from Flaubert's Orient in *Salammbô*, where 'Flaubert uses the function of detail, the relation of part to whole [...] as a hyperbolic imitation, and critique, of Orientalism's cumulative, synthesizing use of details'. Critics desiring to find a 'phantasmatic lost totality' encounter instead '[a]n excess (of detail) and yet a lack (of a whole), a textual hole in place of an epistemological whole'.[89] In *L'Éducation sentimentale* the lost totality of the exotic 'whole' becomes a source of humour. Rosanette's lack of taste is suggested by her wearing a North-African cape under a pagoda-shaped Chinese-style parasol (and in any case '[elle] croyait le Liban situé en Chine', 265). In a similar *bricolage* of incompatible geographical metonymies, the Alhambra, whose name evokes Moresque architecture, incorporates 'galeries moresques [...] toiture chinoise [...] lanternes vénitiennes' (122).[90] The same pattern occurs when Frédéric has to choose the style of M. Dambreuse's tomb architecture: should it be Greek, Egyptian, Moresque? (457); the cemetery itself is full of incompatible exoticisms (460), all serving to sublimate the commerce that has paid for them. Arnoux's downfall is partly the result of his own obsessive search for an elusive oriental object, the mysterious red Chinese glaze—'le rouge de cuivre des chinois'—an alchemy that would allow him to transform mud (pottery) into gold. His search is diluted into seriality and random

[88] Nigel Leask, '"Wandering through Eblis"; absorption and containment in Romantic exoticism', in *Romanticism and Colonialism: Writing and Empire, 1780–1830*, ed. by Tim Fulford and Peter J. Kitson (Cambridge: Cambridge University Press, 1998), 165–88 (p. 174). Leask argues that the exotic curio, separated from its original context, leads to an aesthetics of the sublime in the disruption of the spectator's aesthetic command and suspension of points of comparison (pp. 169–74).

[89] Constable, 'Critical Departures', p. 627, p. 629. She suggests that Flaubert's 'hyperbolic use of detail might not only represent, but persistently critique as it represents, Orientalist strategies' as defined by Edward Said (p. 625).

[90] The drafts refer instead to a dance hall called 'La Chaumière', which did in fact exist in Paris at the time; the pseudo-exoticism of the 'Alhambra' was Flaubert's own invention. For Victor Brombert, the mixed architecture of the Alhambra 'is not merely a sign of vulgarity. It represents the particular attempt at facile poetry, or rather at facile estrangement, which is the special function of all purveyors of bought pleasures. In this light, the bordello [sic] becomes the convenient metaphor for any catering to the thirst for illusion.' (*The Novels of Flaubert: A Study of Themes and Techniques* (Princeton, NJ: Princeton University Press, 1966), p. 131). The real Alhambra in Granada had been restored in 1828, and 1836–45 saw the publication of Owen Jones's *Details and Ornaments from the Alhambra*.

exotic variety, as he attempts 'des majoliques, des faënza, de l'étrusque, de l'oriental [...] Aussi remarquait-on, dans la série, de gros vases couverts de mandarins, des écuelles d'un mordoré chatoyant, des pots rehaussés d'écritures arabes, des buires dans le goût de la Renaissance' (256). Once again a *series* of disparate pseudo-exotic objects aims to capture a transcendent oriental truth, and falls short in the quest for the absolute.

Lowe refers to this *bricolage* as a series of 'incomplete quotation[s]' from different exoticisms,[91] while Richard Terdiman sees the fragmentary quality of such oriental signifiers as defining them 'precisely by the possibility of *extracting* them from the whole'. This involves a double movement of penetration and appropriation through which the dominant subject appropriates parts extracted from a distant territory.[92] It is important not to forget, however, that in Flaubert's hands this process is self-consciously exposed to our gaze. The fragmentary nature of the exotic signifier in the novel cannot be reduced to a mere appropriation; it deliberately points to a gap. In *La Peau de chagrin* this gap is situated not only between the multiple objects and their distant geographical origins, but more importantly between their incompleteness and the ecstatic glimpse of human history as a whole, which can only be supplied by the momentary poetic vision. This gap shows us the problematic nature of a 'realist' writing project: if writing gives us only fragments, the totality of the 'real' can only be reached via a leap of subjectivity. And the gap between desire and satisfaction is of course also a sexual one: Frédéric leaves the Alhambra, like the brothel run by 'La Turque', without sexual satisfaction. Of course, Flaubert's use of metonymic series that leave us with fragments and no whole is not restricted to oriental/exotic objects. As Leo Bersani has argued, nineteenth-century Realism embodies desire in its heroes in order to annihilate it.[93] But exotic objects are more emphatically fragmentary than other objects, because they are detached from their origin. While the Romantic Orient is a figure for the plenitude of desire, in its belated form, confronted with the (capitalist, colonial) Real, it stands for the impossibility of such plenitude.[94]

The frustration of desire can, however, amount to a reinstatement of transcendence. Never quite possessed, Mme Arnoux remains an unknown object: she is always only potentially reducible to a housewife from Chartres, and the unknown takes up new residence in the gap between the impossible exotic and the bathetic metropolitan everyday. The imported object is a fetishist metonymy, since it points towards a meaning that is not contiguous and present, but (conceptually) contiguous and (geographically) absent.[95] By a miraculous sleight of hand, the imported object thus reintroduces absence itself as a form of transcendence within the realist

---

[91] 'Nationalism and Exoticism', p. 231.

[92] Richard Terdiman, *Discourse/Counter-Discourse: The Theory and Practice of Symbolic Resistance in Nineteenth-Century France* (Ithaca/London: Cornell University Press, 1985), pp. 238–9.

[93] Leo Bersani, *A Future for Astyanax: Character and Desire in Literature* (Boston/Toronto: Little, Brown and Company, 1969), pp. 66–7. See also Brook, *Reading for the Plot*, pp. 183–4.

[94] '[L]'Orient affiche le désir dans sa plénitude' (Laforgue, *1830*, p. 251).

[95] This is of course reminiscent of sexual fetishism, whose links with realist description are discussed by Naomi Schor in 'Fetishism and its ironies', *Nineteenth-Century French Studies*, 17:1 (1988) 89–97 (p. 93).

mode. It is no coincidence that Henry James's 'Figure in the Carpet' (1896) is suggestive of an elaborately patterned *Persian* rug. As Todorov puts it, James's narratives are always based on 'la quête d'une cause absolue et absente', where the 'cause' could be a character, an event or an object; the effect of this 'cause' is the story we are told; the story is the quest for the initial (but ill-defined) cause. 'L'essentiel est absent, l'absence est essentielle.'[96] The exotic object, pointing towards a significant absence, looks forward to symbolism; such 'aesthetic religion', Jameson tells us, is a nineteenth-century mode of nostalgia for the lost imaginary wholeness of a now impossible faith, that displaces the sacred into aesthetic objects.[97]

Seen from a postcolonial perspective, this might at first glance seem merely an internal affair, a polemical settling of accounts between Romanticism and Realism, or an aesthetic sleight of hand by which to reintroduce transcendence as an aspiration towards an absent object of desire. We have however seen that the double metonymy of the imported object, and the clash of the *effet d'exotisme* with the *effet de réel*, are deliberately used by writers working in the realist mode in order to test it from within. It is, in other words, part of the 'realist' stance to stretch the boundaries of Realism's own generic possibilities. This deliberate introduction of tension has important consequences for a mode of writing that is too often seen as simply declaring its mastery of the world. This doubt, which plays an important role in the realist canon, has significant political and ethical ramifications which will be further explored in Chapters 3 and 4. In any case, as we have seen, the imported exotic object itself marks a consciousness of the emerging world-system that is present within the nineteenth-century metropolitan novel: it is part of a 'catalogue of effects or motifs at the level of narrative form: discrepant encounters, alienation effects, surreal cross-linkages, unidentified freakish objects' that make up the 'typology of combined and uneven development'.[98]

---

[96] Tzvetan Todorov, *Poétique de la prose, suivi de Nouvelles recherches sur le récit* (Paris: Seuil 1978 [1971]), p. 83.
[97] *Political Unconscious*, pp. 241–2.   [98] WReC, p. 17.

2

The Real Cost of Sugar

Ethics, the Slave Trade, and the Colonies

Slavery is not generally thought of as one of the many concerns of the author of *La Comédie humaine*. He is almost absent from Christopher Miller's study of slavery in French literature (Flaubert and Zola are entirely absent).[1] Balzac, of course, is not alone in failing to confront the issue head on. Even British Realism produced no novel fully devoted to slavery. Nevertheless, postcolonial critics such as Aravamudan or Parry have followed Macherey in suggesting that the unsaid in literature is sometimes as important as what is said.[2] I shall argue here that, in the case of slavery in the *Comédie humaine*, the 'unspoken' occupies rather more words than one might think. Its oblique nature is not silence, but rather is concomitant with the situation of colonial issues offstage in the realist novel. The slave trade could in fact serve as emblematic of this present absence. In the realist novel, characters leave France in pursuit of a fortune and return with or without profits, but their activities remain offstage. So too the third leg of the 'triangular trade'—the voyage that brought slaves from Africa to the Caribbean—never touched metropolitan French territory.[3] This chapter aims to demonstrate that the *Comédie humaine*'s many passing references to the offstage realities of slavery reveal a much more complex set of responses than is immediately apparent. Narrative distanciation echoes the effect of geographical distance—and of perceived racial distance—in making the offstage imperial space one in which metropolitan morality does not apply. Balzac is complicit in this ethical prevarication, but at the same time he holds it up for questioning.

* * *

Slavery in the French colonies was abolished for the first time, in theory at least, by the Revolutionary *Convention* in 1794. In fact, forced labour replaced the slaves in

---

[1] Christopher L. Miller, *The French Atlantic Triangle: Literature and Culture of the Slave Trade* (Durham, NC: Duke University Press, 2008).

[2] Srinivas Aravamudan, 'Introduction', in *Slavery, Abolition and Emancipation: Writings in the British Romantic Period*, ed. by Peter J. Kitson and Debbie Lee, 8 vols (London: Pickering and Chatto, 1999), vol. 6, pp. vii–xxii. According to Parry, an understanding of the imperial imaginary must take into account the way empire marks novels 'in cryptic or oblique or encoded ways' (*Postcolonial Studies*, p. 107).

[3] Symptomatic of the occultation of the third side of the triangle in the French consciousness is the absence of slavery from Pierre Nora's 'lieux de mémoire' (see Miller, *French Atlantic Triangle*, p. xi; on the silence about the slave trade, pp. 38–9).

those places where the abolition was applied, and in any case Napoleon reinstated slavery in 1802. Britain abolished the slave trade (though not slavery itself) in 1807, and after the Treaty of Vienna in 1815 France theoretically followed suit, officially banning the trade in 1818. In practice, the abolition of the slave trade increased its profitability and the number of French trading voyages. This illegal trade was at a peak between 1820 and 1829,[4] when Balzac's first great novels were in gestation. There was no widespread popular abolitionist movement in France, as there was in Britain; the abolitionists were a relatively small and elite group. This was partly due to the association of abolition with revolutionary violence because of the Haitian revolution of 1791–1804, and partly to the fact that abolition had been imposed after Waterloo by the victorious British and was therefore unpatriotic.[5] The 1820s did however see new abolitionist agitation, and a 'Comité pour l'abolition de la traite' was founded within the 'Société de la Morale chrétienne' in 1822. But the Comité's abolitionist campaigns encountered hostility in the *chambre des députés* and indifference in the broader public.[6]

The literature of the 1820s is often ambivalent about slavery, but reveals a new interest in the issue: in 1823 the Académie française took the abolition of the slave trade as the theme of its annual poetry competition, and the decade saw an increasing number of novels dealing with slaves or Africans.[7] Under the July Monarchy the slave trade (though not slavery) was made illegal with the 'loi du 4 mars 1831'. The year 1833 saw the emancipation of slaves in the British Empire, as well as the publication of Balzac's *Eugénie Grandet* (which will be the focus of the first part of this chapter); the French 'Société française pour l'abolition de l'esclavage' was founded a year later. French anti-slavery campaigns gained strength in the early 1830s (reflected in increasingly pro-abolitionist comments in literary works[8]), and that is when Balzac shows the most interest in slavery—or, more specifically, in the slave trade.

When Balzac expressed opinions on the slave trade in his journalism or letters, he was explicitly critical of the abolitionists.[9] The eventual abolition of slavery by France in 1848 provoked his fear and regret,[10] and passing comments in his novels are extremely sarcastic about liberal abolitionist campaigns.[11] This cynicism was

---

[4] See Miller, *French Atlantic Triangle*, p. 31, p. 198.

[5] See Lawrence C. Jennings, *French Anti-Slavery: the Movement for the Abolition of Slavery in France, 1802–1848* (Cambridge: Cambridge University Press, 2000). On the role of British-French antagonism in relation to literary reflections on the slave trade, see Said, *Culture and Imperialism*, p. 107.

[6] See Miller, *French Atlantic Triangle*, p. 254, as well as Claude Liauzu, *Histoire de l'anticolonialisme en France, du XVIᵉ siècle à nos jours* (Paris: Armand Colin, 2007), p. 35. Hoffmann has a more positive view of French public opinion in the 1820s (*Nègre romantique*, p. 150).

[7] Most notably Victor Hugo, *Bug-Jargal* (first version 1820, revised 1826); Claire de Duras, *Ourika* (1823); and Prosper Mérimée, *Tamango* (1829).

[8] Francis Arzalier, 'Les mutations de l'idéologie coloniale en France avant 1848', in *Les Abolitions de l'esclavage*, ed. by M. Dorigny and B. Gainot (Paris: Éditions UNESCO, 1995), pp. 301–08 (p. 303).

[9] Feeding the French working classes more meat would, he declares, be a better philanthropic project than 'la suppression de la traite des nègres' ('Le Catéchisme social', in *Œuvres complètes*, vol. 27, pp. 101–22 (p. 112)).

[10] *Lettres à Mme Hanska*, letter of 24 June 1848 (vol. 2, pp. 875–6); also 9 July 1848 (vol. 2, p. 905).

[11] Among other examples, in *Le Député d'Arcis* there is a list of the preposterous rhetorical stances adopted by the party of 'Progress' that includes declaring oneself for 'l'indépendance des nègres', and modern philanthropists ignore problems nearer home in favour of the 'noix creuses de la négrophilie'

part of his general disaffection with philanthropists and *bien-pensants*. The abolitionists included many leading figures of the liberal opposition to the legitimist
monarchy, and Balzac's derision stemmed from his anti-liberal politics as well as his
patriotic Anglophobia. There was, however, some critical debate in the 1960s and
1970s about whether or not he should be seen as a straightforward opponent of
abolition. In 1966 Hoffmann pointed out Balzac's resolutely anti-abolitionist attitude and his use of mockery and insult rather than argument.[12] The 1970s saw a
reaction to this clear-cut denunciation. Ade Kukoyi argued that in his treatment of
Africans, 'la pensée de Balzac n'est pas simple mais double': Balzac defended slavery, as he defended all institutions, against the menace of revolution; but this is
balanced by a contradictory movement in which he rejects any threat to individual
liberty.[13] There have also been more extreme 'revisionist' approaches, albeit with
little textual justification: one includes Balzac in a list of 'young Romantic writers'
who 'all seem to have agreed from at least the beginning of the decade that slavery
was an inherently evil institution that should be abolished';[14] and more recently
another asserts that *La Cousine Bette* invites 'criticism of slavery and social hierar-
chies based on racial difference'.[15]

To what extent, then, can we take seriously the idea that Balzac was critical of
the institution of slavery? His writings of the 1820s do reflect the fashion for characters of African origin. Two chapters of *Le Vicaire des Ardennes*, published in 1822
under the pseudonym Horace de Saint-Aubin, recount the protagonist's childhood
in Martinique, and the figure of the escaped slave or *nègre-marron* is treated as a
Romantic symbol of union with nature and exclusion from society.[16] In the same
year and under the same name he wrote a play called *Le Nègre*, a melodrama whose
black villain, Georges, is not without Romantic grandeur.[17] In *La Fille aux yeux*

(VIII: 736; 749). In *La Cousine Bette* 'on s'occupe beaucoup trop des nègres' (VII: 436). Balzac's
anti-British satire, *Peines de cœur d'une chatte anglaise* (1841), makes fun of the abolitionist movement:
the hypocritical English cats establish a 'Société Ratophile', but English cats have a hidden economic
agenda, preventing others from eating rats in order to see the prices fall. Hoffmann gives further
examples of Balzac's passing sarcastic references (Léon-François Hoffmann, 'Balzac et les noirs',
L'Année balzacienne (1966), 297–308 (pp. 304–5)).

[12] 'Balzac et les noirs', pp. 303–5. The Pléiade edition of *Le Père Goriot*, by Rose Fortassier, unac-
countably claims that Hoffmann's article shows Balzac to have taken position against the trade (III:
1271 n. 2).

[13] Ade Kukoyi, 'A propos d'une réflexion sur "Balzac et les noirs"', *L'Année balzacienne* (1976),
53–68 (p. 63).

[14] David O'Connell, 'The Black Hero in French Romantic Fiction', *Studies in Romanticism*, 12:2
(1973), 516–29 (p. 516).

[15] Carol Colatrella, 'The Significant Silence of Race: *La Cousine Bette* and "Benito Cereno"',
Comparative Literature, 46:3 (1994), 240–66 (p. 243).

[16] In Balzac, *Premiers romans, 1822–1825*, ed. by André Lorant, 2 vols (Paris: Robert Laffont,
1999), vol. 2, pp. 216–17, p. 220, p. 307. On *Le Vicaire des Ardennes* see Hoffmann, *Nègre romantique*, p. 198; 'Balzac et les noirs', p. 299 n. 1.

[17] *Le Nègre*, inspired largely by *Othello*, was refused by the Théâtre de la Gaîté in 1823 and never
performed. It offers little direct reflection on slavery, although the passionate Georges, demanding that
his master's wife see him as a man, not a 'nègre', protests against the trade that brought him to his
current position: 'Courbé sous le joug dans ma patrie, j'étais heureux de mon malheur, c'est Monsieur
qui trafiqua de moi, qui me transporta dans un pays où le rire le plus insultant m'apprit que j'étais un
être en dehors de l'humanité' (*Œuvres diverses*, vol. 1, pp. 1004–5). See Kukoyi, p. 61 on the centrality
of Georges in the play and his Shakespearian inspiration.

d'or (1835), Christemio, the mighty mulatto who is devoted to Paquita Valdès, is a similarly melodramatic character who, like Georges, is compared to Othello. These Romantic black characters, and slavery in general, have most often been approached by critics in relation to Balzac's Orient of talismans and harems. (Indeed Balzac's Orientalism has, understandably, attracted much more critical attention than his treatment of slavery.) But Balzac's attitude to slavery and colonialism oscillates between wish-fulfilment and the *undermining* of exotic fantasy. The ambivalence that Kukoyi has pointed out is of course no news to Balzac specialists, and it is this 'double' Balzac that I shall pursue here. Balzac was no abolitionist, and the *Comédie* does not represent slavery directly, but the slave trade is associated with a form of evil, a thwarted promise, or a fascinating temptation that is destructive to those who pursue it. And as Lawrence Schehr has argued more recently, Balzac's introduction of the exploited, dehumanized other, albeit in a shadowy and peripheral form, does have the effect of including them 'within the realm of the discursively possible'.[18]

Some of Balzac's ambivalence concerning the narrative motif of the 'colonial fortune' may well arise from his mixed feelings towards his younger brother Henry, his mother's preferred child and the son of her lover. Citron calculates that Honoré discovered his brother's illegitimacy, and therefore his mother's adultery, in 1831, and traces the impact of this 'blessure interne' over the years 1831–6, after which it seems less acute.[19] This corresponds to the period when Balzac was most fascinated by the slave trade. Henry Balzac embarked for the colonies in March 1831, and in 1832 was in Mauritius where, albeit briefly, he owned slaves;[20] he was doing well and his example may have encouraged his brother to dream of colonial adventures leading to fortune, like those of Charles Grandet (*Eugénie Grandet* was published in 1833). But in June 1834 the spendthrift Henry was back in France, needing money from his family. Perhaps not coincidentally, it is in August 1835 that Balzac made revisions to the tale that was to become *Gobseck* (first written in 1830), introducing a whole new colonial side to the eponymous character. By November 1835 Balzac thought the only solution was for his brother to leave his wife and child in the Seychelles while he undertook trade 'aux Indes'.[21] It would however be hasty to assume that in Balzac's world art always imitates life, rather than the other way around. Graham Robb gives 'Henry's decline and fall' as 'a splendid example of Balzac's habit of taking one of his characters as the model for a real person': *before* urging Henry to head back to the colonies, he had written

[18] Lawrence R. Schehr, *Figures of Alterity: French Realism and its Others* (Redwood, CA: Stanford University Press, 2003), p. 24.

[19] Pierre Citron, 'Sur deux zones obscures de la psychologie de Balzac', *L'Année balzacienne* (1967), 3–27 (pp. 4–10).

[20] For Hoffmann the fact that Henry was a slave-owner in Mauritius may have encouraged Balzac to defend his interests ('Balzac et les noirs', p. 304). Henry cannot ever have felt much security as a slave-owner: his marriage to a wealthy widow who owned seventeen slaves occurred in December 1831, shortly *after* the emancipation of the slaves of Mauritius had been declared; following a period of unrest, the emancipation was confirmed in February 1835. See Madeleine Fargeaud and Roger Pierrot, 'Henry le trop aimé', *L'Année balzacienne* (1961), 29–66 (pp. 45–6 n. 7).

[21] See Graham Robb, *Balzac: A Biography* (London: Picador, 1994), p. 203, pp. 250–1; Fargeaud and Pierrot, pp. 47–8.

Le Contrat de mariage, which ends with Paul de Manerville's departure for Calcutta.[22] Balzac's attitude to the 'colonial fortune' theme was perhaps partly inspired by a feeling that he, Honoré, would have succeeded had he been the one to leave rather than his feckless brother. He certainly imagined himself successfully acquiring a fortune in Brazil or the West Indies, notably in the early 1840s.[23] Nevertheless, alongside colonial wish-fulfilment one finds signs of disenchantment, and this is true as early as 1830, before Henry had even left France.

EUGÉNIE GRANDET, SUGAR, AND THE SLAVE TRADE

Unusually among Balzac's novels, *Eugénie Grandet* has been read as entirely detached from history. It remains silent, for example, on the subject of the 1830 revolution; for Nicole Mozet, it represents 'le degré zéro du rapport à l'Histoire'.[24] And yet the novel is in fact implicated in history indirectly, through metonymy that points to the slave trade. As I have noted, the two sides of the triangular trade that touched metropolitan France carried not slaves, but merchandise: 'pacotille' or cheap goods for trading with Africa on the outgoing leg of the voyage, and sugar, its by-product rum, or other colonial products such as tobacco, coffee, or indigo, on the homebound leg. The slave trade itself happened elsewhere, out of sight and out of mind, and the moral questions raised by a crime committed at a distance are a recurrent theme of the *Comédie humaine*, particularly in the 1830s. In *Eugénie Grandet* the slave trade is evoked explicitly, though offstage. Balzac has Eugénie's adored cousin Charles leave in pursuit of a fortune, bound not for the West Indies but for the East, the 'Grandes Indes' (what we would call South and South-East Asia: III: 1084; 1085; 1095); and explicitly Java (III: 1139). But he rapidly realizes that 'le meilleur moyen d'arriver à la fortune était, dans les régions intertropicales, aussi bien qu'en Europe, d'acheter et de vendre des hommes. Il vint donc sur les côtes d'Afrique et fit la traite des nègres en joignant à son commerce d'hommes celui des marchandises les plus avantageuses à échanger sur les divers marchés où l'amenaient ses intérêts' (III: 1181). Eugénie has invested her hopes with Charles in these global trading networks, and on his return eight years later, when she receives the boorish letter in which he breaks off their engagement, a maritime metaphor recounts the fate of their engagement: 'Le vaisseau sombrait sans laisser ni un cordage, ni une planche sur le vaste océan des espérances' (III: 1188). This is a novel that may seem detached from metropolitan history, but is one in which the freight of domestic psychology is firmly tied to world geography.

Metonymy is the key to entering into the detail of the text, just as it is key to reading the rhizome-like *Comédie humaine* itself. I shall begin therefore with what may seem a detour into a typically realist detail, an everyday foodstuff that acts as

---

[22] Robb, p. 250.

[23] See Dupuy, 'Balzac colonial', p. 258. On dreams of departure to the Antilles, see Balzac's letters of 19, 21, and 25 March 1843 (*Lettres à Mme Hanska*, vol. 2, p. 655; pp. 657–8; p. 659).

[24] Nicole Mozet, 'De sel et d'or: *Eugénie Grandet*, une histoire sans Histoire', in *Corps/décors: Femmes, orgie, parodie*, ed. by Catherine Nesci (Amsterdam: Rodopi, 1999), 203–20 (p. 215).

a reminder both of material needs and of the cost of living: sugar. In *Eugénie Grandet* the word 'sucre' appears nineteen times, the verb 'sucrer' four times, and 'sucrier', sugar bowl, three times. But why?

In nineteenth-century Britain sugar had become a basic product consumed by the middle classes and aspiring poor, but this was not the case in France where its consumption remained limited to a largely Parisian elite until well into the second half of the century.[25] Sugar 'connoted a bourgeois food. Working-class antagonism to sweetness functioned as a building block in its lived identity and social experience beyond its objective class position.'[26] For Eugénie's father, the miser Félix Grandet, sugar is a sore point since he can get most of the basic foodstuffs required by his household—fruit, and even poultry and fish—from his tenant farmers by abusing his position of power (III: 1034, 1107–8), while sugar, along with butter, wood, candles, and flour (III: 1077–9), must be bought, requiring him to relinquish his precious hoard of cash. Sugar is emphatically not indigenous to Grandet *père*'s hometown, provincial Saumur. On the contrary, Saumur is from the outset associated with salt, feminine simplicity, and 'salt of the earth' working-class values: here one can purchase 'deux ou trois baquets pleins de sel et de morue' offered by a clean young girl with red arms (III: 1029), and the town's name itself reminds us of its salty homonym.[27] Sugar, on the contrary, was mostly imported from France's colonies in the Caribbean, where it was cultivated until 1848 by slave labour.

The novel's insistence on the basic material needs of life (food, heat, light) makes the circulation of goods an element of the plot in its own right. Sugar however is no basic foodstuff. It stands for the softness of little luxuries, for refinement, and also for nurture and care; all things that are denied by the miser Grandet. Eugénie's dying mother could have had her life prolonged by it (a 'régime doux', that is, based on milk and sugar, III: 1170). Even the cassis sold by apothecaries for medicinal purposes contains more sugar than that of the Grandet household (III: 1134).[28] But sugar figures in the novel above all as the small domestic luxury that Eugénie is desperate to offer her elegant Parisian cousin Charles. She bends the household's strict rules to give their visitor sugar in his own room, where it was the custom to take sugared water before going to bed (III: 1060), and family meals become the scene of a silent war. Eugénie sets the table for Charles's first breakfast with love, including 'le sucre amoncelé dans une soucoupe' (III: 1086); she removes the

---

[25] See Elizabeth Abbott, *Sugar: A Bittersweet History* (London/New York: Duckworth, 2009), pp. 178–9; Martin Bruegel, 'A Bourgeois Good? Sugar, Norms of Consumption and the Labouring Classes in Nineteenth-Century France', in *Food, Drink and Identity: Cooking, Eating and Drinking in Europe since the Middle Ages*, ed. by Peter Scholliers (Oxford/New York: Berg, 2001), pp. 99–118 (pp. 100–6).

[26] Bruegel, p. 102.

[27] The homonymy of Saumur and 'saumure' is flagged for our attention towards the end of the novel, when we are given the explanation for the servant Nanon's invincible youth: 'elle s'est conservée comme dans de la saumure' (III: 1177).

[28] In his *Traité des excitants modernes* (1839), Balzac includes sugar as one of five substances, introduced in the preceding two centuries, that significantly modify human society: distilled alcohol; sugar; tea; coffee; and tobacco (XII: 306–7). Four of these have exotic or colonial origins. Balzac followed the majority of medical opinion in seeing sugar as beneficial if not taken in excess (XII: 327).

saucer hastily when she hears her father coming back, but Grandet sees some sugar that remains on the table and asks his wife where it comes from (III: 1090). Charles, oblivious, looks for more sugar and Grandet refuses it, but Eugénie dares to defy her father and brings back the saucer, displaying extraordinary courage in the service of love. Grandet sneers at this 'pillage' of his house and is able to put a stop to all sweetness immediately, telling Charles he wants to speak to him (to tell him of his father's death and his own sudden penury): 'j'ai à vous dire des choses qui ne sont pas sucrées' (III: 1091). Only afterwards does he settle the question with his womenfolk—'Le père Grandet regarda sa femme, Eugénie et le sucrier'—forbidding them to continue: 'Je ne vous donne pas MON argent pour embucquer de sucre ce jeune drôle' (III: 1094). Charles's short-lived love for Eugénie is born when she passes him a pot of coffee, that other colonial product (III: 1107). But it is the association of *sugar* with love that proves the most enduring and ironic, since many years later, when Charles breaks off their engagement, Eugénie finds a bitter reminder of her cousin in 'une certaine soucoupe dont elle se servait tous les matins à son déjeuner, ainsi que du sucrier de vieux Sèvres' (III: 1189).

Grandet *père*, meanwhile, keeps tight control of sugar, taking pleasure in cutting it himself and doling out cubes weighing only a few grams (III: 1083). 'Malgré la baisse du prix, le sucre était toujours, aux yeux du tonnelier, la plus précieuse des denrées coloniales, il valait toujours six francs la livre, pour lui. L'obligation de le ménager, prise sous l'Empire, était devenue la plus indélébile de ses habitudes' (III: 1078–9). The value Grandet attributes to sugar is a hangover from the Napoleonic wars, when the price of imported sugar from the colonies had become exorbitant because of the British blockade, and sugar beet was only beginning to offer an alternative supply. This fits neatly into the current of Anglophobia that underlies *Eugénie Grandet*, while explicitly reminding us that sugar is a colonial merchandise. Thanks to state subsidies under the Restoration, however, 'French colonial sugar producers experienced a steady increase in fortunes in the late 1820s', which 'were known as the golden age of sugar production in the West Indies. French imports from the colonies and the number of ships involved in colonial trade doubled between 1816 and 1829.'[29]

Sugar and slavery had been linked via the theme of 'blood sugar' used by British abolitionist campaigners in the eighteenth century. They sought a popular boycott by linking the consumption of sweetened beverages to the symbolic drinking of the blood of slaves. Thus sugar worked as a metonym for the suffering body of the slave who had produced it.[30] This theme of collective guilt is famously evoked by Voltaire in *Candide*: 'C'est à ce prix que vous mangez du sucre en Europe.' But Balzac was even less an abolitionist than Voltaire. His use of sugar as a motif is

---

[29] Jennings, p. 26. The fledgling beet industry was temporarily ruined by the return of colonial sugar imports after 1815 (see also Abbott, pp. 181–3). Competition from sugar beet grown in France began to be an economic threat to the colonial trade from the mid-1830s.

[30] As Timothy Morton writes, in the blood sugar motif the 'metonymic chains which relate the colony to colonial power [...] are condensed into a powerful and ambiguous metaphor, in which sugar stands for the blood of the slaves' ('Blood Sugar', in *Romanticism and Colonialism: Writing and Empire, 1780–1830*, ed. by Tim Fulford and Peter J. Kitson (Cambridge: Cambridge University Press, 1998) pp. 87–106 (p. 88)).

highly ambivalent. In his hands it is a polyvalent signifier that stands in metonymic relation to expenditure as well as to the bodies of slaves, while slavery itself is used metaphorically, as we shall see.

Sugar, as a sign of luxury, is value in a consumable form that does not accumulate but opens up capital to wastage. In contrast to salty Saumur, it is associated with Charles's extravagant Parisian lifestyle. How does he keep his boots so shiny? 'J'ai entendu dire qu'on fourre du sucre dans leur cirage pour le rendre brillant' says Grandet (III: 1079). And when he learns that Eugénie has given her gold away he guesses that it is to Charles: 'tu auras jeté notre fortune aux pieds de ce va-nu-pieds qui a des bottes de maroquin' (III: 1155); 'votre Charles avec ses bottes de maroquin et son air de n'y pas toucher' (III: 1158). The opposition salt/sugar maps onto an opposition between true but unrecognized worth (Eugénie's beauty, Nanon's faithfulness) and Parisian prettiness. Charles, like the objects he brings with him, is described as 'joli' or even 'mignon', whereas Eugénie 'n'avait [...] rien du joli qui plaît aux masses' (III: 1054; 1076–7). Salt gazes at sugar with admiration and desire, and—if we are to believe Naomi Schor—with narcissistic identification.[31]

Sugar is associated with Parisian excess in opposition to what Mozet calls the provincial 'négation des valeurs romantiques d'énergie et de dépense'; it is the 'signe d'un luxe obscène'.[32] Indeed, the salty, anti-Romantic provinces are a new geographical territory for Realism. And yet one would be wrong to think that the *retention* of gold by the miser is the great theme of the novel. In fact, for the cunning Grandet gold is only of worth insofar as it can increase. 'Grandet' is an anagram of 'd'argent', not of 'or', and money must be made to work. As the miser himself puts it: 'Vraiment les écus vivent et grouillent comme des hommes: ça va, ça vient, ça sue, ça produit.' (III: 1153). He shows his agility in putting his capital to work: learning that the price of gold has doubled in Nantes he travels there secretly by night to sell it at a premium. This opportunity arises because many ships are being fitted out ('par suite de nombreux armements entrepris à Nantes', III: 1121; see also 1132). The aims and destinations of the voyages thus being prepared are not made clear, but Nantes was France's primary port in the triangular trade.[33] Mentioned eleven times in the novel, Nantes is the westernmost point of the Loire valley in which *Eugénie Grandet* is set: it is the point at which the provincial and global networks of exchange meet. From Saumur one turns either North-East towards Paris, where fortunes are dissipated and sugar is consumed, or West towards Nantes, to embark on the high seas.

Charles leaves to regain his family fortune with a capital of gold in the form of Eugénie's preciously amassed dower (needless to say, he accepts the latter without her father's permission). This dower is made up of individual coins that come from

---

[31] Naomi Schor, *Breaking the Chain: Women, Theory, and French Realist Fiction* (New York: Columbia University Press, 1985), pp. 92–95; on Eugénie's identification with Charles as a more beautiful version of herself, pp. 102–03.

[32] Nicole Mozet, *Balzac au pluriel* (Paris: Presses Universitaires de France, 1990), p. 114, and 'De sel et d'or', p. 211.

[33] 'In Nantes, the sugar and slave trades were closely linked; the city's merchants sold slaves in return for tropical produce' (Abbott, p. 180).

the great sea-faring nations: Portugal, Genoa, Spain, and Holland (III: 1127–8; repeated 1153, 1157).[34] India, too, is present ('la magnifique monnaie du Grand-Mogol', III: 1128), perhaps replacing Britain among the great maritime nations because of the trade blockades of the Napoleonic wars. The Indian rupees are printed with zodiac signs, five with the 'signe de la Vierge', and these coins are all 'neuves et vierges' (III: 1128). Offered by the perpetual virgin Eugénie as a gift of love to her cousin, they return symbolically whence they came (the East and West Indies; Latin America). Charles, however, fails to appreciate the human aspect of Eugénie's investment, and treats it as a mere financial transaction, a loan to be repaid at 5 per cent interest (III: 1188).

WOMEN AS SLAVES AND THE 'COMMERCE D'HOMMES'

The virgin coins entrusted to Charles's hands stand metonymically for Eugénie herself, and the 'commerce d'hommes' (III: 1181) in which they are invested is used partly as a parallel with the trade in women back home. It is no coincidence that the coins are her '*douzain* de mariage' (III: 1045), since the novel charts the struggle for the acquisition and management of women as cash value, that is, dowries. It is the rivalry between two Saumur families, the Cruchot and the Grassins, for possession of Eugénie that supplies the satirical backdrop to the entire plot.[35] Grandet's own wealth was founded on his acquisition of his wife's dowry, and he retains it thanks to Eugénie's voluntary abjuration of her own rights after her mother's death.[36] He fails to find his daughter a husband, frustrating what the novel stresses is her innate maternal potential, and reducing her to the sterile accumulation of financial value. Grandet is 'le grand prêtre d'une religion dans laquelle le sacrifice humain apparaît comme une conséquence du rite mécanisé de l'accumulation'.[37] The victims of his sacrifice are women, but we are reminded of the parallel between the 'commerce d'hommes' and the 'commerce de femmes' through apparently fortuitous choices of vocabulary. The Grassins family tries to buy Eugénie's preference, just as a slave trader buys human merchandise in Africa, by offering her a cheap gilt sewing box, 'véritable marchandise de pacotille' (III: 1050). The evocation of 'pacotille', that is, merchandise of bad quality destined for colonial trade, is no coincidence. Indeed, we are reminded of it when Charles scrapes together enough money to establish a 'pacotille composée de curiosités

---

[34] These nations were also slave-trading powers: Genoa was one of the earliest European slave-trading states (initially in North Africa); the Dutch were the first to ship slaves to the Americas, and the most successful slave-trading nation in the seventeenth century.

[35] For a more detailed analysis, see L. and N. Rudich, 'Eugénie Grandet, martyre du capitalisme', *Revue de l'institut de sociologie*, 3–4 (1973) 651–69 (p. 654).

[36] Michael Lucey shows that the Napoleonic Code would in fact have allowed Eugénie (who is no longer a minor) to claim her mother's dowry as her inheritance and choose her own husband, had she not, following a family tradition of feminine abnegation, renounced control over her fortune ('Legal Melancholy: Balzac's "Eugénie Grandet" and the Napoleonic Code', *Representations*, 76 (2001), 1–26).

[37] See Rudich and Rudich, p. 654; also p. 659.

européennes' to start off trading (III: 1139; his *pacotille* is mentioned repeatedly, see 1123; 1127; 1065; 1180). Women are chattels to be bought and sold; they are also locked up (Eugénie and her mother live a life that is 'presque monastique' (III: 1136) in one room of Grandet's house; later Eugénie is literally locked up in her room by her angry father), and the very first sentence of the novel compares the melancholy of the houses of Saumur to that of a cloister (III: 1027).[38] Through constant humiliation he keeps his wife in a state of complete helotism or serfdom (III: 1035; 1045; 1046; 1091). This comparison of married women with slaves is developed in more explicitly radical form in the *Physiologie du mariage* (1829). But Grandet's female possessions also include his servant Nanon, who has belonged to him for thirty-five years and accepts his despotism without quailing; he exploits her 'féodalement' and loves her as if she were a dog who 's'était laissé mettre au cou un collier garni de pointes dont les piqûres ne la piquaient plus' (III: 1042; 1043). Balzac's commentary on the condition of women is also apparent in the anti-romantic focus on material staples such as wood, butter, sugar, fruit, candles: these are the goods that patterned women's everyday life, and which are subject to the tyranny of a man.[39]

In *Eugénie Grandet*, then, the trade and exploitation of African slaves is used partly as a metaphor for the exploitation of women and their purchase through marriage. Elsewhere Balzac uses slavery as a way of thinking about the metropoli-tan class system. In the 1840s he explicitly compares the condition of the modern industrial workforce unfavourably with that of slaves: 'Il existe sous nos yeux des Esclaves innomés plus malheureux que les esclaves nommés, que l'esclave chez les Turcs, que l'esclave chez les anciens, que le nègre. [...] L'industrie moderne ne nourrit pas ses esclaves.'[40] More generally still, in the *Traité de la vie élégante* (1830) a despotic relationship is maintained by those who do not have to work over those who do: 'il est infiniment agréable pour un homme ou une femme de se dire en regardant ses concitoyens: "Je suis au-dessus d'eux; je les éclabousse; je les protège; je les gouverne; et chacun voit clairement que je les gouverne, les protège et les éclabousse..."' Slaves, in this case, are among others in the category of those who are 'éclaboussés' (XII: 219). In many parts of the *Comédie* one finds, too, a third metaphoric use of slavery, which is the enslavement of an individual to passion, either to a domineering beloved figure or to a monomania. So slavery is made to serve as a vehicle for three distinct tenors in Balzac's hands: the exploitation of women in marriage; the exploitation of the proletariat; the dominance of an

---

[38] Grandet employs his wife's dowry to purchase an *abbaye* when the clergy's goods are sold off during the Revolution, and supplies the Republican armies with wine in exchange for land belonging to a 'communauté de femmes que l'on avait reservée pour un dernier lot' (III: 1031)—the singular feminine agreement suggesting that the Republic is selling off the nuns as a job lot, and not just their 'prairies'. The cloister is the dominant image of the novel according to Tim Farrant (*Balzac's Shorter Fictions: Genesis and Genre* (Oxford: Oxford University Press, 2002), p. 172). On the novel's cloister imagery, see also John T. Booker, 'Starting at the End in *Eugénie Grandet*', *L'Esprit créateur*, 31:3 (1991), 38–48.

[39] Grandet's pleasure in controlling his womenfolk could be linked to sadism, which a Freudian analysis would situate, along with avarice, as part of the complex of anality. For a psychoanalytic reading of this kind, see Jean-Pierre Richard, *Études sur le romantisme* (Paris: Seuil, 1970), p. 122 n. 21.

[40] Balzac, 'Le Catéchisme social', p. 110.

individual by an obsession. This use of slavery as a vehicle for metaphor undoubtedly detracts from any sense of its specificity as an issue in itself. Balzac's use of slavery as metaphor not only does not reflect abolitionist sympathies, it denies the historical specificity of slavery in the French colonies by subsuming it into a very general category. The presence of imperialism and slavery as metaphors within the metropolitan novel does however open the door to a broader sense of French history, one that sees it as compromised by economic and political engagements elsewhere. Moreover they also appear through metonymy, and whereas metaphor is comprised of a tenor and a vehicle, metonymy works through chains with multiple links, extending in different directions. Balzac's massive *œuvre*, as we know, can be read against the grain, and more than most works *must* be read in different directions; *Balzac contre Balzac*.[41] For Balzac, slavery is merely an explicit manifestation of exploitation, which he observes to be present everywhere in post-Revolutionary society; it can thus be used freely as a metaphor. But at the same time sugar as a metonym connects the domestic life of the provinces to the global networks of the triangular trade.

Grandet *père* treats his women as chattel or serfs, and in a direct parallel with his nephew's experience of the slave trade we are told that he honed his skills 'dans le commerce des hommes' (III: 1110). His trade in men is described in Biblical terms: a long authorial aside compares the miser's compulsive devouring of others' money to the fattening, slaughter, and contempt reserved for a lamb (III: 1105). The techniques Grandet most successfully employs to get the upper hand in negotiations were learnt from an 'Israélite' a 'malin Juif' (III: 1110–11). Charles Grandet passes himself off under a Jewish name during his years of illicit trading so that he can undertake the most crapulous transactions without undermining his own future respectability. The Grandets, uncle and nephew, have indeed been compared with assimilated Jews as symptoms of a society in a process of transformation,[42] but one might equally suggest that in this case Balzac—who included so many Jewish characters in *La Comédie humaine*—is demonstrating that the *commerce d'hommes* is not a Jewish monopoly. The man that the miser Grandet most obviously buys and sells is his own brother Guillaume, whose bankruptcy is brought about indirectly by fraternal competition; he is guilty of a form of fratricide (III: 1063; 1116; 1131). Grandet then finds it worth his while to appear to 'racheter [son] frère' (III: 1114) for 25 per cent of the amount owed, which he never in fact pays. Grandet's crimes against his brother, his wife, and his daughter lie in his considering them as susceptible to being retained, bought, or sold within a system of monetary values. His nephew Charles's experience of the slave trade sees him operating within a system that is similarly, if more explicitly, dehumanizing.

Charles Grandet leaves France to rebuild his lost family fortune, and in doing so is corrupted, or rather, reshaped in his uncle's image: 'Le sang des Grandet ne faillit

---

[41] Franc Schuerewegen, *Balzac contre Balzac: les cartes du lecteur* (Toronto: Paratexte, 1990).

[42] Marshall C. Olds, 'Globalisation and "la pièce de cent sous": Balzac's nation-state', in *Currencies: Fiscal Fortunes and Cultural Capital in Nineteenth-Century France*, ed. by Sarah Capitanio et al. (Bern: Peter Lang, 2005), pp. 175–91 (pp. 184–9).

point à sa destinée.' His practice of the slave trade dries him up: 'Au contact per-
pétuel des intérêts, son cœur se refroidit, se contracta, se dessécha.' His experience
of trafficking in humans, like his uncle buying and selling both men and women,[43]
denies human values: 'Charles devint dur, âpre à la curée. [...] L'habitude de
frauder les droits de douane le rendit moins scrupuleux sur les droits de l'homme'
(III: 1181). This is of course a reference to the revolutionary *Déclaration des droits
de l'homme*, which Balzac had admired in his youth but soon rejected. Balzac's few
references to the *Déclaration* are generally ironic, but this does not necessarily
appear to be the case here.[44] Balzac is no abolitionist, but neither does he treat the
slave trade as a source of 'magical', untainted money: Charles Grandet is a new
type of capitalist, transformed, and not for the better, by the global economy.[45]

In 1830, a few years before writing *Eugénie Grandet*, Balzac published a fragment called *L'Usurier*, developed as a longer tale under the title *Les Dangers de
l'inconduite*, which was, in 1842, to become *Gobseck*. It was when revising his tale
for the 1835 edition (called *Papa Gobseck*), that Balzac introduced a colonial theme
associated with the early experiences, and seedy death, of the eponymous character.[46] The characters of Gobseck and the Grandets, uncle and nephew, appear in
fact to have mutually influenced each other,[47] and Gobseck's Jewish identity may
explain the Grandets' links with Judaism. Éric Le Calvez offers a sustained
comparison of the two misers, Gobseck and Grandet *père*. In their ferocity and
voraciousness both are compared to surprisingly exotic animals: Gobseck is like a
boa (II: 1010), Grandet like a tiger and a boa (II: 1033; also 1084 and 1167). Le
Calvez devotes little space to the comparison with Charles Grandet's life in the
Indies, except to suggest that it is almost a summary of Gobseck's early experiences.[48] Both men are formed through their apprenticeship on the high seas between
the East and West Indies, although Gobseck's experience comes much earlier in his
life, and directly as the result of a maternal rejection: 'Sa mère l'avait embarqué dès
l'âge de dix ans en qualité de mousse pour les possessions hollandaises dans les
grandes Indes, où il avait roulé pendant vingt années' (II: 967).[49] Gobseck's twenty

[43] On Charles as having engaged in the 'traite des blanches', selling white women among others,
see Schehr, *Figures of Alterity*, p. 73.

[44] See René-Alexandre Courteix, *Balzac et la révolution française: aspects idéologiques et politiques*
(Paris: Presses Universitaires de France, 1997), pp. 128–40. Miller points out the 'problem of irony in
the handling of the slave trade' (in the case of Sue and Staël), *French Atlantic Triangle*, p. 282.

[45] His corruption through the experience of the slave trade is comparable to that of Philippe Bridau
in *La Rabouilleuse*, though the latter is much less successful (as we shall see in Chapter 6). And his
trade in human bodies includes the wide sexual experience that Balzac's libidinous listing gives as 'les
Négresses, les Mulâtresses, les Blanches, les Javanaises, les Almées, ses orgies de toutes les couleurs' (III:
1181), which erases the memory of his cousin Eugénie.

[46] Gobseck is a highly ambivalent character, whose probity and strict justice make him a 'good'
father-figure to Derville and the young Ernest de Restaud whose property he manages. Before the
1835 revisions he was at the end of the story as much an angel as a demon; it was in 1835, when Balzac
introduced the colonial theme, that Gobseck's death took on its macabre and obsessive quality.

[47] See Bertrand Lalande, 'Les États successifs d'une nouvelle de Balzac: *Gobseck*', *Revue d'Histoire
Littéraire de la France*, 46 (1939), 180–200.

[48] Éric Le Calvez, 'Gobseck and Grandet: Semes, Themes, Intertext,' *Romance Studies*, 23 (1994),
43–60.

[49] It is probable that Balzac identified with narratives of maternal rejection. On a slightly different
note, Raphaël de Valentin, much less energetic and thick-skinned as a young adult than one imagines

years on the high seas, ostensibly 1750–70 (compared to Charles, 1819–27), are evoked indirectly, via a list of names of people he frequented that includes historical as well as fictive recurring characters (the latter were added in 1842). These names suggest actions and experiences that are left unspecified in an open metonymic series whose chains span the entire globe, rather like Eugénie's coin collection. They encompass India and the Caribbean, the East and West Indies. The period corresponds to the loss of France's first colonial empire (the Treaty of Paris was signed in 1763), and many of the references evoke the British and French at war in India. Anachronistically, and on the other side of the world, Gobseck had a hand in the American war of independence (1775–83). He also knew Victor Hugues, the Revolutionary commissioner who abolished slavery in Guadeloupe only to replace it with forced labour, and later re-established slavery in Guyana as well as arming corsairs to pillage British ships in the 1790s. Gobseck was a long-term resident of the Danish Caribbean colony Saint-Thomas, a hub of the slave trade whose economy depended on sugar; Charles Grandet also trades there. Gobseck seems to have made his way thanks to treason as well as illicit trade: 'Il peut avoir été corsaire, il a peut-être traversé le monde entier en trafiquant des diamants ou des hommes, des femmes ou des secrets d'État' (II: 995).[50] Certainly, he has used every means to make a fortune, and survived through 'ces déterminations dont la rapide urgence excuse la cruauté'; and he is loathe to talk about it: 'quand il parlait des Indes ou de l'Amérique [...] il semblait que ce fût une indiscrétion, il paraissait s'en repentir' (II: 967). Still, the narrator of the tale, the honest Derville, is convinced that, excepting his firmly amoral stance in relation to money, Gobseck is an honest man (II: 995).[51] The slave trade and treason are extreme extensions of free-market capitalism, and as such they both fascinate and repel Balzac.

What their colonial experience gives Charles Grandet and Gobseck, and what Grandet *père* seems to have acquired without it, is a lesson in amorality. As Aimé Dupuy observed long ago, among Balzac's many migrants are some who, 'livrés à eux-mêmes ou au contact de gens de sac et de corde, se sont amoindris, pollués aux pays lointains'.[52] The experience of distant trade apparently removes its perpetrators from the concerns of humanity: as Derville says of Gobseck, 'Si l'humanité, si la sociabilité sont une religion, il pouvait être considéré comme une athée' (II: 967). In Charles's case this derives from the discovery of moral relativism: he loses his 'prejudices'—that is, his principles—at the 'baptême de la Ligne' (a sailors' ceremony on crossing the Equator). 'A force de rouler à travers les hommes et les

Gobseck to have been even as a child, was threatened by his strict father with a similar fate: 'il m'avait menacé de m'embarquer à ma première faute, en qualité de mousse, pour les Antilles' (in *La Peau de chagrin*, X: 122).

[50] In the 1835 Béchet edition Gobseck explicitly sold 'Tippoo-Saëb' or Tipu Sultan, the French ally, to the English (II: 1583).

[51] Gobseck does however extend his trafficking in human lives to the young Derville himself, lending to him at a cruel 15 per cent interest.

[52] 'Balzac colonial', p. 264. Others have tended to minimize the effect of such experiences on characters: Bordas, for example, sees Balzac's 'Orient' as nothing more than a useful source 'd'enrichissement presque toujours'; 'Sur leur vie là-bas [...] on ne sais jamais rien, reste le profit, capitalisable à Paris' ('L'Orient balzacien', p. 329 n. 29).

pays, d'en observer les coutumes contraires, ses idées se modifièrent et il devint sceptique. Il n'eut plus de notions fixes sur le juste et l'injuste, en voyant taxer de crime dans un pays ce qui était vertu dans un autre' (III: 1181). Gobseck himself expresses a similar moral flexibility: 'Mes principes ont varié [...] j'en ai dû changer à chaque latitude. Ce que l'Europe admire, l'Asie le punit. Ce qui est un vice à Paris est une nécessité quand on a passé les Açores. Rien n'est fixe ici-bas, il n'y existe que des conventions qui se modifient suivant les climats' (II: 969). In both cases, then, the lesson of moral relativism is understood as following logically from the experience of geographical and cultural diversity; the only remaining yardsticks for behaviour are self-interest and gold.

Balzacian ambivalence here cuts both ways, since amorality, far from being entirely negative, is linked to near-supernatural clairvoyance. Gobseck has gained an extraordinary ability to 'posséder par la pensée la terre qu'il avait parcourue, fouillée, soupesée, évaluée, exploitée' (II: 968). The material appropriation and exploitation of distant lands gives him calm and detachment. In both his ability to live vicariously and his reliance on gold as the only measure of value, Gobseck resembles the antiquarian of *La Peau de chagrin*,[53] who shows 'la tranquillité lucide d'un Dieu qui voit tout, ou la force orgueilleuse d'un homme qui a tout vu'. He too has reached a position of amorality through the experience of different moral values: 'Les mœurs de toutes les nations du globe [...] se résumaient sur sa face froide' (X: 78). Gobseck is similarly, though less supernaturally, hardened by his experiences: 'aucune âme humaine n'a été ni plus fortement trempée ni mieux éprouvée' (II: 995).

Other characters, too, gain insight through travel. In *Modeste Mignon* (1844), Charles Mignon returns from his experience of colonial trade on the high seas with near-visionary clairvoyance, a rare figure of a wise and perceptive 'good' father in the *Comédie humaine*; but he made his money in the 'innocent' trade of opium to China, and indigo, not in human merchandise.[54] In *Le Père Goriot*, Vautrin's clairvoyance is not explicitly attributed to the experience of travel, but in the eyes of his fellow boarders his knowledge of the world includes 'les vaisseaux, la mer, la France, l'étranger, les affaires, les hommes, les événements, les lois, les hôtels et les prisons' (III: 61). He marks his cynical good humour by singing 'J'ai longtemps parcouru le monde, / Et l'on m'a vu de toute part ...' (III: 82; see also 84 and 85).[55] So distant

[53] The earliest versions of *Gobseck* date to 1830, when Balzac was beginning to plan *La Peau de chagrin* (see X: 1221–2). Citron's introduction offers a full comparison of the miser with the antiquarian of *La Peau de chagrin* (X: 31–4).

[54] Charles Mignon leaves in 1826 for Constantinople, and then trades in Malaysia and China, returning in 1829 (the first Opium War, between China and Britain 1839–42, shortly preceded the writing of the novel; France was to obtain the same commercial rights as Britain at the Treaty of Whampoa in October 1844). Mignon returns wiser than ever, and as Mozet points out, money earned through the opium trade allows him to buy back his lost family home (*Balzac au pluriel*, p. 114); elsewhere she mentions the fairytale nature of *Modeste Mignon*, in which the absence of the Father gives way to his triumphant return (*La Ville de province*, p. 266). Jean-Hervé Donnard, however, considers that Charles Mignon 'n'est honnête qu'en France' (*Les Réalités économiques et sociales dans La Comédie Humaine* (Paris: Armand Colin, 1961), p. 327).

[55] This air from the 1827 opera *La Joconde, ou les coureurs d'aventures* is seen by Carol Mossman as conveying no specific allusions ('Sotto voce-Opera in the Novel: The Case of *Le Père Goriot*', *The*

travel may be the source of his uncanny clear-sightedness too: 'son œil semblait aller au fond de toutes les questions, de toutes les consciences, de tous les sentiments' (III: 61). And of course Vautrin is a past master in the moral relativism learnt by Charles Grandet on the high seas: 'Il n'y a pas de principes, il n'y a que des événements' (III: 144).

The experience of travel and moral relativism give these characters extraordinary detachment and insight, affording them an overview like that of a writer manipulating a fictional world to reveal the secret mechanisms of the real one. But for our well-travelled visionaries, particularly if they have been tainted by the slave trade, this stance proves unsustainable. Gobseck claims that he is invulnerable: 'je possède le monde sans fatigue, et le monde n'a pas la moindre prise sur moi' (II: 970). The antiquarian of *La Peau de chagrin* claims invulnerability with even greater hubris (X: 85–7). But they are both proven wrong: the antiquarian falls in love with a dancer; and Gobseck dies in premature dotage. Charles Grandet, one might add, loses his moral values in the slave trade without gaining any perspicacity, since he misses out on a bigger fortune hidden beneath his nose.

CRIME AT A DISTANCE

Balzac does not treat the slave trade as a unique or even specific phenomenon; for him it reveals the basis of all wealth in the new world of mobile capital, that is, the exploitation of others. In metropolitan society too, as Gobseck tells us, anyone who would ape the aristocratic luxury of having a carriage and horses to raise him above the mud must first 'prend[re] une bonne fois un bain de boue' (II: 974). This mud is that of crime at one remove in *L'Auberge rouge* (1831), where the narrator asks in anguish whether or not he can marry a young woman who will inherit the fortune her father, the banker Taillefer, founded on a murder committed before her birth.[56] As Vautrin puts it, 'Le secret des grandes fortunes sans cause apparente est un crime oublié, parce qu'il a été proprement fait' (III: 145–6). For Balzac, in the new post-Revolutionary world where wealth is acquired rather than inherited, and based on mobile capital rather than land, the acquisition of a fortune involves moral compromise somewhere on a sliding scale between mud and murder. Trading slaves on the high seas is an extreme version of the individualism that he

French Review, 69:3 (1996), 387–93 (p. 390, p. 392)). It does however evoke a vast experience of the world expressed in terms of travel, and possibly deportation. The character Vautrin had his origins in Balzac's first works in the figure of the pirate Argow (in *Le Vicaire des Ardennes* and *Annette et le criminel*), which helps to explain his knowledge of ships and sea life.

[56] In 1838 Balzac revised *La Peau de chagrin* to incorporate the guilt of the banker Taillefer, amphitryon of the orgy of part II: in an inversion of the purification of the Catholic mass, the guests participate in Taillefer's guilt: they will 'manger les entrailles' and 'boire le sang d'une famille' and will thus be 'complices' (X: 97). In effect Taillefer père is already in the position of having accepted the diabolical pact that Rastignac refuses in *Le Père Goriot*. *L'Auberge rouge* gives the backstory of Taillefer's fortune, along with a condensed version of several Balzacian obsessions, including the temptation scene and the tainted fortune.

saw as being one of the flaws inherent in the new society. The financial transaction is a banal version of the diabolical pact.[57]

Selling oneself to the devil—or at least accepting a pact in which one renounces certain moral values in order to acquire a fortune—leads us directly to *Le Père Goriot* and its famous temptation scene in which the disguised criminal mastermind Vautrin offers Rastignac a fortune to be had at the cost of a murder to be committed by someone else. Shortly after Vautrin's offer, Rastignac asks his friend Bianchon how he would respond to a moral dilemma he attributes to Rousseau: '—Te souviens-tu de ce passage où il demande à son lecteur ce qu'il ferait au cas où il pourrait s'enrichir en tuant à la Chine par sa seule volonté un vieux mandarin, sans bouger de Paris.' Bianchon jokes 'J'en suis à mon trente-troisième mandarin', then asks if the mandarin is really very old; but when pressed he finds he would in fact refuse (III: 164).

Rastignac's situation is one we encounter time and again in the Balzacian world, and one that Vautrin sums up with damning clarity: 'Une rapide fortune est le problème que se proposent de résoudre en ce moment cinquante mille jeunes gens qui se trouvent tous dans votre position' (III: 139). This is the 'nœud gordien' that could be cut by the sword of a hidden crime (III: 165). The illegal slave trade—which presented higher risks but, potentially, a dramatic rate of return on a successful voyage[58]—appealed to those pursuing this fantasy of a sudden fortune. Rastignac's choice is vividly embodied in the contrast between Vautrin, who would kill the mandarin without hesitation, and Goriot, who is himself a variant of the old Chinaman, sacrificed by his daughters in the depths of the *quartier Latin* where high society will know nothing of the crime.[59] The contrast is one that Balzac returns to in *Eugénie Grandet*: Eugénie, like Goriot, sacrifices herself; Charles Grandet's slave trade, like Vautrin's pact, is based on the sacrifice of others.

Balzac was mistaken in attributing the ethical dilemma of the Chinese mandarin to Rousseau. His most immediate source was a passage in *Le Génie du christianisme* where Chateaubriand used a comparable dilemma as proof that we have innate feelings of morality, thus arguing for the immortality of the soul and the existence of God.[60] Chateaubriand himself borrowed the reference to China from a brief mention by Diderot that demonstrates how distance weakens our feelings of moral accountability, so that 'The murderer transported to the coast of China is too far

[57] The comparison is made by André Vanoncini in reference to *L'Auberge rouge*: 'une société qui s'est vendue au diable recourt constamment à cette forme banalisée du pacte que représente la transaction' ('Le Pacte: Structures et évolutions d'un motif balzacien', *Année balzacienne* (2002), 279–92 (p. 286)).

[58] Olivier Pétré-Grenouilleau's imposing overview of the slave trade dispels the myth that the profits of the Atlantic trade were consistently very high. The illegal trade of the 1820s seems instead to have attracted 'un capitalisme aventureux' prepared to run the risks of making a loss in order to have a chance at making a sudden fortune (*Les Traites négrières: essai d'histoire globale* (Paris: Gallimard, 2004), pp. 326–7).

[59] Mme Vauquer even calls Goriot 'ce chinois-là' (III: 82) in the derogatory slang of the time.

[60] Chateaubriand does not refer to a mandarin, simply to China. See Laurence W. Keates, 'Mysterious Miraculous Mandarin: Origins, Literary Paternity, Implications in Ethics', *Revue de littérature comparée*, 40:4 (1966), 497–525 (pp. 504–6), and before him Paul Ronai, 'Tuer le mandarin', *Revue de littérature comparée*, 10 (1930), 520–3.

away to make out the corpse he has left bleeding on the banks of the Seine.'[61] Chateaubriand argues, against Diderot, for the existence of an absolute sense of morality. The response of the honest Bianchon, who would choose not to kill the mandarin, is the equivalent of Chateaubriand's moral imperative. But Rastignac himself hesitates, and when Bianchon asks him later 'Nous avons donc tué le mandarin?' replies 'Pas encore [...] mais il râle'; Bianchon 'prit ce mot pour une plaisanterie et ce n'en était pas une' (III: 181). Rastignac hesitates too long and the victim is killed, though without his having accepted the pact. This is a far cry from the absolute moral integrity of *Le Génie du christianisme*, which Balzac did not much admire.[62] Indeed, Lucien de Rubempré later accepts the pact with Vautrin that Rastignac rejects. Levin contrasts Balzac's stance with Dostoevsky's uncompromising position that 'no one can be happy while others are suffering': 'For Balzac compromise is the precondition of happiness, which is invariably paid for by others. Instead of renouncing the bargain, he computes the cost; instead of sparing the mandarins, he reckons the casualties.'[63] It is Balzac's fascination not with the response, but with the hesitation in giving an answer, that implicates his characters in the networks of the emerging capitalist world-system.

In the absence—or at least weakness—of any inner moral imperative or immediate social sanctions, the refusal to accept a fortune at the cost of another's life can be based on the fear of judgement after death. Rastignac, we are told, 'croyait en Dieu' (III: 177). But Balzac reduces the idea of eternal judgement to a jest told at second hand when Goriot, teased by Vautrin, tells him 'vous payerez cela bien cher quelque jour...' and another lodger adds 'En enfer, pas vrai?' (III: 93). In *Eugénie Grandet* the narrator's own voice asserts the necessity of belief in the afterlife because of its fundamental role in social cohesion; it is on this belief that 'l'édifice social est appuyé depuis dix-huit cents ans' (III: 1101). Faith, in other words, is necessary for social cohesion, rather than having importance in its own right; the moral context is relativist, not divine.[64] Whatever the faith of its author, the morals of the *Comédie humaine* are profoundly secular.

The scenario of the Chinese mandarin is discussed by Carlo Ginzburg as part of a fascinating study of how distance affects our sense of ethics. Geoffrey Baker develops Ginzburg's brief suggestion of how this moral dilemma is applicable to

---

[61] Diderot, *Entretien d'un père avec ses enfants, ou du danger de se mettre au-dessus des lois* (1773), quoted by Carlo Ginzburg, 'To Kill a Chinese Mandarin: The Moral Implications of Distance', in *Wooden Eyes: Nine Reflections on Distance*, trans. by Martin Ryle and Kate Soper (New York: Columbia University Press, 2001), p. 161. Diderot's *Lettre sur les aveugles* also suggests the relative ease of killing someone far away (see Ginzburg, p. 162; pp. 164–5). In *La Peau de chagrin* a supernatural version of the temptation scene sees Raphaël choose between the portrait of Christ by his namesake and the diabolical Skin. To choose the painting would mean following Chateaubriand in asserting the victory of inner morality. But Balzacian characters tend to make more equivocal choices.

[62] See his note, probably dating to 1830, in 'Pensées, sujets, fragmens [sic]', fol. 12, in *Œuvres complètes*, vol. 28, 653–721 (pp. 666–7).

[63] *Gates of Horn*, p. 208.

[64] 'Un crime, c'est l'athéisme en action. On ne croit pas à l'avenir.' And 'La foi catholique est un mensonge qu'on se fait à soi-même [...] La piété est un calcul d'enfant qui se tient sage pour avoir des confitures.' In 'Pensées, sujets, fragmens [sic]', *Œuvres complètes*, vol. 28, fol. 31, p. 681; fol. 46, p. 691.

imperialism.[65] Diderot and Chateaubriand use China primarily as shorthand for extreme geographical and cultural difference, but Ginzburg links the dilemma to issues of imperialism by suggesting its applicability to today's 'global economic system' where there are 'real opportunities for people to grow rich across distances immeasurably greater than ever Aristotle had imagined or could imagine'.[66] Balzac himself, meanwhile, associates the idea of a distant, secret crime with the colonialism of his own day. Ten years before *Le Père Goriot*, in 1824, he situated the crime in 'la Nouvelle-Hollande' (Australia),[67] a more obviously colonial reference than China.

While Baker argues that the ethical dilemma of the Chinese mandarin is a way of thinking through 'imperial violence' and 'the imperial allusions [...] serve to contextualize the crime in global terms',[68] the dilemma can be understood more specifically in relation to the issue of slavery. In the period 1830–5 the theme of the slave trade is as much a preoccupation of Balzac's as the diabolical temptation.[69] They are linked by the word 'traite'—which can signify either the slave trade or a bill of exchange such as the one Vautrin gets Rastignac to sign—and in other ways as well.

If Rastignac accepted Vautrin's pact, the latter's share of the spoils would allow him to emigrate and purchase two hundred slaves to work his own American plantation. Baker points out that Vautrin's aspirations are 'literally colonial',[70] but they are of course more specifically linked to the fantasy of slave-ownership:

> Mon idée est d'aller vivre de la vie patriarcale au milieu d'un grand domaine, cent mille arpents, par exemple, aux États-Unis, dans le sud. Je veux m'y faire planteur, avoir des esclaves, gagner quelques bons petits millions [...] en vivant comme un souverain, en faisant mes volontés, en menant une vie qu'on ne conçoit pas ici, où l'on se tapit dans un terrier de plâtre. [...] Je possède en ce moment cinquante mille francs qui me donneraient à peine quarante nègres. J'ai besoin de deux cent mille francs, parce que je veux deux cents nègres, afin de satisfaire mon goût pour la vie patriarcale. Des nègres, voyez-vous? c'est des enfants tout venus dont on fait ce qu'on veut, sans qu'un curieux de procureur du roi arrive vous en demander compte. Avec ce capital noir, en dix ans j'aurai trois ou quatre millions. (III: 141)

As Baker puts it, 'by dint of recalling the allegory of the Mandarin, Vautrin's plan again summons the idea of colonial abuses into the local murder underway'.[71] Vautrin is once again contrasted with Goriot, that sacrificial victim to paternal

---

[65] Ginzburg, *Wooden Eyes*; Baker, *Realism's Empire*, pp. 48–64.

[66] *Wooden Eyes*, p. 166.

[67] In *Annette et le criminel*. See Rose Fortassier's notes to *Le Père Goriot* (III: 1280, n. 2), following the article by Ronai, 'Tuer le mandarin', pp. 521–2.

[68] *Realism's Empire*, p. 53, p. 55.   [69] See Vanoncini, 'Le pacte', p. 288.

[70] *Realism's Empire*, p. 55. In *Son Excellence Eugène Rougon*, Zola's eponymous statesman indulges in a colonial fantasy very much like Vautrin's, though his dream of absolute power is placed in the French provinces; it too comes to nothing. For Naomi Schor, Rougon's 'old fantasy of running a model farm' is 'in fact a kind of colonial empire or enclave on French soil' (*Zola's Crowds* (Baltimore, MD: Johns Hopkins University Press, 1978), p. 145); on the provinces as a form of 'Far West' like the colonies, see Pierre Citti, *Contre la décadence* (Paris: Presses Universitaires de France, 1987), pp. 244–5.

[71] *Realism's Empire*, p. 56.

love, for the 'patriarchal' life he seeks is based on the dominance of slaves: he is an anti-father like Taillefer or Grandet.[72] And Vautrin's aspiration to increase his (hypothetical) fortune through the labour of slaves suggests a further parallel with the Grandets and Gobseck. For Ginzburg, Balzac is showing that bourgeois society makes us complicit, at least indirectly, in crime.[73] In Balzac's hands slavery is a way of looking at how distance changes moral attitudes; it also shows us an extreme version of the individualism that he sees as the basis of the new capitalist society.

Much later, in *Modeste Mignon* (1844), Balzac revisits the role played by distance in our moral perceptions, specifically in relation to the colonies. Here, the geographical distance from Paris to the Provinces is mapped over the distance from France to South and South-East Asia. Le Havre is the meeting point of both trajectories, just as Nantes pins Saumur to the wider world in *Eugénie Grandet*.[74] Whereas Saumur is closed and stifling like a convent, Le Havre looks out towards the sea, which Mozet calls 'l'anti-province', in this later, much more cosmopolitan, 'roman de la circulation'.[75] Modeste's father, Charles Mignon, leaves to make good the family's lost fortunes through trade in China and Malaysia. His return to Le Havre is crucial to the plot, as is the arrival there, from Paris, of the poet Canalis and his secretary La Brière. For them, the provinces are a foreign country, 'autant que la Chine' (I: 635), where people's opinion matters 'autant que celle du roi de Bornéo' (I: 681). And the cynical Canalis expresses the relativism of moral sensibility explicitly, in terms that echo Charles Grandet's: 'Il y a pour les vérités morales, comme pour les créatures, des milieux où elles changent d'aspect au point d'être méconnaissables' (I: 646). He mocks the faithful family friend who tries to move him concerning the fate of the provincial girl who has fallen in love with him:

> ... cette jeune fille est tout pour vous... Mais dans la société, qu'est-ce?... rien. En ce moment, le mandarin le plus utile à la Chine tourne l'œil en dedans et met l'empire en deuil, cela vous fait-il beaucoup de chagrin? Les Anglais tuent dans l'Inde des

[72] Jean Borie sees Vautrin as aspiring to play the role of dominating father to slaves to compensate his failure as a creator in his own right (*Zola et les mythes ou de la nausée au salut* (Paris: Seuil, 1971), p. 182). Levin suggests that despite, or because of, Balzac's view that the family is the central unit of society, he shows us 'a collection of bad examples' of fatherhood (*Gates of Horn*, p. 170). The opposition between Grandet and Goriot as bad and good fathers is striking in the parallel scenes when Eugénie observes her father secretly transporting gold by night (III: 1120) and Rastignac spies on Goriot crushing his beloved gold dish to sell it for his daughter. The childless Gobseck is also an anti-father figure (in 1835 the tale was called 'Papa Gobseck'), who bleeds his young protégé dry with a loan at extortionate interest rates.

[73] *Wooden Eyes*, p. 66.

[74] R. Anthony Whelpton asks rather plaintively what the point of the many foreign references in *Modeste Mignon* might be ('L'Atmosphère étrangère de *Modeste Mignon*', *L'Année balzacienne* (1967), 373–5). I suggest that Balzac's provincial port cities are carefully portrayed as two-faced, looking outwards to the wider routes of global trade as well as inwards to the Paris–Provinces axis so familiar to readers of the French realist novel. Watts underlines the role of Le Havre as 'a gateway to the wider world' (*Preserving the Provinces*, p. 270).

[75] *La Ville de province*, p. 267, p. 265. In Maupassant's story 'Boitelle' (1889), Le Havre plays a similar role of opening to the wider world, in contrast to the narrow-minded Norman village inland: on its quay is a shop selling parrots imported from the Amazon and Senegal, and a 'café des Colonies' where the protagonist meets his adored 'négresse' (II: 1087–8).

milliers de gens qui nous valent, et l'on y brûle, à la minute où je vous parle, la femme la plus ravissante; mais vous n'en avez pas moins déjeuné d'une tasse de café?... En ce moment même, on peut compter dans Paris beaucoup de mères de famille qui sont sur la paille et qui jettent un enfant au monde sans linge pour le recevoir!... voici du thé délicieux dans une tasse de cinq louis. (I: 593)

Balzac's echo of his own earlier Chinese mandarin dilemma underlines that Canalis is unlike Bianchon and Chateaubriand, but like Vautrin and Charles Grandet, in his willingness to trade in the suffering of others. In this passage colonial contexts are again used to note the dulling effect of distance on empathy. Canalis also repeatedly evokes the enjoyment of those key colonial imports, coffee and tea, in a way that harks back to the use of sugar in *Eugénie Grandet*. Here bourgeois consumption of colonial goods is juxtaposed with contempt for individual women; and once again metonymy draws in the wider world of imperial domination and transaction.

SLAVERY AND AUTOCRATIC PASTORAL

We have seen that Balzac links the slave trade to a loss of moral values, but without taking an abolitionist stance, and indeed that amorality is not always, or not only, understood in a negative light. In a further instance of moral ambivalence, the *Comédie* holds up the ownership of slaves as a sort of wish-fulfilment. Baron Montès, in *La Cousine Bette*, owns a hundred slaves in Brazil, and as he himself says 'je suis un roi, mais pas un roi constitutionnel, je suis un czar, j'ai acheté tous mes sujets, et personne ne sort de mon royaume' (VII: 415). He also has a coach driven by 'des nègres parfaitement esclaves et très bien battus' (VII: 404).[76] In slightly more moderate terms, Charles Mignon brings back from his travels not only a fortune but also 'un cuisinier et un cocher, nègres tous deux, une mulâtresse et deux mulâtres sur la fidélité desquels il pouvait compter' (I: 613). The fantasy of the submissive 'nègre' plays to bourgeois nostalgia for a lost never-never land of aristocratic domination.[77] Indeed, the melodramatic Montès represents an ideal aspired to by many struggling metropolitan characters in *La Comédie humaine*.

Unexplained fortunes are often associated with the Americas, which Citron contrasts with Balzac's oriental exoticism 'qui se rattache à l'indolence, à la passivité'. The Far West, on the other hand, is a place to go to remake oneself: 'Le mythe américain, il faut insister là-dessus, en est totalement différent: les sauvages, les Indiens, le côté Fenimore Cooper et chasse à l'homme, cela, c'est autre chose, c'est l'action.'[78] Citron only discusses slavery in its Oriental form, but the domination

---

[76] Colatrella asserts that these 'enslaved blacks' in *La Cousine Bette* 'appear powerful and dangerous' and that the reader is being asked to 'reinterpret the significance of racial difference', but does not give evidence for either of these assertions (p. 241).

[77] As Hoffmann says of black servants in the metropolis: 'Plutôt que de véritables personnages, ce sont les symboles d'une opulence et d'une fantaisie dont la France bourgeoise de Louis-Philippe avait la nostalgie' (*Le Nègre romantique*, p. 223).

[78] 'Le Rêve asiatique', p. 307.

of others is in fact a central part of the American fantasy too. Vautrin's plan, like Montès' self-definition as a Tsar, presents the New World as a heterotopia of autocracy in which the individual can escape the laws of the metropolis and achieve perfect liberty. In striking contrast to the idea of America as representing democracy, such liberty appears to depend on the domination of others, of which enslavement is an extreme version.[79] Unsurprisingly, then, critics of the mid twentieth century tended to emphasize Balzac's references to distant lands as a form of wish-fulfilment, in which the figure of the 'aventurier'[80] represents the strongman who rejects the constraints of the law, while the colonial space is 'le dernier refuge où le Surhomme puisse laisser libre jeu à ses instincts de domination absolue'.[81] This fantasy is akin to the Romantic view of near-supernatural insight gained through amoral detachment described above. Both are aspects of the 'homme fort' that contribute to the undoubted seductions of piratical figures in the literature of the 1830s and 1840s, when the distinction between the *corsaire* and the *négrier* was not always clear-cut.[82] Moreover, if we follow the analysis of slavery offered by Orlando Patterson, the slave-owner is an exemplary figure of the strongman because he accumulates 'honour' in proportion to his slaves' *loss* of honour. The slave-owner, not the metropolitan bourgeois, experiences his own freedom fully because the very concept of freedom depends on the presence of its opposite.[83] There are no doubt parallels to be made with early American literature, in which, Toni Morrison argues, the oft-recounted immigrant dream comprised a yearning not only for freedom, but also for power: by leaving the Old World for the New, '[o]ne could move from discipline and punishment to disciplining and punishing; from social ostracism to social rank'.[84]

Distance allows the high seas or the Far West to operate as a semi-magical space into which to project a fantasy of self-realization in the form of mini-despotism and non-accountability. This bourgeois fantasy of individual autocracy is a response to the hypocrisies and constraints of the constitutional monarchy, the 'terrier de

---

[79] Prendergast sees this as 'a classic projection of an essentially bourgeois fantasy and no different from the fantasies of wealth and domination that haunt other members of Balzac's world' (*Balzac: Fiction and Melodrama*, p. 88). Unlike other bourgeois fantasies, however, the colonial heterotopia offers scope for complete self-realization, individualism pushed to the point of autocracy.

[80] For Silvestre de Sacy, Balzac's adventurers reveal his own obsession, indeed identification, with pirates; they also free him from the constraints of his own determinist literary doctrine and the 'servitudes de la vraisemblance' ('Balzac et le Mythe de l'Aventurier', *Mercure de France* (1 January 1950), 115–28 (p. 126)).

[81] Hoffmann, 'Balzac et les noirs', p. 304.

[82] A *corsaire* sailed at his own cost, but with the authorization of his government, to intercept trading vessels belonging to an enemy nation and to confiscate any goods found. The *négrier*, or slave trader, took on some of the piratical glamour of the *corsaire* when the slave trade was made illegal and slave ships ran the risk of interception by the British navy. Balzac's admiration for the *corsaire* is part of this glamorous conception of a figure of derring-do and anarchic liberty, an *hors-la-loi* who is nevertheless patriotic. See Hoffmann, *Nègre romantique*, p. 252. As an example of his identification with the *corsaire* and the 'Mohican' because of their 'vies d'opposition', see his letter to Victor Ratier, 21 July 1830 (*Correspondance*, I, p. 461).

[83] Orlando Patterson, *Slavery and Social Death: A Comparative Study* (Cambridge, MA: Harvard University Press, 1982), pp. 11–12, pp. 340–2.

[84] Toni Morrison, *Playing in the Dark: Whiteness and the Literary Imagination* (New York: Vintage, 1993 [1992]), p. 35.

plâtre' that Vautrin despises as being for the weak. In the post-revolutionary world individuals are theoretically equal, while in the natural world that Balzac saw as determining real human behaviour, inequality rules. As a result, the distant pastoral setting of the Americas offers a return to Nature in the anti-Rousseauist sense of a return to 'natural' inequality,[85] where the individual frustrated by the regime of Louis-Philippe can assert his will to power over others. We find here a variant on the eighteenth- and nineteenth-century novel's ongoing temptation towards pastoral: colonial heterotopias are reminiscent of Bakhtin's view of the pastoral as one form of the 'Idyllic Chronotope', which offers a model for 'restoring folkloric time' with its 'immanent unity'.[86] Slaveholding in antebellum America represents a promise of salvation both from the threat of levelling in the post-Revolutionary world and from the Biblical condemnation to work. The pastoral impulse thus takes on the sinister form of desire for an imagined land of aristocratic/autocratic self-fulfilment in the enslavement of others, an anti-Rousseauist idyll. But the wish-fulfilment implicit in this sinister pastoral is only half the story.

In French (though not British) realist fiction, the urge towards the pastoral gives way to satire,[87] which helps to explain why the move towards colonial heterotopias is so often a failure. For Brooks, Vautrin will never realize his dream because he—like Realism itself—is wholly urban, and 'there are no worlds elsewhere anymore' in which the pastoral dream derived from Rousseau would be possible.[88] In Balzac's hands the fantasy of colonial autocracy, like the fantasy of absolute detachment and second sight, is frustrated. The *Comédie* does not allow Vautrin satisfaction; the convict is forced back into the metropolitan net of law and order, which he will eventually be able to manipulate from within.[89] Montès claims to enjoy autocratic power, but that is in far-off Brazil and he is, in more ways than one, a foreigner in the narrative world of *La Cousine Bette*, in which the petty rules of the July Monarchy apply. In the same novel, Hulot disregards these rules but—as we shall see in the next chapter—his dream of a miraculous colonial fortune is thwarted; at another moment, when he proposes to leave to 'faire fortune en Amérique' it is only a pretext to extort money from Josépha (VII: 362). Of course, Balzacian 'spéculateurs d'outre-mer' are sometimes successful in regaining lost fortunes, as we see in the case of Charles Mignon, the Marquis d'Aiglemont (six years of trade in Latin America in *La Femme de trente ans*), and Mongenod (who gains a fortune and good health after purchasing land in America in *L'Envers de l'histoire contemporaine*);

---

[85] See Courteix, p. 131 on Vautrin as symptomatic of Balzac's anarchic tendencies and rejection of Rousseau.

[86] *Dialogic Imagination*, p. 224, p. 225.

[87] See Levin, *Gates of Horn*, p. 39. Prendergast also mentions the 'ironic cancellation' of pastoral imagery in the hands of Balzac and Zola, though he sees Balzac's use of pastoral as primarily 'casual and opportunistic' (*Paris and the Nineteenth Century*, p. 9, p. 62).

[88] *Realist Vision*, p. 131.

[89] In *Le Père Goriot* Vautrin's fantasy of slave-ownership is a dead end, and in Balzac's later play *Vautrin*, staged in 1840, the eponymous hero rejects an offer to flee the metropolis in order to manage large holdings in Latin America under a false name, and is in any case then arrested. This ending was however imposed by the censors: the play was originally to have ended with Vautrin's departure in search of a fortune, along with his faithful followers. See Balzac, *Œuvres complètes*, vol. 23, pp. 4–126 for *Vautrin*, and for the censored first version of the play see the annex, pp. 356–440.

but Philippe Bridau returns disillusioned and impoverished from his attempt at the American dream (in *La Rabouilleuse*), while the Tascheron family are successful but disappointed and nostalgic for France (in *Le Curé de village*).[90]

'À quoi sert l'Afrique': this chapter-title of one of Balzac's abandoned projects, *Le Programme d'une jeune veuve* (XII: 373–8), hesitates between the interrogative form and the pronouncement of a whole programme. In that piece of writing Africa (like trade on the high seas) seems to offer General Giroudeau the possibility of refurbishing a tarnished reputation; the case is similar for Oscar Husson in *Un début dans la vie*, or Savinien de Portenduère in *Ursule Mirouët*; but at the same time the form suggests an open question. Indeed, Balzac often situates departure for the colonies at an end-point to a narrative (*Le Contrat de mariage*; *Z. Marcas*) as a negative commentary on the metropolitan regime, and a solution of some uncertainty or desperation, rather than a promise of fortune and self-fulfilment. Interestingly, though this is not the place to explore the comparison in detail, Zola also evokes variations on the Far West fantasy which generally remain frustrated; notably, a variation in which an illicit couple dreams of running away together, usually to America, but fails to do so (a possibility also envisaged briefly in Balzac's *Le Cabinet des Antiques* and *La Rabouilleuse*).[91] One recalls Said's evocation of colonial territories as 'realms of possibility' that 'have always been associated with the realistic novel'.[92] Balzac and Zola certainly evoke these realms of possibility, but often in a negative mode, thus discrediting Romantic narrative tropes of magical fortune or self-fulfilment.

COLONIAL GUILT AND THE TAINTED FORTUNE

In a particularly striking variant on the 'colonial fortune' theme Gobseck, with his clear-sighted amorality acquired in illicit trade across the globe, late in life builds up a colonial fortune in Paris. The tale deals with an issue on which French literature has remained relatively taciturn; Miller sees this silence as a 'calculated plan for forgetting' about the Haitian Revolution.[93] What is at stake in this elision of the Haitian Revolution is analysed by Michel-Rolph Trouillot in *Silencing the Past:*

[90] Jameson's argument that Balzacian narrative is primarily wish-fulfilment (*Political Unconscious*, pp. 148–9) does not take into account the fact that so many colonial fantasies are frustrated in his novels.

[91] In *La Bête humaine*, Séverine and Jacques dream of leaving for America, 'le paradis rêvé', where they hope to make a fortune and Jacques imagines fulfilment as becoming a 'patron' in his own right (that is, dominating others; see IV: 1232; 1235; 1294). But emigration is only a dream; Jacques and Séverine cannot escape the heredity which binds them to their metropolitan past. In *La Joie de vivre*, Lazare at various times expresses regrets at not having left for Australia, America, or 'Océanie'; in that last fantasy he imagines living with Pauline in a *Paul-et-Virginie* fantasy of work-free island life where monkeys would be their servants (III: 904; 1038; 1069–70). We learn in *Le Docteur Pascal* that he does in the end leave for America, but on his own (V: 1017). Flaubert, in the 1845 *Éducation sentimentale*, has his illicit couple get much further away, not to an autocratic pastoral but to disillusionment in a very urban New York.

[92] *Culture and Imperialism*, p. 75.

[93] *French Atlantic Triangle*, ch. 10, particularly p. 246.

Power and the Production of History.[94] In Balzac's tale, however, metonymic detail stands as silent witness to the legacy of slavery in the neocolonial predicament of Haiti in the 1820s.

Having won its independence from France in fact if not *de jure* during the world's first successful slave revolution in 1791–1804, the young republic of Haiti (ex-Saint-Domingue) finally received Charles X's recognition of its independence in 1825. In exchange, Haiti agreed to pay an indemnity of 150 million gold francs to reimburse the ex-slaveholders. 'Balzac n'a pas oublié cet épisode' writes Hoffmann, 'lui qui imagine l'usurier Gobseck faisant partie de la commission chargée de fixer le montant de l'indemnité réclamée à Port-au-Prince.'[95] Gobseck is in fact on the committee that distributes the indemnity to individual claimants:

> Lors du traité par lequel la France reconnut la république d'Haïti, les connaissances que possédait Gobseck sur l'état des anciennes fortunes à Saint-Domingue et sur les colons ou les ayant cause auxquels étaient dévolues les indemnités le firent nommer membre de la commission instituée pour liquider leurs droits et répartir les versements dus par Haïti. Le génie de Gobseck lui fit inventer une agence pour escompter les créances des colons ou de leurs héritiers, sous les noms de Werbrust et Gigonnet avec lesquels il partageait les bénéfices sans avoir besoin d'avancer son argent, car ses lumières avaient constitué sa mise de fonds. (II: 1009)[96]

In this brief paragraph Balzac evokes what is effectively a new form of imperialism. France as a nation-state only appears in the initial clause; it is rapidly replaced by individual financial interests and the private-sector infrastructure that administers those interests. Through the system by which bills with monetary value ('des traites') can be traded, Parisian high finance has an immediate interest in Haiti's payments; and of course money is to be made administering the collection and redistribution of funds.[97] Gobseck receives what Balzac here discreetly calls 'bénéfices', but later 'cadeaux' or 'présents' (II: 1012)—in other words bribes from claimants. His avidity is described in terms of devouring orality, as Owen Heathcote shows.[98] 'Gobseck fut donc l'insatiable boa de cette grande affaire' (II: 1010). The

---

[94] Michel-Rolph Trouillot, *Silencing the Past: Power and the Production of History* (Boston, MA: Beacon Press, 1995). The omission of Haiti in French accounts of the Revolution is also discussed by Léon-François Hoffmann ('Representations of the Haitian Revolution in French Literature', in *The World of the Haitian Revolution*, ed. by David Patrick Geggus and Norman Fiering (Bloomington, IN: Indiana University Press, 2009), pp. 339–51).

[95] *Nègre romantique*, p. 151.

[96] This passage, in Citron's Pléiade edition of 1976, is given one brief footnote (II: 1582) that misleadingly refers the reader to the unification of the island in 1822 rather than to the 1825 indemnity. This is a startling occultation of France's imposition of an impossible debt burden on Haiti, but the blind spot is not Balzac's.

[97] For background on this new system of debt farming and trading in debt, see Benoît Joachim, 'La reconnaissance d'Haïti par la France (1825): Naissance d'un nouveau type de rapports internationaux', *Revue d'histoire moderne et contemporaine*, 22:3 (1975), 369–96 (p. 385); and 'L'indemnité coloniale de Saint-Domingue et la question des rapatriés', *Revue Historique*, 246:2 (1971), 359–76: 'l'indemnité coloniale était destinée à profiter principalement à la haute banque et aux manieurs d'argent qui pratiquaient l'escompte et la spéculation' (p. 374).

[98] Heathcote notes the violence of Gobseck's formative years, and examines the conjunction of orality and violence, linking them with the Eastern piracy of his youth ('From Cannibal to Carnival: Orality and Violence in Balzac's Gobseck', *The Modern Language Review*, 91:1 (1996), 53–64 (p. 56)).

voracious boa suggests the complexity of the faceless financial system that is manipulated by Gobseck. While roughly 8,000 slave-owners had escaped the Haitian revolution and returned to France, their numbers were swollen by relatives, heirs, and creditors so that in 1833 there were officially 25,838 claimants to indemnity payments by Haiti. Many of them were members of France's most influential families, capable of swaying public policy in their own interests. The sum initially agreed on represented ten times the fledgling republic's annual budget, obliging it to contract an immediate debt of 30 million francs in order to meet the first payments; the agreement stipulated that this loan had to be from Paris-based banks. As Balzac shows us, management of debt offered all kinds of neocolonial possibilities that did not entail as many risks as direct colonial domination.[99]

So Gobseck makes a fortune from Haitian debt slavery. As if he were a character in the *Arabian Nights*, '[c]haque matin il recevait ses tributs et les lorgnait comme eût fait le ministre d'un nabab avant de se décider à signer une grâce' (II: 1010); but Balzac carefully grounds the acquisition of his fortune in colonial history and financial manipulation.[100] Moreover, Gobseck's fortune proves to be no magical means to self-realization: at his death his apartment is full of decomposing merchandise, crawling with worms and insects, along with receipts for 'des caisses de thé [...] des balles de café [...] marchandises consignées en son nom au Havre, balles de coton, boucauts de sucre, tonneaux de rhum, cafés, indigos, tabacs, tout un bazar de denrées coloniales!' (II: 1011–12). He has engaged in petty disputes over prices rather than re-selling immediately, and 'pendant la discussion les marchandises s'avariaient'. Gobseck's name, one of Balzac's most suggestive, is ambivalent: *gober sec* could mean swallowing something whole, or dry swallowing.[101] The 'insatiable boa' swallows up the colonial merchandise that should be converted into liquid capital, but it sticks in his dry throat; indeed, Gobseck himself is frequently described as 'dry', just as Charles Grandet is dried up by his experience of the slave trade. Money is the life-blood of the brave new world of post-Revolutionary France, but the fortune Gobseck amasses in administering Haiti's indemnity payments

[99] Joachim, 'Reconnaissance d'Haïti', p. 394, p. 395. In 1838 the debt was reduced to 90 million francs, 60 million to the French state plus the 30 million in loans taken out with Parisian banks in 1825. On the cost to the Haitian economy in the long term of the indemnity payments, see David Patrick Geggus and Norman Fiering, eds, *The World of the Haitian Revolution* (Bloomington, IN: Indiana University Press, 2009), p. 327. See also Miller, p. 484 n. 11; he sees the indemnity as serving to purchase France's forgetting of Haiti (p. 247). On the debt as ushering in a new era of French neocolonialism, see François Blancpain, 'L'Ordonnance de 1823 et la question de l'indemnité' and Gusti Klara Gaillard-Pourchet, 'Aspects politiques et commerciaux de l'indemnisation haïtienne', both in *Rétablissement de l'esclavage dans les colonies françaises, 1802: Ruptures et continuités de la politique coloniale française (1800–1830)*, ed. by Yves Bénot and Marcel Dorigny (Paris: Maisonneuve et Larose, 2003), pp. 221–9 and 231–7. See also Frédérique Beauvois, 'L'indemnité de Saint-Domingue: "Dette d'indépendance" ou "rançon de l'esclavage"?', *French Colonial History*, 10 (2009), 109–24. And on the broader importance of the 1804 revolution in Haiti, see *Yale French Studies*, 107 (2005), 'The Haiti issue', particularly Nick Nesbitt, 'The Idea of 1804', 6–38.

[100] Balzac is, for example, remarkably precise in his use of the name 'Saint-Domingue', to refer to France's colony, and 'Haïti' for the new state, at a time when the latter term was not yet in common usage in France (see Joachim, 'Reconnaissance d'Haïti', pp. 371–2). The speculator Werbrust, a Jew like Gobseck, also appears engaged in doubtful financial schemes in *La Maison Nucingen*.

[101] On his name, see Le Calvez, p. 44; Citron, 'Le Rêve asiatique', p. 320.

remains stagnant so long it is reduced to abjection. So too Charles Grandet returns with barrels of gold powder that appear to be a perfect sublimation of the slave trade, but this gold is sterile, offering no flow of energy into the metropolitan vital system; it purchases his loveless marriage with an aristocrat whose unwomanly physique is strikingly contrasted with that of the adoring Eugénie.

Like the coffee and tea mentioned mockingly by Canalis, Gobseck's colonial products point metonymically back to their distant origins. At the same time, they suggest the failure of his economic vision: 'chaque objet donnait lieu à des contestations qui dénotaient en Gobseck les premiers symptômes de cet enfantillage, de cet entêtement incompréhensible auxquels arrivent tous les vieillards chez lesquels une passion forte survit à l'intelligence' (II: 1012). For Marx, Balzac is using Gobseck to illustrate a misinterpretation of the workings of capital, since he hoards commodities rather than putting them to work as Grandet *père* does with his *écus*.[102] Gobseck, as we saw earlier, had shown a remarkable, almost supernatural, degree of insight into the workings of finance and the human heart; in the management of the Haitian indemnity his own investment is not money but his 'lumières', this same famous insight; but any light is dramatically lost in his obsessive hoarding of colonial products as he sinks into senility. His 'enfantillage' neatly parallels his early experiences on the high seas (II: 967) in a figure of chiasmus that sees him lose in his second childhood the clear-sightedness gained in his first, and waste a colonial fortune just as he made one earlier. The experience of slave trafficking afforded him mastery of money and himself, but it is in pursuit of the blood money of slavery that he loses that mastery.

Heathcote sees *Gobseck* as a tale of restorations,[103] and I would add the Haitian indemnity as another restoration. If a fortune is to be had in such a way, it is a tainted fortune. Miller uses the expression 'Atlantic or colonial "blowback"' for 'the notion that the sins of the slave trade will return to haunt France'.[104] Such a system of 'blowback' seems to be operating in the case of Balzac's devouring miser who proves unable to digest his tainted merchandise. Of course, what is almost entirely absent from Balzac's passing references is any conception of the suffering of individuals; slavery is as distant and abstract as the death of an elderly mandarin in China. This is no abolitionist writing; nor does Balzac write in opposition to the payment of an indemnity by Haiti. Nevertheless, *Gobseck* incorporates a precisely grounded historical reference to the indemnity which foregrounds metropolitan corruption and disenchants the magical possibilities of the exotic fortune. We are very far from the moral certainties of Chateaubriand, who asked, after the Haitian revolution, 'qui oserait encore plaider la cause des Noirs après les crimes qu'ils ont commis?'[105] And we are also far from the evocation of the distant colonies as a

---

[102] *Capital*, vol. 1, p. 735 n. 15.

[103] 'Cannibal to Carnival', p. 55. He also stresses that the ending of the novella, as revised by Balzac for the 1835 Bechet edition, is a victory for chaos and not, despite initial appearances, for patriarchal order (p. 60).

[104] *French Atlantic Triangle*, p. 298.

[105] François-René de Chateaubriand, 'Mission des Antilles', in *Essai sur les Révolutions/Génie du christianisme*, ed. by Maurice Regard (Paris: Gallimard, 1978 [1802]), p. 1000.

means to consolidate metropolitan order that, according to Said's famous essay, characterizes Jane Austen's *Mansfield Park*, where the restoration of domestic harmony follows the return to 'productivity and regulated discipline' in Sir Thomas's Antiguan slaveholdings.[106] Very different are the ideological implications of Gobseck's demise in an unheated room, his apartment full of rotting, worm-ridden colonial merchandise. The tale sheds what is, to say the least, an ambivalent light on France's relationship with what was once its most profitable colony.

ZOLA'S COLONIAL EXPERIMENTS AND THE ETHICS OF DISTANCE

We have seen Balzac's ambivalence towards sinister pastoral, which remains a fantasy even as he unpicks its credibility. There are both comparisons and contrasts to be drawn with Zola. The latter's attitude to France's colonies fluctuated over time, but he too registered the impact of distance on ethics, notably in a brief, chilling evocation of medical experimentation in the colonies. Zola famously argued that the naturalist novel should function as a scientific experiment, based on the experimental science of medicine that was emerging at the time, and his manifesto *Le Roman expérimental* (1879) was calqued on Claude Bernard's *Introduction à l'étude de la médecine expérimentale* (1865). Doctor figures in Zola's novels are frequently partial figurations of the author (Dr Pascal, in the novel of that name, being the most developed case). As early as the second edition of *Thérèse Raquin* (1868) he compares the novelist's work with dissection: 'J'ai simplement fait sur deux corps vivants le travail analytique que les chirurgiens font sur des cadavres.'[107] The cruelty of the surgical metaphors he employs in his theoretical writing stands as a guarantee of scientific honesty.[108]

Among the doctor-figures of the Rougon-Macquart is Dr Cazenove in *La Joie de vivre* (1883), an intelligent man who feels real tenderness for the heroine Pauline. His formative experiences were in the four corners of the world, or at least the 'quatre coins de nos colonies', and the sentence that lists his activities begins pragmatically enough: 'il avait soigné les épidémies du bord, les maladies monstrueuses des tropiques'; and adds, in more picturesque mode 'l'éléphantiasis à Cayenne, les piqûres de serpent dans l'Inde'. Then comes an abrupt shift from the verb *soigner* to the description of experimentation on live subjects: 'il avait *tué* des hommes de toutes les couleurs, *étudié* les poisons sur des Chinois, *risqué* des nègres dans des *expériences délicates de vivisection*' (my italics, III: 919).[109] Cazenove, like Balzac's

---

[106] *Culture and Imperialism*, p. 104. There has been energetic critical debate over Said's analysis of the role of slavery in *Mansfield Park*, but there is no space here to do justice to it.

[107] Preface to the 2nd edition of *Thérèse Raquin* [1868] (*Thérèse Raquin*, ed. by Henri Mitterand (Paris: 'GF' Flammarion, 1970), p. 60.

[108] See François-Marie Mourad, '*Thérèse Raquin*, roman expérimental', *Les Cahiers naturalistes*, 84 (2010), 157–64 (p. 161).

[109] Later, in a rare moment of sociable relaxation, Dr Cazenove 'racontait des histoires de sauvages' III: 993). This storytelling may be a deliberate reminiscence of the story her uncle told the child

Gobseck, has travelled so much he no longer believes in anything.[110] The aging doctor is however hesitant and fearful about the difficult labour endured by Louise, Pauline's rival, initially suggesting a procedure that would sacrifice either the mother or the child because he remembers 'quelques négresses qu'il avait accouchées, aux colonies' including one who died 'pendant qu'il la délivrait d'un paquet de chair et d'os'. It is not clear whether this delivery was by an attempted caesarean, for which he had had no medical training; such procedures were not considered necessary for navy doctors, for whom these are 'les seules *expériences* possibles, des femmes *éventrées* à l'occasion' (my italics, III: 1092–3).[111] Here the word *expériences* is used in the narrower sense, that is, not as referring to experience but to experiments that the kindly Dr Cazenove has deliberately undertaken in order to test the effects of surgical procedures on a living African woman (*éventrer* means to disembowel, rather than to perform a caesarean, although *ventre* can mean womb by association; Zola's use of the word suggests a deliberately fatal operation). In such an experiment the surgeon-doctor operates on the living female body just as the naturalist novelist operates on a fictive one.[112]

Claude Bernard had explored the moral question of experimentation on living subjects in a chapter of the work on experimental medicine that Zola so admired, but he drew cautious conclusions.[113] Zola's novels fantasize, and attempt to enact in the form of fiction, the possibility of such experimentation. Dr Pascal is able to conduct dissections because a cholera epidemic furnishes him with the corpses of a series of pregnant women (V: 944). More privileged, Dr Cazenove has had access to living African or Chinese bodies in what would appear to be the best laboratory for unimpeded experimentation: the colonies. *La Joie de vivre* was initially planned as a novel about 'l'idée de bonté et de douleur' (III: 1746), and the mini embedded narratives that constitute Cazenove's colonial recollections set up an implicit parallel between the suffering bodies of Pauline and Louise and the subjects of his colonial experimentation. But in this pessimistic novel—where male creative

---

Pauline in the kitchen of her family home in *Le Ventre de Paris*, a story which also included the monstrous tropics of Cayenne and its serpents, and which is discussed in Chapter 4 of this book.

[110] In his preparatory work for the novel, Zola writes: 'Il en a tant vu, qu'il dit de Dieu lui-même: Est-ce qu'on sait!' (N.A.F. 10311 fol. 248, in *La Fabrique des Rougon-Macquart: édition des dossiers préparatoires*, ed. by Colette Becker and Véronique Lavielle, 6 vols to date (Paris: Honoré Champion, 2003–13), vol. 4, p. 1054).

[111] In Zola's plan Cazenove is 'effrayé' by Louise's situation and the need to choose between the life of the mother or the child, despite having some experience on 'les négresses qu'il a pu éventrer aux colonies' (N.A.F. 10311 fol. 122, in Becker, *La Fabrique*, vol. 4, p. 928).

[112] As Baguley reminds us, one of the 'most significant paradigms of naturalist fiction' is that of the (male) doctor analysing the (female) patient; and the narrator is often a substitute for that doctor's analysis (*Naturalist fiction*, p. 106). On the gendered nature of the naturalist experiment, see Dorothy Kelly ('Experimenting on Women: Zola's Theory and Practice of the Experimental Novel', in *Spectacles of Realism: Gender, Body, Genre*, ed. by Margaret Cohen and Christopher Prendergast (Minneapolis: University of Minnesota Press, 1995), pp. 231–46) though she does not mention *La Joie de vivre*. On childbirth and male violence in Zola, see Susie Hennessy, '(Re)producing Death in Emile Zola's Rougon-Macquart', in *Aimer et Mourir: Love, Death, and Women's Lives in Texts of French Expression*, ed. by Eilene Hoft-March and Judith Holland Sarnecki (Newcastle upon Tyne: Cambridge Scholars, 2009), pp. 48–63.

[113] See Mourad, p. 161.

powers are thwarted, the male protagonist fails to complete his study of medicine, and Dr Cazenove is acutely aware of the limitations of contemporary medical methods—the possibility of true experimentation, to be conducted in the moral void of the colonies, seems to suggest a rare promise of progress. In this sense *La Joie de vivre* already points towards the unpopulated Sudan of *Fécondité* (1899), where the march of progress can continue unimpeded by inconvenient ethical concerns.

Envisaging human vivisection reflects the militantly secular outlook, and the foregrounding of experimentation and anatomy, that are central to Zola's *œuvre*. Cazenove is unable to pursue his experiments, but no moral impediment is suggested, and the choice of vocabulary points to the liberating effect of both geographical and racial distance. Zola was aware enough of the shock-value of these ideas to have kept the references brief and ambivalent, so that readers could skim over them should they be so inclined, and they play only a minor role in *La Joie de vivre*.[114] Nor, having learnt the Flaubertian lesson of authorial impartiality, does he explicitly ask moral questions; but in striving for an 'experimental' terrain on which to base a forward-looking literature, like a forward-looking science, he offers the colonial space as one that is exempt from moral obstacles. This is in stark contrast to Balzac's frequent and explicit examinations of the question of ethics at a distance. Nevertheless their treatment of space and of distance has a common basis. Balzac's intense focus on a specific milieu founded the realist novel in 'everyday time' and with it, 'everyday space'. In Zola's works too, characters are defined by carefully delimited space—in Hamon's term, Zola's characters are 'territorialisé[s]'.[115] Henri Mitterand prefers the term 'terrain' to Hamon's 'territoire', emphasizing the competitive game that is played out in a spatially defined arena, but he too stresses the tight relation between character and milieu, which he calls 'une relation... sui-spatiale'.[116] It is the determining nature of this grounding of characters in everyday space—be it called milieu, terrain, or territory—that makes the potentially transformative nature of distance so striking. For if milieu defines a character, a radical rupture with that milieu triggers his or her equally radical transformation and, as we have seen, a suspension of the metropolitan moral framework. Distance has long been understood, as Ginzburg shows, to dull our sense of identification and thus remorse for murder. But whereas Zola's colonial bodies seem entirely removed from metropolitan ethical space, Balzac asks us to ask ourselves the moral question faced by his characters.

In *The Political Unconscious*, Fredric Jameson dismisses the idea that one can separate the 'greatness of a given writer' from 'his deplorable opinions', which is

---

[114] The novel is sufficiently ambiguous in its wording concerning Cazenove's experimentation on African women for Harrow, for example, to refer in a much more positive light to 'native women he helped deliver in the colonies' (*Zola: The Body Modern*, p. 37 n. 26).

[115] Hamon, *Personnel*, p. 33, p. 35; characters are even 'assigné[s] à résidence' (p. 316). Hamon points out the curious parallel established between this obsessively reiterated territorialization and the classical conventions of the unity of space, time and action (p. 33).

[116] Henri Mitterand, 'Pour une poétique de l'espace romanesque: l'exemple de Zola', in *Zola and the Craft of Fiction*, ed. by Robert Lethbridge and Terry Keefe (Leicester: Leicester University Press, 1990), pp. 80–8 (p. 85, p. 82).

'not possible for any world-view [...] that takes politics seriously'. His chapter on Balzac claims that the crucial feature of Balzacian narrative is 'libidinal investment or authorial wish-fulfilment', particularly in the earlier works that we have been examining.[117] There is much to be said for both of these claims, but my reading of slavery and imperialism in *La Comédie humaine* does, I hope, encourage us to nuance them. In the case of Balzac and the *Comédie*, even more strikingly than elsewhere, the work is greater than the man, and while it encompasses his personal views, it also exceeds them. The outward-reaching nature of metonymy, with its multiple meanings, is one key to how this works in practice. Objects, like money itself, do not exist in isolation in Balzac's world: they have a history; they come with baggage. In the *Comédie humaine* slave-ownership and the slave trade are associated with forms of wish-fulfilment, but they frequently bring with them the *frustration* of that same 'libidinal investment'. Indeed, despite its monumental, totalizing breadth and ambition, the *Comédie humaine* is striking for the precariousness of its positions. The Balzacian novel simply cannot be reduced to what Said calls the 'consolidation of authority'. He argues that Austen's references to Sir Thomas Bertram's Antiguan slaveholdings show her subscribing to his values;[118] but the *Comédie* does not offer any such fixed position. Balzac himself might well have accepted the death of the Chinese mandarin for the sake of an instant fortune; but what his writing does, much more interestingly, is ask *us* to ask ourselves that question.

---

[117] *Political Unconscious*, p. 279, p. 141, p. 157.
[118] *Culture and Imperialism*, p. 92, p. 73.

3

The Great Imperial Scam

Realist narrative, from Balzac onwards, exposes a post-Revolutionary world that is subject to a regime of legal contracts and monetary transactions, suggesting the ever-present threat of the fraud or swindle.[1] While this contractual regime is now broadly recognized as central to the nineteenth-century novel, it is not often acknowledged quite how frequently fraud, and dubious or outright criminal acts, figure in narratives of French *colonialism*. Before turning to fraud proper, this chapter will begin by harking back to metonymy and the imported objects of Chapter 1, but this time focusing on objects or products that are only pseudo-exotic, orientalizing rather than actually Oriental, or authentically imported but used for some sort of cover-up or trickery. These fraudulent products will then lead us to a discussion of colonial financial scams. The fact is that exotic objects and imperialist enterprises alike are repeatedly linked with duplicity and fraud. This can be explained partly in generic terms: since the realist novel relies on conceptual and spatial contiguity, introducing the distant space of the colonies creates a gap into which ruse or falsehood slips, an 'alibi' (the word comes to us, after all, from the Latin word for 'elsewhere'). From a more political perspective, meanwhile, although the association of imperialism with fraud does not necessarily indicate an anticolonial stance, the cynicism thus suggested undermines the idea that there was a single imperialist discourse summed up by the rhetoric of the *mission civilisatrice*. This chapter examines elements of a very different discourse on imperialism, one that is intent on denouncing the Great Imperial Scam.

ORIENTAL LUXURY, METROPOLITAN FRAUD

From the late eighteenth century onwards there was dramatic growth in the European market for 'populuxe' products, that is, cheaper copies of luxury goods, aimed at the growing middle and urban working classes.[2] Exoticism was frequently

---

[1] The importance of the contractual regime that underlies both narrative and legal contracts in the Balzacian novel has been widely acknowledged since Christopher Prendergast's crucial study (*Order of Mimesis*, pp. 83–118). He does not discuss it in relation to imperialism.

[2] The term 'populuxe', coined by Cissie Fairchild, is used by Morag Martin in *Selling Beauty: Cosmetics, Commerce, and French Society, 1750–1830* (Baltimore, MD: Johns Hopkins University Press, 2009), p. 3). The seventh chapter of Martin's book, 'Selling the Orient: From the Exotic Harem to Napoleon's Colonial Enterprise' (pp. 134–54) traces the changing uses of orientalist imagery, and in particular imagery drawn from the Turkish seraglio, by the French cosmetics industry.

used in marketing such products, because exotic imports had until then been reserved for the elite. The democratization of exotic imports was so popular that Eastern and African images were used to market non-exotic products such as 'confectionery, soap and medicine'.[3] 'Populuxe' products appear frequently in the nineteenth-century realist novel, alongside new social phenomena that are now so familiar to us that we risk not noticing them: advertising campaigns, shop window displays, and, later in the century, department stores. As we saw in Chapter 1, consumerist exotic ersatz plays a part in Flaubert's *L'Éducation sentimentale* which is set in the 1840s when, as Walter Benjamin noted, the Parisian fashion for Orientalist décor was partly propaganda for the Algerian campaign.[4] Orientalist motifs and décor had also been used by the First Empire, and would be used by the Second, as part of a calculated public relations strategy. The great realist novelists do not, however, simply repeat these exotic motifs: they hold them up for our attention and they frequently associate them with duplicity. Long before Flaubert wrote of Arnoux buying identical cashmere shawls for his wife and mistress, Balzac's travelling salesman Gaudissart sold cheap French-made pseudo-cashmere shawls in order to be able to afford to buy an authentic (Indian) cashmere shawl for his own mistress (*L'Illustre Gaudissart*, IV: 569; 573). The social hierarchy revealed in the contrast of authentically imported object and local imitation has been studied by Susan Hiner: so-called 'cashmere' shawls could be made in Lyon or Nîmes, though they were not as exuberantly 'oriental' as those made in Paris. Hiner also argues that the yellow cashmere shawl that plays a key role in *La Cousine Bette*, as well as being 'linked to Bette's "imperialist" fantasy of conquest', is part of her attempt at a fraudulent masking of social identity: the shawl's movement between the different characters reveals the 'essential theme of social imposture'.[5]

Balzac uses a range of more-or-less authentic and prestigious objects to reflect shifts in social class; he also exposes new marketing techniques that appeal to the growing urban population. It is in the marketing of cosmetics that we can best see the role played by exoticism as an antidote to the drab metropolitan realities of age, grime, banality, and (relative) democratization. César Birotteau, in the 1837 novel of that name, rises to fortune selling perfume in a shop called 'La Reine des Roses'. The shop's name suggests Birotteau's royalist sympathies, and it soon becomes advisable to display them less openly. His move from merely trading, to producing perfume, corresponds with a shift to less politically charged references, borrowing from the fashionable discourses of Orientalism and science with two products that

---

[3] Joanna de Groot, 'Metropolitan desires and colonial connections: reflections on consumption and empire', in *At Home with the Empire: Metropolitan Culture and the Imperial World*, ed. by Catherine Hall and Sonya O. Rose (Cambridge: Cambridge University Press, 2006), pp. 166–90 (p. 187). Advertising using exotic motifs, according to de Groot, shaped not only images of the colonial other, but how the British saw themselves (p. 189); her comments can be applied, albeit with caution, to the French market too. On advertising as developing under the July Monarchy (so used by Balzac in *César Birotteau* a little anachronistically) and on Orientalism in advertising for perfume in the 1820s, see Donnard, p. 255 and p. 257.

[4] Benjamin, p. 214, p. 215.

[5] *Accessories to Modernity*, p. 97; also 'Lust for Luxe', pp. 84–7. On the growth of the French industry producing imitations, see 'Lust for Luxe', p. 78, pp. 82–3.

he calls the 'Double Pâte des Sultanes' and the 'Eau Carminative'. The purported Turkish origin of Birotteau's perfumed cream, the 'Pâte des Sultanes', is of course false: 'L'eau de rose prétendue de Constantinople se faisait, comme l'eau de Cologne, à Paris' (VI: 70). Birotteau's inspiration comes from a book which was itself marketed under false Orientalist pretentions, going by the name *Abdeker ou l'Art de conserver la beauté*. It is a 'prétendu livre arabe, espèce de roman fait par un médecin du siècle précédent' (VI: 63).[6] According to Balzac, such Orientalist marketing strategies appeal to the French consumer's desire to escape from pseudo-democratic levelling in the metropolis, since in France 'tout homme tient autant à être sultan que la femme à devenir sultane' (VI: 64). Morag Martin, less cynical than Balzac, prefers to see the Orientalist marketing of cosmetics as evoking 'resistance against despotism'.[7] Birotteau's strategy is not alone of its kind: his ambition is to defeat a rival 'exotic' product, 'l'huile de Macassar' (VI: 46; 94), whose strengths lie in its novel square-shaped bottles and possession of 'un nom séduisant': 'On la présente comme une importation étrangère', he worries, 'et nous aurons le malheur d'être de notre pays.' He proposes to counter-attack by selling his own product abroadmau, where it will be exotic, because 'il paraît que Macassar est réellement aux Indes' (VI: 94).[8] Balzac had already joked that the Makassar oil sold in Europe was fake, and not really from the Indies (Indonesia), in the *Voyage de Paris à Java* (OD, II: 1147), a text that plays on its own problematic relationship with authenticity (as we shall see in Chapter 4). In *César Birotteau* Balzac focuses on the tension between probity and dishonesty: the intrusive narrator tells us Birotteau is honest, but he is shown engaged in procedures that challenge our conception of 'honesty'.[9] The narrator of *César Birotteau* explicitly points out the moral ambivalence of marketing strategies 'que l'on nomme peut-être injustement charlatanisme' (VI: 64), a comment that makes the accusation even as it apparently pleads against it.[10]

---

[6] Balzac was referring to a real Orientalist fake, *Abdeker* (1754). Its author, Antoine Le Camus, used an Oriental tale as the context for beauty advice, claiming the book was an authentic fifteenth-century Arab manuscript brought to Paris in 1740 by the Turkish ambassador's doctor. See Martin, p. 139.

[7] *Selling Beauty*, p. 139.

[8] Makassar is an international trading port city in Sulawesi, Indonesia. Makassar Oil was a real product, very successfully marketed by British companies during the nineteenth century. Martin suggests that the attraction of Makassar as a name was its association with wildness, and thus an abundance of hair, since it was mainly used by men to treat baldness (p. 167).

[9] John P. Greene offers an interesting 'oppositional' reading of the novel as showing a conflict of narrative intention and narrative practice ('Cosmetics and Conflicting Fictions in Balzac's *César Birotteau*', *Neophilologus*, 83:2 (1999) 197–208 (p. 198)). Barbéris's more classic reading shows a much higher opinion of Birotteau's integrity, and of the new advertising methods that his successor Popinot puts into place (Pierre Barbéris, *Le Monde de Balzac* (Paris: Arthaud, 1973), pp. 234–5).

[10] Greene emphasizes that 'The claim that the product hails from the "mysterious East" is a blatant lie' (p. 199). Balzac's ambivalence about the honesty of his perfumer reappears in *La Cousine Bette*, when the nouveau-riche Crevel, proposing a dishonest pact, proudly proclaims himself '[a]ncien parfumeur, successeur de César Birotteau, à la Reine des Roses' and claims that he is 'absolument comme [s]on prédécesseur' (VII: 69). When Crevel later learns that he is dying of an obscure (sexually-transmitted) exotic disease, he does not seem entirely surprised and hypothesizes 'On n'a pas été commis voyageur pour la parfumerie impunément' (VII: 434).

By employing fiction in his marketing, Birotteau arguably becomes a creator in his own right. Although he is too ill-educated to have an artistic appreciation of his own exotic perfumery, using marvellous ingredients to fabricate it in complete ignorance of where they come from, he is able to manipulate their effect on his public. He uses scientific claims with equal ignorance, though he is careful to get authoritative backing from experts. Interestingly, the same appropriation of Orientalism and science is found in the marketing strategies employed by Jantrou, the journalist/PR manager of Zola's 1891 novel *L'Argent*, which will be discussed later in this chapter. The prospectus for Birotteau's Cephalic Oil is written by Finot, a minor *homme de lettres* just as Zola's Jantrou is a failed academic, excluded from the university for unspecified sexual misdemeanours. Both Finot and Jantrou understand the new power of advertising, and know how to manipulate the press to serve it. In these instances one finds a certain degree of autoreferentiality (both Balzac and Zola were journalists as well as novelists), but one in which it is implicit that the 'true' writer, unlike his second-rate fictional counterpart, does not descend into advertising.[11]

Anne McClintock's influential study *Imperial Leather* argues that the last decades of the nineteenth century saw a shift in the culture of imperialism from scientific racism to 'commodity racism', which 'converted the narrative of imperial Progress into mass-produced consumer spectacles', a category in which she includes advertising for products such as soap.[12] The expression 'commodity racism' is suggestive, but the transition is not as neat as McClintock implies: scientific racism did not disappear or even decline in the last decades of the nineteenth century (or the first decades of the twentieth) and, as we have seen in the case of Balzac, 'commodity racism'—or at least 'commodity Orientalism'—appears much earlier. Balzac's commodity Orientalism is already part of an 'Orientalist capitalist narrative'[13] that sees the East as in decline but providing artefacts to feed the devouring hunger of Western capitalism. It tells us more about capitalist corruption than it does about desires for imperial expansion, but it is already a sign of popular culture's response to the ongoing 'question d'Orient'—that is, the question of how the European Great Powers could safely profit from the decline of the Ottoman empire.

When Oriental cosmetics appear in Zola, too, they are primarily signifiers of fraud or delusion. In *Son Excellence Eugène Rougon*, Zola's most overtly political novel on the Second Empire, the *femme fatale* Clorinde has her maid rub her body with aromatic oils and unguents 'connus d'elle seule, achetés à Constantinople,

---

[11] For Balzac, Orientalist daydreaming is the sign of an imagination beyond the reach of the petty capitalist Birotteau. A true 'poète', in the street where the perfumers work, 'peut en y sentant quelques parfums rêver l'Asie. Il admire des danseuses dans une chauderie en respirant du vétiver. Frappé par l'éclat de la cochenille, il y retrouve les poèmes brahmaniques, les religions et leurs castes. En se heurtant contre l'ivoire brut, il monte sur le dos des éléphants, dans une cage de mousseline, et y fait l'amour comme le roi de Lahore. Mais le petit commerçant ignore d'où viennent et où croissent les produits sur lesquels il opère' (VI: 70). On the parallels between Finot et Jantrou, see Corinne Saminadayar-Perrin, 'Fictions de la Bourse', *Les Cahiers naturalistes*, 78 (2004), 41–62 (pp. 48–51).

[12] Anne McClintock, *Imperial Leather: Race, Gender and Sexuality in the Colonial Context* (New York/London: Routledge, 1995), p. 33 (chapter 5 deals with 'commodity racism').

[13] Gallois, *Zola*, p. 138.

chez le parfumeur du sérail, disait-elle, par un diplomate italien de ses amis. [...]
Cela devait lui donner une peau blanche, lisse, impérissable comme le marbre; une
certaine huile surtout [...] avait la propriété miraculeuse d'effacer à l'instant les
moindres rides' (II: 301–2). The credulity that leads Clorinde to believe in the
miraculous properties of this oil is signalled to us by the indirect free discourse,
the verb 'devait', and the suspicious Italian intermediary, whose very existence she
implicitly denies later when she claims that she obtained the product directly ('elle
parla des essences qu'elle tenait du parfumeur même des sultanes', II: 305).
Commodity Orientalism here warns us of naïve consumerism; it also stands metonymically for Clorinde's own doubtful origins. 'Oriental' cosmetics are sold as an
aspiration to transcend age, dirt, and banality, but reminders of their status as
commodities reconfirm that the world of the novel is one of contingency and
deception. Her desire to appropriate the beauty of the seraglio women also shows
her eagerness to assume their role in relation to the Master (later, when she becomes
the Emperor's mistress, she wears a gold and diamond dog collar and chain that he
gives her, II: 333) and implicitly situates Napoleon III as would-be despot in relation to a would-be harem beauty. The seraglio theme should not however lead us
to think of all Orientalist cosmetics as gendered in one direction; Balzac's aging
dandy Maxime de Trailles has jet-black hair thanks to 'un cosmétique indien fort
cher, en usage dans la Perse, et sur lequel Maxime gardait le secret' (*Le Député
d'Arcis*, VIII: 808). What the dandy and the *femme fatale* have in common is their
idolatry of their own youth and beauty and their willingness to employ masquerade. Commodity Orientalism underlines their social and sexual ambivalence.[14]

There is no particular reason to think Maxime de Trailles' hair dye is a 'fake'
import; it stands for deceit in other ways. So too, authentically exotic imports
stand for falsity and the unnatural in elements of luxury décor. One notable variant on the association of exoticism and duplicity, which would merit a whole study
in its own right, is the theme of imported tropical plants in metropolitan green-
houses. Removed from their natural habitat, such plants function as a metaphor
for unnatural desire in Zola's *La Curée* and for the hypocrisy and masquerade of
social climbing in Maupassant's *Bel-Ami*. Most famously, in Huysmans' *À Rebours*,
the disjunction of tropical origin and metropolitan setting is part of an attack on
realist aesthetics. In *Bel-Ami* hothouse plants, and exotic décors more generally,
mark Duroy's rise in society. He begins in a shabby room overlooking the railway
(that central motif of unadorned realism), but papers it over with cheap *japonaiserie* to welcome his mistress, Clotilde de Marelle. She herself seeks distraction
from her life married to a railway inspector and dresses in a Japanese kimono
(251). Duroy uses authentically exotic Japanese *bibelots*—prints, fans, screens,
even cut-outs of printed boats and birds stuck on the windows and the ceiling—
for the purposes of concealment or masquerade (264).[15] Mme de Marelle later

---

[14] On *maquillage* and the dandy as the 'point of maximal ambiguity' of the new social mixture, see
Prendergast, *Order of Mimesis*, p. 93.
[15] For a discussion of Maupassant's Orientalism, including *japonaiserie*, see Susan Barrow, 'East/
West: Appropriation of Aspects of the Orient in Maupassant's *Bel-Ami*', *Nineteenth-Century French
Studies*, 30:3–4 (2002), 315–28 (p. 326).

rents a flat for their meetings in the rue de Constantinople (266), whose name
suggests the Orientalism of the Turkish seraglio—appropriately enough, since he
ends up using it for *rendez-vous* with both her and another mistress.[16] Duroy's
vertiginous rise is marked by the décor of his future father-in-law's house, with its
orientalist paintings, tropical greenhouse, and Chinese carp that make his heart
beat faster with envy and desire. Maupassant maps the Parisian cityscape over
exotic geography to chart Duroy's rise by the degree to which stark realities (such
as the railways) are concealed by exotic façades (I shall return to *Bel-Ami* below, to
discuss imperialism itself as a scam).

Commodity Orientalism is deliberately framed and exposed by realist writers.
In other words, rather than taking the Orientalist capitalist motif as a sign that a
novel is necessarily complicit with imperialist rapacity, we need to consider its
deliberate narrative distancing and ironic framing. Nor is the theme of commodity
Orientalism to be mistaken for the racist stereotype of Oriental duplicity, since
falseness lies in the metropolitan use that is made of exoticism. So too, as we shall
now see, the realist novel frequently portrays imperialist ventures not as heroic
activities, civilizing missions, or sources of marvellous fortunes, but as themselves
tainted with duplicity and hypocrisy.

THE DEBUNKING OF MAGICAL MONEY

In the nineteenth-century novel exotic lands ostensibly hold out the promise of
foreign adventure and space for economic self-realization. I discussed the (usually
frustrated) 'sinister pastoral' aspiration in Chapter 2; alongside it must be considered what might be called the 'oncle d'Amérique' narrative function, in which the
combination of geographic distance and metropolitan ignorance permits the
inheritance of a fortune whose origins need not be explained. This is part of what
Moretti calls 'the mythic geography—*pecunia ex machina*—of a wealth that is not
really produced [...] but magically "found" overseas whenever a novel needs it.'[17]
These functions of exotic space often correspond to a 'Romantic' world-view,
and indeed the magical quality of luck has been seen as part of the essence of
Romanticism; but they are to be found long after Romanticism proper.[18] In contrast, however, French Realism examines the conditions in which money is
acquired, and debunks the myth of the magical fortune. It undermines the *conte
fantastique* by denouncing the century's *comptes fantastiques*.

---

[16] Claudine Giacchetti sees *Bel-Ami* as the story of a conquest of space, and mentions the low space
of the rue de Constantinople, but emphasizes vertical ascension rather than colonial or exotic space
(*Maupassant, Espaces du roman* (Geneva: Droz, 1993), p. 86, pp. 102–4).

[17] Moretti, *Atlas*, p. 27.

[18] On luck as part of the essence of Romanticism, see Fernand Baldensperger, *Orientations
étrangères chez Honoré de Balzac* (Paris: Champion, 1927), p. 20. In many late nineteenth-century
adventure stories fortunes are also achieved miraculously; see notably Seillan on Africa as 'un cof-
fre-fort géologique empli de trésors amassés par la nature et destinés, par une sorte de finalisme naïf, à
être raflés par un Blanc' (*Aux sources*, p. 133).

For Moretti, the colonial fortune theme is simply a way of avoiding the issues of metropolitan class struggle, in other words a form of disavowal. Jameson, however, points out that from the last decades of the nineteenth century onwards colonialism located elsewhere a significant part of the 'new imperial world system'. The resulting 'spatial disjunction' and the invisibility of the colonial space in metropolitan representation made it impossible 'to grasp the way the system functions as a whole'.[19] Recognizing the presence of colonial lands *offstage* in the metropolitan realist novel, as we do here, may provide a means of mitigating Jameson's view. It is through colonial heterotopias offstage that Realism engages with the emerging world economy and links it to the circulation of metropolitan capital. The 'question d'Orient' was asked not just by politicians, but more specifically by ambitious western financiers from the eighteenth century onwards.[20] The point of the present study is not to *deny* the near-invisibility, in the metropolitan novel, of the colonial side of the economic balance sheet, but to show that many novels themselves dwell on the spatial disjunction of the emerging global system.

Many realist novels thus debunk the 'oncle d'Amérique' function, the narrative sleight of hand by which a character abruptly acquires a disproportionate fortune. The colonial fortune generally originates in the Americas or in the Orient, almost indifferently: in the archetypal ironic-Romantic tale of wish-fulfilment, Gautier's *Fortunio* (1837), the hero's fortune comes not from an 'oncle d'Amérique' but from an uncle established in India, but when the novel was first published in 1836 it was entitled *El Dorado*.[21] It is not that the realist colonial comedy ceases to be haunted by the dream of a sudden wealth. Rather, it satirizes the meeting point of two antithetical systems: the miraculous Oriental fortune and the unforgiving financial balance sheet of the metropolis. Balzac has been seen as a Romantic in whose writing the Oriental dream triumphs over the real world of figures and accounts,[22] but he was rather contemptuous of *Fortunio*.[23] In *La Peau de chagrin* he himself took up the magic Oriental fortune but set it jarringly in an emphatically materialist context. While he was clearly fascinated by the Romantic potential of the Oriental dream, he was also intent on denouncing the destructive potential

---

[19] 'Modernism and Imperialism', p. 11.

[20] See Hentsch, p. 168.

[21] On *Fortunio*, see Catherine Champion, 'Fortunio, un rêve romantique indien dans le Paris d'Haussmann', *Corps Écrit*, 34 (1990), 57–64. The Indian nabob uncle is briefly explained in chapter 17 of the novel.

[22] Baldensperger, for example, saw Balzac's Romantic Orientalism as being opposed to his detailed use of 'chiffres [...] de la comptabilité, de la banque, de la faillite, de la banqueroute'; he sees Balzac as essentially on the side of the Romantic Orient against this realist accountability (*Orientations étrangères*, p. 21). This seems to be favouring an author's individual sympathies rather than the deliberate strategies revealed in his work: like Flaubert after him, Balzac consciously undermines his own Romanticism.

[23] For Balzac's opinion of Gautier's *Fortunio*, see his letter of 15 October 1838 (*Lettres à Mme Hanska*, vol. 1, p. 469). Nevertheless, Gautier's novel borrows extensively from Balzac himself (see Moïse Le Yaouanc, 'Échanges romantiques: Balzac et "Gamiani", Balzac et "Fortunio"', *L'Année balzacienne* (1976), 71–86. If we follow Levin's analysis, in which the epic, romance, and novel forms correspond to successive military, courtly, and mercantile estates, *Fortunio* is a throwback to the romance form, while commerce is the great subject of the realist novel (*Gates of Horn*, p. 32, pp. 34–5).

of speculation in the post-Revolutionary world where wealth is no guarantor of social cohesion but rather 'responsible for the emergence of a fluid, shifting, disordered social reality'.[24] So his novels repeatedly take up the tropes of the mysterious fortune and imperial self-realization in order to undermine them.

Much has been written on Balzac's use of the *Mille et une Nuits*,[25] but it is not always acknowledged that this use has a two-fold effect: references to the *Arabian Nights* stand for the fabulous potential of the Orient, but also for the false, misleading nature of the Oriental mirage (we shall see that this dual usage is replicated by Zola). So Balzac evokes an Oriental fortune to indicate that something has financially doubtful origins. Thus, in *Illusions perdues*, the witty courtesan Mme du Val-Noble, showing off her luxurious apartment, declares 'Voilà les comptes des Mille et Une Nuits!' (V: 493).[26] In *César Birotteau* the perfumer evokes the power of a magic wand in the preparation of the marvellous ball that will ruin him, allowing himself 'un geste asiatique digne des *Mille et une Nuits*' (VI: 101). When Rastignac suddenly appears in fine new clothes in *Le Père Goriot*, Vautrin ironically asks their fellow lodgers, 'combien cette merveille, me direz-vous, messieurs? deux sous! Non. Rien du tout. C'est un reste de fournitures faites au grand-Mogol' (III: 168). By mockingly evoking Oriental opulence, Vautrin is neatly reminding Rastignac of the actual cost of his outfit, for which he has appropriated his family's scarce financial resources. That very evening Delphine de Nucingen puts on a façade of Orientalist luxury, wearing a 'robe en cachemire blanc à dessins perses de la plus riche élégance' (III: 169), before, in desperation, asking Rastignac to gamble the last of her money in the Palais Royal.

The Palais Royal is also the setting for the opening scene of *La Peau de chagrin*, where Raphaël de Valentin, in a doomed third attempt at gambling, risks his last gold coin before exchanging his life itself for a magic Oriental talisman. Gambling and the Oriental fortune are associated, for what is a fortune gained on the gaming table but fantastic (that is, inexplicable)? The Orient, and to a lesser extent the Americas, stand for riches acquired outside the tyrannical equations that dictate the finite nature of energy and money in the Balzacian world. Through the Oriental motif, his novels mourn the ultimate impossibility of such a miracle. Indeed, *La Comédie humaine* self-consciously stages the secularization and disenchantment of money. The gambling den is crucial because financial speculation was itself initially seen as a form of gambling. As Prendergast writes, 'the analogy between gambling and modern economic practice is a recurrent motif in nineteenth-century European literature'. *La Comédie humaine* uses gambling, like the stockmarket, to show us a mysterious meeting of chance and necessity.[27]

[24] Prendergast, *Balzac*, p. 51.
[25] The main overviews date back to the 1960s (Citron, 'Le Rêve asiatique') or even the 1920s (Baldensperger, *L'Appel de la Fiction Orientale*).
[26] Brooks comments 'This is the Arabian Nights of protocapitalist Paris' (*Realist Vision*, p. 30).
[27] Prendergast, *Balzac*, p. 51, p. 52. See also Roger Bellet, 'La Bourse et la littérature dans la seconde moitié du XIXe siècle', *Romantisme*, 40 (1983), 53–64 (p. 57). Gambling is also used by George

BALZAC AND (FAILED) COLONIAL FRAUD

In Balzac's merciless universe where money is needed for the basic necessities of life, to keep up appearances, or to acquire sexual and marital partners, colonial heterotopias appear to offer a refuge in which the accounts can be manipulated, whether it is by the agile trader or authorial providence. Indeed, his colonial fortune-hunters do sometimes succeed. But more often Balzac checks his colonial accounts and finds them wanting. It is in Paris, not some distant El Dorado, that one should seek a fortune, as Henri de Marsay writes to Paul de Manerville (too late, since the latter only reads the letter when already en route for Calcutta, in *Le Contrat de mariage*, 1835, III: 621). The fabulous, though real, Bolivian silver mine of Potosí is not to be sought abroad, De Marsay tells him: '[l]e Potose est situé rue Vivienne, ou rue de la Paix, à la place Vendôme, ou rue de Rivoli', and it is only in Paris that 'tout homme, même médiocrement spirituel, aperçoit une mine d'or en mettant ses pantoufles' (III: 650). Colonial speculation on the other hand is a high-risk business, in which those who succeed often do so at the cost of their integrity. The wily banker Nucingen declares bankruptcy for a third time, ruining some of his associates, in order to buy up Mexican precious metals following the collapse of the Spanish American empire (*La Maison Nucingen* VI: 386, 388). Charles Grandet, as we saw in Chapter 2, makes a fortune but loses his humanity in the slave trade.

In *La Cousine Bette* (1846), Baron Hulot attempts to avert the financial ruin into which his womanizing has plunged his family by making a quick fortune in France's new colony, Algeria. Here the Algerian subplot is used for a realist debunking of the idea that a fortune can be made, as if by magic, in a legal and moral vacuum. Hulot thinks that, with his wife's uncle Johann Fischer as his agent, he can act in Algeria according to his Bonapartist faith in the power of the sword (VII: 298). He does not grasp that in the new political regime, not only post-1815 but post-1830, a new set of conditions apply.[28] He engages the elderly Fischer in what he later sums up as 'des razzias en Algérie' (VII: 341): the basic necessities, grain and fodder, are to be taken from the Arabs 'sous une foule de prétextes'—that is, in raids targeting civilians ('razzias'); or through spurious administrative fees ('l'achour, les khalifas')—and sold to the French army, under official commission, with a profit margin of 30 per cent (VII: 176). This is a double crime: violent theft committed against the Arabs and fraud against the French State. It is the latter that leads to exposure and Fischer's suicide in an Algerian prison. Balzac's sources included scandals that had come to tarnish the military

---

Eliot in *Daniel Deronda*, as a dramatic incipit conveying economic instability and the amoral nature of money.

[28] Fredric Jameson plays down the importance of Balzac's colonial embedded narrative, claiming that his emphasis 'is less on the actual situation in Algeria than on Hulot's mistaken assessment of it' ('*La Cousine Bette* and Allegorical Realism', *Publications of the Modern Language Association of America*, 86:2 (1971), 241–54 (pp. 245–6). For Scott McCracken, 'Hulot fails to bring off the scheme because the techniques of accumulation which worked so well before 1815 are not applicable to the new conditions of North Africa' ('Cousin Bette: Balzac and the Historiography of Difference', *Essays and Studies*, 44 (1991), 88–104 (p. 101)).

administration of Algeria: the 'affaire Brossard' of 1838, and the 1844 revelation of the systematic use of pillaging, which was hotly topical at the time he was writing.[29]

As is very often the case in the Balzacian novel, moral judgement on this Algerian affair is split. Fischer's honesty is affirmed in the narrator's own voice, and he himself sees no harm in stealing grain worth a fortune from the 'Bédouins', because '[c]ela se faisait ainsi sous l'Empire' (VII: 177).[30] The golden-hearted courtesan Josépha admires Hulot's extreme passion, which has driven him to 'mange[r] la grenouille du gouvernement en Afrique' (VII: 358). And yet critics have seen anti-colonialism in Balzac's 'admirable picture of the infamies and horrors of incipient French colonial policy'.[31] Writing in 1950, Aimé Dupuy had no doubts of Balzac's pro-colonial stance, but saw these pages of *La Cousine Bette*, 'd'une remarquable densité', as having exposed 'l'un des aspects les plus choquants de la "présence française"', that is, the fact that in the 1840s the French occupation of Algeria relied on systematic pillage. For Dupuy, Balzac's novel was defending France's Algerian colonialism by suggesting that the administration would be honest in the future.[32] There are however serious reasons to doubt the future honesty of the colonial administration as portrayed by Balzac. Its change of heart depends on the role of the press in denouncing corruption, and the newspaper that denounces the crime is a Republican one, which hypocritically vaunts the role a free press (as established by 'la Charte de 1830') can play in keeping the administration of Algeria honest (VII: 317). This must be understood in the context of Balzac's disapproval of both Republicanism and the shift of responsibility in Algeria from military to civilian administration. In addition, although the fraud is uncovered it is also largely hushed up by the Ministry of War, and a new civilian 'bureau des subsistances en Afrique' is created in order to avoid such 'désordre' in the future, but the intention is for it to be run by the despicable, civilian M. Marneffe, whom we have already seen acting as pimp for his own wife (VII: 348).[33] In other words, although Balzac's personal attitude was pro-colonial, *La Cousine Bette* suggests the present and future corruption of the French administration of Algeria, 'an Algeria

---

[29] See Anne-Marie Meininger, Introduction, VII: 37–9, and Donnard, pp. 328–30. Brossard, one of the generals in the Algerian campaign, accepted bribes in order to pay his debts.

[30] He is contemptuous of a government agent who questions the morality of such actions (VII: 288), and he has no hesitation in going to Africa because of the Napoleonic precedent in Egypt: 'Les Français y sont allés avec le petit caporal' (VII: 177).

[31] Lukács, *Studies in European Realism*, p. 89.

[32] Dupuy, 'Balzac colonial', p. 274. Pillaging and theft were in fact employed as standard means of provisioning the army in Algeria. See Pierre Darmon, *Un siècle de passions algériennes: une histoire de l'Algérie coloniale 1830–1940* (Paris: Fayard, 2009), p. 69, and Gallois, *History of Violence*.

[33] In fact Marneffe's posting in Algeria is part of a threat by the Prince de Wissembourg to try to make him reimburse 200,000 francs that the too-charming Mme Marneffe has extracted from Hulot, but Marneffe prefers to tender his resignation, and dies of natural causes in Paris (VII: 345–6, 368). Dupuy points out that 'le sinistre Marneffe' is the only French civilian Balzac associates within North Africa; the many other characters with Algerian connections are attached to the army (Aimé Dupuy, 'Balzac et l'Algérie', *Documents algériens*, 52 (1 March 1951), no p. ref.). This suggests where Balzac's sympathies lay in the tensions between civilian and military rule in Algeria, rather than revealing an anticolonialist attitude.

populated by criminals and has-beens', as Bell puts it.[34] Balzac removes the process of making a fortune from the realm of oriental magic and places it firmly under the heading of doubtful financial undertakings and dubious morality: money is always taken from someone.[35] Although his intention was not specifically anticolonial, Balzac's novels deflate the colonial rhetoric of the July Monarchy.

In *La Rabouilleuse* (1842) too, colonial heterotopias are associated with spectacular failure and fraud. The young Philippe Bridau takes part in the abortive 1818 colonization of the *Champ d'Asile* in Texas by ex-Napoleonic officers. The call on public and private finances to fund the emigration—and then, when the colony failed six months later, the repatriation—of the ex-soldiers was, in Balzac's view, 'une des plus terribles mystifications connues sous le nom de Souscriptions nationales' (IV: 300).[36] His virulence was aimed at the Liberal opposition to Louis XVIII, which had organized the subscription: the problem, in his eyes, was not colonization as such, but the hypocrisy of the Liberals who did not put enough of their own money into the project (IV: 304). The *Champ d'Asile* is, moreover, the project of orphans: Napoleon is imprisoned and in exile in 1818, while Philippe's father is dead. The fatherless son, who has not known 'cette royauté patriarcale que la Femme ne remplace [pas]' (IV: 271) risks sinking beyond recall into the chaos of 'la spéculation et l'individualisme' (IV: 303). Philippe Bridau is a victim, the dupe of the Liberals, rather than himself to blame for the catastrophe, but the experience helps to form his vicious criminal character (and his violent nature, which will be discussed in Chapter 6). He goes on to build up a fortune through the most dubious means possible, but loses it as the victim of manipulative stockbrokers in the 1830 Revolution and leaves for the colonies a second time in order to escape the consequences of his own bankruptcy. His newfound adherence to the July Monarchy brings him no luck and he meets a gruesome end on an Algerian battlefield in 1839.

The fictional brothers Joseph and Philippe Bridau have been seen as the positive and negative sides of a self-portrait.[37] But in *La Rabouilleuse* more than in any other novel we see Balzac working through his jealousy of his own brother, their mother's favourite. Since the colonial connection is, as we noted in Chapter 2, associated with Henri Balzac, Philippe Bridau's dramatic death seems a striking form of wish-fulfilment. Jameson sees this death as 'prophetic' of France's colonial

---

[34] 'Balzac's Algeria', p. 39.

[35] In *La Cousine Bette* melodramatic Orientalism is also associated with fraud (and murder) when the death of Valérie Marneffe is paid for by Victorin Hulot with cash given to Jacques Collin in Levantine disguise: 'Un jour, dans trois mois, un pauvre prêtre viendra vous demander quarante mille francs pour une œuvre pie, un couvent ruiné dans le Levant, dans le désert!' (VII: 388).

[36] In *L'Envers de l'histoire contemporaine* Balzac also denounces the 'souscriptions patriotiques' for the *Champ d'Asile* as 'tromperies politiques' degenerating into 'des vaudevilles de police correctionnelle' (VIII: 328).

[37] The argument that the Bridau brothers reflect opposite sides of Balzac himself is developed by René Guise in his introduction to the Pléiade edition, p. 261, following Citron; both neglect the double colonial destiny of Philippe Bridau, though Citron looks at the links between him and Henri Balzac elsewhere ('Sur deux zones obscures').

expansion to come.[38] He then turns from a prophetic reading towards a psychoanalytic emphasis on the novel as wish-fulfilment concealed beneath a superimposed plot, but he also suggests that the 'so-called reductionism' of psychoanalysis should in fact be 'a two-way street': 'the model may be reversed, and the archaic fantasy content seen [...] as the motor force of public actions [...] and values'.[39] If one applies this reversal to the colonial context Jameson began by evoking, it becomes apparent that the fantasy of a maternal rejection of the rival sibling is replaced by a reiterated rejection-of-rival-sibling-by-foreign-land. The fraudulent basis and ultimate failure of Philippe Bridau's colonial ventures map onto the fraudulent basis, and the much-desired failure, of his mother's preference for him. And his violent death in the army of the July Monarchy, like the failure of the attempt at Texan colonization by the orphaned Bonapartistes, reveals a failure in the restoration of lost patriarchal authority. But to subsume the historical/political reading under the individual psychological reading would be to traduce the workings of the 'two-way street'. The episode can be read not only in terms of prophecy or individual psychology, but as reflecting Balzac's historical vision: as in the case of Algerian embezzlement attempted in *La Cousine Bette*, he is situating the remnants of the Napoleonic old guard within the changing ebb and flow of history, and in doing so showing up the weakness of colonialism after the Restoration.

DAUDET, TUNISIAN DEBT, AND THE AMBIVALENT STOCKBROKER HERO

The second half of the century saw the rise of a new realist subgenre focusing on a figure who inspired fascination as well as wariness within the public: the stockbroker or 'literary financier' novel.[40] The figures of the gambler and the stockbroker are variants on that key character of the French realist novel, the adventurer or *parvenu*, whose career serves a structural, organizational function in the 'adventure novel of everyday life'.[41] Balzac also shows us adventurers, of course, but the later novel of financial speculation attributes even more importance to the role played by newspapers, and has been called a 'roman de scandale'.[42] These novels reflect—

---

[38] Fredric Jameson, 'Imaginary and Symbolic in *La Rabouilleuse*', *Social Science Information*, 16:59 (1977), 59–81 (p. 65).

[39] 'Imaginary and Symbolic', pp. 69–70, p. 78. Jameson reads the plot of *La Rabouilleuse* in terms of Lacan's Symbolic order superimposed on top of the inner truth of the Imaginary. For further discussion of the need for a two-way street between historical and psychological analysis, see also *Political Unconscious*, pp. 158–9.

[40] See Harold James, 'The Literary Financier', *The American Scholar*, 60:2 (1991) 251–7, and Saminadayar-Perrin, 'Fictions de la Bourse'. On changes in financial mechanisms in nineteenth-century France, see Hélène Gomart, *Les Opérations financières dans le roman réaliste: Lectures de Balzac et de Zola* (Paris: Champion, 2004), pp. 7–9. The novel of stockmarket speculation appears with the Second Empire and becomes more frequent following the sharp rise in financial speculation in the 1870s (see Bellet, pp. 53–4).

[41] Bakhtin, *Dialogic Imagination*, pp. 125–6, p. 111.

[42] See Guillaume Pinson, *L'Imaginaire médiatique: histoire et fiction du journal au XIXe siècle* (Paris: Garnier, 2012), pp. 93–7. Levin points out that Realism's approach is primarily iconoclastic, and is far

and no doubt contributed to—a certain normalization of financial speculation, but they also show uneasiness about the increasingly intangible nature of financial operations, often taking as their inspiration scandals or stockmarket crashes. The new novel of high finance is a largely male-dominated subgenre, and as has been pointed out in relation to the Victorian novel, critics now tend to neglect the 'discourses of prosperity that are largely white, male, metropolitan, and middle class in distinction from the contemporary academy's present interests in other, often opposite, terms of identity'.[43] But the striking presence of colonial elements in the nineteenth-century financial novel has also been relatively neglected. These colonial elements clearly point to emergent economic globalization. In France under the Second Empire, as Sartre puts it, 'le capitalisme lui-même devient colonialiste', with the foundation of the great colonial banks and companies.[44] The novel addresses financial speculation alongside rapid industrialization, notably the development of railways abroad (in the Middle East, North Africa, and the American Far West). This geographical distance, as I have pointed out, shocks the realist aesthetics of contiguity and familiarity: it leaves a gap between the metropolitan centre and the site of the industrial project. Into this (geographical and mimetic) gap steps the speculator. Of the novels I shall look at, there has been much recent critical interest in Zola's *L'Argent* and Maupassant's *Bel-Ami*, but the imperialist contexts of these novels can be usefully understood by beginning with a brief discussion of a less well-known earlier novel, Alphonse Daudet's *Le Nabab* (1877).[45]

A generation after Balzac's death, Daudet's novel focuses on the questionable nature of money made through economic imperialism in North Africa. *Le Nabab* was inspired by a *fait divers*, and although it also reflects his reading of Zola's 1876 *Son Excellence Eugène Rougon*,[46] Daudet gives full expression to the colonial theme that was only implicit in that novel. *Le Nabab* recounts six months following the arrival in Paris of Bernard Jansoulet, a Frenchman of humble origins from Marseille, who has made an enormous fortune in the service of the *Bey* of Tunisia. The first half of the novel focuses on the difficulties of his new young secretary in reaching a clear moral judgement of Jansoulet, the nabob of the title. In direct discourse, or free indirect style, various characters opine that Jansoulet exploited

from idealizing the business man: with the bourgeois regime of 1830, 'the romantic individualist went underground' (pp. 62–3).

[43] Francis O'Gorman, *Victorian Literature and Finance* (Oxford: Oxford University Press, 2007), p. 13.
[44] Jean-Paul Sartre, 'Le colonialisme est un système', in *Situations, V: Colonialisme et néo-colonialisme* (Paris: Gallimard, 1964), pp. 25–48 (p. 28).
[45] References are to Alphonse Daudet, *Œuvres*, ed. by Roger Ripoll, 3 vols (Paris: Gallimard 'La Pléiade', 1986–94), vol. 2. Daudet's more famous novel *Tartarin de Tarascon* also associates fraud with North African colonialism. This includes economic fraud in the case of the false Montenegrin prince, but other forms of fraud abound and will be discussed in the next chapter. The term *nabab* refers to a European who has come back with a fortune, usually from India; it was borrowed from the English word 'nabob', itself derived from the Urdu via the Portuguese. In Balzac's *Splendeurs et misères des courtisanes* even the nabobs and their mulatto servants are false (VI: 626, 631–2).
[46] Daudet began writing *Le Nabab* in 1874, interrupted it to write *Jack*, and took it up again for final publication in 1877 (Murray Sachs, *The Career of Alphonse Daudet: A Critical Study* (Cambridge, MA: Harvard University Press, 1965), pp. 96–7, p. 104). The influence of Zola's 1876 novel is apparent particularly in Daudet's treatment of key female characters.

the *Bey* shamefully; more worryingly, he is accused of setting up a harem of European women for him, something, it is insinuated, of which he had experience from running a brothel in Paris (II: 535–6). As the novel continues, the reader is increasingly pushed to judge in favour of the man's moral integrity and he is presented as the innocent victim of others' corruption. Nevertheless the initial novelistic tension depends on hesitation over the moral status of the central figure. Is he, or is he not, morally besmirched? 'qu'en fallait-il croire?' (II: 538). In the end evil doubles are shown to have committed all the crimes of which he is accused: it is not him, but his enemy and one-time friend, who has exploited the Tunisians, or 'tondu le Turc un peu trop ras' (II: 546); the brothel in Paris was run not by him, but by his corrupt elder brother, their parents' favourite. The novel increasingly takes the form of a case made by the defence in favour of the neglected younger child, the betrayed loyal friend, the unloved husband; like many of Daudet's novels, it seems to revisit a private narcissistic wound. But the first part of the novel focuses on the questionable origin of the nabob's Tunisian fortune (for which we are never given a satisfactory explanation) and, in the trial that marks his downfall, he is later accused of having imported foreign corruption into France: 'Établi depuis si longtemps en Orient, il a désappris les lois, les mœurs, les usages de son pays. Il croit aux justices expéditives, aux bastonnades en pleine rue, il se fie aux abus de pouvoir, et, ce qui est pis encore, à la vénalité, à la bassesse accroupie de tous les hommes' (II: 796). The novel ends by asserting the complete innocence of the nabob, but it does so in the face of the ambivalence it has spent much energy exploring.

The real-life model for Daudet's nabob, François Bravay, made his fortune in serving the viceroy of Egypt, mostly in the 1850s–1860s. By transferring the origins of this fortune to Tunisia Daudet sought to cover his tracks, but he also drew on recent history in ways that suggest the nabob's millions derive from a spectacular and very topical economic crisis.[47] The novel is set over six months of the year 1864, which is the year the Tunisian financial crisis and escalating public debt reached such a point that the Tunisian constitution itself was suspended; the State was, as Daudet of course knew when writing, going to be declared bankrupt in 1869, when an international (French-Italian-British) commission was set up to reform its finances. This in turn paved the way for France's annexation of Tunisia (which was made a protectorate in 1881, four years after the publication of the novel).[48] Although Daudet's novel is set entirely in France and has been read as

---

[47] François Bravay served the viceroy Said from 1851 until the latter's death in 1863. His relationship with the next viceroy, Ismail, was less successful, his forays into French politics were marred by trials for electoral fraud, and he was accused of having run a brothel. He died in December 1874, just three years before Daudet published his novel. Daudet changed the names and used Tunisia instead of Egypt, causing the *Bey* of Tunisia to protest at the smear on his good name. In fact, though Daudet raises questions concerning the legitimacy of his protagonist's actions both in North Africa and in France, he made his nabob a much more honest figure than his real-life model, and softens his responsibility in driving the (fictive) *Bey* into debt. See Auriant, *François Bravay ou le 'Nabab'* (Paris: Mercure de France, 1943).

[48] The 1881 intervention is treated by Maupassant in *Bel-Ami*, as we shall see.

having Paris itself as its true hero, or rather villain,[49] it returns time and again to the dubious North-African past of the European adventurers and their rather less European wives. The central target of Daudet's irony is the moral ambivalence of a fortune made in Tunisia.[50]

ZOLA'S *L'ARGENT*, THE STOCKBROKER HERO, AND THE MIDDLE EAST

This leads us to another novel whose action begins in 1864, Zola's *L'Argent* (1891). Zola's novel is also set entirely in Paris, but throughout we are reminded of the newly global nature of the financial world: rumours concerning the Suez canal and the Mexican expedition rock the stockmarket and the novel charts the rise and fall of a bank, *L'Universelle*, whose apotheosis coincides with the opening of the 1867 *Exposition universelle* (V: 228).[51] Paris is at the centre of a web of global finance: when the protagonist Saccard (aka Aristide Rougon) asks his brother, the states-man, to help set him on his feet again after the financial catastrophe recounted in *La Curée*, Eugène Rougon offers to make him a colonial governor, but Saccard sees this as equivalent to deportation (V: 20) and resolves to struggle on in France. And yet the brief, dramatic rise of his *Banque Universelle* is based on proto-imperialist projects in the Middle East.

Zola's portrayal of the collapse of Saccard's *Banque Universelle* was based on the 1882 *Krach* of the *Union générale*, and its founder Bontoux provided much of the detail for Saccard's role. Zola took extensive notes on Bontoux and the *Krach*, dwelling on details of the banks and railways founded by the *Union* in Eastern Europe and the Balkans. His notes betray excitement at the idea of furthering progress in a 'pays neuf', a process described as 'La marche vers l'Orient', '2 pas vers l'Orient', or as part of a 'Programme d'Orient'.[52] Zola shifted the period (1878–82) to 1864–8, so that it would fit with his focus on the Second Empire, and transposed the bank's investment activities to the Middle East, which reflects—somewhat anachronistically—the newly imperialist attitudes of the 1880s.[53] We have here a foretaste of the Zola who, after the Rougon-Macquart series, was to

[49] Murray Sachs' analysis of the novel, for example, does not mention Tunisia at all (*Career of Alphonse Daudet*, pp. 103–11).

[50] On Daudet's irony, and the influence of Balzac on his writing, see Françoise Court-Pérez, 'Figures de l'ironie chez Daudet', *Écritures XIX/La Revue des Lettres modernes*, 1 (2003), 67–81.

[51] For a discussion of economic imperialism and xenophobia in *L'Argent*, see Emily Apter, 'Speculation and Economic Xenophobia as Literary World Systems: The Nineteenth-Century Business Novel', in *French Global: A New Approach to Literary History*, ed. by Christie McDonald and Susan Rubin Suleiman (New York: Columbia University Press, 2010), pp. 388–403 (pp. 396–401).

[52] MS 10268 fol. 546; fol. 547; fol. 558 (*L'Argent*, dossier préparatoire, Bibliothèque Nationale de France, N.A.F. 10268 and 10269).

[53] See Henri Mitterand's notes to the Pléiade edition, particularly pp. 1238–42, 1251, 1258, 1263, 1270. As Jean Bouvier writes, the transposition to the Middle East shows that Zola was inspired by later events: 'quand Zola écrit *L'Argent* les chemins de fer de l'Empire Ottoman sont à l'ordre du jour' ('*L'Argent*: roman et réalité', *Europe*, 468–9 (1968), 54–64 (p. 62)). The colonialist attitude implicit in the Middle-Eastern projects of *L'Argent* can be dated to after 1885 (see Brunschwig, *Mythes et réalités*, pp. 60–1). See also David Baguley, 'Le Capital de Zola: Le Fétichisme de la monnaie dans *L'Argent*',

become an unabashed apologist for French imperialism and the ideology of progress (in *Fécondité*, 1899). In *L'Argent*, however, he deliberately sets this idealistic view of social and industrial progress within a portrayal of the dual, and morally doubtful, nature of the energy that fuels it: money, or more precisely, speculation.

Saccard's ambitions and world-view are broadened to include the Orient when he encounters his idealistic neighbours, the engineer Georges Hamelin and his sister Caroline. They have lived and worked in Egypt and Syria, where they shared '[d]es projets de réveil' aiming to wake up lands that they see as asleep beneath the ashes of dead civilizations, essentially through industrialization (V: 59). Georges Hamelin is the source of a flurry of ideas that Saccard will seize on: a consortium that would hold the monopoly to Mediterranean travel (V: 61–2);[54] a silver mine to exploit in the Holy Land; a rail network that would criss-cross all of Asia Minor (V: 63);[55] and a new bank in Constantinople (V: 64). These projects are overtly, even naïvely, imperialist: 'c'était l'Orient conquis, donné à la France' (V: 62). The vocabulary used is that of exploitation, invasion, and conquest, and money is the aim as well as the means: 'On conquérait l'Asie à coups de millions, pour en tirer des milliards' (V: 253). Saccard and the Hamelin siblings present three contrasted visions of economic imperialism in the Middle East. Georges Hamelin dreams of making Palestine into a Christian kingdom that will be the new home of the Papacy. Saccard and Caroline Hamelin, on the other hand, share a secular conception of the project, the former motivated by personal financial gain and the latter by the improvement of humanity; but the borderline between these two motivations is blurred. This ambivalence at the foundation of the imperialist enterprise is mapped onto the ambivalence that founds the novel as a whole: financial speculation is both a destructive, deforming power and a tremendous, constructive force. As with Daudet's *Nabab*, our reading of the novel focuses on the question of how to judge the protagonist, the literary financier. Where Daudet's judgement hinged on an individual personality, however, Zola asks us to consider the new capitalist system of financial speculation itself.

Saccard's genius lies in what we would now call 'PR'. He translates the engineer Hamelin's daydreams into language that will appeal to the public, slogans that are resonant with myth, classical learning, or—most powerfully—Catholic symbolism. He knows that the idea of silver found in the earth is 'toujours passionnante pour le public, surtout quand on pouvait y accrocher l'enseigne d'un

in *Currencies: Fiscal Fortunes and Cultural Capital in Nineteenth-Century France*, ed. by Sarah Capitanio, et al. (Oxford: Peter Lang, 2005), pp. 31–42 (pp. 34–5).

[54] Gallois (*Zola*, pp. 135–6) sees this plan to unite the transport companies that exploit the Mediterranean as a vision that combines capitalism and socialism for the glory of the French nation, but one should note that the project is not for a State monopoly but for private initiatives to combine, a vision in which the market economy itself tends away from both the State and the liberal ideal of free competition, and towards the accumulation of capital.

[55] Zola's emphasis on the construction of railways in the Middle East is born of the concerns of his own period and is anachronistic when transferred back into the 1860s. Direct European investment in the lands of the Turkish empire began primarily in 1888–96, two-thirds of it in railways. See Zürcher, p. 89. Borie argues that Zola's fascination with doomed machines and engineering projects reflects his Œdipal anxieties concerning his dead father, the engineer of the Zola canal (*Zola et les mythes*, pp. 78–83).

nom prodigieux et retentissant comme celui du Carmel' (V: 75); he instinctively masters the colonialist rhetoric of classical learning, which makes the Eastern half of the Mediterranean seem destined for domination by the West (V: 64–5); and he finds a catchy name for Hamelin's naïve dream of a Catholic bank ('Le Trésor du Saint-Sépulcre', V: 80). As their enterprise gathers momentum, Saccard employs a failed academic, Jantrou, to excite public opinion by using the latest marketing techniques: advertising, brochures, the increasingly influential genre of travel writing,[56] an inhouse journal, and a press agency to touch the provinces (V: 231). He even buys up a reputable newspaper that will sing its praises (V: 252).[57]

The triumphant rise of the *Universelle*'s stocks also depends on covert financial operations, for which Saccard employs an 'homme de paille', Sabatani. Sabatani's physical appearance is ambiguous: he is handsome, but with 'une bouche mauvaise, inquiétante' that spoils his face (V: 13); he has a 'grâce caressante d'Oriental mâtiné d'Italien' (V: 19; repeated 301, 352); sensual and effeminate, he is the subject of fascination for women because of a rumour that he is extraordinarily well-endowed (V: 263; 352). Hélène Gomart's Freudian reading sees Sabatani as Saccard's alter-ego, a phallic extension of the man himself.[58] There are indeed evident links between Saccard's exploitative sexuality and his financial projects. The wild success of his bank is due to its ability to arouse in women a crusading passion that leaves their menfolk untouched; this passion 'violentait' 'les pères, les maris, les amants', suggesting that Saccard (and the phallic Sabatani) are symbolically fornicating by appealing to the women's fantasies (V: 253). Now Sabatani, Saccard's exaggerated appendage, is a seedy foreigner, a Levantine.[59] The model for the character was Bontoux's henchman, Izoard, whose name is of Germanic origin.[60] The transformation Zola applied to this secondary character is thus part of his general shift of the activities undertaken by the investment bank from central and Eastern Europe to the Middle East.

The civilizing work of the *Universelle* is, ironically, already undermined by the corruption of which this ethnic mixing is symbolic. Like Daudet's *Le Nabab*, or

---

[56] They exploit 'un extrait d'un voyage en Asie Mineure, où il était expliqué que Napoléon avait prédit' the bank's success (V: 231).

[57] On the crucial importance of publicity, see also David F. Bell, *Models of Power: Politics and Economics in Zola's* Rougon-Macquart (Lincoln, NE: University of Nebraska Press, 1988), pp. 136–41. On the role of corruption and political influence in relation to the press in Zola's novel, see Adeline Wrona, 'Mots à crédit: *L'Argent* de Zola, ou la presse au cœur du marché de la confiance', *Romantisme*, 151 (2011), 67–79.

[58] She also suggests a link between sexual desire and bull markets (*Opérations financières*, pp. 169–71).

[59] In Zola's notes Sabatani claims to have been born in Alexandria: 'Un levantin. [...] Ne parle pas d'où il vient. On sait, ou du moins il dit qu'il est né à Alexandrie. On sent en lui le mélange du sang italien et du sang turc' (MS 10268 fol. 355). For a discussion of ethnic 'types' used to characterize the financier, see Christophe Reffait, *La Bourse dans le roman du second XIXe siècle: discours romanesque et imaginaire social de la spéculation* (Paris: Champion, 2007), pp. 127–8, pp. 162–4.

[60] Zola's notes on the 1882 *Krach* frequently mention Izoard by name, e.g., MS 10268, fols 355 and 480. The name Zola chose for his character links him by sibilance with Saccard, and both names are heavily suggestive: Saccard = 'mettre à sac'; Sabatani = 'saboter'; but perhaps still more, 'sabbat', with its connotations of Judaism or devilry.

Anthony Trollope's *The Way We Live Now* (1874–5), *L'Argent* can be read as an instance of the new 'global capitalist novel' or 'novel of breached metropolitan sovereignty' in which the domestic economic sphere is invaded by outsiders.[61] Trollope's protagonist Melmotte is of undecidable, but certainly foreign, origin (Jewish, Irish-American...?). French literature too plays on the foreignness of its financial adventurers, though perhaps a little less overtly. Daudet's nabob is of humble Southern French origins, but he is a dark-skinned, short-nosed giant with '[d]es cheveux crépus', who looks like 'un sauvage de frontières' (II: 500). Saccard is part of the familiar Rougon family, but dark-skinned ('noir', V: 15; 67) and, as we have seen, his alter-ego Sabatani embodies foreign seediness. This suggestive racialization of his stockbroker pair may actually contribute to what Dorian Bell has recently argued is Zola's work towards 'uncoupl[ing] the imperial from the realm of Jewish financial domination' by setting up the anti-semitic Saccard in rivalry with the Jewish speculators whose traits he shares.[62]

In *L'Argent* Zola's repeated references to the *Arabian Nights* have inspired various conflicting interpretations. Gomart sees Saccard as a figure of the naturalist novelist transforming the poetry of the *Arabian Nights* (along with the Papal crusade and the Ottoman empire) into prose. For her, the entire novel is an allegory for the way in which the naturalist novel moves beyond poetic inspiration, Saccard's financial operations represent proper prose, and his ultimate failure in the stockmarket shows the failure of the naturalist novel to be transposed into theatre.[63] The argument that Saccard represents the novelist is made more convincingly by Saminadayar-Perrin, for whom Saccard is a creator 'par la force de l'imagination et l'efficacité de sa parole', though his 'rêve oriental' is counter-utopian because it is embodied only at the cost of financial catastrophe. The *Arabian Nights* theme, she argues, attests his ability to transform financial operations into art, but also his captivation by a fantasy of easy riches: he abuses his own powers of mythical invention and falls into his own trap.[64] Christophe Reffait, for whom Saccard is both poet and novelist, takes the opposite approach to Gomart: Saccard does not transform Orientalist poetry into prose, instead the multiple references to the *Arabian Nights* are evidence that the whole Oriental project is concentrated in 'le genre merveilleux'.[65]

The references to the fantastic are indeed signs of deliberate generic tension incorporated into Zola's Realism. Zola's references to the *Arabian Nights*, like Balzac's, warn us that Saccard's project is a fairytale that cannot subsist within the

[61] Lauren M.E. Goodlad, 'The Trollopian Geopolitical Aesthetic', *Literature Compass*, 7:9 (2010), 867–75 (p. 868). Baker also sees *The Way We Live Now* as showing us the new world of globalization in terms of diminishing distance (*Realism's Empire*, p. 144).

[62] Dorian Bell, 'Beyond the Bourse: Zola, Empire, and the Jews', *Romanic Review*, 102:3–4 (2011), 485–501 (p. 493, also p. 495).

[63] Gomart, pp. 283–5, pp. 291–2.

[64] Saminadayar-Perrin, 'Fictions de la Bourse', p. 62, p. 41; on Saccard as a failed writer, see p. 57. Of course the 'real' novelist of *L'Argent* is the humble, hard-working Jordan, who does not play the stockmarket and whose first novel begins to sell well just as the *Universelle's* shares are reduced to nothing.

[65] *La Bourse*, p. 383, p. 385.

rules of finance or the realist mode. Saccard is so taken up in dreams of fantastic Oriental riches that on the day he heads out to launch his great affair, he is surprised by the cold wind of Paris, but is comforted by the sound of gold in a workshop '[qui] semblait sortir des entrailles de la terre, continu, léger et musical, comme dans un conte des *Mille et une nuits*. [...] Il y vit un heureux présage' (V: 83). The strongboxes of the *Universelle* are 'comme les tonneaux des contes, où dorment les trésors incalculables des fées' (V: 229); the Parisians buy its shares as if 'les cavernes mystérieuses des Mille et une Nuits [...] s'ouvraient', offering them 'les incalculables trésors des califes' (V: 252); the bank seems to turn everything it touches into gold (V: 232). Colette Becker highlights the fairytale quality that underlies much of Zola's writing.[66] In this case, however, the references to fantastic Oriental fortunes are used to *expose* the fabricated, and precarious, nature of Saccard's success, just as the Second Empire itself shows an 'apothéose de féerie', 'un mensonge de féerie' on the eve of its downfall (V: 228, 254).

Given this emphasis on fairytale implausibility, is Saccard's Middle-Eastern project just so much hot air? Our judgement is complicated by the Hamelin siblings' authentic desire to further the cause of 'progress'. Caroline herself embodies humanity's energy and capacity for renewal (V: 74), but her idealism is travestied by a deforming echo coming from less exceptional women, who transfer her secular vision of progress back to its Christian roots ('l'Éden reconquis, la Terre sainte délivrée, la religion triomphante, au berceau même de l'humanité'); women's whispering gives the impression that 'les trésors retrouvés des califes resplendissaient, dans un conte merveilleux des *Mille et une Nuits*' and that their jewels, dreamlike, are flooding into the *Universelle*'s strongboxes (V: 233).

Zola's Orientalism thus has a double—and apparently contradictory—significance: it tells us that the Middle East is a wasteland that could be brought into flower by the vital energy of Western civilization and technology, but at the same time that the dream of Oriental wealth is a naïve fairytale delusion. Caroline herself dreams of the 'coup de baguette tout-puissant dont la science et la spéculation pouvaient frapper cette vieille terre endormie, pour la réveiller' (V: 77): fairytale magic is not impossible, if the conjunction of those two vectors of progress, science and speculation, can be made successfully. And yet, as we have seen, speculation is based on Saccard's inventive PR, and Caroline herself is eventually horrified by the corrupt means that he uses. This ambivalence is part of the novel's treatment of money itself as both a vital force necessary for life and creativity, and at the same time the source, and product, of dangerous delusions. Critics have tended to focus on the positive side of money in *L'Argent*, which is part of the 'élan moderne' for Auguste Dezalay;[67] for Brian Nelson, it validates the 'magic qualities of science' and even the comparisons with the Napoleonic conquest are not necessarily ironic (Saccard

---

[66] Colette Becker, *Zola: le saut dans les étoiles* (Paris: Presses Universitaires de la Sorbonne Nouvelle, 2002), pp. 210–11. Auguste Dezalay also studies the fairytale elements, and references to the *Arabian Nights*, in Zola; but he does not see them as operating in a negative sense to underline implausibility ('Les mystères de Zola', *Revue des Sciences Humaines*, 160 (1975), 475–9 (particularly pp. 477–8)).

[67] Auguste Dezalay, *L'Opéra des Rougon-Macquart: Essai de rythmologie romanesque* (Paris: Klincksieck, 1983), p. 24.

comes to see himself as accomplishing the conquest of the East that the Crusaders and then Napoleon had attempted, V: 78); Saccard is a prototype of the messiah in Zola's 'latent messianism'.[68] Nevertheless Saccard, and money itself, retain their ambiguity, and Nelson emphasizes that the question of how to judge Saccard is the novel's thematic centre.[69] So too Zola's portrayal of imperialism as furthering the progress of humanity is fraught with ambivalence.

Capitalism is expressed most fully, in *L'Argent* at least, in 'les rêves impérialistes de Saccard et de Georges Hamelin',[70] and the question of how to judge these imperialist projects of industrialization in the Middle East is tied to divergent understandings of the nature of Progress. In his preparatory notes Zola jotted down: 'Les croisades de la science, l'expédition de Napoléon, mais par la civilisation'; the march of civilization must return to the East and give new life to the cradle of humanity, the 'paradis terrestre' (MS 10269, fol. 220). But in the novel itself he was careful to ascribe these triumphalist views of progress to specific characters. The neo-Hegelian vision of the march of history from East to West (which is at the foundation of the new Imperialist ideology) is put into the mouth of Saccard (V: 78). Gallois sees even Caroline's enthusiasm as being subject to irony, and Zola as critical of narratives of progress and imperial regeneration.[71] Caroline herself feels the force of 'la marche en avant', but it is a blind energy, 'sans savoir au juste où l'on va' (V: 77), that inspires her 'admiration effrayée' (V: 225).[72] Zola portrays the imperialist dream as double in nature, at once corrupt and idealistic.[73]

L'Argent's reflection on the role of imperialist capitalism has an interesting precursor in *La Curée*, Zola's novel of 1871, which also has Saccard as one of its protagonists. Here an entirely fictive investment fund, the 'Société générale des ports du Maroc' (I: 340; 396), is used to rip off the metropolitan investor. Saccard is not the inventor of this scam, which he knowingly mocks as a 'Compagnie générale des Mille et une Nuits' (I: 418), but he uses it himself when lying to his wife about

---

[68] Brian Nelson, 'Energy and Order in Zola's *L'Argent*', *Australian Journal of French Studies*, 17:3 (1980), 275–300 (p. 286); see also 'Zola's Ideology: The Road to Utopia', in *Critical Essays on Emile Zola*, ed. by David Baguley (Boston, MA: G.K. Hall and Co., 1986), pp. 161–72 (p. 165).

[69] 'Energy and Order', p. 293.

[70] Baguley, 'Le Capital de Zola', pp. 36–7.

[71] Gallois, *Zola*, pp. 137–8.

[72] Éléonore Reverzy suggests that 'Zola veut en tout cas et à tout prix dire que l'argent est une bonne chose', but contradicts this by quoting amply from his drafts, where he intends the novel to be '[s]ur l'argent, sans l'attaquer, sans le défendre'; 'Ne pas frapper sur l'argent. La pire et la meilleure des choses' (*La Chair de l'idée: Poétique de l'allégorie dans Les Rougon-Macquart* (Geneva: Droz, 2007), p. 160, p. 161.) As Baguley puts it, 'l'argent, assimilé à la vie même, se situe au-delà du bien et du mal' ('Le Capital de Zola', p. 41). Zola's ambivalence about financial speculation reflects contemporary attitudes to the subject (Bell, *Models of Power*, p. 152).

[73] The novel is also carefully mapped over another French attempt at indirect colonization, this one a dramatic failure. It begins in 1864, the year that saw Napoleon III establish the Archduke Maximilian as Emperor of Mexico, and Saccard buys shares in the Mexican expedition. The downfall of the Mexican 'empire' and the execution of Maximilian in 1867 mark the beginning of the downfall of Saccard's financial empire. In his notebooks Zola wrote, of the last years of the Second Empire: 'L'affaire du Mexique, l'exécution de Maximilien (67?) semble avoir été le signal de la débâcle' (*Carnets d'enquêtes: une ethnographie inédite de la France, par Émile Zola*, ed. by Henri Mitterand (Paris: Plon 'Terre humaine', 2005 [1986]), p. 104).

having invested her dowry (I: 462).[74] Like the largely fictive South Central Pacific and Mexican Railway in *The Way We Live Now*, on which the protagonist is able to build a vast but precarious fortune, the 'Société générale des ports du Maroc' flourishes thanks to the mysteries of distance. The 'stockbroker novel' thus portrays economic imperialism as a form of speculation 'in which the absence of the material commodity in any recognizable form' increases profitability;[75] here speculation is intransitive, without any material referent, nothing but a 'mirage'.[76] In *L'Argent*, however, there remains the tantalizing possibility that speculation and private entrepreneurship will indeed bring progress and rebirth to the Middle East, and the *Universelle*'s projects do seem to be bearing fruit slowly. In 1891 *L'Argent* thus marks an ideological midpoint between the cynicism of *La Curée* in 1871 and the colonial utopianism of *Fécondité* in 1899. The ending of *Fécondité* departs from the examination of capitalism to initiate a new, explicitly colonialist, mythology of progress, returning to a quasi-magical use of distant lands as offering limitless potential for self-realization.[77]

MAUPASSANT'S *BEL-AMI*: AN ANTICOLONIAL NOVEL?

Whereas *L'Argent* and *Le Nabab* recount the *disappearance* of a dubious fortune, Maupassant's *Bel-Ami* shows us its conquest. It has often been read as a novel about the drive to power and social advancement in a pitiless, Darwinian struggle. *Bel-Ami* is also a striking portrayal of corrupt speculation in the Parisian political world, made possible by the obscuring factor of colonial distance and the new power of the press. The connections of *Bel-Ami* with France's newly prominent colonialism have been well known since 1954, when André Vial gave a detailed exposition of Maupassant's transposition of the real Tunisian affair of the 1880s into the Moroccan scandal that forms a pivotal episode of his novel.[78] Following Vial, Astier Loutfi examined how revelations concerning behind-the-scenes manipulations in the run-up to the Bardo treaty (by which France forced the *Bey* of Tunisia to accept a protectorate) 'frappèrent d'un "discrédit moral" l'entreprise africaine et les mœurs parlementaires'; in *Bel-Ami* Maupassant holds up a portrait

---

[74] Zola's preparatory notes show his careful historical grounding of the property expropriations and constructions that are the main theme of *La Curée*; in contrast, he took few notes related to the 'Société générale des ports du Maroc', mostly connected with the seedy minor character Toutin-Laroche. See Becker, *La Fabrique*, vol. 1, p. 480 (N.A.F. 10282 fol. 327); p. 488 (fol. 335); p. 518 (fol. 352); p. 556 (fol. 377).

[75] Bell, *Models of Power*, p. 142.   [76] Reffait, *La Bourse*, p. 386.

[77] On *Fécondité* as initiating the new colonial literature and reflecting the turn towards nationalism, despite being published at a time when Zola's colonial utopianism flew in the face of evidence of both fraud and disease, see Steins, 'L'épisode africain de *Fécondité*' and 'Zola colonialiste'. On myth-making tendencies in *Fécondité*, see Baguley, *Fécondité*, p. 167 and Seillan, *Aux sources*, pp. 357–78. Yet Zola had again associated the colonies with corruption only a year earlier, in *Paris* (1898), where a murky scandal concerning African railways is based on the model of the Panama affair ('un pot-de-vin de cinq millions, deux ministres vendus, trente députés et sénateurs compromis' (*Paris*, ed. by Jacques Noiray (Paris: Gallimard 'Folio', 2002), p. 63)).

[78] André Vial, *Guy de Maupassant et l'art du roman* (Paris: Nizet, 1954), pp. 316–29.

of these 'machinations politico-financières dont les entreprises coloniales étaient l'objet'.[79] Although the colonial events always remain offstage, the distant space of North Africa and the urban, Parisian space of newspaper offices and salons are 'tous deux soumis à une même structure de base, la fraude'.[80] The media magnate Walter is able to exert his influence on government cabinets, the stockmarket, and public opinion alike. He and his ally the new minister of foreign affairs, Laroche-Mathieu, buy up the debt of the Moroccan government at low prices through straw men, and make a fortune overnight when the French State takes control of Morocco and guarantees its debt. The protagonist, budding journalist Georges Duroy, nicknamed Bel-Ami, is himself the instrument of the coterie's manipulation of public opinion.

Vial considers Maupassant's satirical naturalism to be prophetic of the expansionist policies to come; he also situates Maupassant within the contemporary anticolonial opposition party.[81] Some more recent critics have been exercised by debate as to whether or not Maupassant should be deemed 'anticolonial', which seems to be largely a matter of definition.[82] Astier Loutfi for example finds his anticolonialism inadequate because he simplifies his observations of colonial policy

---

[79] Astier Loutfi, pp. 12–13. Her concern is largely with 'la valeur documentaire de *Bel-Ami*', p. 22. The historian Henri Brunschwig expressed doubts about the plausibility of this financial plot scenario, but he does quote a contemporary source on the Tunisian *Bey* giving out contracts to 'des aventuriers': 'On obtient à titre gratuit [...] ou moyennant quelque redevance illusoire, la concession de vastes domaines, de mines inexplorées etc.' He shows how this directly brought about a financial crisis and debt which in turn led to the International Commission and thence the French Protectorate and loss of sovereignty (*Mythes et réalités*, p. 53, p. 49). For background to the French intervention in Tunisia, see also Charles-André Julien, *Histoire de l'Algérie contemporaine*, vol. 1, p. 31 as well as *L'Affaire tunisienne 1878–1881* (Tunis: Dar el-Amal, 1981); and Gilbert Meynier and Jacques Thobie (*Histoire de la France coloniale II: L'Apogée, 1871–1931* (Paris: Armand Colin, 1991), p. 46).

[80] Giacchetti, p. 128.

[81] Vial, p. 329, p. 323. Gérard Delaisement also sees his observations on France's colonial policy as prophetic (*Maupassant journaliste et chroniqueur* (Paris: Albin Michel, 1956), p. 16).

[82] Maupassant travelled to Algeria in 1881 as a special correspondent for *Le Gaulois*, and returned to North Africa as a tourist (probably) October 1887–January 1888 and again 20 October 1888–end February 1889; these trips furnished him with the material for journalism and short stories. His journalism certainly took on a polemical tone. 'Rien ne peut donner une idée de l'intolérable situation que nous faisons aux Arabes', he wrote: 'Le principe de la colonisation française consiste à les faire crever de faim' ('Autour d'Oran', *Le Gaulois*, 26 July 1881, p. 1, not included in the 10/18 edition of his *Chroniques* but available through Gallica). Nevertheless, since he never rejected colonization in principle, many recent critics consider him not to be an anticolonial writer (e.g. Roger Little, '"Tiens, Forestier!": Maupassant et la colonisation', *Plaisance: rivista di letteratura francese moderna e contemporanea*, 3:8 (2006) 75–87 (p. 81); Michèle Salinas, *Guy de Maupassant, Lettres d'Afrique (Algérie, Tunisie)* (Paris: La Boîte à documents, 1990), p. 39; Marie-Claude Schapira, 'Guy de Maupassant en Algérie: critique du fait colonial et portrait du colonisé', in *L'Idée de 'race' dans les sciences humaines et la littérature (XVIIIe et XIXe siècles)*, ed. by Sarga Moussa (Paris: L'Harmattan, 2003), pp. 329–41 (p. 340)). Others however have seen him as anticolonialist: Delaisement, *Maupassant journaliste et chroniqueur*, p. 16 and 'Les chroniques coloniales de Maupassant', in *Maupassant et l'écriture*, ed. by Louis Forestier (Paris: Nathan, 1993), pp. 53–9 (p. 56); Liauzu, pp. 89–90; Mireille Gouaux-Coutrix, '*Au Soleil* de Guy de Maupassant ou un romancier face à la colonisation', *Actes du Colloque international 'Entre l'Occident et l'Orient'* (Nice: Laboratoire d'Histoire Quantitative, 1983), p. 275, p. 282. *Bel-Ami* was considered sufficiently anticolonialist for a film adaptation by Louis Daquin in 1955 to be censored, and to remain censored in the French *territoires d'outre-mer* even when it was passed in France (on the anticolonialist stance of the Daquin film, and its fidelity to Maupassant, see Susan Hayward, *French Costume Drama of the 1950s: Fashioning Politics in Film* (Bristol: Intellect, 2010), pp. 332–5).

for the purposes of social and moral critique, in order to denounce 'la puissance et les mœurs d'un capitalisme effréné'.[83] (Four decades after Astier Loutfi was writing, it no longer seems quite so useful to consider capitalism and colonialism separately.) *Bel-Ami*, along with other novels dealing with financial speculation, has also been read in a new wave of studies on literature and the press, which stress late Realism's focus on its own relationship with newspapers and 'actualité'.[84] In any case it is striking that Maupassant situates the fraudulent manipulation of public opinion for the purposes of individual profit specifically in relation to the colonial sphere. Indeed, this is striking independently of the question of the degree of documentary accuracy with which Maupassant portrays this specific money-making scam.[85]

A recent post-Freudian reading of *Bel-Ami* by Andrew Counter suggests that it reveals 'the play of inconvenient knowledge and of strategic ignorance—disavowal' in what he neatly terms the 'epistemology of the mantelpiece'.[86] Following Jameson's argument that we should see the relationship between psychoanalytic and political interpretations as a 'two-way street',[87] Maupassant can in fact be seen as repeatedly interweaving individual *sexual* disavowal (of adultery) and collective *political* disavowal (of the role of financial speculation and short-term individual profit in State imperialism). The 'epistemology of the mantelpiece' can be understood, following Counter, through analysis of a simile Maupassant puts into the mouth of a right-wing opposition MP, Lambert-Sarrazin, who suggests the new government will want to send an army to Tangiers to balance the one previously sent to Tunis, out of a foolish and costly desire for symmetry, 'comme on met deux vases sur une cheminée'. In this simile Tangiers and Tunis are two symmetrical vases on the mantelpiece of North Africa, with France as a hostess decorating her salon with taste (405–6). The 'bibelot marocain' that France aspires to place opposite her 'bibelot tunisien' (406) provides material for ten of George Duroy's articles on Algeria.[88] Counter's analysis of this simile reveals the image to be mapped over

---

[83] Astier Loutfi, pp. 15–17.

[84] See Edmund Birch, 'Maupassant's *Bel-Ami* and the Secrets of *Actualité*', *The Modern Language Review*, 109:4 (2014), 996–1012, which discusses Maupassant's portrayal of the Tunisian affair (in the novel the Moroccan affair) in relation to newspaper coverage. See also Pinson, *Imaginaire médiatique*.

[85] In fact it seems that there was more than one underhand deal marking the beginnings of the Tunisian protectorate, which was followed by press denunciation, mockery, and disaffection for Jules Ferry's government in France (see Julien, *L'Affaire tunisienne*, pp. 47–62, for an account that suggests scandals even racier than those of Maupassant's novel; he also points out that it is hard to distinguish financial motivations from political motivations, since the two are so tightly interwoven, p. 61).

[86] Andrew Counter, 'The Epistemology of the Mantelpiece: Subversive Ornaments in the Novels of Guy de Maupassant', *Modern Languages Review*, 103 (2008), 682–96 (p. 682).

[87] Jameson's two-way street is discussed above. The need to take into account a two-way process between individual psychic factors and political, societal factors in considering colonialism is also discussed by Ania Loomba, pp. 126–7, who follows Jacqueline Rose in emphasizing the 'two-way process between the field of psychoanalysis and politics'. Emily Apter also points out that certain overtly sexual forms of colonial literature, such as harem narratives, 'emerge as the premier literary conduit for "veiled" allusions to France's territorial conquest of North Africa' (*Continental Drift*, p. 106).

[88] Louis Forestier suggests that Lambert-Sarrazin's speech may be calqued on one made by the duc de Broglie in July 1882 about Egypt, but which used a simile of twins rather than knick-knacks (see

that of Duroy's new wife Madeleine placing two bouquets—one from her lover and one from her husband—in symmetrical vases on her mantelpiece. The unpalatable truth that Duroy strives to disavow is thus his own cuckolding.

One should not, however, forget that the simile itself also leaves another gap—a gap situated precisely in the middle of France's (North African) mantelpiece, and which disavows not a psychoanalytical truth but a political one: that is, France's most important colony, Algeria. It is while marauding as part of the French army in Algeria that Duroy, just before the beginning of the narrative, learnt the cynicism that serves him so well in his conquest of French society. And the immediate pretext for French military intervention in Tunisia, on which the novel's Moroccan affair is calqued, was the security of French Algeria. Maupassant's knick-knacks demand a political reading. Before writing *Bel-Ami* he himself, like Duroy, had used the parallel between colonial wars and knick-knacks in his journalism, but with entirely the opposite intentions: in 1881, in response to the Tunisian expedition, he published an article called 'La Guerre', giving horrifically graphic descriptions of the pointless suffering caused by war, in which he refers to the invasion as 'la petite guerre d'étagère que nous allons nous offrir sur la côte d'Afrique'.[89] In 1883 he re-used some of the same material for another article, this time on the imminent war with China following France's occupation of Tonkin. After describing an eye-watering amputation, and atrocities committed against the Chinese, he concludes with a sarcastic final paragraph: 'Si nous avons la guerre avec l'empire du Milieu, le prix des vieux meubles de laque et des riches porcelaines chinoises va baisser beaucoup, messieurs les amateurs.'[90] So there is no doubt that in Maupassant's prose domestic metonymy, in the form of the *bibelot*, has a directly and polemically political purpose. Duroy's clever wife Madeleine herself tells us, 'il ne faut pas dire: "Cherchez la femme," mais: "Cherchez l'affaire"' (388).

In fact psycho-sexual and socio-political disavowal are tightly worked together throughout *Bel-Ami*. Duroy assiduously disavows his own acceptance of money from women (and thus from the other men who have given money to those women), and he insists on a legal sleight-of-hand in order to accept in his own name the money left to his wife by her long-term lover. Interwoven with this personal disavowal of the exchange of money for sex is the parallel blinding of public consciousness to the financial speculation that drives political decisions. Duroy's

his introduction in *Romans*, p. 1418). On Broglie as a model, see also Vial, p. 328. I think it has other (earlier) sources in Maupassant's own journalism, as I explain below.

[89] 'La Guerre', *Le Gaulois*, 575 (10 April 1881), p. 1 (not included in the 10/18 edition of his *Chroniques* but available through Gallica). See also Michel Lambart, 'Maupassant et la politique coloniale ou Maupassant le pacifique', *Bulletin Flaubert-Maupassant*, 21 (2007), 41–51.

[90] 'La Guerre' (first published in *Gil Blas*, 11 December 1883), in Maupassant, *Chroniques*, ed. by Hubert Juin, 3 vols (Paris: '10/18' Union générale des éditions, 1980), vol. 2, 292–9 (p. 299). On the escalating conflict between France and China over the French occupation of Tonkin, which led to Jules Ferry's defeat, see Pierre Brocheux and Daniel Hémery, *Indochine: la colonisation ambiguë 1858–1954* (Paris: Éditions de la découverte, 2001), pp. 50–3. The virulent opposition to the North African expedition expressed in Maupassant's journalism 1881–4 is part of his general opposition to war, including colonial wars (see Marie-Claire Bancquart, 'Maupassant, la guerre, la politique', *Magazine littéraire*, 156 (1980), 18–21 (p. 19)). See also Gérard Delaisement, 'Les chroniques coloniales de Maupassant', in *Maupassant et l'écriture*, ed. by Louis Forestier (Paris: Nathan, 1993), pp. 53–9.

older mistress Mme Walter, wife of the media magnate, convinces him he is not a 'kept' man because he only accepts her money in order to buy up Moroccan shares before the secretly planned conquest of Morocco and France's guaranteeing of the Moroccan debt (416). And the Moroccan affair comes to a head, to the immense profit of Laroche-Mathieu and Walter himself, at exactly the moment when Duroy contrives to put in his own name half of the money his wife has been given by her lover (432). It is thanks to his experience 'de maraudages en Afrique, de bénefs illicites, de supercheries suspectes', passed off with military ideas of honour, patriotism and glory, that his conscience has become 'une sorte de boîte à triple fond où l'on trouvait de tout' (225), another instance of a collectible object, this time serving as a wonderful image for disavowal. It is no wonder that the public mind confuses the means Duroy (by now rebaptized Du Roy de Cantel) has employed to achieve his crowning success (marriage with the heiress Suzanne Walter): public perception, ignorant that he has seduced and eloped with her, supposes that he has blackmailed her father with the threat of revealing 'des cadavres découverts... des cadavres enterrés au Maroc' (476). In the fictive world concealed colonial atrocities stand in for concealed extra- or pre-marital sex, but the novel itself performs the opposite, *showing* us illicit sexuality and *implying* the colonial skeletons in the closet.

COLONIAL FRAUD AND CRITICAL ORIENTALISM

What does the association of imperialism with fraud imply for our reading of colonial discourse—and of the realist novel? It would of course be both misleading and naïve to take the category 'colonial discourse' as a single and homogeneous object of study, unchanging between nations and across time. What we have seen in the French realist novel are reflections of colonial doubt, hesitation and satire that must be understood within a specific historical context. In the heyday of the French realist novel, roughly 1830–90, it was common to adopt what was, at least in part, a satirical or oppositional stance towards colonialism. Even Balzac, that self-avowed pro-colonialist, writes with an 'increasingly equivocal note' about scandals arising from France's ongoing colonial enterprise in Algeria in the 1840s.[91] This literary stance of doubt about the colonies was part of a more general attitude in France. A certain type of anticolonialism sought to protect not the rights of the colonized, but French economic interests: before 1885 liberal economic theorists were on the whole doubtful that France stood to gain from an aggressive colonial policy.[92] In the context of the international rivalry between the 'Great Powers' at

---

[91] See Bell, 'Balzac's Algeria', p. 40.

[92] See Liauzu, pp. 45–7. Brunschwig also writes of the lack of popularity of colonialism until the Third Republic, and even then, 'les milieux économiques n'ont pas encouragé les premières expéditions coloniales de la Troisième République. Ils n'ont poussé ni à l'intervention au Tonkin en 1873, ni à l'action en Tunisie en 1880, ni à l'exploration de l'Afrique centrale' (p. 25; see also p. 50). It is only from 1885 onwards that economic doctrine 'justifia la politique d'expansion et que, dans l'impérialisme colonial, le moteur économique commença de tourner à côté du moteur politique' (pp. 60–1).

the end of the century this stance was however to lead not to a rejection of imperialist expansion per se, but to a modified form of imperialism. The 1880s and
1890s, which are often seen as heralding the rise of a real 'colonial culture' in
France, in fact saw a partial reversal of the policy of *direct* colonial intervention that
had been pursued at such great cost in Algeria. The new wave of French imperialism encouraged private financial initiatives, a secondary colonialism or imperialism in the broader sense. This is the subject taken up by the late-realist or naturalist
novel. What Zola shows us, with the project of the *Universelle* which he somewhat
anachronistically situates in the 1860s, is privately funded speculation, rather than
State intervention, as the way to make the most of the decline of the Ottoman
empire: here at last is 'une manière pratique de trancher l'éternelle et encombrante
question d'Orient' (*L'Argent*, V: 79). The new imperialism also saw the imposition
of protectorates (in Annam, Tahiti, the Comoros, Madagascar, West Africa,
Tunisia, and Morocco), rather than direct rule. The stockbroker novels of
Maupassant and Daudet explore the path that leads from proto-colonial economic
imperialism to direct political intervention to establish protectorates. The term
itself has a certain slipperiness: *protectorat* was a 'formule nouvelle [...] et dénuée
de toute précision' whose elasticity allowed welcome relief from politically onerous
conquests such as that of Algeria;[93] protectorates were, in other words, a useful
fiction.[94] In any case, opposition to government policies, and suspicions of financial manipulation, are widespread in realist and naturalist novels; they reflected,
and contributed to, a certain scepticism in public opinion.

In the novels we have looked at it is the practice of colonialism that comes under
fire, not the principles behind it. Zola and Daudet focus on the difficulty of judg-
ing their protagonists and do not actually denounce or expose them. And to some
extent these novels follow a narrative of unmasking through which the machinations of the financial world are exposed to the reader, which may imply that some
degree of transparency is ultimately possible. Yet they do not leave us with the
feeling that the world in general, or the zone of France's imperial influence in particular, has become more honest after the events recounted.

The primary focus of the realist novel is on the exposure of the power of money
in the metropolitan context, but that context itself is increasingly part of a broader
geopolitical framework. Any clear-cut division between metropolitan finance and
colonial or proto-colonial enterprises is itself brought into question. The existence
of a conceptual category labelled 'colonial discourse' should not lead critics to take
their object of study to be separable from metropolitan concerns, as if European
texts discussing colonies in Africa, say, were entirely distinct from European texts
discussing Europe. Aijaz Ahmad regrets this tendency to study colonial traces separately from other sorts of traces, which he attributes to the influence of Edward
Said's *Orientalism*.[95] Stuart Hall also regrets postcolonial criticism's (partial) failure

[93] Daniel Rivet, *Le Maghreb à l'épreuve de la colonisation* (Paris: Hachette, 2002), p. 214.
[94] Brunschwig, p. 57; see also p. 53 on the protectorate as 'la forme typiquement française de
l'impérialisme colonial' in the 1880s.
[95] Aijaz Ahmad, *In Theory: Classes, Nations, Literatures* (London: Verso, 1992), p. 172.

to take into consideration the relationship between the postcolonial and global capitalism, while Laura Chrisman calls for a new critical analysis of imperial/colonial discourse that would 'begin to address questions of capitalism and political economy'.[96] It is in part a tendency to see imperialism as divorced from the new global capitalism that has led to the relative neglect of the French realist novel's treatment of the colonial sphere. Charting the rise of advertising and the new power of journalism, the patterns of speculation and their impact on the everyday, the realist novel exposes the intertwined histories of the metropolitan world of finance and the wider world of imperial ambition, and thus points towards the paths of our own economic globalization.

The widespread association of imperialism and fraud also obliges us to re-examine any vision of colonial discourse as universally triumphalist and self-confident. Notably it suggests that we need to look again at one of Said's definitions of Orientalism as a corporate institution that constructs the European in contrast to the Oriental as 'rational, virtuous, mature, "normal"'.[97] In the French realist novel, as we have seen, Orientalist discourse itself is frequently deployed by literary fiction as a means of casting doubt on the honesty or rationality of the European subject and Western institutions. Elsewhere, Said asserts that the English presence in the colonies is 'never' viewed as anything but 'regulative and normative', an extension of metropolitan order into the colonies.[98] This is strikingly not the case in the French novel, where there is so often a deliberate focus on the uncertain financial outcomes and moral ambiguity of imperialist enterprises. It seems to me then that there is a particular strand of 'Orientalism'—widespread from at least the 1830s onwards—that is missing from Said's discussion, and which I am calling 'Critical Orientalism'. Critical Orientalism is Orientalism *au second degré*; it undermines Orientalist discursive practice, even as it engages in a form of it, by citation, framing, or satire. This chapter began by examining literary representations of exoticism used by fraudulent Western entrepreneurs as a deliberate marketing ploy, which suggests awareness of the existence of an Orientalist discourse long before Said himself denounced it. The next chapter, focused on Critical Orientalism, will show that Realism employs Orientalist motifs and colonialist discourse self-consciously in ways that question the credibility of the text itself.

---

[96] Stuart Hall, 'When was "the post-colonial"? thinking at the limit', in *The Post-Colonial Question*, ed. by Iain Chambers and Lidia Curti (London: Routledge, 1996), pp. 242–60 (p. 257); Chrisman, 'The Imperial Unconscious?', pp. 40–1.
[97] *Orientalism*, p. 40   [98] *Culture and Imperialism*, p. 89.

4

Critical Orientalism
Misreading and Miswriting the Colonies

The discourse of Orientalism was seen by Said in 1978 as a form of 'radical realism' through which an aspect of the Orient was fixed with a word or phrase that was 'then considered either to have acquired, or more simply be, reality'.[1] This view of Realism as reifying its object and asserting its own claim to 'being' reality is belied by the subtlety of Said's own more focused and less polemical individual studies. Among the rich debates inspired by his claims, critics have argued that the conception of Orientalism as a cohesive and univocal discourse must also be nuanced by the specificity of literature itself. Unlike most 'political tracts or statesmen's memoirs', which 'offer no internal resistance to the ideologies they reproduce', literary texts are capable of self questioning or 'internal ideological distanciation'.[2] As has been argued more recently, it is time for us to 'formulate an alternative notion of literary *realism*, as a modality that maintains a formal balance between reflexiveness and representativity'.[3]

The present chapter explores literature's capacity for internal resistance. More specifically, it argues that much nineteenth-century writing on 'the Orient' or 'the colonies' was engaged in a self-conscious polemic aimed at the very same Orientalist tradition that Said himself was later to attack. Both literary Realism and its late-Romantic precursor effectively introduce a critique of Orientalist discourse within Orientalism itself. The view of Realism that sees it asserting that the phenomena it describes are perfectly knowable is belied by closer study. In fact the realist mode can better be thought of in terms of a dialectical movement between the assertion of knowability on the one hand, and epistemological doubt on the other. Realist texts reveal an 'anxiety' that 'turns on the uncertain status of representation as such',[4] and oriental or colonial motifs are frequently used to expose this anxiety. They are by no means the only way by which epistemological doubt is foregrounded in the nineteenth-century novel. Indeed, as Jameson shows in *The Antinomies of Realism*, demystification is one of the central functions of the realist novel, which is marked from the outset by its secular vocation as a response to romance. He

---

[1] *Orientalism*, p. 72.

[2] Dennis Porter, '*Orientalism* and its Problems', in *The Politics of Theory*, ed. by Francis Barker (Colchester: University of Essex Press, 1983), pp. 179–93 (pp. 181–2).

[3] Sorenson, p. 57.

[4] Prendergast, *The Order of Mimesis*, p. 14. Prendergast's discussion of anxiety and uncertainty within mimesis, though invaluable for this chapter, does not specifically address Orientalist/colonial motifs.

emphasizes that the realist novel must first construct the very forms that it aims to dismantle.[5] The novel incorporates its opposites (melodrama, journalism, travel writing, romance) in a knowing and self-conscious way. Among these opposites is Orientalist discourse, portrayed as a pre-existing textual tradition whose adequacy as a response to the 'real' is repeatedly cast into doubt.[6] This secondary, belated or self-aware Orientalism is what I am calling 'Critical Orientalism'.

Critical Orientalism appears in the novel primarily as an incorporation of prior textual traditions within an ironic frame and with polemic intent. The nineteenth-century novelist writing on 'the Orient' is bent on picking apart his or her forbears, not—as Said was to do in 1978—using the tools of structuralism and Foucauldian discourse analysis, but through literary devices such as pastiche, parody, and narrative framing. These can be understood in terms of what Bakhtin calls 'incorporated genres' within the novel.[7] They are not to be mistaken for the modernist concept of *mise en abyme*, where self-referentiality reaches a higher degree of formal perfection. In addition, the framed stories and instances of misreading and miswriting that we shall see here have a contrastive relation with the main narrative in which they are embedded, rather than mirroring it.[8] But *mise en abyme* is not the only criterion for textual self-awareness; parody too introduces a significant nuance within the referential function, since it 'works by showing up the referential inadequacy of the parodied language'.[9]

As we have seen, the realist mode foregrounds not only the referential function but also verisimilitude. Now the theme of colonial misreading focuses the reader's attention on a conflict between two modes of verisimilitude. On the one hand there is prior textual verisimilitude, which fulfils expectations derived from travel writing or Orientalist tradition: stories about the Orient contain lions and intense Romantic passion, therefore it is plausible to encounter them there. On the other hand there is on-the-terrain verisimilitude, whose references are either metropolitan (Paris and the everyday imperatives of work and money), or colonial (the actual reality of the colonial regime and its effects). The incompatibility of these two types of verisimilitude is staged within the realist text as a conflict between Romanticism and Realism.

---

[5] Jameson, *Antinomies*, p. 139, and his earlier 'Beyond the Cave' [1975], reprinted in *Ideologies of Theory*. On Realism's incorporation of its own counter-discourses, see also Brown, 'The Logic of Realism'.

[6] Recent critical approaches based on close reading show that the novel foregrounds the problematic foundations of knowledge of the other. See, for example, Baker, *Realism's Empire*; and Célestin, *From Cannibals to Radicals*.

[7] On 'incorporated genres', see *The Dialogic Imagination*, pp. 320–3; on the incorporation of other genres as signifying a 'relativizing of linguistic consciousness', see ibid., pp. 323–4.

[8] According to Lucien Dällenbach's definition, 'est mise en abyme toute enclave entretenant une relation de similitude avec l'œuvre qui la contient' (*Le Récit spéculaire: Essai sur la mise en abyme* (Paris: Seuil, 1977), p. 18). On a possible contrastive function of the *mise en abyme*, see Dällenbach, p. 77.

[9] Ann Jefferson, 'Realism Reconsidered: Bakhtin's Dialogism and the "Will to Reference"', *Australian Journal of French Studies*, 23:2 (1986), 169–84 (p. 181). Jefferson argues that novelistic dialogism, far from being incompatible with the referential function of the novel, depends on it; she unpicks the widespread assumption that mimesis and self-consciousness are incompatible literary traditions (p. 183).

Realist writers make ironic use of travel narratives, whose reliability is revealed to be doubtful, and exotic daydreams, whose lack of reality is underlined. Narratives of exploration, discovery, and intelligibility are doubled by narratives of recursion, misinterpretation, and doubt. The opening scene of Flaubert's 1869 *L'Éducation sentimentale* is paradigmatic of this process: we begin with the outward signs of a nautical journey, a chance encounter with an exotically-accoutred, experienced traveller, and a glimpse of a tantalizing, exotic object of desire; but it turns out to be a bathetic return home to the provinces. Exotic sign-posting causes the reader to misread the promises held out by the novel, just as exotic daydreams encourage the protagonist Frédéric to misread his own life. This chapter will begin by examining exotic misreading in more detail, before turning to a more active form of exotic misinterpretation, that is, mis*writing*—the deliberate invention of false discourse about the colonies. After this two-sided analysis of misinterpretation as a topos we shall then turn to look at one of the *formal* means of introducing doubt or hesitation, via embedded stories and the use of a double narrative focus. Both the thematic and formal approaches reveal the knowingly derivative and self-questioning nature of the Orientalist tradition.

It is perhaps surprising to find this self-conscious and often anti-mimetic approach to the colonies and the Orient within the nineteenth-century realist tradition. Aravamudan has recently argued that we should see the eighteenth- and nineteenth-century novel as an ongoing war of genres between Enlightenment Orientalism and 'domestic realism'.[10] This is a productive and compelling reading, but it neglects the possibility of civil war: 'domestic realist' writers like to use Oriental referents as a means of incorporating a challenge to the very genre within which they are working. There is another significant, if rather different, contrast between eighteenth- and nineteenth-century exotic writing that one must point out here. The eighteenth-century exotic novel used a foreign protagonist to create an effect of defamiliarization (*Lettres persanes*, *Lettres d'une Péruvienne*, etc.), whereas nineteenth-century writers using the realist mode tend to adopt a French focalizer. The Enlightenment foreigner-in-France/Indian-in-the-City figure is a variant on the 'wise fool' tradition; in the nineteenth century the foreigner is replaced by the foolish European enamoured of the exotic. And the new fool of the nineteenth century is far from wise, because he or she cannot escape the clutches of earlier discursive traditions, in particular Romanticism.

MISREADING: EXOTIC BOVARYSM IN FLAUBERT AND DAUDET

Realism was shaped by its critique of the movement from which it was born, Romanticism, and its oppositional stance was all the more emphatic because it had to work hard to obscure the fact that it actually prolonged many aspects of Romanticism rather than rejecting them. So writing about the colonies and

[10] Aravamudan, *Enlightenment Orientalism*, p. 6.

the 'Orient' in a realist mode meant challenging the Orientalism of an earlier generation through critical (but often nostalgic) incorporation. This frequently takes a form that we shall call 'Exotic Bovarysm'. The term 'Bovarysm', inspired by Flaubert's most famous heroine, was coined by the philosopher Jules de Gaultier, who in turn was to influence Victor Segalen's theories of exoticism.[11] For Gaultier, Bovarysm is the need to conceive of oneself as something one is not, and rather than being a pathology it is a fundamental part of what makes us human. The term suggests something that is harmfully misleading but also enriching, or even necessary.

Exotic Bovarysm has a comic effect because of the discrepancy between dreams or textually derived expectations on the one hand and reality on the other. But the realist denunciation of Romantic Exotic Bovarysm is in fact a *continuation* of Romanticism's own ironic tendency to question exoticism. After all, the most 'Romantic' of the Romantics, Byron, was himself extremely cynical about his own Orientalist practice. French Romantic poetry, in the hands of Victor Hugo ('Novembre', last poem of *Les Orientales*) and Alfred de Musset ('Namouna'), also emphasizes its construction of an Orient without any direct connection to the real. This 'Romanticism of disillusionment' comes to dominate the nineteenth-century novel, according to Lukács.[12] So Romantic self-deprecation leads directly to Realism's doubts about our ability to address the real world of the colonial here-and-now.

There are two main modes of exotic misreading, one predominantly feminine, one determinedly masculine—though they sometimes overlap. The first, clearly derived from Romantic exoticism, draws on a heady mixture of Byron, Bernardin de Saint-Pierre, Chateaubriand, and Hugo. (The second, which I shall return to below, draws on adventure stories, *Robinson Crusoe*, and Fenimore Cooper's novels of the American frontier.) Exoticism in the broadest sense—historical as well as geographical exoticism—is the hallmark of Emma Bovary's reading during her convent childhood. Even more than Walter Scott's novels, Bernardin de Saint-Pierre's Mauritian idyll figures in pride of place at the beginning of the recapitulative chapter 6: 'Elle avait lu *Paul et Virginie* et elle avait rêvé la maisonnette de bambous, le nègre Domingo, le chien Fidèle, mais surtout l'amitié douce de quelque bon petit frère.'[13] Her reading awakens her to idealized passion, associated with an

[11] Jules de Gaultier put forward his theory in *Le Bovarysme: La Psychologie dans l'œuvre de Flaubert*, ed. by Didier Philippot (Paris: Éditions du Sandre, 2008 [1892]) and *Le Bovarysme: Essai sur le pouvoir d'imaginer* (Paris: Société du Mercure de France, 1903, first published as *Le Bovarysme*, 1902). See also Deborah Jenson, 'Bovarysm and Exoticism', in *The Columbia History of Twentieth-Century French Thought*, ed. by Lawrence D. Kritzman and Brian J. Reilly (New York: Columbia University Press, 2006), pp. 167–70.

[12] See the chapter 'The Romanticism of Disillusionment', in *Theory of the Novel*, pp. 112–31. Lukács implies that Balzac is exempt from this form of Romanticism, which is not entirely convincing.

[13] III: 179–80; at the end of the previous chapter she asked about the meaning of 'félicité', which will later be the name of her new maid. The connections between the name, and an ironic reference to the ideal happiness of exotic young love in Bernardin de Saint-Pierre's island paradise, will be teased out further in 'Un cœur simple', where the maid-of-all-work Félicité cares deeply for the children in her charge, Paul and Virginie, whose very names gesture ironically towards the island idyll.

exotic wilderness;[14] but as Larry Schehr points out, misreading is evident not only in what Emma reads and remembers, but also in what she forgets or omits. In the case of *Paul et Virginie*, he argues, she keeps only the idyllic love of the beginning and omits the ending.[15] In fact Emma's reading occludes not just sexuality, but also economic realities. Her idealist sublimation offers substitutes for material needs (the bamboo hut) and work (the devoted slave), alongside sex (pre-pubescent love that perishes on the eve of adolescence). Here Flaubert's exotic referent again has the dual function we saw in Chapter 1: it appears to offer transcendence of material realities, but in fact affirms the impossibility of such transcendence.[16]

Happiness, Emma imagines, is like a plant that only grows well in particular climates (III: 184). Alongside the island idyll, Emma's fantasies are peopled with the Romantic Orientalist fantasies of Flaubert's own youth, of which he offers a merciless caricature:

> Et vous y étiez aussi, sultans à longues pipes, pâmés sous des tonnelles, aux bras des bayadères, djiaours, sabres turcs, bonnets grecs, et vous surtout, paysages blafards des contrées dithyrambiques, qui souvent nous montrez à la fois des palmiers, des sapins, des tigres à droite, un lion à gauche, des minarets tartares à l'horizon, au premier plan des ruines romaines, puis des chameaux accroupis;—le tout encadré d'une forêt vierge bien nettoyée, et avec un grand rayon de soleil perpendiculaire tremblotant dans l'eau, où se détachent en écorchures blanches, sur un fond d'acier gris, de loin en loin, des cygnes qui nagent. (III: 182–3)

In Flaubert's negative poetics the accumulation of clichés becomes the very substance of literature and the raw material from which a new form of beauty can be painstakingly constructed. We are also reminded of the textually derivative nature of Emma's daydreams: Bovarysm is part of what Genette proposes could be called '[la] folie romanesque'.[17] Later, as the debt-collectors threaten and her life is on the point of collapsing around her, Emma retires to her room, returning to her books and a daydream world of Orientalist intensity: 'Elle restait là tout le long du jour, engourdie, à peine vêtue, et, de temps à autre, faisant fumer des pastilles du sérail qu'elle avait achetées à Rouen, dans la boutique d'un Algérien. [...] elle lisait jusqu'au matin des livres extravagants où il y avait des tableaux orgiaques avec des situations sanglantes.' She herself is burning like the 'pastilles': 'brûlée plus fort par cette flamme intime que l'adultère avivait, haletante, émue, tout en désir, elle ouvrait sa fenêtre, aspirait l'air froid, éparpillait au vent sa chevelure trop lourde, et, regardant les étoiles, souhaitait des amours de prince' (III: 404–5). Emma's reading

---

[14] On the dangers of reading *Paul et Virginie* in Flaubert (and Balzac), see Sarah Hurlburt, 'Educating Emma: A Genetic Analysis of Reading in *Madame Bovary*', *Nineteenth-Century French Studies*, 40:1–2 (2011–12), 81–95.

[15] Lawrence R. Schehr, *Subversions of Verisimilitude: Reading Narrative from Balzac to Sartre* (New York: Fordham University Press, 2009), pp. 78–9; for a substantial discussion of Bovarysm, see pp. 68–79.

[16] As Anne Green points out, when Flaubert mocks orientalist cliché he is 'both borrowing the popular myth of the Orient as an imaginative or erotic escape, and at the same time subverting it by stressing its illusory quality—it is a myth presented as a myth, shown to be unattainable and unreal, and even slightly absurd' ('Flaubert's myth of civilisation and the Orient', p. 217).

[17] Gérard Genette, *Palimpsestes: La littérature au second degré* (Paris: Seuil, 1982), p. 206.

transforms her into Delacroix's bloody and orgiastic prince, Sardanapalus. But the Orientalist 'pastilles du sérail' (where the seraglio evoked is the imperial seraglio of the Ottoman Empire) is undercut by the fact that she has bought them in the local provincial capital in a shop run by an early colonial immigrant, probably a French colonist returning from Algeria.

L'Éducation sentimentale also exposes Exotic Bovarysm in the form of Frédéric Moreau's daydreams of interior decoration and orientalist accessories. Like many of Emma's daydreams of escape, Frédéric's are Romantic, pseudo-Turkish fantasies inspired by Hugo and Byron—the very readings that had moved the young Flaubert. Frédéric and Emma yearn for an Orient that they know only through pre-existing textual frames; what the novels highlight is the misfit of these frames with their reality. This is why, as we have seen, Flaubert introduces reminders of real colonial encounters as a foil for the textually derived Romantic Orient: Emma's 'pastilles du sérail [turc]' are bought in the shop of a migrant from colonial Algeria; she dreams of a sublimated Byronic, Turkish Orient, but buys an Algerian shawl (and will have to pay for it later); Frédéric dreams of Mme Arnoux dressed for a Turkish harem, but sees her with an Algerian purse in her hair. As early as the *Éducation sentimentale* of 1845, one finds an incongruous meeting of the two Orients (the Romantic Middle East, and the post-Romantic colonial North Africa). At the end of the novel Jules renounces the world and departs to tour the Orient, taking with him two pairs of shoes that he intends to 'user sur le Liban, et un Homère qu'il lira au bord de l'Hellespont'. From this Byronesque, Chateaubriandesque gesture the novel slips towards satire of a properly *colonial* encounter: 'S'il passe par Alger il y rencontrera Bernardi, établi directeur d'une troupe de vaudeville et amusant les Arabes civilisés avec les couplets de M. Scribe, et la prose de MM. Mélesville et Bayard' (I: 1079–80).

Bovarysm does not reside in novels or poems, but in the use that is made of them. In a variant that one might call 'naïve Bovarysm', the interpreter is hampered not by excessive imagination but by childlike naïvety. The Exotic Bovarysm of childhood is famously evoked by Baudelaire in 'Le Voyage': 'Ah! que le monde est grand à la clarté des lampes! / Aux yeux du souvenir que le monde est petit!' A naïvety like that of childhood is encountered in 'Un cœur simple' where Félicité's 'éducation littéraire' is limited to the child Paul's explanations of the prints in a geography book given by the untrustworthy M. Bourais: its engravings 'représentaient différentes scènes du monde, des anthropophages coiffés de plumes, un singe enlevant une demoiselle, des Bédouins dans le désert, une baleine qu'on harponnait, etc.' (48–9). Later she imagines her nephew Victor, who has left for South America, participating in these terrible scenes. In a cartographical variant on naïve Bovarysm, she also wants to be shown Victor's house portrayed in an atlas (the innocence of her mistake is implicitly contrasted with the medical error that results in Victor's death, and the deliberate misappropriation of funds committed by the smug Bourais).[18]

---

[18] Arden Reed discusses the geography book and atlas of 'Un cœur simple' as a paired source of visual images in *Manet, Flaubert, and the Emergence of Modernism: Blurring Genre Boundaries* (Cambridge: Cambridge University Press, 2003), pp. 215–16.

Though it is a form of misreading that he evokes more than once, cartographical Bovarysm was not invented by Flaubert.[19] Balzac showed us Eugénie Grandet also succumbing to the illusion of presence provided by maps: 'le lendemain du départ de Charles [...] elle prit, chez le libraire de la ville, une mappemonde qu'elle cloua près de son miroir, afin de suivre son cousin dans sa route vers les Indes, afin de pouvoir se mettre un peu, soir et matin, dans le vaisseau qui l'y transportait, de le voir, de lui adresser mille questions' (III: 1147). The map gives her a false feeling of proximity that is mentioned again later, when she and her mother ask themselves where he is, but 'ignoraient complètement les distances' (III: 1160, 1161). The misreading of the map as offering presence is a synecdoche for the misreading of the world's vast geographical distances, and also for the untold miles that separate one human heart from another.

Post- or late-Romantic mockery of Exotic Bovarysm becomes even more common in the second half of the century. With colonial expansion, and increased opportunities for travel thanks to technological advancement, the trope focuses increasingly on the contrast between Orientalist presuppositions and colonial realities. Emma Bovary's successor is thus Tartarin de Tarascon; indeed, he has been called 'la Madame Bovary de l'exotisme'[20] (though as we have seen Emma herself has some claims to that title).

In the 1860s–1870s, seeking to exploit the experience of a trip to Algeria (1861–2, aged twenty-one), Alphonse Daudet published a short comic story called 'Chapatin le tueur de lions',[21] and planned to write a much more 'realist' novel, based on detailed observation, that was to be 'le roman de l'Algérie coloniale'.[22] As it turned out, it was not Algeria, but the illusions of the novel's protagonist, that would eventually be the focus of the novel, *Tartarin de Tarascon*, that he did eventually publish in 1872 after the trauma of the Commune: 'Chapatin' had become 'Barbarin' and then 'Tartarin'. Daudet later returned to his most famous creation in two other novels, written primarily to exploit the commercial success of the first. Where *Tartarin de Tarascon* (1872) parodies the adventure story, *Tartarin sur les Alpes* (1885) parodies the story of heroic mountaineering, and

---

[19] In *Madame Bovary*, too, Emma buys a map of Paris and imagines her life there, following the lines of the roads with the tip of her finger (III: 199–200). The rest of the world comes to seem vague, even inexistent for her, and 'Plus les choses [...] étaient voisines, plus sa pensée s'en détournait. [...] Ne fallait-il pas à l'amour, comme aux plantes indiennes, des terrains préparés, une température particulière?' (III: 201).

[20] Jacques-Henri Bornecque, *Les Années d'apprentissage d'Alphonse Daudet* (Paris: Nizet, 1951), p. 370. Flaubert was, incidentally, an enthusiastic admirer of *Tartarin de Tarascon*.

[21] 'Chapatin le tueur de lions', published in *Le Figaro* (18 June 1863), is the first version of the Tartarin story. The character was inspired by Daudet's travel companion, his cousin Henri Reynaud. 'Chapatin' mocks the Southern provincial type in a way that appealed to his Parisian readers; it is also a reaction against his own earlier Romanticism, belonging to the 'genre de roman anti-romanesque que l'on pourrait nommer "roman de désillusion critique"' according to Bornecque (*Années d'apprentissage*, p. 369).

[22] Alphonse Daudet, *Œuvres*, ed. by Roger Ripoll (Paris: Gallimard 'La Pléiade', 1986–94), 'Notice', I: 1433. In *Histoire de mes livres*, Daudet later pointed to a missed opportunity for what could have been a realist satire on Algerian colonial society (see I: 574).

Port-Tarascon (1890) parodies the colonial novel—the latter two being relatively new genres at the time.[23]

In the first, 1872 novel, Tartarin's Bovarysm, like Emma's, derives from the Turkish, Byronic/Hugolian model of Orientalism, so that in Algeria he pursues a *mauresque* and expects to be attacked by 'une dégringolade d'eunuques et de janissaires' (I: 518).[24] Tartarin's Exotic Bovarysm is however decidedly masculine, and his misreading includes *Robinson Crusoe*[25] and the adventure novels of Fenimore Cooper, Gustave Aimard, and Gabriel Ferry (mostly situated in the wilds of America). In addition, he is influenced by hunting manuals and travel writing (the *Voyages* of Captain Cook; and, in preparation for his voyage to Africa, the writings of explorers, or 'récits des grands touristes africains' I: 491). In Daudet's spoof colonial novel of 1890, *Port-Tarascon*, comic effects also arise from the disjunction of Tartarin's experience with his prior reading. Meeting a chieftain who claims to be a Polynesian king, he applies what he has learnt through reading Cook, Bougainville, and d'Entrecasteaux and rubs noses with him; the king, who speaks Tarasconnese fluently, is somewhat surprised as this custom is no longer in use among his people. Tartarin has committed the classic error of the anthropologist who, as Johannes Fabian tells us, sees the human object of his study as frozen in an unchanging, ahistorical, timeless identity.[26] Tartarin's reading also includes practical handbooks on the skills needed to establish a successful colony, none of which prove of any use. And along with novels, travel writing, and colonial manuals, Daudet parodies scientific taxonomy. In the opening scene of the first novel, the fearsome exotic weapons in Tartarin's famous collection are identified by neatly-written labels that pastiche the classificatory systems so dear to the nineteenth-century collector/explorer.[27] Collecting and displaying exotic weapons is part of the new consumer culture that seeks to incorporate that which is precisely its opposite: in his safe bourgeois home, the collector is able to identify himself with the lost virile values of violence and danger. In any case, it is clear that Bovarysm, or the ability to imagine the world other than it really is, is nourished by sources that are textual, but not by any means exclusively literary.

If Realism exposes misreading or lack of critical faculties, is there—if only by implication—an alternative stance that would provide a true reading? Within the

---

[23] On the trilogy as a parody of travel writing, see Anne-Simone Dufief, 'Voyages et rêverie dans l'œuvre de Daudet', in *Apprendre à porter sa vue au loin: Hommage à Michèle Duchet*, ed. by Sylviane Albertan-Coppola (Lyon: ENS Éditions, 2009), pp. 331–42.

[24] *Tartarin de Tarascon*'s origins as a joyously irreverent mockery of Romanticism are suggested by the fact that the full novel was originally announced under the title 'Barbarin de Tarascon/Raconté par un témoin de sa vie' (*Le Petit Moniteur*, 1869), a pastiche of Adèle Hugo's *Victor Hugo raconté par un témoin de sa vie* (1863). See Anne-Simone Dufief, *Alphonse Daudet romancier* (Paris: Champion, 1997), pp. 505–7.

[25] Alphonse Daudet's autobiographical novel recounting his childhood, *Le Petit chose*, dwells on the importance of *Robinson Crusoe* to his imaginary world.

[26] *Time and the Other*, particularly p. 31, p. 80.

[27] Tartarin's neatly labelled collection includes Malaysian daggers or *kris*, just as Gautier's antique shop in 'Pied de momie' (1840) has a *kris* for sale. Frédéric Moreau decorates his cosy bachelor pad with a *kris* and a collection of Mongol arrows in *L'Éducation sentimentale* (p. 247, p. 280). The *kris* signals a self-consciously ironic Romantic lineage leading back at least as far as Balzac's *Voyage de Paris à Java* (1832), which will be discussed later in this chapter.

comic tale of Exotic Bovarysm that is *Tartarin de Tarascon* one finds traces of the novel of 'observation' that Daudet wanted to write, and Tartarin's blindness is held up as antithetical to a potential empirical stance. The novel that Daudet did not write would have been 'une étude de mœurs cruelle et vraie', revealing the corruption and petty rivalries of 'la France algérienne'.[28] Between two major paths taken by literary Realism—claiming to see the truth on the one hand, and denouncing not seeing correctly on the other—Daudet opted for the latter. Nevertheless, throughout we are given, often explicitly, a double focalization in which the anonymous narrator has a truer grasp of outside realities than the protagonist. This double focalization and ironic perspective are also present, though in a less explicit form, in Flaubert's use of indirect free discourse.

In Daudet's hands, double focalization gives the implied reader a comfortable sense of superiority to the naïve Tartarin. Nonetheless, when Daudet's narrator points out Tartarin's blindness to the reality of poverty and exploitation in colonial Algeria, our attention is focused on the splitting of the western self in relation to the new global world order: on the one hand we have Tartarin's exotic impulse, and on the other the 'neutral observation' of the real. The truth to which Tartarin is blind, but which the narrator exposes, are the effects of the colonial military regime and its delegation of power to corrupt local authorities. 'Curieux spectacle pour des yeux qui auraient su voir... Un peuple sauvage et pourri que nous civilisons, en lui donnant nos vices... L'autorité féroce et sans contrôle [...] La justice sans conscience [...] tout autour, des plaines en friche, de l'herbe brûlée [...] Des douars abandonnés, des tribus effarées qui s'en vont sans savoir où, fuyant la faim, et semant des cadavres le long de la route.' In the rare French villages the fields remain uncultivated while in the café the colonists drink absinthe and discuss projects for reform.[29] This is what Tartarin could have seen, but did not, 'l'œil obstinément fixé sur ces monstres imaginaires' (I: 542–3). What Daudet wrote, then, is not a novel about the real effects of colonization, but a novel about the splitting of our perceptions between textually derived Orientalist tradition and colonial reality. In the 1920s the emphasis on a distinction between 'littérature exotique' on the one hand, and 'littérature coloniale' on the other, was to lead to a critical stand-off concerning the degree to which Daudet had actually observed with his own eyes while in Algeria, rather than slavishly 'copying' his models.[30] But it is in fact the tension between illusion and observation that is the main focus of Daudet's novel.

Any attempt to recuperate *Tartarin de Tarascon* as an anticolonial text must be careful to distinguish between satire and parody. The novel's energy is primarily directed towards parody of the Romantic oriental dream and of adventure narratives; this is to be distinguished from satire of an extra-textual (institutional) reality.

[28] 'Histoire de mes livres' (I: 574).
[29] Some historians estimate that the French invasion wiped out half of Algeria's pre-colonial population between 1830 and 1872, through a combination of direct violence and famine induced by *razzias* that destroyed local cultivation patterns. See Gallois, 'Genocide', p. 74.
[30] The 1920s debate focused on whether or not *Tartarin de Tarascon* was a novel of observation or of literary inspiration; Bornecque gives a rather humorous summary of the discussion (*Années d'apprentissage*, pp. 338–9). See also his introduction to the *Aventures prodigieuses de Tartarin de Tarascon* (Paris: Garnier, 1968), pp. xvii–xviii.

Satire of the disastrous effects of French colonialism in Algeria is certainly present, but it is a secondary consideration. In the 1860s, when *Tartarin de Tarascon* was written (and indeed throughout the 1870s), there was considerable opposition to colonial expansion from within France, including within the government; Brunschwig has gone so far as to call this a 'colonisation anticolonialiste'.[31] Daudet's novel reflects the hesitations over Algerian policies that were current at the time. Astier Loutfi sees French colonial writing of this early period as a literature of doubt and hesitation, and although she belittles Daudet's satirical intentions, she acknowledges that 'néanmoins, pour qui savait lire, Daudet faisait nette-ment de l'exemple algérien un épouvantail sur la route des prochaines tentatives d'expansion'.[32]

Anne-Simone Dufief has argued that while *Tartarin de Tarascon* can be understood partly as a satire of colonization in Algeria, *Port-Tarascon* (1890) is not anticolonial because it is not based on first-hand observation. She also argues that it cannot be considered to be a parody of the colonial novel since the genre did not yet exist.[33] This is strange, since it is usually considered that the French colonial novel began its rise in the 1880s. Daudet certainly parodies an immediate precursor of the *roman colonial*, Pierre Loti's *Le Mariage de Loti*, which dates to 1880 (Loti's novel is targeted in the love affair between the fat, aging Tartarin and a barely nubile Polynesian princess). Certainly, neither *Tartarin de Tarascon* nor *Port-Tarascon* is primarily a work of political satire. But they must be understood within an ongoing generic concern that is at the heart of the realist project in the nineteenth century, and their epistemological question—to what extent can we 'know' a foreign land and people?—is also political.

Exotic Bovarysm's staging of epistemological doubt falls short of a fully political *prise de position* that would satisfy our postcolonial expectations, because it is charac-terized by ambivalence. This is a *dialectical* Realism, born of a very French form of Romantic irony, which derides what it loves (that is, the textually derived tradition of Orientalism/adventure stories). The comic denunciation of not seeing correctly is mitigated by the fact that the daydreams—Emma's, Tartarin's—are more attract-ive than the reality. Furthermore, although Exotic Bovarysm implicitly suggests that perception *can* in theory correspond to the realities of the outside world, it does so *a contrario* by dwelling on the difficulties that are encountered in the attempt. Critical readings of *Tartarin de Tarascon* are divided on whether it recounts a victory for dreams[34] or is a pedagogical novel that shows the formation of an individual consciousness through a process of disillusionment.[35] The answer would

---

[31] *Mythes et réalités*, p. 10.

[32] Astier Loutfi, p. 12. She sees Daudet as a propagandist for empire and a racist, despite his satirical asides attacking both the French military and civilian regimes (pp. 5–12).

[33] *Alphonse Daudet romancier*, p. 474. Elsewhere ('Voyages et rêverie') Dufief argues that *Port-Tarascon* should be read instead as a philosophical tale and counter-utopia.

[34] Bornecque saw it as the story of 'le rêve apparemment vaincu par la réalité banale, mais vainquant à son tour cette réalité par la toute-puissance de l'imagination heureuse', *Années d'apprentissage*, p. 370.

[35] Adriano Marchetti sees the novel as destroying the reader's illusions entirely; the narrator's posi-tion (of having learned the 'truth') is the dominant one. But he does emphasize the inheritance of Daudet's novel in Decadent writing, where the word and the sound of the word take precedence over

seem to hang on the nature of the double focalization. Is Exotic Bovarysm—indeed, any kind of Bovarysm—an error specific to characters who are perceived as having a 'weak' grasp on reality, such as provincials, or worse, provincial housewives? Flaubert for one followed his provincial Emma with the male, bourgeois Frédéric, installed in Paris and in possession of a private income; if Frédéric is guilty of Bovarysm, anyone or everyone can be. In *L'Éducation sentimentale* Flaubert also went further in removing suggestions of the presence of an all-seeing narrator capable of superior judgement. This careful refusal to allow the narrator—and reader—a sense of superiority requires a technical mastery that Daudet does not even attempt. The sheer beauty of the language of Emma's lyrical exotic day-dreams in *Madame Bovary* also renders their impact ambivalent, since it makes it hard for the reader to dismiss them with undiluted contempt. Who are we to judge her illusions?

The Tartarin of Daudet's first novel boasts of his adventures in Shanghai, where he has never been, but 'L'homme du Midi ne ment pas, il se trompe. Il ne dit pas toujours la vérité, mais il croit la dire…Son mensonge à lui, ce n'est pas du mensonge, c'est une espèce de mirage' (I: 487). The reader is allowed to believe that Northerners are less self-deluding, and to feel a comfortable sense of superiority when confronted with the comic Tartarin, but the character is effective precisely because it is possible to identify with him despite our laughter.[36] It is not for nothing that Henry James, who translated *Port-Tarascon*, identified with Tartarin as presenting the essential ambiguity that opposes an idea and its application.[37] Tartarin's Exotic Bovarysm is a form of Platonic idealism whose constant failure to correspond to our experience of the outside world is part of our own comic, but universal, predicament. Dualism is inherent in all Bovarysm, which loves the thing that is denigrated, and asserts the value of the dream over reality, the lie over the truth.

Bovarysm or misreading is not simply one trope among others, but part of a major generic mainstay of the novel: the anti-novel tradition. From its outset the modern novel has invented itself in opposition to earlier writings. While modernism tended to declare its own unique invention of the anti-roman, more recently critics have acknowledged the broad historical scope, or even 'transhistoricity' of the anti-roman.[38] The topos of misreading, part of the realist denunciation of the

the real (see 'La tentazione esotica nel romanzo filosofico di Alphonse Daudet', *Questione Romantica: Rivista Interdisciplinare di Studi Romantici*, 12–13 (2002), 129–40 (p. 130, p. 140)).

[36] Indeed, Daudet's early writing shows a tendency to portray himself, including his negative sides, and the figure of Tartarin may well be inspired as much by himself as by his cousin Reynaud. See Sachs, *The Career of Alphonse Daudet*, pp. 66–70.

[37] Henry James, 'Translator's Preface' to *Port-Tarascon*, *Harper's New Monthly Magazine*, 81 (June 1890), p. 3.

[38] See Ugo Dionne and Francis Gingras, 'Présentation: l'usure originelle du roman: roman et anti-roman du Moyen Âge à la Révolution', *Études françaises*, 42:1 (2006), 5–21; and Pierre-Olivier Brodeur, 'Pourquoi l'anti-roman?', *French Studies Bulletin*, 119 (2011), 28–31. Dionne and Gingras point out the lack of historical perspective of those critics who see the 'anti-novel' as being 'new' in a given period, rather than constantly renewing itself (p. 8); in particular, Ian Watt's division of 'romance' from 'novel' (the former mistaken, close to folk tradition; the latter tending towards Realism, serious) is in error because it seeks to give a specific historical date to such a separation, which

Romantic or heroic stance, is a variant of the anti-novel. Harry Levin, while acknowledging the longevity of the novel's deflation of romance, also emphasizes the foundational role played by parody in the realist text. It is almost inevitable that writing sets itself up in opposition to a literary precursor ('True literature…deprecates the literary'; 'Fiction approximates truth, not by concealing art, but by exposing artifice'), but at the same time it is of particular importance for the realist novel: 'No writers have been more intensely conscious of what was already written.'[39] Daudet himself was so self-conscious about writing an anti-novel that *Tartarin de Tarascon* incorporates a sustained parallel with *Don Quixote*, the paradigmatic example of the tradition. His marvellous comic invention was to include in the single person of Tartarin both the heroically inspired, if misguided, Don, and his pragmatic, cowardly servant Sancho Pancha.

Genette makes a distinction between the *real* anti-novel, which attacks, or takes as its 'hypotext', an entire genre, and the *pseudo* anti-novel, which takes a specific novel as its hypotext.[40] In the case of Exotic Bovarysm, however, the attack is aimed neither at a single novel nor at the genre as a whole: the real target would appear to be inappropriate modes of reading. At fault is the Romantic/heroic belief in the immediate application of text to world.

MISWRITING: ORIENTALISM AND THE INVENTION OF THE COLONIES

From misreading exoticism, a natural step takes us to misrepresenting, or miswriting. We move from the domain of Bovarysm to something more like the fake exotic objects, duplicitous advertising campaigns, and pseudo-exotic perfume we saw in Chapter 3. Orientalism is not a one-way process, and a textually based Orientalist tradition—itself perhaps fraudulent—is held up as a source for active invention, as we saw with César Birotteau's 'Pâte des Sultanes'.

The imperialist applications of this derivative Orientalism are more obvious later in the century. In Zola's *L'Argent* the speculator Saccard begins to daydream about Middle-Eastern engineering projects and investment banks while gazing at watercolours of the Orient and a folder of engineering plans, produced by the siblings Caroline and Georges Hamelin. The novel repeatedly links Caroline's intensely personal instinct for colour with the firm, mathematically precise lines of her brother's plans. However Caroline's watercolours, along with her verbal 'descriptions colorées', are the main source of Saccard's feverish inspiration and colonial aspirations in Syria (V: 60; 75; see also 223–4). Gomart sees these watercolours as giving views of the Orient that are merely poetic, or 'inertes', and which must be transformed into muscular prose by Saccard, who she sees as a figure for

---

would thus be at the origins of a single linear movement (p. 10). One nevertheless continues to find, among specialists of the modern period, the sort of ahistorical naïvety that can claim: 'la parodie est un genre très moderne car c'est une forme sophistiquée' (Dufief, *Alphonse Daudet romancier*, p. 523).

[39] Levin, p. 51; p. 66.　　　[40] *Palimpsestes*, p. 209.

the naturalist novelist.[41] Had she turned to Zola's notes, however, she would have found that the muscles are in fact on the female side: Zola's plan emphasizes Caroline's 'aquarelle énergique' that complements the pure 'matérialisme' of her brother's technical sketches.[42] The conjunction embodies what Zola sees as the double basis of human creativity in science and individual creative genius. As Saminadayar-Perrin puts it, Zola's fiction itself relies on a comparable combination of scientific discourse with 'les puissances de l'illusion, seules capables de susciter la croyance'.[43] In *L'Argent*, Zola thus emphasizes the (dual) textual, secondary derivation of the imperialist project, born of the conjunction of orientalist art and engineering projects. Saccard's dreams of grand Napoleonic conquests in the Orient are moreover exacerbated when he begins to read 'des livres sur l'Orient' and in particular 'une histoire de l'expédition d'Égypte' (V: 78). This sounds like Exotic Bovarysm, and one is not surprised by Saccard's fall after the hubris of taking himself for a new Napoleon; but Zola does not see Orientalism as mere delusion. In the closing pages of the novel Caroline's own Orientalist watercolours cause her to meditate on the future of the Middle East, developed and at peace thanks to private French companies financed by French financial speculation. Zola's carefully maintained ambivalence about the role of speculation does not prevent him from inclining towards economic imperialism in this ending, whose explicit message suggests the tendency of his late works towards the *roman à thèse* (notably foreshadowing *Fécondité* (1899)). But he also emphatically shows us that imperialism has its roots in artistic Orientalism.

Our new focus on the Orientalist invention of the colonies brings us back to Tartarin. In *Tartarin de Tarascon* he composes a love letter to a supposed 'Mauresque', striving for an amalgam of 'la rhétorique apache des Indiens, de Gustave Aymard, avec le *Voyage en Orient* de Lamartine, et quelques lointaines réminiscences du *Cantique des cantiques*' (I: 523).[44] In 1890 Daudet's last Tartarin novel, *Port-Tarascon*, shows the town's entire population succumbing to what one might call collective Bovarysm. One of the main targets of the novel's parody was precisely the kind of rhetoric that was, by the 1880s, encouraging French people to leave for colonial ventures afar (without a great deal of success, it must be said).[45] *Port-Tarascon* includes parodies, sometimes very close to their source texts, of colonial

---

[41] *Les Opérations financières*, p. 284.

[42] MS.10268 fol. 281. Caroline's dynamic watercolours are linked to the energy of a new Napoleonic-style conquest of the East, this time by Science and Civilization (cf. MS.10269, fols 217–20; see Pléiade V: 1300–1, notes to p. 59). For a longer analysis of the watercolours, see Monica Lebron, 'Madame Caroline: Expéditions discursives dans *L'Argent*', *Les Cahiers naturalistes*, 73 (1999), 217–25 (pp. 219–21).

[43] 'Fictions de la bourse', p. 51.

[44] Tartarin's letter begins with 'Comme l'autruche dans les sables' and ends with 'Dis-moi le nom de ton père, et je te dirai le nom de cette fleur.' The ending is taken directly from Lamartine's *Voyage en Orient*.

[45] The Northern 'Duc de Mons' (*mens-onge?*) publishes enticing advertisements for cheap land, guaranteed profits, and ready-built houses on a paradisiacal Polynesian island. The story was based on a real case of fraud in which a swindler had sold land in a non-existent colony called 'Port-Breton', in 1877. In the novel, the 'Duke' sets up 'un comité d'actionnaires marseillais' presided by a Greek banker, Kagaraspaki, with sums to be paid into 'la banque ottomane Pamenyaï-ben-Kaga, maison de toute sécurité' (III: 871). The invented names hide a scatological joke in Provençal, perhaps

journalism and administrative rhetoric.[46] Tartarin himself, still in Tarascon, publishes
a newspaper called the *Gazette de Port-Tarascon*, for which he gets Pascalon, the
pharmacist's apprentice, to write daily reports of the colony and its resources. The
Gazette is perfectly adapted not to any external reality (there is in fact no news
from the colony) but to the hopes and expectations of its readers: there are travel
stories and tales of fights with the savages 'pour les esprits aventureux'; tales of
hunting and fishing for the 'gentilshommes campagnards'; and tales of pleasant
picnics and exotic fruit for the more peaceable (III: 874). Tartarin himself is the
colony's governor, and later makes administrative pronouncements that are embedded word for word in italics in the text of the novel.[47] In times of crisis, which is
the norm once he reaches the actual colony, these pronouncements take the form
of promises that cannot be carried out, and which the population *knows* cannot be
carried out, but which reassure everyone nevertheless.

Daudet also satirizes what David Cannadine has called 'Ornamentalism': the power
of props in the management of colonial relations.[48] The aging Tartarin, governor of
the fictive colony Port-Tarascon, accords his fellow colonists pompous-sounding
new ranks, 'ce qui lui permettait de satisfaire le goût de ses compatriotes pour tout
ce qui est titre, honneur, distinction, costume et soutache' (III: 873; even the
English are impressed by Tartarin's use of 'Ornamentalism', III: 939). In *Tartarin
de Tarascon*, already, we learned that the gilt military cap plays a crucial role in 'nos
relations avec les Arabes': 'pour gouverner l'Algérie [...] pas n'est besoin d'une forte
tête, ni même d'une tête du tout. Il suffit d'un képi, d'un beau képi galonné, relu-
isant au bout d'une trique...' The kepi with its shining braid covers the realities of
the cudgel, a synecdoche for the violence of the French invaders, and as such it
works wonders: 'Les indigènes qui passaient s'inclinaient jusqu'à terre devant le
képi magique...' (I: 539).

The town of Tarascon subscribes joyously to the collective delusion, while
Tartarin himself, along with his loyal sidekick and scribe Pascalon, merrily invents
misrepresentations of the colonial venture. Wishful thinking takes Tartarin from
misreading to miswriting, or from exotic naïvety to colonial lies. When he is, eventually, taken to court, what is put in the dock is in fact the triumphalist rhetoric of
colonialism. Daudet's novel in the end exonerates Tartarin in the name of sheer
inventiveness and imagination, and his innocence was clear all along in the lamb-
like name of his accomplice Pascalon. But in the process the rhetoric of France's
emerging colonial culture is exposed as a form of collective Bovarysm.

Daudet's attempt to conciliate the victims of his burlesque by showing he was one of them (see
notes, III: 1346).

[46] Dufief discusses the Tartarin novels as parodies, but does not mention colonial rhetoric as among
the languages parodied ('Voyages et rêverie').

[47] Tartarin also fabricates a treaty between himself and a self-declared king, and sells hectares of
land to various colonists, demonstrating his mastery of administrative fictions as a crucial element
of the colonial power base. The narrator comments on the success of empty administrative rhetoric:
'ce n'est pas pour rien qu'un proverbe dit chez nous: "L'homme par la parole et le bœuf par les cornes"'
(III: 927).

[48] David Cannadine, *Ornamentalism: How the British Saw their Empire* (London: Allen Lane,
2001).

Tartarin de Tarascon, as we have seen, included brief passages of observation that give a stark image of the effects of French colonization on Algeria. A much more open criticism of French policy in North Africa is to be found in the journalism and travel narratives of Maupassant.[49] We saw in Chapter 3 how he uses the real-life Tunisian 'affair' as the model for his satirical treatment of the 'affaire marocaine' in *Bel-Ami*. Despite the novel's thoroughly Parisian focus, it begins the tale of George Duroy's social climbing just after his return from service in the French army in Algeria. Duroy is invited to begin his career in journalism by recounting his recent African experience, but he proves incapable of writing the chronicles required. The title, 'Souvenirs d'un chasseur d'Afrique', is given to him by his future mistress Mme Walter (217), and the articles themselves are composed, and dictated to him, by his future wife, the very Parisian Madeleine Forestier, who is able to fabricate a convincing account not of the colonial experiences that he has really had, but of those that her readers expect him to have had:

> Elle imaginait [...] portraiturait [...] ébauchait [...]. Puis, s'étant assise, elle interrogea Duroy sur la topographie de l'Algérie qu'elle ignorait absolument. En dix minutes, elle en sut autant que lui, et elle fit un petit chapitre de géographie politique et coloniale pour mettre le lecteur au courant et le bien préparer à comprendre les questions sérieuses qui seraient soulevées dans les articles suivants.
>
> Puis elle continua par une excursion dans la province d'Oran, une excursion fantaisiste, où il était surtout question de femmes, des Mauresques, des Juives, des Espagnoles.
>
> 'Il n'y a que ça qui intéresse', disait-elle. (231)

This passage has been cited as confirmation of Said's claims that writing about Algeria is a form of colonization.[50] Nineteenth-century authors' critiques of oriental discourse are often confused with first-degree oriental discourse itself. And yet there can be no doubt that what we have here in fact *frames* colonial discourse, exposing its fabrication according to the rules of textual verisimilitude (that is, verisimilitude that conforms to what readers already expect because they have read it elsewhere), and suggesting that this textual construction has dubious motivations in vicarious sexual tourism. As Giacchetti argues, Algeria and Morocco function in Maupassant's novel as extra-diegetic spaces that exist only through the speech and writing of the characters, and Africa is thus not only a 'modèle actantiel' but also a model for writing that produces false discourse.[51]

The 'truth' status of the colonial events thus recounted is *ipso facto* brought into doubt. Not only are the journalistic accounts of Duroy's North African experience false, but Maupassant shows us a doubly derivative discursive act: when the

[49] *Tartarin de Tarascon* and Maupassant's *Bel-Ami* are compared by Alain Ruscio, for whom both denounce the colonies as 'des lieux malsains et amoraux'; he sees *Tartarin de Tarascon* in particular as a ferocious denunciation of the military regime, the colonists themselves, and colonial propaganda ('Littérature, Chansons et colonies', in *Culture coloniale: la France conquise par son Empire*, ed. by Pascal Blanchard and Sandrine Lemaire (Paris: Autrement, 2003), pp. 67–80 (p. 70)).

[50] Jared Hayes, *Queer Nations: Marginal Sexualities in the Maghreb* (Chicago: University of Chicago Press, 2000), p. 33.

[51] *Maupassant, Espaces*, p. 128, p. 129.

Moroccan 'affair' comes to a head and more copy is needed, Duroy simply recycles 'his' first article which, 'débaptisé, retapé et modifié, ferait admirablement l'affaire, d'un bout à l'autre' (402). This satirical exposition of the derivative origins of colonial discourse is complicated by the fact that Madeleine's journalism resembles Maupassant's own, and critics have long pointed out parallels between the arriviste Bel-ami/Georges Duroy and his creator.[52] Indeed, in his North African short stories, Maupassant sometimes follows the same formulae that he satirizes in *Bel-Ami*.[53] The ambivalence—and the lack of narratorial comment—are part of the lesson Maupassant had learnt from Flaubert. But when Duroy does attempt to write without the assistance of Madeleine's superior intelligence, his writer's block is the occasion for a list of farcical journalistic platitudes and clichés about Algiers, in free indirect discourse: 'Alger, cette antichambre de l'Afrique mystérieuse et profonde [...] les autruches, ces poules extravagantes, les gazelles, ces chèvres divines...'.[54] The paragraph of purple prose fizzles out when Duroy is reminded of another, more prosaic piece of writing: 'la note de sa blanchisseuse' (224).

As Gerald Prince argues, the choice of journalism as the first step in Duroy's conquest of Parisian society through his influence on women is not incidental. *Bel Ami* is in part about the novel's own definition as a serious new form, in opposition to journalism, which is akin to the literary novelist's 'ultimate enemy: narrative (and the novel based on narrative)'. Attacking journalism is, in other words, part of Maupassant's general rejection of adventure novels and idealist novels.[55] Nevertheless, one should not underestimate the frequency with which *Bel Ami*'s exposure of narrative pandering to readers' expectations takes as its focus France's military and economic imperialism. A more experienced journalist, 'Saint-Potin' writes an article ('Inde et Chine', 246)[56] supposedly based on interviews with a Chinese

[52] See notes by Louis Forestier in the Pléiade edition (*Romans*, p. 231), and Delaisement, *Maupassant journaliste et chroniqueur*, p. 126. Armand Lanoux, in *Maupassant, le 'Bel-Ami'* (Paris, Fayard: 1967), made the argument that Maupassant himself was the model for Duroy. If Duroy's journalism is in some respects (though without the vivid anti-war stance) like Maupassant's, the journal *La Vie française* is based in part on the journal *Gil Blas* in which Maupassant published his regular chronicles and in which *Bel-Ami* itself appeared in serial publication.

[53] Soubias emphasizes the stereotypes reiterated by Maupassant's African short stories, and sees Duroy as 'une sorte de duplication inconsciente, sous forme de personnage, du narrateur-voyageur, tel que nous le révèlent les nouvelles africaines' (pp. 37–8). On Maupassant's pandering to readers' expectations, particularly in the emphasis on Oriental women, see also Astier Loutfi. For an alternative, and much more positive, view of Maupassant's North African writings, see Henri Mitterand, *L'Illusion réaliste de Balzac à Aragon* (Paris: Presses Universitaires de France, 1994), pp. 173–82. In Maupassant's metropolitan stories, in any case, the colonies are a perfect pretext for manipulative fiction of all kinds: in 'Les Tombales' the protagonist falls for a prostitute's pickup line based on her claim to be an honest widow who lost her husband in Tonkin (II: 1238–45).

[54] This passage has, oddly enough, and despite the 'poules', been read as being in the voice of Maupassant himself, with no ironic framing; see Barrow, p. 317. Her apparent face-value acceptance of Duroy's failed attempt at writing journalism as Maupassant's own is all the more surprising since she goes on to show how the newspaper for which Duroy works, *La Vie française*, 'provides exactly the fantasy version of the Orient and its peoples demanded by its target audience' (p. 319).

[55] Gerald Prince, '*Bel-Ami* and Narrative as Antagonist', *French Forum*, 11:2 (1986), 217–26 (p. 220, p. 223).

[56] France had regained parts of its earlier colonial footholds in India in the form of trade-posts or *comptoirs* in 1816. There had also been renewed imperialist interest in China since the 1820s, which is when Balzac had his Charles Mignon engage in the opium trade: in 1844 France had demanded the

general and an Indian rajah who are visiting Paris, but he does not bother to conduct the interviews, since he knows better than these exotic dignitaries what readers of *La Vie française* want and expect them to say; he has already conducted hundreds of fictive interviews of the kind, and need only copy out his latest article word for word, being very careful to adjust the factual details of name, title, and age. The name of the newspaper itself suggests that it functions simply as a mirror of what the French know and expect, just as the journalist's own name, 'Saint-Potin', suggests mere gossip. Idle social chit-chat in Mme Walter's salon follows the same pattern: when the conversation turns to the 'question du Maroc et de la guerre en Orient' as well as British difficulties in South Africa, '[c]es dames discutaient ces choses de mémoire, comme si elles eussent récité une comédie mondaine et convenable, répétée bien souvent' (286); Mme Walter herself always has her opinion 'prête d'avance' (287). Maupassant repeatedly underlines that in order to enter into the seamless pattern of metropolitan life—*la vie française*—colonial events are reduced to the reiteration of expected truths, or the *vraisemblable*. In his novel the realities of imperialism, like those of adultery, are subject to a repeated process of disavowal.

In Chapter 3 we saw that in *Bel-Ami*, the great novel of false appearances, fraud was presented as the structuring principle that provides a tangible link between financial speculation in the capital and realities in the colonies. The new imbalance of power, colonial in fact if not yet always by name, allows narratives of distant lands, fabricated and repeated in the salons and newspapers of the French metropolis, to have a terribly real effect. But by the last third of the century exposure of the fraudulent *invention* of the colonies has become a central trope of the realist mode. This is Critical Orientalism: the denunciation, usually without direct narrative comment, through the presence of irony in indirect free discourse or reported speech, of the mindless repetition of Orientalist truisms.

NARRATIVE EMBEDDING AND GEOGRAPHICAL DISJUNCTION

The realist novel often employs a third-person narrator who is implicitly in possession of specialist knowledge (as seen in the use of technical jargon, for example). This might seem to jar with the recurrent emphasis on misreading and miswriting that we have seen, but it is in fact combined with it through the use of a double perspective: there is a focalizer who is misled (Emma, Tartarin) and a narrator who is implicitly or explicitly possessed of a more authoritative vision. Pushed a little further, this double focalization takes the form of a double narrative structure, that is, an outer or 'framing' narrative, and within it an embedded tale told

same commercial concessions earlier obtained by Britain (Treaty of Whampoa); France then fought alongside Britain in the Second Opium War (1856–60), which ended with the burning of the Chinese imperial Summer Palaces, legalization of the opium trade, and the forced establishment of international legations in Beijing.

by a secondary or diegetic narrator, a 'récit second'.[57] In the last part of this chapter I shall look at narrative embedding or framing that brings together metropolitan and colonial contexts.

Realist narrative embedding is often not of entire stories but of fragmentary conversations, for example where the characters position themselves competitively as possessors of specialist knowledge about the colonies.[58] At the other extreme, whole colonial narratives are framed, as in some of Maupassant's stories. The most common pattern is for the context of the narration (the framing story) to be in metropolitan France, while the events of the distant colony are part of a secondary, framed narrative.[59] In this case the experience of distant lands belongs to a space–time that is part of the fictional world, but excluded from direct representation within the main narrative.[60]

In the nineteenth century, the narrators of these exotic narratives are generally French, which helps to ground them firmly in the metropolitan experience that is familiar to readers: any exotic traits of the embedded narrative are literally framed and *au second degré*.[61] And yet embedded narratives seem at odds with the dominant realist mode: they call attention to their own status as fiction, and could be seen as either a return to an earlier (eighteenth-century) form, or as precursors of the 'revolution started by a return to first-person narrative' in modernism.[62] In fact since the eighteenth century Orientalism has had a privileged relationship with narrative framing because of the role of the *Arabian Nights*, and in particular Galland's translation (1704–17), as one of the Ur-texts of the modern Orientalist tradition.

In the cases looked at here the formal disjunction between two narrative levels underlines the contrast of geographical and cultural contexts. Indeed, narrative embedding is a means of bringing together the two different chronotopes that

---

[57] See Genette, *Figures II*, p. 202; also *Figures III*, pp. 238–9, and *Nouveau discours du récit*, (Paris: Seuil, 1983), pp. 55–64. He uses the terms 'diegetic' or 'intradiegetic' to refer to the events of the first narrative level, and 'metadiegetic' (some critics prefer 'extra-diegetic') to refer to the events of the embedded narrative. He also employs the term 'au second degré' to refer to this embedded narrative.

[58] These colonial conversations are striking, for example, in the 1869 *Éducation sentimentale* and in *Bel-Ami*.

[59] Maupassant offers some interesting exceptions, using a North African setting for the framing narrative and a metropolitan setting for his embedded story in 'Un soir' and 'L'Épingle'.

[60] These experiences are most often recounted by a diegetic narrator through analepsis (e.g. a character recounting an earlier colonial experience, as occurs at the end of Zola's *Fécondité* with the return of a son from Sudan); but they can also be proleptic (e.g. a character planning or daydreaming a future departure to the colonies), in which case they may look forward to experiences that do not in fact materialize (for example the 'Far West' fantasies discussed in Chapter 2).

[61] The narrators of Maupassant's North African tales are either French travellers or long-term colonists; a narrator of the first type (a tourist) sometimes gives way to a narrator of the second type (a colonist), so that the second narrator's perspective is effectively framed. See Soubias, pp. 35–6.

[62] Schehr, *Subversions*, p. 4. In her work on frames, Mary Ann Caws suggests that the use of ekphrasis or embedded literary genres offers a means to 'concentrate upon the entire question of framing itself' in a way that is 'inevitably self-referring; they may be seen to make a frame-up of the reader, as of their own textuality' (*Reading Frames in Modern Fiction* (Princeton, NJ: Princeton University Press, 1985), p. 26). Exotic ekphrasis, such as descriptions of Orientalist paintings, is another form of framed discourse that would merit separate study.

Bakhtin calls 'adventure-time' and 'everyday time'.[63] I shall argue here that this conjunction is far from being comfortable, and in so doing I position myself against a certain critical tradition that has tended to consider the use of narrative framing as having an inherently conservative effect. Sartre, notably, dismissed narrative frames as a reassuring device in which a brief past disorder is evoked simply to reassert the comfort of present stability. One imagines a worldly, knowing narrator telling a story to titillate his cigar-smoking friends.[64] Todorov, approaching narrative embedding from a more formalist and less political perspective, also sees it as a form of control, '[un] cas particulier de la subordination' in which embedded stories serve to advance the arguments, or the action, of the main narrative.[65]

These conceptions of the effect of narrative framing leave little space for the polyphony that arises out of the double narrative form. For Jameson, Sartre's view depends on seeing the form of the traditional novella or storytelling plot as 'closed', and neglects the disruptive potential of the frame. The Romantic/Balzacian revival of 'the Renaissance art-story or novella', he claims, 'already bears within itself formally the powers of the uncanny', because the duality of the form itself marks an unexpected return of the archaic. The uncanny tale is thus 'an interference or a contamination between two distinct cultural principles, which are structurally incompatible, but whose forced conjunction yields a text to be thought of less in terms of hybridization than of anamorphosis'.[66] The very brevity of the 'tale' arguably lends itself to irony, doubt, and ambivalence,[67] all the more so when it includes a narrative frame.

Of course, when the narrative frame does suggest a community of attitudes between the narrator and the implied reader it can be, as Tim Farrant puts it, 'perhaps the archetypally reassuring narrative form'.[68] An uneasy fit between the attitudes of the two narrators is however a common feature of framed stories, and there may also be a disjunction between the attitudes of the addressees—the implied reader

[63] The mixing of these two types is to be found in the 'adventure novel of everyday life', which focuses on the metamorphosis of a character through the course of travel (*Dialogic Imagination*, p. 111).

[64] Sartre, *Qu'est-ce que la littérature?* (Paris: Gallimard, 1948), pp. 142–6. Sartre claims that the effect of narrative framing is to give us a story that is 'déjà pensée, c'est-à-dire classée, ordonnée, émondée, clarifiée' (p. 143).

[65] Tzvetan Todorov, *Poétique de la prose, suivi de Nouvelles recherches sur le récit* (Paris: Seuil [1971], 1978), in particular the essay on 'Les hommes-récits: Les Mille et une nuits', p. 37, p. 40. Genette, more nuanced, distinguishes six different functions of the 'récit métadiégétique' (*Nouveau discours du récit*, pp. 62–3).

[66] *Ideologies of Theory*, p. 55, p. 57. The uncanny that appears in the fantastic tales of the 1830s has much in common with exotic narratives. The uncanny effect of the narrative frame is also suggested by Janet Beizer, in her study of Balzac's 'Une Passion dans le désert' (*Family Plots*, pp. 51–7, p. 82, p. 95).

[67] Seillan notes that the short tale form is in itself 'hostile à l'esprit du roman d'aventures tel que le pratique la fin du XIXe siècle: 'il répugne à adopter la dogmatique positiviste, à épouser le sérieux et la crainte de l'ambiguïté qui le caractérisent. Par essence le conte doute et fait douter. Perplexe, sceptique, il fait appel à l'intelligence critique du lecteur, l'invite à regarder l'envers des idées et des choses' (*Aux sources du roman colonial*, p. 189).

[68] *Balzac's Shorter Fictions*, p. 105; he goes on to emphasize that in some cases the frame serves to ask questions rather than answer them, p. 107.

of the overall narrative, and the diegetic audience of the embedded tale. Brooks emphasizes cases where the fictional audience is contaminated by an unwanted narrative act whose motivations—seduction, aggression, abjection, inability to free oneself from the speaker—are far from consensual and reassuring, and he gives the key example of Coleridge's 'Ancient Mariner'. Narrative embedding does not, Brooks argues, offer us a neat sense of closure, and by the late nineteenth and early twentieth century narrative framing is clearly used with the modernist implication 'that all stories are in a state of being retold, that there are no more primary narratives'.[69]

Critical disagreement over whether narrative framing is inherently conservative, or uncanny and destabilizing, acquires particular intensity in the case of postcolonial theory. Much debate has been inspired by what is perhaps the most famous example of narrative framing of a colonial tale, Joseph Conrad's *Heart of Darkness*, in which a nameless first-person narrator recounts the seafarer Marlow telling the story of his voyage upriver into inland Africa. Chinua Achebe famously attacked Conrad's novella on the grounds that the use of Africa as a metaphorical resource for literary purposes that are alien to it (evoking the break-up of one European mind) is Eurocentric and racist. Through the narrative framing, Conrad attempts to set up 'layers of insulation between himself and the moral universe of his story', but he fails to provide readers with 'an alternative frame of reference'.[70] An insightful overview of the critical debates that have followed Achebe's denunciation is given by Nicholas Harrison, who argues that we need to read *Heart of Darkness* in the historical context of its first publication, when the horrors of King Leopold's Congo were being exposed. He also comments more briefly on the effects of narrative framing, suggesting that Conrad's careful avoidance of the omniscient narrator, and deliberate emphasis on unreliability, is in fact a modernist way of eliminating a coherent 'frame of reference'.[71] Other postcolonial critics such as Chrisman have also argued that the frame story must be taken into account in our reading of *Heart of Darkness* and that it problematizes any straightforward allegorical reading.[72] Abdul R. JanMohamed, despite his own best efforts to read colonialist literature in terms of 'Manichean allegory', also sees Conrad's work as 'reflexive' in its 'rigorous examination of the "imaginary" mechanism of colonialist mentality'. He cites Conrad's use of the narrative frame as one of the ways in which his novella is set apart from colonialist literature.[73] It would appear that narrative framing can, like free indirect discourse, support the ironic purposes of Critical Orientalism.

[69] Brooks, *Reading for the Plot*, pp. 216–36, p. 256, p. 261.
[70] Chinua Achebe, 'An Image of Africa: Racism in Conrad's *Heart of Darkness*' [1977], reprinted in *Heart of Darkness*, Joseph Conrad, ed. by Robert Kimbrough (New York/London: W.W. Norton & Company, 1988), pp. 251–62 (p. 256).
[71] *Postcolonial Criticism*, pp. 22–61, in particular pp. 28–31. See also Nicholas Harrison, 'Who Needs an Idea of the Literary?' *Paragraph*, 28: 2 (2005), 1–17.
[72] 'Rethinking the Imperial Metropolis', p. 403, p. 405.
[73] 'The Economy of Manichean Allegory: The Function of Racial Difference in Colonialist Literature', in *'Race', Writing, and Difference*, ed. by Henry Louis Gates, Jr (Chicago, IL: University of Chicago Press, 1986 [1985]), pp. 78–106 (pp. 84–5, p. 89).

In the light of these debates over the effects of narrative framing, I shall now turn to some less well-studied examples taken from nineteenth-century French literature. There are many others that could have been studied here, notably several tales by Maupassant in which narrative framing brings together colonial and metropolitan contexts, but because of limited space I have chosen to concentrate on two very different examples, one by Balzac and one by Zola.

FRAMED NARRATIVES: BALZAC'S ANTI-TRAVEL TALE, THE *VOYAGE DE PARIS À JAVA*

Balzac frequently used narrative frames, often in a situation where several people are part of a conversation.[74] Farrant argues that he sought to reanimate 'the problematic relation between framed narrative, frame, and the real world' in his tales.[75] In the *Voyage de Paris à Java* (1832) the conventions of the narrative frame are deployed in a strikingly slippery way. Balzac's tale of a voyage to the Dutch colony of Java was written just as he was turning towards a more emphatically materialist approach, but it puts forward a cynical view of the mimetic claims of the travel narrative. At the very point where the Romantic and realist traditions join, we find irony undermining claims to portray the colonial/exotic real. The *Voyage* may seem peripheral to Balzac's vast *œuvre*, but it is in some ways a test case for Realism: like the fantastic short story which was such a fashionable genre at the time it was written, it tests the boundaries of materialism and verisimilitude.

At the outset of the *Voyage de Paris à Java*, there appears to be only one narrator, who tells the tale of his voyage to Java. Nothing signals the separation of frame and embedded story except a line of dots. But by the end of the narrative, when a further line of dots separates the framing story, we learn of the existence of a second 'je' who thanks 'ce voyageur' (whose name is given as 'M. Grand-B***n'), for the account of his travels.[76] Now the real Balzac, like the fictive 'je' of this last section, spent a short time with friends in Angoulême where he met a M. Grand-Besançon, 'commissaire aux poudres' who recounted his trip to Java. But the 'je' of the framed narrative (the metadiegetic narrator), who recounts his experiences with Javanese women and the mysterious, Romantic flora and fauna of that country, can be reduced neither to the travelling ordnance representative,[77] nor to the final 'je' who has heard the tale but has never been to Java. The truth-status of the tale remains ambiguous: while the outer narrator has definitely *not* been to Java, the inner

---

[74] 'Gobseck', of which the first version dates to 1830, only two years before the *Voyage de Paris à Java*, is the first in the series (see Citron, 'Introduction' to 'Gobseck' (II: 946)).

[75] *Balzac's Shorter Fictions*, pp. 133–5; p. 107. Schuerewegen emphasizes the role of this 'capacité de réflexivité' in Balzac's texts, and discusses his use of narrative frames (*Balzac contre Balzac*, pp. 12–13, p. 18).

[76] *Voyage de Paris à Java*, in *Œuvres diverses*, vol. 2, pp. 1141–71 (p. 1171). Further references, to this edition, will be given in parentheses.

[77] The real Grand-Besançon was probably travelling to negotiate deals on Javanese sulphur, a crucial ingredient in gunpowder.

(metadiegetic) narrator both has and has not been there.[78] An epigraphic quotation, probably invented, suggests what we are about to read is comprised of mere 'arabesques, qui commencent par une tête de femme et finissent en queue de crocodile' (*OD* II: 1141). This suggests not only the tale's progression from reptilian Javanese women to crocodiles but also its hybrid and slippery nature, ending *en queue de poisson*.[79]

However slippery it may be, Balzac's *Voyage* employs the realist mode by fore-grounding material necessities involved with travel, food, and everyday life. Balzac in fact plays on the referential ambiguity of his text in order to question the validity of scientific description and technical terminology. The tale's negative energy is partly derived from a rejection of what Colin Smethurst calls 'le voyage ency-clopédique': it parodies scientifically-minded travellers' claims to depict the real empirically.[80] In some sections Balzac both plagiarizes and mocks a written travel narrative by the botanist Samuel Perrottet that he used to supplement Grand-Besançon's oral account.[81] The narrator proposes to write up the story of his travels 'de manière à lui donner des teintes fabuleuses, afin d'être également lu par les savants, par les enfants, et cru par ceux qui croient tout ce qui est incroyable', and he expresses cynicism about the 'grands charlatans' who have claimed to bring back precise scientific knowledge of the world (*OD* II: 1144). The first obstacle to such scientific knowledge is language, and the narrator dwells ironically on the obscu-rity of scientific terminology used by travellers, rejecting the language of botany (*OD* II: 1145–6, 1161), and attacking the account of 'un naturaliste très distingué' who spent only a short period of time in Java and is thus much less well qualified to describe it than the metadiegetic narrator, who has lived there (if only in dream) much more fully (*OD* II: 1149). Indeed, he dwells on three aspects that are absent from Perrottet's account: the allure of Javanese women (Perrottet declares them

[78] Because of the blurring between the two narrators, the *Voyage* may provide the example sought by Genette of a text where the demarcation of embedded and primary narrative is silent or misleading (*Nouveau discours du récit*, p. 58). Perhaps one could even say that this is an example of the irony mixed with uncertainty that Barthes praised in Flaubert and found missing in Balzac (*S/Z*, p. 649). In the manuscript, however, a longer title resolved the ambivalence of the narrator: 'Le Voyage fait à l'Isle de Java en Xbre 1831 par M. de Balzac' (see *OD* II: 1141 n. 1).

[79] Schehr argues (albeit of a different Balzacian text) that 'Balzac makes detours in his narrative, or, more precisely, makes a move toward verisimilitude an impossibility because of the ways in which narrative works, fails, disrupts, teases, and seduces the narratee' (*Subversions*, p. 12). The slippage between possible identities for the 'je', in which neither definitive answer would be entirely adequate, could also be seen as a form of 'enallage', which Schehr sees as one of Balzac's challenges to verisimilitude, although there is no grammatical shift in this case (see pp. 11–30).

[80] Colin Smethurst, 'De Java à Kiew: Le moi du voyageur', *L'Année balzacienne* (2002), 269–78 (p. 270). Véronique Bui also explores the rejection of 'la scientificité, du vérisme, du réalisme' in her article 'D'Issoudun à Java ou l'Inde en Indre-et-Loire', in *Balzac voyageur: parcours, déplacements, mutations*, ed. by Nicole Mozet and Paul Petitier (Tours: Publications de l'Université François Rabelais, 2004) pp. 259–75.

[81] Samuel Perrottet, 'Souvenirs d'un voyage autour du monde. Île de Java', *Revue des Deux Mondes* (October–November 1830), 21–56. Perrottet visited Java during his 1819–21 voyage, so his account—and Balzac's tale—do not reflect any experience of the bloody 1825–30 Java War that pitted the Dutch East India Company against Javanese resistance. Balzac mentions checking, and modifying, Grand-Besançon's account of Java in a letter to Zulma Carraud on around the 25 November 1832 (*Correspondance*, vol. 2), pp. 177–8.

ugly[82]); the poison tree; and the Javanese song-bird or bengali, an object that defies scientific knowledge.[83] The outer narrator does admit that: 'il est possible d'avoir été plus réellement à Java que je n'y suis allé' (*OD* II: 1171). Even the metadiegetic narrator states, of the impossibly long hair given to him by his Javanese wife and brought back to Paris, 'moi-même, il y a des jours où je ne crois plus à ce cheveu; mais ce sont les jours où, pour moi, les cieux sont déserts !' (*OD* II: 1149). Like the mysterious objects so often left over, in fantastic short stories, as tantalizingly ambiguous proof of the reality of a dream, this frail single hair is the support for a hallucinatory reconciliation of empirical and subjective knowledge. Exotic Bovarysm in this case is fully welded with self-conscious Romantic irony, and what is implicit in Bovarysm is explicitly expressed: it is better to dream, and be deluded, than not to dream at all.

Mozet astutely calls Balzac's *Voyage* 'un bréviaire de l'anti-exotisme, avec le refus de tous les "Voyages en Orient" passés et à venir'.[84] This anti-exoticism—a form of Critical Orientalism—is a central element of the Romantic exotic writing of the 1830s. The *Voyage de Paris à Java* is in fact an *anti*-travel narrative, a deliberate attempt to undermine a newly prominent genre.[85] This helps to explain why the title itself is a phonetic echo of one of the founding texts of French Romantic travel writing, Chateaubriand's *Itinéraire de Paris à Jérusalem*.

The *Voyage*'s ironic assertion of the inner truth of subjective experience, and at the same time the difficulties of sustaining such a truth, should not be dismissed as irrelevant to Balzac's later work.[86] His Romantic irony leads directly to the later realist tendency to express epistemological doubt. Like *La Peau de chagrin*, *Voyage de Paris à Java* yokes together Orientalism and Realism in a deliberately uncomfortable partnership. This text, by the 'father' of Realism, written at a time (1831–2) when

---

[82] Perrottet, p. 47; he does however include anecdotes about murderous jealousy, pp. 50–2.

[83] The bengali bird of which he declares 'Moi seul l'ai compris, entendu' (*OD* II: 1151) was part of a code Balzac used to indicate his own genitals; the 'divin oiseau' lives by sucking the nectar of roses, and is faithful to one rose in particular: 'Il la baise, la suce, la piétine, lui chante ses plus douces roulades' (*OD* II: 1151). On the erotic side of Balzac's tale, see Mozet, 'Yvetot vaut Constantinople', p. 104; Bui, pp. 263–71; Beizer, *Family Plots*, 69–71. The bird is not mentioned in Perrottet's account.

[84] *Balzac au pluriel*, p. 109.

[85] The irony of Balzac's anti-travel narrative was typical of a certain kind of French travel writing in the 1830s, which Thompson argues had an increasingly playful, self-consciously satirical bent (see *French Romantic Travel Writing*, in particular p. 79 and pp. 90–128). Far from neglecting the question of the adequacy of writing to reflect the real, Thompson argues, Romantic travel writers kept reminding readers of the need to ask it (pp. 171–2). For discussion of Balzac's *Voyage* as an anti-travel narrative, see also Roland Le Huenen, 'Dans le sillage de Sterne et Nodier: le *Voyage de Paris à Java* de Balzac et l'écriture du supplément', in *Apprendre à porter sa vue au loin: Hommage à Michèle Duchet*, ed. by Sylviane Albertan-Coppola (Paris: ENS Éditions, 2009), pp. 311–29; and Aude Déruelle, '"L'Égypte, c'est tout sables": Balzac et le récit de voyage', in *Voyager en France au temps du romantisme: poétique, esthétique, idéologie*, ed. by Allain Guyot and Chantal Massot (Grenoble: ELLUG, 2003), pp. 325–41 (pp. 326–7).

[86] Citron ('Le Rêve asiatique de Balzac', pp. 303–5, pp. 313–23) argues for the importance of the *Voyage* as a sort of Ur-text foreshadowing many of the orientalist motifs of the *Comédie humaine*, but considers it to be a route abandoned shortly afterwards (p. 316). We have however seen that ironic exoticism is to be found elsewhere in Balzac, and an argument for re-centering the *Voyage de Paris à Java* within the Balzacian canon is made by Smethurst in 'De Java à Kiew'. Mozet sees the *Voyage*'s reliance on a chance earlier experience as a 'postulat non réaliste par excellence' that paradoxically constitutes 'le fondement du roman réaliste du XIXᵉ siècle' (*Balzac au pluriel*, p. 109).

he was on the cusp of producing his first great works, uses the theme of the voyage to reject objectivity, scientific precision, and observation. This is not an exceptional text that Balzac went on to dismiss in later life: rather, it shows us how the tradition of French exotic writing incorporates anti-exoticism and at the same time how emerging Realism incorporates a critique of scientific objectivity and the language of observation.

This strand of Romantic irony, self-consciously aware of the saturation of the field of literary production, is thus rich in Critical Orientalism. One finds a parallel phenomenon in Balzac's 1842 novella, *Un début dans la vie* (I: 717–887). While the *Voyage de Paris à Java* used ironic Romanticism in a polemic against 'scientific' Realism, *Un début dans la vie* frames Byronic Romantic micro-narratives within a realist narrative of sociological observation. Young people travelling in a small public coach tell tall tales of their exploits under invented names; these tales offer two variants on Byronic orientalist heroism, one military and heroic (including fortunes gained and lost, pirates, seraglios, Turkish *beys* whose homosexual passion for the narrator must be thwarted), the other romantic and self-deprecatory (a failed attempt at an affair with that essential Byronic figure, *la belle Grecque*, complete with jealous husband). These tales are a collection of orientalist clichés that take the weakening Ottoman empire as their backdrop; and they are framed by the banal context of the provincial coach. They are 'self-consciously parodic', as Heathcote puts it; they can be seen as a radical questioning of the act of representation itself.[87] The young men's boasts include an exquisite *idée reçue* that would surely have met with the approbation of Flaubert: 'L'Égypte, c'est tout sables' (I: 779). This literary-derived Orientalism-as-tall-tale is also a distorting mirror to the later military career of the youngest and most foolish of the tricksters, Oscar Husson, who goes on to lose an arm in the French defeat at La Macta in Algeria (I: 878). This brief interlude of colonial warfare is itself heroic and presented without irony; but its specific colonial grounding sets it up in ironic juxtaposition with the Turkish/Balkan Orientalism of the earlier Byronic model.[88] And at the end of the tale, the framing narrative neatly returns to the same characters, in another coach, years later.

In both the *Voyage de Paris à Java* and *Un début dans la vie*, Balzac sets up an ironic parallel between distant Oriental travel and banal provincial travel; in both, he uses Orientalist discourse polemically; but the nature of the polemic has shifted so that in 1842 the Romantic discourse that was celebrated—albeit

[87] Owen Heathcote, 'Verbal Hygiene for Oscar: The Expression and Containment of Violence in Balzac's *Un début dans la vie*', in *Confrontations: Politics and Aesthetics in Nineteenth-Century France*, ed. by Kathryn M. Grossman et al. (Amsterdam: Rodopi, 2001), pp. 107–30 (p. 123).

[88] Heathcote, in a slightly different reading, sees the fictional oriental narratives as preparing the reader for the real violence suffered by Oscar Husson ('Verbal Hygiene for Oscar', p. 113). Déruelle gives an interesting discussion of these embedded micro-narratives, citing as the orientalist sources that are being mocked Montesquieu and Volney ('L'Égypte, c'est tout sables', pp. 336–9), and reading them as part of Balzac's polemic against the genre of the travel narrative. The novella was based on an earlier short story by Balzac's sister Laure ('Le Voyage en coucou', reproduced in the Pléiade edition I: 1448–68), but where Laure uses Spain and Ariosto her brother substitutes Orientalism and Byron; the Algerian military episode is also his invention.

ironically—ten years earlier has become the target of the attack. This polemical use of framed discourse is to be found in other instances of narrative framing later in the century.

FRAMED NARRATIVES: THE PENAL COLONY AND ZOLA'S *VENTRE DE PARIS*

Balzac's tale is a commentary on Realism itself, written at the moment of the 1830s realist 'turn'. I shall turn now to look at the use of disjunction between a metropolitan outer narrative and a framed colonial tale in a much later novel that is definitely not an anti-roman, Zola's *Le Ventre de Paris* (1873). This emphatically Parisian novel centres on the market in Les Halles, and an opposition between *les gras* and *les maigres*, the new 'haves' and 'have-nots' of the Second Empire. Its chief focalizer is Florent, who returns after seven years in Cayenne,[89] having been deported after being accidentally involved in the resistance to Louis-Napoléon's *coup d'état* in December 1851.[90] A traumatized outsider in his own city, Florent's gaze on the new Paris of the Second Empire defamiliarizes it like that of Montesquieu's Persians.[91]

The colonial dimension of *Le Ventre de Paris* has often been neglected. Reading it as a novel about Paris, critics have been reluctant to accommodate the jarring effect of Florent's tale of his suffering in the Guyanese penal colony, recounted in the vast kitchen of his brother's Parisian charcuterie where the owners and their employees are preparing 'le boudin' for the year.[92] And yet Zola's preparatory notes show that the clash of the comfortable Parisian setting and the horrific distant story was, from very early in the writing process, fundamental to his conception of the novel. The dramatic juxtaposition of sausage-making and embedded narrative was originally intended to be a whole 'chapitre du boudin et de Cayenne'.[93] As Schehr points out, Devil's Island and Cayenne are 'signs of a colonial economy that

---

[89] In fact five years in the penal colony of L'île du Diable and two in mainland Dutch Guyana after his escape. The penal colony, established there in 1852, was referred to by shorthand as the *bagne de Cayenne*, although Cayenne is more properly the name of the capital of French Guyana.

[90] On the frame in *Le Ventre de Paris*, see Christopher Prendergast, 'Le Panorama, la peinture et la faim: Le Début du *Ventre de Paris*' (*Les Cahiers naturalistes*, 67 (1993), 65–71), though he does not deal with the embedded story itself.

[91] The comparison is made by Jameson, who compares Florent to the ideal reader of the Russian Formalists: a reader for whom everything is estranged (*Antinomies*, pp. 55–6).

[92] For example Borie, *Zola et les mythes*, pp. 162–3. Hamon mentions the 'bagne' briefly (*Personnel*, p. 233).

[93] In Zola's notes, the scene is climactic and long-awaited: 'Enfin la grande scène du boudin.' 'Puis enfin, la soirée pendant laquelle on fait le boudin.' In the very first plan, the third chapter is to be 'le chapitre du boudin et de Cayenne' (N.A.F. 10338 in *La Fabrique*, vol.1, fol. 19 (p. 682); fol. 22 (p. 686); fol. 83/37 (p. 758)). While Zola intended Lisa (as a synecdoche for the well-fed Second Empire) to be the focal point of the novel, the character of Florent and his experience of the penal colony provided a crucial contrast: 'Il me donne Cayenne, dans mon histoire de l'empire, et il me le donne de façon à opposer les souffrances atroces des proscrits, [au] à l'engraissement des [gens] bourgeois qui ont courbé la tête sous [l'emp] le coup d'état et qui en ont profité largement' (*La Fabrique*, vol.1, fol. 58/12 (p. 730); fol. 59/13 (p. 732)).

is far more extensive than the local economy that the text would have us believe is self-sufficient'.[94] The noun 'Cayenne' becomes a shorthand for all that is excluded from the comfortable world of the Second Empire.[95] Zola uses the geography of *colonial* imperialism to map out the exclusion and false claims to self-sufficiency that are the basis of the French Second Empire's *metropolitan* imperialism. And the tale Florent recounts is an essential part of the novel's dominant theme of digestion, with deportation to the penal colony itself being a process of expulsion and abjection. Absorbed into Paris's vast stomach, Florent is in the end excreted a second time as indigestible, a representative of that doomed species, *les maigres*.

The 'boudin' scene is one of Zola's triumphant set-pieces. He makes resounding rhetorical use of the disjunction between the embedded narrative and the situation of its utterance, exploiting to the full the technique of juxtaposition learnt from Flaubert. In the kitchen of the Parisian charcuterie the all-pervading fat and grease and the fresh blood are described in detail. The technical terms, and the process of the fabrication of blood sausage, are observed with the precision that enthrones the naturalist novelist as informed observer. The gas, the heat of the stove, and the fat shining in the kitchen take on the human qualities of their well-fed owners: 'tran-quille'; 'la chaleur [...] très douce'; 'un bien-être de digestion large' (I: 685). It is in markedly different language, however, that the child of the house, Pauline, asks her newly arrived uncle for 'l'histoire du monsieur qui a été mangé par les bêtes' which she associates with the pig's blood (I: 684; repeated 685, 688). This reiterated phrase, both childlike and Gothic in its horror, is a macabre inversion of the novel's focus on human eating. And the fairytale form that Florent gives his tale, addressed to his niece, exaggerates its air of unreality and lack of verisimilitude—in other words its departure from the naturalist mode.[96]

Zola insists on the contrast, but also the permeability of the two narrative levels, with frequent interruptions of Florent's tale. *Le Ventre de Paris* is rightly famous for calling on the reader's experience of sight and smell, and smells permeate from one narrative level to another: 'Ce ventre [de l'homme qui a été mangé par les bêtes], plein d'un grouillement de crabes, s'étalait étrangement au milieu de la cuisine, mêlait des odeurs suspectes aux parfums du lard et de l'oignon' (I: 689). The sensory experiences of the narrated tale and of the moment of narration overlap in an

---

[94] *Subversions*, p. 94. Still, in the absence of any discussion of the real human inhabitants of Guyana it is hard to see this as a deliberate focus on imperialism or (as Schehr does) slavery in itself.

[95] This synecdochical function is clear from the fact that the single word 'Cayenne' is used as a header for Zola's preparatory notes about Florent more generally (*La Fabrique*, vol.1, fol. 199 (p. 882)).

[96] Zola seems, in fact, to have taken his inspiration partly from melodramatic novels by Eugène Sue (*Les Aventures d'Hercule Hardi*, 1857) and Adolphe Belot and Ernest Daudet (*La Vénus de Gordes*, 1866), as well as authentic memoirs of the experience of political deportation, which were more freely available after the press liberalization of 1868. On the melodramatic sources and narrative choices of the Cayenne episode, see Geoff Woollen, 'Les transportés dans l'œuvre de Zola', *Les Cahiers natural-istes*, 72 (1998), 317–33. Dällenbach points out that Zola tends to deploy various other genres or subgenres (such as the fairytale) rather than focusing on the novel itself as a genre to be *mise en abyme*. He judges Zola's self-reflexivity to be heavy-handedly explicit (*Le Récit spéculaire*, p. 97, p. 64). This is undoubtedly true of the more self-reflexive elements in his writing, but he uses contrastive narrative embedding in an altogether more provocative way.

imperfect doubling that creates the sense of the uncanny. Thus the snakes and quicksand of the Guyanese jungle ('quelque boa [...] la queue roulée'; 'cette terre molle' and the hidden 'profondeurs de boue liquide', I: 691, 692) are a ghostly, sinister echo of the *boyau* or blood sausage that Florent's half-brother Quenu and his apprentice are in the process of 'enroul[er]' round a metal dish, filling it with '[une] bouillie [...] toute noire' so that it 'retombait ventru, avec des courbes molles' (I: 692). The new Paris threatens to swallow up Florent just as he was nearly swallowed by the mud of Guyana.[97] The parallels force the reader to live, in visceral terms, the nausea of abjection. The embedded tale in fact reverses the process of *political abjection* as it is played out by the novel as a whole—that is, the expulsion of the undesirable element, Florent himself—and makes us experience abjection at the blood and fat of the Parisian kitchen.

In her study of the scene, Mihaela Marin points out that the juxtaposition is also one of narration (the story of the 'homme mangé par les bêtes') and description (the process of making *boudin*). Strangely, however, she suggests that the effect is to tame any effects of horror or the fantastic because they are incorporated into the precise machine of realist description. The purpose of the story, she claims, is simply to give energy to the narrative and compensate for Zola's excessive use of description.[98] Her—otherwise lucid and useful—formalist reading effectively denies the political content of the juxtaposition. What I am suggesting instead is that Zola is asking the reader to make what Said calls a 'contrapuntal' reading (though one whose polemical intentions are directed at the chasm between the haves and have-nots of the Second Empire, rather than any specific awareness of colonized peoples).

Florent tells his tale in the third person, and his individual presence is progressively reduced to 'la voix', until it too expires: 'Elle mourut, dans un dernier frisson des lèvres' (I: 693). The diegetic narrative act fails: Florent's little niece falls asleep, his brother is too busy to listen, and he himself is so exhausted afterwards that he agrees to accept the pay of the government that imprisoned him. His well-fed sister-in-law Lisa dismisses his story as childishness. For her, having had to eat rotting, worm-ridden foodstuffs is dishonourable. She cannot bring herself to believe that people have ever spent three days without food, and eating one's fill is a prerequisite of honest respectability (I: 687; 690). Florent's oral attempt to deal with the experience of trauma and abjection is a failure. Later he begins to write a 'grand ouvrage sur Cayenne' (I: 732 and 811) but he never completes it. So the embedded story and its immediate frame show us Zola focusing on the limitations of narrative—at least, the limitations of both fairytale and non-fictional forms.

---

[97] On the parallel between the Guyanese 'marécages empestés' and the greasy mud of Paris, see David Baguley, 'Le supplice de Florent: à propos du *Ventre de Paris*', *Europe*, 468–9 (1968), p. 95. He also points out the parallels between Florent's near-death in the quicksand of Guyana and Jean Valjean's passage through the Parisian sewers, and discusses Hugo as a point of inspiration for *Le Ventre de Paris* more generally, pp. 91–6.

[98] Mihaela Marin, *Le Livre enterré: Zola et la hantise de l'archaïque* (Grenoble: ELLUG, 2007), pp. 142–4.

Nevertheless, Florent's framed Guyanese tale has a rather different effect if understood within Zola's novel itself. Telling of the penal colony in the Île du Diable, Florent interrupts his own story to cry 'Ces souffrances crieront vengeance un jour' (I: 687) which makes the sufferings themselves, rather than his weak and effaced self, an active subject emitting a call for political action against the foundational repression of the Second Empire. Moreover the embedding of Florent's failed narration is echoed by a much broader form of frame that is used to give structure to the entire novel: the novel begins with Florent's return from the penal colony, and ends with him deported once again, in 1858.[99] This very Parisian novel is thus framed by deportation to the ultimate space of State violence: what Foucault calls a heterotopia of deviation. State control relies on the existence of spaces in which to enclose individuals whose behaviour deviates from the required norm, and Foucault emphasizes the carefully controlled systems of opening and closing that isolate these spaces, just as Florent's apparently melodramatic escape narrative emphasizes the separateness and closure of the penal space.[100] Florent's inadequate narration of his experience in the penal colony also stands for a *repression* of the memory of State violence, which is relegated outside the metropolitan diegetic space. Zola's intended reader is however asked to be a better audience than the self-satisfied Lisa. His telling of the tale in 1873 is part of the process by which the new Third Republic forged its own identity, rewriting and rejecting the foundational violence of the Second Empire, but also evoking the bloody repression that had marked the end of the Commune in 1871.[101]

Zola's polemically political use of narrative embedding may seem rather distant from Balzac's *Voyage de Paris à Java*. In both cases, however, the use of the frame is profoundly dialogic in nature. It also displays a metatextual awareness that has an uneasy relationship with the mimetic function. This uneasiness is exploited by Zola when he contrasts Florent's childlike narrative style with the precise technical details of sausage-making, and by Balzac through his ironic deprecation of botanical empirical observation. In the *Voyage de Paris à Java* the blurring of identity between two possible narrators, and the resultant uncertainty concerning the status of the narrative as representation, is a rupture of the mimetic contract by which the reader tacitly expects the writer to provide a representation of the real. In its own way, the framed narrative of *Le Ventre de*

---

[99] Ironically Florent will not benefit from the 1859 general amnesty of political prisoners, since his second deportation is due to new accusations of plotting against the government.

[100] Foucault, 'Des espaces autres', p. 757, p. 760.

[101] One of Zola's models for the figure of Florent was the Republican Charles Delescluze, whose life also linked these two moments of violence since he was deported in the early years of the Second Empire but returned and was shot resisting the Versaillais in defence of the Paris Commune in 1871. Florent was originally to have been called Charles, and Zola borrowed many of the details of Florent's Guyanese experience from Delescluze's memoirs, although the portrait of Dutch Guyana is instead partly taken from Eugène Sue. In 'Jacques Damour', a short story published in 1883, Zola revisited the story of a deported man who returns to find himself excluded from Parisian life (the penal colony is situated in Nouméa in this case): Jacques is deported as a Communard in 1871, but his experience is almost identical with that of Florent. One of the sources for both *Thérèse Raquin* and 'Jacques Damour' was *La Vénus de Gordes*, whose plot finishes in the penal colony of Cayenne.

Paris also breaks this contract: Florent's tale is true, but it is *invraisemblable* in the context in which it is narrated. The disjunction between the tale and its frame threatens any naïvely realist relationship to the real.

CRITICAL ORIENTALISM AND SELF-CONSCIOUSNESS

Embedded narrative structures, like the use of literary parody and pastiche, call the reader's attention to the process of writing and reading. In some cases the use of double focalization does have a reassuring effect, reaffirming the shared superiority of reader and narrator. Nor should self-referentiality and irony be taken as amounting to anticolonial critique.[102] I have argued that we must acknowledge Realism's self-awareness, but this self-awareness is of an epistemological rather than a directly political nature. There is some criticism of the practice of colonialism, but little of colonialism in principle. If we take the example of Daudet, we saw that he includes fragments of a realist satire targeting the colonial administration of Algeria and its disastrous effects on the Arab population, but that this was not the main aim of the novel that he in fact wrote. The novel that he *wanted* to write might well have used some of the central techniques of Realism in the service of political *engagement*. But in practice the colonial plots and subplots we have seen, far from focusing on documentary accuracy, tend to emphasize the difficulty of reaching such objective truth-value. They are 'engaged' in a very different kind of polemic.

Through devices such as irony, self-referentiality, parody, and double focalization, these texts lead us to doubt the status of the foreign land as an object immediately accessible to comprehension and recuperation; they ask us instead to pay attention to the construction of the foreign, and to question the validity of our knowledge. They introduce a plurality of voices, and internal polemic within the novel; at times the demarcations between these voices are blurred, in what Barthes sees as one of the key measures of the plurality of the classic text.[103]

Now the realist mimesis of *life* would on the surface seem incompatible with parody, which imitates *texts*. As Baguley acknowledges, '[t]he impulse of realism is to disguise literary conventions, whereas the mainspring of parody is to expose them. [...] parody clearly undermines the mimetic conventions.'[104] Following Levin, however, he goes on to point out that the origins of realist literature are often in parody, and cites a 'target literature' that usually includes Lamartine, George Sand, Walter Scott, and *Paul et Virginie*—to which I would add *Robinson Crusoe*, Byron, and Hugo. Parody is in fact central to the realist aesthetic, and the targeted intertext is frequently Romantic or idealist writing, in which exoticism

---

[102] On a certain critical tendency to over-emphasize the oppositional aspect of modernist writing on these grounds, see Parry, *Postcolonial Studies*, p. 118.

[103] 'La meilleure façon d'imaginer le pluriel classique est alors d'écouter le texte comme un échange chatoyant de voix multiples, posées sur des ondes différentes et saisies par moments d'un *fading* brusque, dont la trouée permet à l'énonciation de migrer d'un point de vue à l'autre, sans prévenir.' Roland Barthes, *S/Z*, in *Œuvres complètes*, ed. by Éric Marty (Paris: Seuil, 1994), vol. 2, p. 582.

[104] *Naturalist Fiction*, p. 156.

often plays a part. Ironic, comic, or polemic effects arise from the conjunction of realist elements (such as observation of specific contemporary colonial realities) with textually derived exotic elements. Exoticism is thus part of a knowing strategy of hypertextual quotation. It shares some of the 'hyper-self-reflexivity' called for by postcolonial critics in response to the anxiety concerning the right to represent others, as expressed by Gayatri Spivak.[105]

We should not leap to the conclusion that all *realist* texts are self-aware, while *exotic* writing falls into the trap, denounced by Said, of mindless repetition of a pre-existing textual tradition. It is in fact not always clear which, of the exotic or realist text, is the hypertext and which the hypotext. Thus Balzac's *Voyage de Paris à Java* could be seen as an exotic text that parodies the realist approach of the botanist-traveller, while his *Peau de chagrin* could be seen as a realist text that incorporates an exotic one (the Skin itself being a text). This would be a misleading opposition. In fact both texts foreground the problematic nature of realist episte-mology, and do so by forcing incompatible literary modes into co-existence. Flaubert, too, parodies exotic writings in his metropolitan fiction, but in *Salammbô* itself he foregrounds realist devices the better to frame and undermine them.[106] Parody, and other forms of knowing hypertextuality, are central to many exotic texts themselves.

Moreover, the oppositional stance at the heart of Realism's identity—its debunk-ing of Romanticism and idealism—does not cancel out the dualism that is inher-ent in Bovarysm. Delusion there is; but it may be inevitable, and it remains alluring. And the delusions of Bovarysm might still be in line with some lingering, Romantic, hidden 'truth'. As Balzac writes in the *Voyage*, 'si je mens, c'est de la meilleure foi du monde' (*OD* II: 1151). The inner truth resides in subjectivity itself. That is why Emma Bovary's most excessive exotic daydreams are couched in Flaubert's most lyrical prose. The realist narrative paradoxically reveals the (Romantic) truth by pointing it out to us and simultaneously telling us that it is a lie. A key element of realist aesthetics is, then, the attention we bring to bear on falsity itself.

This double play, needless to say, takes us very far from the kind of documentary 'truth value' in terms of which, in the period immediately following decoloniza-tion, so many critics evaluated colonial literature. Later, it is Realism itself that bears the brunt of attack: even as subtle a postcolonial critic as Bhabha, who argues that we need to take into account the ironic awareness of the 'repression of discontinuity and difference' that might otherwise mar the 'construction of "sense"', nevertheless equates this construction of 'sense' with the 'discourses of historicism and realism [that] manifestly deny their own material and historical construction'. Strangely, Bhabha gives the example of *A House for Mr Biswas* as moving beyond Realism because of Mr Biswas's fantasies, which are signs of subversion 'unparalleled'

---

[105] Ilan Kapoor, 'Hyper-Self-Reflexive Development? Spivak on Representing the Third World', *Third World Quarterly*, 25:4 (2004), 627–47 (p. 628, and p. 641), commenting on Spivak's ground-breaking essay of 1988, 'Can the subaltern speak?'.

[106] On *Salammbô* as using Realism in order to undermine it, see my chapter on *Salammbô* in *Exotic Subversions in Nineteenth-Century French Fiction* (Oxford: MHRA Legenda, 2008), pp. 63–82.

in the realist tradition.[107] Yet as we have seen, fantasies and their incompatibility with the real are a foundation-stone of nineteenth-century Realism.

French realist literature situates itself in opposition to Romantic Orientalism or adventure stories, plays on the dualism of Exotic Bovarysm, and uses narrative embedding to create disjunction and unease. It unpicks notions of direct access to a transcendent exotic 'Elsewhere'. Yet at the same time, it frequently seems reluctant to take as its referent a non-textually mediated colonial 'real'. Instead, it dwells precisely on the *splitting* in our perception, the discrepancy between the mundane 'real' and the textually derived tradition through which we perceive the wider world. These texts raise an epistemological problem in relation to the new spaces that were being opened up to Western knowledge and control. They expend so much energy denouncing our textual approaches to the non-Western world that we are left in doubt concerning just what a well-founded account would be. In doing this they pre-empt, in very interesting ways, Edward Said's 1978 thesis concerning the textually derivative nature of Orientalism as a discourse. The degree to which they suggest that a more authentic view of other peoples and cultures would be possible, were one only to shed one's misleading discursive framework, varies from one writer to another. But then this ambivalence is familiar to readers of Said himself: he was at some pains to avoid denying the possibility of a valid discourse about Islam or the Middle East, but did not really offer a vision of how to establish it.

Alongside first-degree Saidian Orientalism (the Western construction of the Orient through a textually mediated set of preconceived ideas and reductive binary oppositions) one must therefore place what I have called Critical Orientalism: a discourse on the Orient that foregrounds a critique of its own modes of under-standing. Said himself does not leave space for such a critique within the inherited and endlessly repeating discourse of Orientalism. As Graham Huggan puts it, his idea of Orientalism sees it as a system of representation that 'allowed the Orient to be regularly rewritten, but that effectively prevented it from being critical reread'.[108] Yet, as we have seen, certain aspects of the nineteenth-century Realist treatment of exoticism in effect foreshadow Said's own critical stance. Oppositionality is not situated only in the work of the cultural critic who can read texts against them-selves to establish counter-narratives, but is also deployed as a tool of discursive critique within literary texts themselves.

---

[107] Homi K. Bhabha, 'Representation and the colonial text: A Critical Exploration of Some Forms of Mimeticism', in *The Theory of Reading*, ed. by Frank Gloversmith (Totowa, NJ: Barnes and Noble, 1984), pp. 93–122 (p. 97; and pp. 117–18 for the reference to *A House for Mr Biswas* (V.S. Naipaul, 1961)).
[108] Graham Huggan, '(Not)Reading *Orientalism*', *Research in African Literatures*, 36:3 (2005), 124–36 (p. 127).

5

The Black Maid and Her Mistress

This chapter and the next turn away from representations of colonial space and objects, and focus instead on race or the racialization of difference.[1] Here too, it is necessary to question any neat separation of colonies and metropolis into discrete discursive zones, since the racialization of discourse applies a colonial attitude to France itself. The present chapter will also allow us to approach a figure that was gaining in importance by the end of the nineteenth century, and which is of particular relevance to us today: the immigrant.[2]

The metropolitan novel's central themes, as we have already seen, are linked to the broader geopolitical context by apparently minor details functioning as metonymy. The details examined in this chapter are associated with a central female character, but it is no longer a question of ornament and accessories, as in Chapter 1. Here I turn to a secondary character standing in close proximity to the protagonist: the shadowy figure of the maidservant, and more specifically the *black* maid. We are given little, or none, of her perspective and individual story, but her presence itself is far from neutral.

Bringing into focus the secondary figure of the black maidservant draws her out from her place in the shadows of the background. By removing the central figure from Manet's *Olympia*, the artwork that figures on the cover of this volume, *Untitled (after Manet's 'Olympia')* by Australian artist Julie Rrap (2002), causes a radical shift in our gaze. It renews our 'reading' of a painting that is otherwise in danger of suffering from its own iconic status, by forcing us to acknowledge the presence of the black woman and to question her relation to the empty space left by the white one. We shall turn anew to Manet's painting and, looking at it as a whole, observe the relationship between the secondary figure and the courtesan: the black maid and her mistress. In painting, as well as in realist prose, metonymy plays a crucial role in linking the metropolis to the wider world.

The chambermaid has a symbolic relation of great intimacy with her mistress. According to one study of Parisian nineteenth-century domesticity, they form a

---

[1] A much earlier version of part of Chapter 5 was given as a keynote paper at the Cambridge French Graduate Conference in 2008, with a shorter section published as 'The Black Maid and her Mistress in Manet and Zola', in *The Monstrous and The Beautiful: Essays in French Literature*, ed. by Amaleena Damlé and Aurélie L'Hostis (Bern: Peter Lang, 2010), pp. 167–80.

[2] The role of immigration in France in the last decades of the nineteenth century is often underestimated. By 1886 there were already one million immigrants (mostly of European origin) in France, which was at the time one of the countries with the highest rate of net immigration, along with Argentina, the USA and Australia. See Don Dignan, 'Europe's Melting Pot: A Century of Large-Scale Immigration into France', *Ethnic and Racial Studies*, 4:2 (1981), 137–52 (p. 138).

'couple' in which '[l]a femme de chambre est une partie de la personne même de sa maîtresse'.[3] This suggests that the maid is a *synecdoche* of her mistress (that their relationship is one of the part to the whole). But in this example, once again, I find the notion of metonymy more convincing, and more analytically productive, than that of synecdoche. Indeed, at times the maid stands metonymically in lieu of synecdoche, that is, she functions as a way of exteriorizing certain parts of her mistress. Metonymy, with its basis in contiguity, allows sufficient flexibility to distinguish more than one form of relationship. In this case two types of metonymy come into play: *descriptive* metonymy, in which a contiguous object stands for the main one by a relationship of suggested similarity, almost like metaphor; and *contrastive* metonymy, in which a contiguous object stands in a relationship of antithesis to the central one. These two types of metonymy sometimes operate simultaneously. Thus the black maid stands for her mistress's exotic side by descriptive metonymy, and in opposition to her mistress's whiteness by contrastive metonymy. The distinction between these tropes is made explicit in a note Zola wrote on his own technique: 'Peu de personnages: deux, trois figures principales, profondément creusées, puis deux, trois figures secondaires se rattachant le plus possible aux héros, *servant de compléments ou de repoussoirs.*'[4]

The existence of these two distinct metonymic functions is generally neglected in discussions of the role of the maidservant in fiction. One reason for this is that studies of the literary maid have focused on works in which she is the protagonist,[5] or have looked at secondary characters in their own right as if they existed independently.[6] Yet the literary maidservant appears more often as a secondary character than as a prime mover in her own right. And the *black* maidservant, triply relegated to the position of inferior—by her sex, by her race, and by her class—appears, in the nineteenth-century French novel, only in such secondary roles. Black servants in the novel have in fact been largely neglected, a critical oversight that is surprising given the work done by art historians on similar secondary characters appearing in paintings. Even Hoffmann, although he points out the frequent occurrence of (mostly male) black servants in nineteenth-century novels, dismisses it as mere nostalgia for the picturesque opulence of the *ancien régime*: 'Tout cela ne tire guère à conséquence.'[7] Nostalgia, however, is only part of the story.

Black or white, the maidservant in nineteenth-century fiction represents the disturbing meeting point of bourgeois pretention with dirt and sexuality. The new

---

[3] Anne Martin-Fugier, *La Place des bonnes: la domesticité féminine à Paris en 1900* (Paris: Grasset, 1979), p. 219.

[4] 'Notes générales sur la nature de l'œuvre', in *Les Rougon-Macquart*, V: 1742–45, p. 1744, my emphasis.

[5] Susan Yates, *Maid and Mistress: Feminine Solidarity and Class Difference in Five Nineteenth-Century French Texts* (Bern: Peter Lang, 1991); Martine Gantrel, 'Homeless Women: Maidservants in Fiction', in *Home and its Dislocations in Nineteenth-Century France*, ed. by Suzanne Nash (New York: State University of New York Press, 1993), pp. 247–64.

[6] Raymond Lebègue, 'Notes sur le personnage de la servante', *Revue d'histoire littéraire de la France*, 83:1 (1983), 3–14.

[7] *Le Nègre romantique*, p. 223.

urban concentration of population is associated with excremental imagery, and the point at which this filth enters the bourgeoisie is the servant, particularly the maid-servant, purveyor of dirt and sexual debauchery. As Susan Yates puts it, 'Dealing with the waste matter of daily life, the maid is identified with all that is filthy and shameful in the household, and, thanks to the association that is made between dirt and sex, she is identified particularly with illicit sexuality.' The maid is a *souillon*, that is a slattern, but she is also *souillée* or soiled.[8] As the embodiment of filth and sexuality she reminds her masters of that which cannot be entirely eradicated. Julia Kristeva's concept of the abject builds on the idea of 'souillure' as the trace of a partial object that is (imperfectly) expelled by our own body. Anne McClintock applies this Kristevan idea of the abject to 'abject peoples [...] those whom indus-trial imperialism rejects but cannot do without', among whom she includes the domestic servant.[9] In the nineteenth century blackness, too, is frequently por-trayed in terms of abjection, following the ancient stereotypes that associate African origins with excessive sexuality, and darkness with dirt.[10] Such stereotypes coexist with another—more positive, though equally reductive—which is that of the black servant as a shorthand for blind and absolute devotion. Christemio in *La Fille aux yeux d'or* is one such figure, but the supreme incarnation of the faithful black serv-ant is Harriet Beecher Stowe's Uncle Tom (1852), a nineteenth-century adaptation of the 'bon sauvage' inherited from eighteenth-century philosophy.[11] However, as Hayden White has pointed out, the idea of the Noble Savage was frequently 'used not to dignify the native, but rather to undermine the idea of nobility itself'.[12] And the nineteenth-century black maidservant is indeed a latter-day Noble Savage who, unlike the faithful Tom, has a subversive function: she acts metonymically to undermine not nobility, but the obsession of the new century, her mistress's sexual purity.

It would, however, be a gross simplification to see the appearance of immigrant servants in the literature and art of the period *only* in terms of mythic abjection. The black servant is also part of the new urban poor, who are as strange to their bourgeois masters, and in many ways as frightening, as the natives of the New World. However sketchy she is as a character, one must ask to what extent the lit-erary black maid is situated not only within myth (the stereotype that links Africa with sexuality, or dark skin with dirt) but also within history. Immigrants of African origin lived within French society in the nineteenth century, and although

    [8] Yates, pp. 74–6. Emily Apter also emphasizes the association of maids' bodies with dirt and disease (*Feminizing the Fetish: Psychoanalysis and Narrative Obsession in Turn-of-the-Century France* (Ithaca, NY: Cornell University Press, 1991), p. 190).
    [9] *Imperial Leather*, p. 72. See Kristeva, *Pouvoirs de l'horreur*, p. 88. On 'souillure', see also Martin-Fugier, pp. 193–8.
    [10] The association of African origins with excessive sexuality is explored by critics as varied as Léon-François Hoffmann and Sander L. Gilman.
    [11] See Hoffmann, *Nègre romantique*, p. 138, p. 207; Léon Fanoudh-Siefer, *Le Mythe du nègre et de l'Afrique noire dans la littérature française de 1800 à la 2e Guerre Mondiale* (Paris: Klincksieck, 1968), p. 44.
    [12] Hayden White, 'The Noble Savage Theme as Fetish', in *First Images of America: The Impact of the New World on the Old*, ed. by Fredi Chiappelli, 2 vols (Berkeley, CA: University of California Press, 1976), vol. 1, pp. 121–35 (p. 129, p. 130).

their literary footprint, like their real numbers, was as yet very small indeed, they were part of the modern urban landscape. The shadowy figure of this minor character contains in embryonic form some of the 'transnational histories of migrants, the colonized, or political refugees' that Bhabha sees as the terrain of world literature.[13] The coexistence of mythic and historicizing portrayals is negotiated very differently in the works I shall look at here. I shall begin by looking at Manet's *Olympia* (1863), which has attracted considerable critical attention, then turn to a much more neglected black maid in Zola's *Son Excellence Eugène Rougon* (1876), and finally compare both with Flaubert's treatment of the black maid in the second *Éducation sentimentale* (1869).

MANET'S *OLYMPIA*: INTERPRETING THE BLACK MAIDSERVANT

Manet's *Olympia* (1863) has long been seen as a keystone of emerging modernism, partly because of its uncompromisingly painterly style, and partly because of its transformation of the traditional figure of the reclining naked woman-as-classical-goddess into a confrontational image in which a recognizably contemporary woman gazes back out at the spectator. The background figure of the black maidservant was remarked on immediately by the overwhelmingly hostile, mocking critical responses to the painting when it was exhibited in the 1865 Salon. She was then long relegated to relative invisibility by a critical tradition that emphasized formal traits such as the painting's visible brushstrokes and the use of blocks of contrasting colour and tone—traits that were antithetical to the academic painting tradition. In 1976, however, Theodore Reff's monograph devoted to the painting emphasized the connotations of the black woman (and the black cat) for contemporary viewers: the 'Negress' made explicit what was 'already implied' in the role of the courtesan, connoting 'a primitive or exotic sensuality'.[14] Visual responses by other artists (including Picasso and the Pop artist Larry Rivers[15]) had already refocused the painting with the black maid at its centre, and in the following decades gender studies criticism continued to ask questions about her role. In 1985 Sander L. Gilman saw Olympia's black maidservant as a continuation of the earlier iconographic tradition in which the black servant's central function was 'to sexualize the society in which he or she is found'. By the nineteenth century, Gilman also claimed, the black woman had come to stand not only for sexuality, but for 'the female as the source of corruption and disease', and *Olympia* includes a 'black female as the emblem of illness', revealing 'Manet's debt to the pathological model

---

[13] According to Bhabha, the subject of a true world literature is neither the 'sovereignty' of national cultures, nor the universalism of human culture: it should show us 'freak social and cultural displacements' in 'unhomely' fictions (*Location of Culture*, p. 12).

[14] Theodore Reff, *Manet: Olympia* (London: Penguin, 1976), pp. 92–3.

[15] Picasso, *Parody of* Olympia (1901) and Larry Rivers, *I like Olympia in Blackface* (1970). See Reff, *Manet: Olympia*, p. 37, pp. 40–1.

of sexuality present during the late nineteenth century'.[16] I began by evoking the theme of dirt and its links to dangerous sexuality, and I shall return to them. We shall see, however, that in comparison with other uses of the black maidservant, such as Zola's, it would in fact be reductive to read the maid in *Olympia* as simply standing for disease.

A decade after Gilman, Charles Bernheimer follows some of Reff's arguments, and argues against T.J. Clark's influential study of *Olympia* in *The Painting of Modern Life*, which emphasized class issues. For Bernheimer, *Olympia* portrays the dangers of female sexuality rather than class.[17] He interprets Manet's black maid as a fetish, part of a series of displacements that figure Olympia's sexuality. The courtesan's genital area is covered only by one firmly placed hand that is, in Bernheimer's terms, the agent of a repression that is not entirely successful. Bernheimer's Freudian analysis suggests that the multiplication of penis symbols signifies castration, and that substitutes for Olympia's missing phallus are to be found everywhere, from the flowers to the black cat, whose erect tail was emphasized in contemporary satirical sketches.[18] The slippage from 'chatte' to 'chat' is the kind of visual-verbal pun, associated with animals, that Manet liked to include in the details of his paintings.[19] Along the same lines, a more recent 'queer black feminist reading' of *Olympia* by Jennifer DeVere Brody also sees the cat as 'an index of what we must/must not see', standing for 'what lies underneath Olympia's hand'.[20] The black cat was also seen by contemporary viewers as a parallel with the black maid, who can similarly be understood as a displacement of her mistress's sexuality: her darkness, like that of the cat, replaces Olympia's missing pubic hair. Both Gilman and Bernheimer read the black maidservant as serving to arouse the viewer's 'fantasy of a dark, threatening, anomalous sexuality lurking just underneath Olympia's hand'.[21] But Ali Behdad is astute in criticizing Gilman's analysis, which he otherwise admires, for its occlusion of the political in favour of the psychological.[22]

A renewal of Clark's political/historical reading of *Olympia* was undertaken by Griselda Pollock in 1999. Pollock foregrounds Manet's attempt to situate the black woman in contemporary urban life, in other words his portrayal of her as the product of history rather than physiology. Despite the threatening sexuality she potentially embodies, Olympia's black maidservant is also depicted in terms of the particular and contemporary, rather than in the absolute of tonal or racial difference. This is dramatically apparent when one contrasts Manet's painting with the

---

[16] Sander L. Gilman, 'Black Bodies, White Bodies: Toward an Iconography of Female Sexuality in Late Nineteenth-Century Art, Medicine, and Literature', in *Race, Writing, Difference*, ed. by Henry Louis Gates (Chicago, IL: University of Chicago Press, 1985), pp. 223–61 (p. 228, pp. 250–1).

[17] Bernheimer, *Figures of Ill Repute*, pp. 110–12; T.J. Clark, *The Painting of Modern Life: Paris in the Art of Manet and his Followers* (London: Thames and Hudson, 1984).

[18] Bernheimer, pp. 118–20.

[19] On these puns in 'Le Déjeuner sur l'herbe', see Alan Krell, *Manet and the Painters of Everyday Life* (London: Thames and Hudson, 1996), p. 34. On the black cat and Zola's use of it in *Thérèse Raquin*, see Robert Lethbridge, 'Zola, Manet and *Thérèse Raquin*', *French Studies*, 34:3 (1980), 278–99 (pp. 289–92).

[20] Jennifer DeVere Brody, 'Black Cat Fever: Manifestations of Manet's *Olympia*', *Theatre Journal*, 53 (2001) 95–118 (p. 107).

[21] Bernheimer, p. 123.   [22] *Belated Travelers*, p. 9.

Orientalist paintings that in the following decades repeatedly portrayed a white odalisque with her black slave, such as Jean-Léon Gérôme's two famous paintings of the *Bain maure* (1870 and *c.*1880–5), or Édouard Débat-Ponson's *Le Massage* (1883). Despite the surface 'Realism' of such paintings, with their close attention to detail and observation of the play of light on different surfaces, they portray a remote, unchanging world without history.[23] Where the white odalisques of Orientalist paintings are passive and limp, seen from behind or at an angle so that their bodies are full stage while their faces are turned away, Olympia's gaze is infamously direct. And where the Orientalist paintings clothe the black slave in little but an exuberantly exotic madras, the black maidservant of Manet's painting wears a discreet headscarf along with a contemporary, everyday dress.[24] Manet's maidservant is also shown gazing at her mistress: politely self-possessed, she is implicitly interrogative, waiting for a response to the bouquet of flowers that she bears: this is very much the portrait of a servant, not a slave. In 1862 Manet had also painted a separate portrait of the woman who modelled for the maid.[25] Both portrayals are lively and individualistic, far from caricature, and it is hard to follow Clark in seeing Olympia's black maid as 'inert and formulaic, a mere painted sign for Woman in one of her states', in this case the state of 'compliance'.[26] Pollock traces the model for the maid to a woman named Laure, who appears to have been registered as an orphan *in Paris* in 1839. Her metropolitan identity, evident in the everyday clothing and context in which she is situated by Manet, suggests that he is attempting a 'de-Orientalising and anti-Africanist project', working to 'disturb both the Orientalist fantasy and the Africanist discourse in which women such as Laure were typically reconfigured in Western painting'.[27] Pollock argues that class and sexuality are inseparable in this painting. For her, *both* the women in *Olympia* are seen as belonging to the contemporary urban proletariat, and Manet rejects Orientalism, locating racial difference within time, space, and class. His black woman is no absolute other, but an immigrant in a modern urban world. Given the bathetically everyday setting and clothes, the idea that the black maid simply brings to *Olympia* 'an otherness, an exoticism, a sexual freight'[28] does not do justice to Manet's Realism.

Everyday contextualization of the immigrant begins to situate her within history rather than in an essentialist view of her 'racial' nature; it normalizes her presence as part of an ironic deflation of Romantic exoticism. Something similar is at work in the 'négresse, amaigrie et phtisique' of the famous poem 'Le Cygne' (1861) by Manet's friend Baudelaire, which is nearly contemporary with *Olympia*. Although

---

[23] See Nochlin, *Politics of Vision*, pp. 35–7.

[24] On the function of the modest and understated 'bandanna' as part of the de-Orientalizing stance of the painting, see Pollock, p. 285 and p. 294.

[25] The portrait is known as *La Négresse* (Pinacoteca Giovanni e Marella Agnelli, Turin, 1862). See Stéphane Guégan, 'Le moment Baudelaire', in *Manet, inventeur du moderne* (Paris: Gallimard/Musée d'Orsay, 2011), pp. 135–57 (p. 138 n. 25, p. 156); and Reff, *Manet: Olympia*, pp. 93–4.

[26] *The Painting of Modern Life*, p. 133.   [27] Pollock, p. 277, p. 257.

[28] Pollock, p. 255.

it draws on a recognizable Romantic topos of nostalgia in exile,[29] the poem also gives a fleeting suggestion of historical context and weight to the figure of the African immigrant among the urban poor of Paris's changing cityscape. Later, Maupassant's short story 'Boitelle' (1889) also normalizes the presence of the immigrant, by pointing an ironic figure at the French *response* to racial difference, rather than focusing on difference itself.[30] The racism of the Norman peasants is 'quoted' or framed by the story, in a gesture reminiscent of Flaubert's collection of *idées reçues*.[31]

The critical emphasis on stark tonal contrast of black and white in *Olympia*—which owes a lot to Zola's influential response to the painting—is not entirely incompatible with a more political reading. Brody suggests the black maid 'grounds the figure of whiteness' so that the contrast of white and black is not simply formal but also political. The black maid is the 'vehicle needed for the (re)productive performance of "white" sexuality' and serves to make the white figure whiter.[32] Along similar lines, the performance artist and cultural critic Lorraine O'Grady sees the black maid as 'the chaos that must be excised' so that the Western construction of the female body may be stabilized and the femininity of the white female body ensured.[33] Both these critics see the black and white figures in terms of contrastive metonymy, and—despite their political agendas—are indebted to formalist readings of the painting as binary, contrasting tones. It seems that Manet himself, however, was thinking in terms of descriptive rather than contrastive metonymy, since he included in the Salon catalogue entry for the painting a stanza taken from Zacharie Astruc's poem, 'La Fille des Îles', which emphasizes the 'creolity' reflected onto the reclining nude by the presence of the black servant.[34] The poem, influenced by Baudelaire, combines a newly urban, modern context with (largely imaginary) tropical erotic languor. And as Brody acknowledges, it 'suggests a

---

[29] Christopher Miller's reading of the poem, though admiring its 'profoundly sympathetic role for the black', emphasizes its belatedness and its view of Africa as synonymous with absence, rather than seeing Baudelaire's 'négresse' as a figure of the immigrant (*Blank Darkness*, pp. 127–36).

[30] For a reading of 'Boitelle' as anti-racist, and some interesting parallels with Baudelaire, see Daniel F. Ferreras, 'Amour noir et mort blanche: "Boitelle" de Maupassant, ou le naturalisme contre le racisme', *Excavatio*, 8 (1996), 185–93.

[31] The parallel with Flaubert is underlined by Maupassant's humorous, but tender, homage to his mentor (dead nine years earlier): 'Boitelle' includes a whole paragraph devoted to a lyrical description of parrots (II: 1087), and the protagonist's home village is near Yvetot (II: 1089).

[32] Brody, p. 100, pp. 104–5.

[33] Lorraine O'Grady, 'Olympia's Maid: Reclaiming Black Female Subjectivity' [1992], in *The Feminism and Visual Culture Reader*, ed. by Amelia Jones (London: Routledge, 2003), pp. 174–87 (p. 175).

[34] The lines of the poem that concern the maidservant are: 'Le printemps entre au bras du doux messager noir; / C'est l'esclave à la nuit amoureuse pareille'. On the poem, the stanza, and its relation to the painting, see E.D. Lilley, 'Two Notes on Manet', *The Burlington Magazine*, 132 (1990), 266–9. Manet had himself seen slavery first-hand during his trip to Brazil in 1848–9 as a youth. His letters home recount his disgust: 'j'ai vu un marché d'esclaves, c'est un spectacle assez révoltant pour nous'. He notes that the 'négresses', mostly naked to the waist, take great care of their appearance, some wearing turbans, and that the 'Brésiliennes' go out 'suivies de leur négresse'. Édouard Manet, *Lettres de jeunesse, 1848–1849. Voyage à Rio* (Paris: Louis Rouart, 1928), pp. 52–3. Brody sees this as 'one of the painting's preposterous precedents' (pp. 105–6).

correspondence between the female figures'.[35] Indeed, many (shocked or mocking) contemporary reactions tended to see the white courtesan Olympia herself as dirty (her body is compared to a corpse; her feet are said to need washing), and she was described in racist terms explicitly associated with Africa by contemporary critics who called her 'that Hottentot Venus, with a black cat', or 'a sort of female gorilla, a grotesque in India rubber outlined in black' and 'a sort of monkey'.[36] This suggests that the presence of the black woman does not function only as a *contrastive* metonymy but rather, and perhaps more immediately, as a *descriptive* metonymy. The white courtesan is *less* white, not *more* so, because of the proximity of her maidservant.

MANET AND ZOLA

Following the scandal provoked by *Olympia* in 1865, Manet's submissions to the Salon of 1866 were rejected, and Zola, then a young journalist with a nose for publicity, spearheaded a campaign in his defence.[37] In 1868 the grateful Manet painted a portrait of Zola, in the background of which can be seen a black and white print of *Olympia*.[38] Contemporary with the portrait, Zola's novel *Thérèse Raquin* was directly influenced by *Olympia*.[39] Later, Manet's 1877 painting *Nana* refers to the end of Zola's *L'Assommoir*, published earlier the same year, where Nana/Anna Lantier appears as a secondary character (the novel *Nana* itself dates to 1880). Zola's *Son Excellence Eugène Rougon* (1876), although it is not generally read as reflecting the influence of Manet, also fits within this general pattern of mutual influence and insider references.

Zola was the first to see Manet as one of the foremost painters of the day. He clearly identified with Manet's choice of contemporary subjects and rejection of idealism, but he also dwelt at length and with great enthusiasm on his painterly

[35] Brody, pp. 104–05.

[36] Quoted by Bernheimer, *Figures of Ill Repute*, p. 102, p. 112, p. 116.

[37] Zola and Manet do not appear to have met before 1866. Zola's first article on Manet, 'M. Manet', was published in 1866 in *L'Événement*, under the pseudonym 'Claude'. An expanded version, 'Une nouvelle manière en peinture: Édouard Manet', was published on 1 January 1867 in the *Revue du XIXe siècle* and then again as a separate pamphlet, *Édouard Manet, Étude biographique et critique* (Paris: E. Dentu, 1867). See Zola, *Œuvres complètes*, ed. by Henri Mitterand, 15 vols (Paris: Cercle du livre précieux, 1969), vol. 12, pp. 801–06 and pp. 821–45.

[38] In the portrait, Olympia gazes not at the spectator, but sideways, at Zola. Although it would appear on the surface to be an extremely sympathetic portrait, this and other *clins d'œil* to the viewer have led recent critics to see Manet as implicitly mocking his sitter. See Theodore Reff, 'Manet's Portrait of Zola', *The Burlington Magazine*, 117 (1975), 35–44 (p. 40, p. 41); Alexandra K. Wettlaufer, 'Metaphors of Power and the Power of Metaphor: Zola, Manet and the Art of Portraiture', *Nineteenth-Century Contexts*, 21:3 (1999), 437–63; Robert Lethbridge, 'Zola and Contemporary Painting', in *The Cambridge Companion to Emile Zola*, ed. by Brian Nelson (Cambridge: Cambridge University Press, 2007), pp. 67–85 (pp. 74–5).

[39] See Lethbridge, 'Zola, Manet and *Thérèse Raquin*', and Tracy Denean Sharpley-Whiting, *Black Venus: Sexualized Savages, Primal Fears, and Primitive Narratives in French* (Durham, NC: Duke University Press, 1999), pp. 78–80.

style and the formal 'honesty' of his work.[40] In 1866, holding up *Olympia* as Manet's supreme achievement to date, he even denied that Manet had any intention of including 'ideas' in his paintings. This may be feigned innocence, a way of whitewashing the sulphurous reputation Manet had acquired with his portrayal of a contemporary prostitute.[41] Instead, Zola read the painting as a formal contrast of dark and light tones. Olympia herself is 'cette note blonde emplissant la toile de lumière'; 'couchée sur des linges blancs, [elle] fait une grande tache pâle sur le fond noir; dans ce fond noir se trouvent la tête de la négresse qui apporte un bouquet et ce fameux chat qui a tant égayé le public'. The black maid is nothing more than contrasting tone: 'il vous fallait des taches noires, et vous avez placé dans un coin une négresse et un chat. Qu'est-ce que tout cela veut dire? Vous ne le savez guère, et moi non plus.'[42] Zola identifies lack of authorial comment and judgement, embodied in a formalist play of contrasting tones, as being central to Manet's modernity. This emphasis on formalism in Zola's view of Manet's painting seems to be at odds with his own writing which, though it includes striking painterly tableaux and contrasting colours, also advances ideas of social reform, explores scientific theories, and relies heavily on symbolism and myth. Zola may have painted his own self-portrait in his articles on Manet,[43] but it is only a partial one.

Bernheimer reconciles this emphasis on form with his own 'sexual' interpretation thanks to Georges Bataille's response to *Olympia*. Bataille sees the text or idea, in this case the theme of impurity, as being effaced by the painting: 'And what the painting signifies is not the text but the effacement.'[44] It is, then, the effacement of the conceptual that is constitutive of the painting's modernism. Pollock, on the other hand, seeks to nuance Zola's emphasis on the contrasting tones of dark and light: each tone's meaning is relative, not absolute. While the cat in the painting *is* black—that is, painted in black pigment—the maidservant is not: she is 'manufactured in paint' that is in reality a 'deep chestnut brown'.[45] Where Manet painted nuances of colour, Zola, I would suggest, saw the painting in terms of formalist, binary contrast partly because he was reluctant to accept its portrayal of the two women in terms that are both specific and contingent. His own brand of Realism depended on a powerful myth-making urge that is a far cry indeed from the effacement of symbolism to be found in Manet and, as we shall see, Flaubert.

[40] It was not clear to contemporaries whether Manet should be considered an Impressionist or a Realist. He had reasonably warm relations with Champfleury, the champion of so-called 'Realism', but the latter did not see him as 'a Realist in the mould of Courbet'. In the 1860s, however, critics began to associate him with Courbet and increasingly, in the 1870s, affirmed his 'Realism' (see Krell, p. 173, pp. 164–5).
[41] Guégan suggests 'la feinte innocence d'un Zola, qui s'est ingénié à blanchir le tableau en 1867' (p. 136). Reff emphasizes that Zola's study diverted attention 'from the imagery and meaning of *Olympia* to its form and style' (*Manet: Olympia*, p. 21).
[42] Zola, 'Édouard Manet', *Œuvres complètes*, vol. 12, p. 832, p. 838, p. 839. On Zola's rehabilitation of the (hitherto pejorative) word 'tache', see Reed, pp. 56–91.
[43] See Lethbridge, 'Zola, Manet and *Thérèse Raquin*', p. 279.
[44] Bernheimer, p. 113. On Zola's reading of Manet in formalist, painterly terms that excludes his 'literary' or narrative side, and this rejection of 'ideas' or perhaps of referentiality itself as founding his modernity, see Reed, pp. 2–3.
[45] Pollock, pp. 282–3.

ZOLA: THE BLACK MAID AND ABJECT FEMININITY

Son Excellence Eugène Rougon (1876) is perhaps the least read of the twenty novels in Zola's Rougon-Macquart cycle. It is also the most overtly political: Eugène Rougon lusts after power just as his brothers Saccard and Pascal lust after money or knowledge. Baguley warns us, however, that it is not *simply* a satire of the politics of the Second Empire.[46] The novel contrasts painterly, impressionist art with 'bad' academic art, and itself demonstrates an impressionist approach through its strikingly visual depictions, notably the chapter-long account of the baptism of the Imperial Prince.[47] Zola's myth-making is also in evidence in the novel's staging of the battle of the sexes in the rival wills to power of the antagonistic couple comprised by Eugène Rougon and Clorinde Balbi.[48] Clorinde embodies the destructive power of the *femme fatale*, and the sexual threat she poses is all the more vividly suggested for being split in two: it is portrayed directly, but also metonymically, through the figure of her maidservant Antonia.

Clorinde herself is not vaguely Creole, like Olympia (or Flaubert's Mme Arnoux), but definitely Italian, though her exact background remains mysterious. Italy, like Spain, was still the bearer of Romantic tropes of exoticism, and understood as being halfway to the Orient or to Africa. Italy is in fact a double signifier for the French nineteenth century: its Greco-Roman inheritance, mediated by classical art, stands in contrast to the perceived 'primitive' side of the contemporary Italian South (one of Europe's inner Africas). These two sides, the white/classical and the black/primitive, are reflected in the pairing of the white-skinned, sculptural mistress and her black maid. Antonia's function is thus partly one of contrastive metonymy: far from Olympia's greyish, angular pallor, Clorinde's body, emphatically white, is constantly seen through the frame of classical statuary. In one of Zola's great set-pieces, she even poses, nearly nude, for the goddess Diana hunting, and in her 'pose de déesse' her limbs have 'un luisant de marbre' (II: 64, 65); like Diana, she belongs to 'cette race de viriles amazones qui menacent le héros de dévirilisation'.[49] Naomi Schor describes the destructive powers of the heroine's 'chair de marbre' in Zola's 1888 *Nana*, with its 'réseau sémantique comprenant la femme, l'écriture, et le marbre'. What Schor calls an inverted Pygmalion myth

[46] David Baguley, *Zola et les genres* (Glasgow: University of Glasgow French and German Publications, 1993), p. 43.
[47] For a discussion of Zola's painterly, impressionist set-pieces, see Patricia Carles and Béatrice Desgranges, '*Son Excellence Eugène Rougon* ou la métairie des Beaux-Arts', *Nineteenth-Century French Studies*, 21:1–2 (1992–3), 114–29.
[48] The 'subplot' with Clorinde was given primacy by the use of the title *Clorinda* for the novel's 1880 translation into English by Mary Neal Sherwood.
[49] Baguley, *Zola et les genres*, p. 45; he also points out that Clorinde is wearing 'une amazone' in the attempted rape scene, and emphasizes the theme of hunting that reaches its culmination in the imperial hunt scene at Compiègne. Diana, goddess of virginity and the hunt, who has men killed if they see her naked, is both an ironic role for the exhibitionist Clorinde and a suitable one for a woman engaging in a battle of the sexes; when we first meet her she is infamous for having appeared at a ball disguised as a 'Diane chasseresse' (I: 22). Clorinde was conceived in terms of classical sculpture in the preparatory sketches: 'Type romain'; 'Un marbre. Brune avec une peau très blanche' (N.A.F. 10292, fols 143–4, in Becker, ed. *Fabrique*, vol. 2, p. 592).

could equally be applied to Clorinde, Nana's marmoreal precursor: 'avant que la statue puisse se faire femme, il a fallu que la femme se fasse statue'.[50] Rougon, watching Clorinde pose, seeks at first to criticize her proportions, and the sketch being produced has the statuesque immobility that characterizes academic paintings of antique-inspired nudes, far from the impressionism and moving canvasses of Zola's own writing.[51] But Rougon is briefly subjugated by a vision of the naked Clorinde as a giant statue (II: 67).

Clorinde's chambermaid Antonia is a late addition to the work, absent from the lists of characters in Zola's preparatory notes.[52] Generally ignored by the critical literature, she is nevertheless a revelatory minor figure.[53] Antonia may be a Southern Italian and not literally African, but she is constantly described in terms associated with racist stereotypes of Africans.[54] She is a 'petite femme noire, mal coiffée, traînant une robe jaune en loques, qui mordait dans une orange comme dans une pomme'. When Rougon asks if her mistress is home, '[e]lle ne répondit pas, la bouche pleine, agitant la tête violemment, avec un rire. Elle avait les lèvres toutes barbouillées du jus de l'orange; elle rapetissait ses petits yeux, pareils à deux gouttes d'encre sur sa peau brune' (II: 61). The slatternly maid and her gaping mouth are again associated with sticky substances when she brings Clorinde two slices of buttered bread, one on each hand. 'La servante les lui tendit, comme sur un plateau, avec son rire de bête qu'on chatouille, un rire qui fendait sa bouche rouge dans sa face noire. Puis, elle s'en alla, en essuyant ses mains contre sa jupe' (II: 74). Clorinde offers to share the sticky buttered bread with Rougon; one guesses his mixture of repulsion and fascination. The butter, like the juice of the (Southern) oranges, is intimately associated with the bodily contact of the maid-servant and with her red mouth in her black face (she has a 'rire de chèvre noire' II: 122). Indeed, Antonia's open red mouth and the contrast of white teeth/black skin reflect the racist imagery that was to become increasingly commonplace in popular advertising for chocolate or coffee. Her unexplained laughter is also witchlike or mad, and madness itself had long been associated with Africa.[55] Clorinde's sexual 'otherness' is, in other words, racialized in the portrayal of her other half, Antonia.

[50] Naomi Schor, 'Le Sourire du sphinx: Zola et l'énigme de la féminité', *Romantisme*, 6:13–14 (1976), 183–96 (p. 192).
[51] See II: 65. This is an implicit critique of a contemporary academic painting of *Diane* by Jules-Élie Delaunay (1872, Musée d'Orsay), according to Carles and Desgranges, pp. 115–16.
[52] The list of characters, along with their age in 1857, includes Clorinde Balbi (twenty-two years old) but not her maid (N.A.F. 10292, fol. 139, in *Fabrique*, vol. 2, p. 586; see also fols 169–70, p. 618).
[53] Clayton Alcorn, in his article on 'The Domestic servant in Zola's novels' (*L'Esprit Créateur*, 11:4 (1971), 21–35) omits to mention her at all, and claims Zola's servants are 'industrious, economical, honest, loyal, and chaste' (p. 27); Antonia does appear to be loyal to her mistress, but one hardly recognizes her in this description otherwise. Bruce Robbins, meanwhile, sees literary servants in English fiction as being characterized by their 'characterlessness' (*The Servant's Hand: English Fiction from Below* (New York: Columbia University Press, 1986), p. 37).
[54] Popular hostility to Italian immigration in France in the late nineteenth century was in fact very similar to the hostility expressed to African immigrants in much of the twentieth. See Dignan, p. 141. Zola's own father was of course an earlier immigrant from (Northern) Italy.
[55] See notably Sander L. Gilman, *Difference and Pathology: Stereotypes of Sexuality, Race, and Madness* (Ithaca, NY: Cornell University Press, 1985), pp. 131–49; also Bernard Mouralis, 'L'Afrique comme figure de la folie', *Cahiers CRLH-CIRAOI*, 5 (1988), 45–59.

Antonia controls visitors' access to her beautiful mistress, with whom she has a remarkably intimate relationship. Clorinde 's'amusait à s'habiller en homme avec sa femme de chambre, sans doute afin de tuer le temps' (II: 318). The phrase 'sans doute' in this passage suggests that the reader ought in fact to doubt the innocent explanation provided. That she should play at dressing up as a man in itself gives a sense of Clorinde's sardonic, imitative engagement in the war of the sexes;[56] that she should do so with her maid hints at her ability to pursue her existence, scandalously, without Rougon or any other man. He, obtusely, concludes from her apparent inactivity that she is obedient to her husband and that 'les femmes doivent rester tranquilles chez elles' (II: 321). Gilman's analysis of *Nana* stresses that the heroine's corruption comes partly through her seduction by a lesbian, but that it is 'the sexual corruption of the male' that is 'the source of political impotence'.[57] In this earlier novel, Eugène Rougon is effectively disempowered by his relationship with Clorinde: her powerful sexuality, with its implicit homoerotic self-sufficiency, is the ultimate challenge to his political potency.

More explicit than her lesbianism, it is Antonia's much-repeated slatternly nature that embodies her mistress's own filth. When Clorinde marries, becoming a wealthy woman, '[e]lle avait gardé sa petite bonne, cette noiraude d'Antonia qui suçait des oranges du matin au soir', and indeed the two women amuse themselves by dirtying Clorinde's elegant apartment together ('des assiettes sales sur les fauteuils, des litres de sirop à terre', II: 146). When Clorinde returns home rain-soaked, 'sa femme de chambre, Antonia, la bouche barbouillée d'une tartine de confiture, la déshabilla en riant très fort de l'égouttement de ses jupes, qui pissaient l'eau sur le parquet.' She sits on the ground to remove her mistress's shoes, and remains sitting there, 'mal peignée, la robe grasse, montrant ses dents blanches dans sa face brune' (II: 301). In the context of the novel's battle of the sexes, the constant references to her red mouth with its white teeth and smeared juices make Antonia a disturbing evocation of a part of Clorinde that is only hinted at by the text. The open mouth is linked to an extended paradigm of holes, cracks, and gaps in Zola's novels in general, and which was to have its most famous instance not long after, in the putrefaction of the dead Nana: her face, too, is gashed by abrupt, oozing openings. Gilman sees Nana's decomposition as a reversion to the pathologically primitive nature of the prostitute or in other words a return to 'blackness'; he claims that the theme of filth confirms perceived parallels between 'the genitalia of the Hottentot' and 'the diseased genitalia of the prostitute'.[58] Like this lingering over decomposition, Antonia's oozing filth is suggestive of the role played by nausea in naturalist aesthetics: unlike the earlier 'realists' (Flaubert, Baudelaire, Manet), 'Naturalism does not delight, or arouse, or broaden moral sympathies. It does not frighten or enrage. Naturalism makes you sick.'[59] Antonia figures the abject side of

---

[56] On Clorinde's masculine behaviour, see Jurate D. Kaminskas, 'De la séduction et du pouvoir: *Son Excellence Eugène Rougon*', *Excavatio*, 15:3–4 (2001), 92–106 (p. 94 and p. 105).

[57] 'Black Bodies, White Bodies', p. 256.

[58] Gilman, *Difference and Pathology*, pp. 104–5; 'Black Bodies, White Bodies', p. 256.

[59] David Trotter, 'Modernity and Its Discontents: Manet, Flaubert, Cézanne, Zola', *Paragraph*, 19:3 (1996), 251–71 (p. 256).

female sexuality, that which a lady's marmoreal surfaces attempt to sublimate. Tellingly, she is inseparable from her mistress, for the abject is 'something rejected from which one does not part'.[60] While it has been claimed that the black maid and the cat in Manet's *Olympia* reinstate what the courtesan's firmly pressed hand so inefficiently denies, it is much more evident that Zola's black maid stands for her mistress's genitals. It is not a maid's feet that serve as a sexual fetish here,[61] but the maid herself.

The simultaneous workings of contrastive and descriptive metonymy are crucial to the sleight of hand by which the abject is both denied and repeated. In this case, as in *Olympia*, the maid's blackness is inseparable from her mistress's apparent whiteness. She gives an external focus to the destructive exoticism of the legendary Clorinda of Torquato Tasso's *Jerusalem Delivered*, a pagan warrior-maiden whose white skin belies her black parentage. But at the same time Antonia's darkness exaggerates the whiteness of Clorinde's body by contrastive metonymy, just as the black slaves serve as foils to the white odalisques in Orientalist painting. Zola explicitly plays on such Orientalist imagery when Clorinde, standing naked before her mirror, has Antonia rub her body with special aromatic oils she claims naïvely to have acquired 'à Constantinople, chez le parfumeur du sérail, disait-elle [...] Et pendant qu'Antonia la frottait, elle gardait des attitudes de statue. Cela devait lui donner une peau blanche, lisse, impérissable comme le marbre' (II: 301). Orientalism is used as a means of creating the perfect(ly) white woman, from whom blackness and permeability are repressed.[62] Antonia is a disavowal of Clorinde's sexuality, and even her name suggests 'antonym', or the function of contrastive metonymy. It is however a disavowal that reiterates the presence of the very thing it purports to deny. Gilman suggests that in Manet's painting of *Nana* Olympia's black servant is still present, hidden within the courtesan herself, in the tell-tale physiological signs of the atavistic prostitute.[63] In the duo Clorinde–Antonia these signs are exteriorized, embodied in the metonym that is the maidservant. The white, smooth statue and the dark, oozing lips represent the two (indivisible) sides of femininity: the classical ideal and the primitive *vagina dentata*.

Zola is of course not alone in his use of racializing imagery to characterize a slovenly maidservant, and he was familiar with the Goncourts' *Germinie Lacerteux* of 1865. Germinie, though French, is a recent migrant from the provinces who has become a Parisian maid. She has dark hair that is frizzy and coarse, with a low forehead that protrudes above 'l'ombre d'orbites profondes où s'enfonçaient et se cavaient presque maladivement ses yeux', and the lower part of her face has a 'caractère presque simiesque' as well as a 'grande bouche, aux dents blanches, aux lèvres pleines, plates et comme écrasées'.[64] Her body nevertheless exudes a mysterious

---

[60] McClintock, *Imperial Leather*, pp. 71–2, following Kristeva.

[61] On foot fetishism, see for example Apter, *Feminizing the Fetish*, pp. 183–5.

[62] On orientalist cosmetics as creating the perfect white woman, see Martin, *Selling Beauty*, p. 141 and p. 152.

[63] *Difference and Pathology*, p. 102.

[64] Edmond and Jules de Goncourt, *Germinie Lacerteux* [1865], ed. by Nadine Satiat (Paris: GF Flammarion, 1990), pp. 95–6.

sexual charm. The description owes much to recent discoveries of fossilized remains of earlier humans, as well as contemporary tendencies to establish an equivalence between them and the increasingly influential racialist discourse. This powerful paradigm was, as we shall see in more detail in Chapter 6, applied to the working classes as well as to Africans. As if to emphasize the link, Germinie is seriously tempted to migrate to Africa when her sister and brother-in-law take her beloved niece there.[65]

To return, however, to Zola: it would be too simplistic to dismiss his portrayal of the black maid and her mistress as mere misogyny, and Naomi Schor astutely calls him a 'romancier de l'obstacle' who leaves space for the unknown.[66] The simultaneous contrast and proximity of Antonia and Clorinde repeats the aesthetic conception of the novel as a whole, which is constructed in painterly terms as a contrast of black and white, from the 'nudité des statues et des sculptures [qui] arrêtait des pans de clarté blanche' (II: 13) to Clorinde's 'draperies noires semées de larmes d'argent', her 'couvertures également noires' (II: 23) or her dramatic black velvet dress, contrasting with her white face.[67] These visual contrasts, that dominate the novel throughout, could have been borrowed from Zola's own analysis of *Olympia*. Moreover, the proximity and contrast of white and black also stand for writing itself. In her black velvet robe, reclining on her white bed, Clorinde combines in herself the black (ink) and the white (surface): 'sa blouse noire, dont l'ampleur faisait sur la couverture blanche une mare d'encre' (II: 311). Earlier it was the maid, rather than the mistress, whose eyes were 'pareils à deux gouttes d'encre sur sa peau brune' (II: 61). Together the mistress and maid figure the tonal contrast of paper and ink, a pairing that echoes the splitting of the female body into white statue and black slit. Far from being a trace or echo of contemporary history, they are embodied text. And Clorinde's role as a protagonist in the battle of the sexes runs parallel with her metatextual role, as Robert Lethbridge has shown. Clorinde is tempted by art, and began, but never completed, a sculpture (II: 64). Not only is she the subject of 'bad' academic painting, she is herself a 'bad' novelist, surrounding herself with disorder, leaving gaps everywhere, fantasizing and lying; she is 'le mensonge absolu'.[68] In Zola's preparatory notes she is described as having 'le besoin d'observation et l'amour d'intrigues d'un romancier. *Elle ment par nature*', this last phrase underlined by Zola himself.[69] Her power, like that of Rougon, and of his master Napoleon III, is based on a lie. Nevertheless, Clorinde is a figure of the novelist-as-powerbroker, transporting her mysterious, bulky,

---

[65] Goncourt, *Germinie*, pp. 100–02. It turns out that her brother-in-law's letters asking for money are a scam, since both her sister and niece have died. Germinie's love for her niece, and the latter's untimely death in the colonies, may be among the sources of Flaubert's 'Un cœur simple'.

[66] Schor, 'Le Sourire du sphinx', p. 193.

[67] Zola no doubt took his inspiration for Clorinde's black robes and décor from the eccentric fantasies of the Countess of Castiglione (see Richard B. Grant, *Zola's* Son Excellence Eugène Rougon (Durham, NC: Duke University Press, 1960), p. 73, p. 76). Like Renée making love to her stepson on a black bearskin in *La Curée*, the use of luxurious black décor is the sign of a society in decadence.

[68] Robert Lethbridge, 'Zola et la fiction du pouvoir: *Son Excellence Eugène Rougon*', *Les Cahiers naturalistes*, 44:72 (1998), 291–304 (p. 299).

[69] Fol. 116/20, in *Fabrique*, vol. 2, p. 558.

unfeminine bag of documents with her everywhere. She belongs to a sinister sister-hood of women who collect documents, human documents like those of the nat-uralist novelist. But unlike Mme Sidonie (sister of Eugène Rougon) in *La Curée* and La Méchain in *L'Argent*, who are variants of the 'hag', Clorinde Balbi—self-made statue and sinister novelist—is also a *femme fatale*.[70]

During the period when Zola was writing *Son Excellence* he was fascinated by Flaubert's 1869 *Éducation sentimentale*, seeing it as the ultimate realist novel: 'Tous nos romans sont des poèmes à côté de celui-là', he observed rather astutely.[71] Yet a comparison of the relationship between maid and mistress in the two novels does not suggest that Zola was attempting to follow Flaubert: he was perhaps writing a poem after all. His own use of blackness as a signifier, his Africanization of female sexuality, seems pure mythopoetics beside Flaubert's deflation of exoticizing and orientalizing impulses. Moving back in time from Zola's 1876 novel to Flaubert's treatment of the black maidservant in 1869 can in turn shed light on Manet's *Olympia*, painted in 1863, which was the scandal of the 1865 Salon—during the period when Flaubert was writing his masterpiece (1863–9). And concluding with Flaubert allows us to see how his procedure is in many ways the opposite of Zola's: while Zola Orientalizes and Africanizes his Italian duo, Flaubert—like Manet—undermines the Orientalism of the black maid and her mistress.

FLAUBERT: THE BLACK MAIDSERVANT AS RED HERRING

In the opening scene of the 1869 *Éducation sentimentale*, when Frédéric first meets Mme Arnoux on the boat taking him from Paris to Nogent, she is accompanied by her black maid: 'Une négresse, coiffée d'un foulard, se présenta, en tenant par la main une petite fille, déjà grande.' The maid's blackness and her creole 'foulard' serve to bring into focus her mistress's splendid 'peau brune', providing circum-stantial evidence that encourages Frédéric to construct her as a figure of Romantic exoticism: 'Il la supposait d'origine andalouse, créole peut-être; elle avait ramené des îles cette négresse avec elle?' (51). The black maidservant who is so succinctly evoked is interpreted by Frédéric as metonymically signifying her mistress's exotic origins, which in turn suggest sensuality. In other words, rather than setting off her mistress's white skin by contrastive metonymy, the black maid in Flaubert's novel serves to *darken* her mistress's skin by descriptive or analogical metonymy, like the

---

[70] On Zola's female document-collectors, see Borie, *Zola et les mythes*, pp. 179–80. Traits belonging to Clorinde reappear much later in two separate secondary characters of *L'Argent*—the hag La Méchain, who carries around a bag of documents concerning the private lives of potential victims, bought in bulk from bankruptcies, and the Baronne Sandorff, a beautiful, frigid brunette.

[71] Zola, 'Gustave Flaubert: "L'Éducation sentimentale"', *Le Voltaire* (9 December 1879), in *Œuvres complètes*, vol. 12, pp. 606–09 (p. 608). Zola had written an article on *L'Éducation sentimentale* at its appearance in 1869, followed by this one ten years later. He began writing a longer study on Flaubert (published in *Le Messager de l'Europe* in November 1875) during the early stages of his work on *Son Excellence Eugène Rougon*, and he seems to have re-read *L'Éducation sentimentale* then. See Lethbridge, 'Zola et la fiction du pouvoir', p. 303 and n. 52, and F.W.J. Hemmings, 'Zola and *L'Éducation senti-mentale*', *The Romanic Review*, 50:1 (1959), 35–40.

maid in *Olympia*.[72] At the same time the interpretative link is carefully framed in indirect free discourse, since the supposition is Frédéric's, not the narrator's. Mme Arnoux's darkness—both her own 'peau brune' and the darkness conferred on her metonymically by her maidservant—is in fact misleading, since she is from prosaic Chartres. Interpreting her maid as an exotic signifier, Frédéric fails to 'read' the latter in more pragmatic and much less erotic terms as a nursemaid looking after the Arnoux's infant daughter. It is crucial not to lose sight of the implicit double perspective provided by the indirect free discourse. Although Said asserts that '[w]oven through all of Flaubert's Oriental experiences [...] is an almost uniform association between the Orient and sex',[73] one must remember that the sexual fantasy of Andalusian or creole exoticism is Frédéric's own. The black maid as a fetish standing for her mistress's sex—which we find in Zola and in later Orientalist paintings—is belied by Flaubert. Such ironic framing through one character's limited perspective is harder to achieve in painting, and it is no doubt pushing things to argue that Manet's inclusion of verses from Astruc's sub-Baudelairean creole-themed poem was ironic. The black maids in *Olympia* and *L'Éducation sentimentale* do however share the trait of pointing in two metonymical directions at once: towards exotic creole identities, implicitly associated with erotic availability; and at the same time towards the everyday context of contemporary Parisian life.

A genetic reading of Flaubert's novel reveals further traces of colonial themes. His technique in writing *L'Éducation sentimentale* involved rewriting and paring down to an often elliptical minimum details that were more fully fleshed out in his manuscripts. Earlier drafts of the boat scene give more details showing that Frédéric's view of both mistress and maid is conceived in racial and colonial terms. The Arnoux couple are constantly associated with false or misleading exoticism, and even their daughter, in the manuscripts, has '[de] jolis cheveux noirs bouclés' (N.A.F. 17599, fol. 58). Frédéric imagines Mme Arnoux to be not just 'créole' but 'de sang créole', which emphasizes the physiological grounding of difference, building on her 'teint légèrement doré' to suppose that she is 'née aux Colonies [sous les tropiques]' (fol. 55V°, partly crossed out). Flaubert also wrote, and rewrote—before crossing out altogether—a passage that emphasizes the maid's slave origins: 'La négresse en effet avait l'air passif des esclaves. [...] Elle riait à l'enfant d'une manière silencieuse [...] en écartant ses dents blanches et ses grosses lèvres bleuâtres [...] qui laissaient voir ses dents' (fol. 55V°; see also fol. 60V°). In the drafts, too, her headdress is described with the exotic term 'madras' (fols 58 and 60V°). This is replaced by the more neutral 'foulard' in the final text, a discretion reminiscent of Manet's treatment of the maid's headscarf. So it seems that Flaubert, at one stage, had in mind a more explicit link with

---

[72] Despite her brown skin, Mme Arnoux has, rather oddly, been seen as the 'ideal image of France' (Tadiar, p. 168). Hiner also sees the presence of a black maidservant as making Mme Arnoux more French and less exotic (it 'whitens her up'), which is to emphasize the contrastive function of metonymy over the analogical or descriptive function (*Accessories to Modernity*, p. 99).

[73] *Orientalism*, p. 188. Lisa Lowe, in *Critical Terrains*, argues that Flaubert parodies in the second *Éducation sentimentale* the orientalizing stance he himself adopted in earlier works like *Salammbô* and his *Voyage en Orient*.

colonial slavery, which was of course still legal in French colonies in the 1840s; this may have underlined Mme Arnoux's own subordination to her domineering husband or the Arnoux couple's affiliation with the property-owning classes. Explicit traces of the theme are removed from the final version of the text, perhaps because Frédéric's Romantic imagination responds not to Atlantic slavery but to the Orientalist image of the black servant as a metonymy for her white mistress's sensuality and availability.

Mme Arnoux's maid is identified as 'une [négresse ou] une femme de couleur' from the very first 'scénario d'ensemble' onwards,[74] which suggests the importance of this apparently minor detail in the process by which Frédéric constructs his ideal woman. Yet as I have just shown, her blackness does not stand as a straightforward metonymy for her mistress. Instead, following Jonathan Culler's reading of Flaubert as deliberately frustrating our attempts at decoding, I would like to suggest that Mme Arnoux's maid is a superb example of the red herring. First her racial identity misleads Frédéric into projecting exoticism onto her mistress. Then the maid becomes an unhelpful clue in his attempt to trace her mistress once in Paris. He glimpses '[u]ne négresse, qu'il croisa un jour dans les Tuileries tenant une petite fille à la main [qui] lui rappela la négresse de Mme Arnoux' (70–1). The scenarios, once again, include this brief non-event from very early in the writing process: 'Les négresses bonnes d'enfant en souvenir de l'autre l'agitaient.—il allait exprès pour en voir aux Tuileries.'[75] In a later draft, the trail is explicitly a false one: 'Il allait aux Tuileries voir les enfants jouer.—chercher les négresses bonnes d'enfant.—une fois en aborde une—mais ce n'est pas celle-là' (N.A.F. 17599, fol. 151V°). In the published version of the novel we do not learn whether or not the woman and child glimpsed in the Tuileries garden are the right ones, but it is probable that, like the windows above Arnoux's shop where Frédéric mistakenly imagines the family to live, this black nanny is a false clue.

The nanny spotted by Frédéric in the Tuileries garden is reminiscent of Manet's painting *Children in the Tuileries Gardens* (1861–2), in which a black nursemaid looks after a little girl. The inspiration for this woman was probably the same Laure who was the model for the maidservant in *Olympia*, and in both paintings the black woman wears a headscarf and a pale pink dress with a white collar.[76] It is unlikely that Flaubert would have seen this painting,[77] but it is tempting to think that he glimpsed Laure herself when she was working as a nursemaid in Paris in the early 1860s, shortly before he began *L'Éducation sentimentale*. In any case there are

[74] Scénarios, fol. 66 (2), in Williams, ed., p. 34.
[75] Fol. 67 (3), in Williams, ed., p. 38; see also scenario V, fol. 5, p. 127.
[76] 'Manet first encountered the woman named Laure working as a nursemaid in the Gardens of the Tuileries' (Pollock, p. 286). *Children in the Tuileries Gardens* is held by the Museum of Art of the Rhode Island School of Design.
[77] The textually confirmed links between Manet and Flaubert are few and far between, despite the fact that they had several acquaintances in common. There is no evidence that they ever met. Flaubert's correspondence makes one reference to Manet (letter to Zola, 27 June 1879, *Correspondance* V: 672) to the effect that he doesn't understand his work. Reed discusses the parallels and intersections between their modernist projects (pp. 6–7). There have even been claims (not fleshed out) of an implicitly antagonistic relationship (Pierre Sorlin, *L'Art sans règles: Manet contre Flaubert* (Paris: Presses Universitaires de Vincennes, 1995)).

parallels between Manet's anti-Orientalist *Olympia* and Flaubert's black-maid-as-red-herring. Frédéric sees an exotic and sexualized 'négresse' in the initial scene on the boat, but the woman in the Tuileries garden is prosaically a children's maid, like Manet's model, Laure. And of course the glimpse of the second 'négresse' *seems* significant to him, but proves a dead end. Misguided quests are recurrent in the frustrating anti-narrative of *L'Éducation sentimentale*. Brooks refers to this as a 'systematic interference' or 'narrative dissonance' that 'takes the forms of missed rendezvous, interrupted meetings, wrong addresses, mistaken objects'.[78] The black maidservant is a key example of this misleading metonymy.

L'Éducation sentimentale refuses to play along with the myth of realist transparency, exposing language as opaque and detail as contingent. Frédéric is mistaken in supplying meaning for the maid's blackness, which in itself means nothing: racial identity loses its mythic content, in this case its links to Romantic exoticism, primitivism, and sexual availability. Racial and exotic markers in Flaubert are slippery signifiers that do not point to any direct determinist meaning.[79] The African or Creole origins of her maid tell us nothing about Mme Arnoux's inner identity: the black woman is a contemporary Parisian nanny, not an exotic symbol of primitive erotic availability. It is hardly surprising, then, to find that elsewhere too Flaubert implicitly mocks the association of African women with sexual passion and availability as a pseudo-ethnographic *idée reçue*. In *Madame Bovary* Homais, lunching with Léon as two men-about-town, teases him about supposedly courting Emma's maidservant and proffers raunchy clichés concerning women of different nations. The callow Léon goes one better: '—Et les négresses ?'; '—C'est un goût d'artiste, dit Homais' (III: 397). And in the *Dictionnaire des idées reçues* the entry 'Négresses' reads 'Plus chaudes que les blanches (v. *brunes* et *blondes*)', a succinct summary of the 'African sexuality' myth, unpicked by cross-referencing to the two neatly symmetrical entries 'Blondes.—Plus chaudes que les brunes (v. *brunes*)' and 'Brunes.—Plus chaudes que les blondes (v. *blondes*)'.[80]

---

[78] *Reading for the Plot*, p. 190. Alison Fairlie has studied such misguided quests more closely, though she doesn't mention the black maid ('La quête de la femme à travers la ville dans quelques œuvres de Flaubert', in *Flaubert, la femme, la ville* (Paris: Presses Universitaires de France, 1983), 77–87). Flaubert may be remembering his youthful erotic adventure with Eulalie Foucaud who had just returned from Lima and who had as a servant 'un négrillon, vêtu de nankin et de babouches'; his later attempts to find the hotel in Marseille where he had this adventure were fruitless, perhaps a model for Frédéric's frustrated pursuit of Mme Arnoux (Goncourts, *Journal*, vol. 1, pp. 535–6 (20 February 1860)).

[79] Flaubert, on the whole, remains aloof from the racialization of identities that was gathering momentum in the second half of the century. On the indeterminate nature of race in the 1869 novel, see Alan Raitt, 'La Décomposition des personnages dans *L'Éducation sentimentale*', in *Flaubert, la dimension du texte*, ed. by P.M. Wetherill (Manchester: Manchester University Press, 1982), pp. 157–74 (particularly pp. 163–4). Even in *Salammbô* there are too many different races, so that the significance of racial difference is largely emptied of meaning: see for example Corinne Saminadayar-Perrin who says of *Salammbô*, 'l'ensemble du roman ne pose d'ailleurs les oppositions de races, de mœurs et de civilisations que pour mieux miner les présupposés qu'ils justifient' ('Antiquité des races et naissance des nations: modèles scientifiques et logiques discursives', in *L'Idée de 'race' dans les sciences humaines et la littérature (XVIIIᵉ et XIXᵉ siècles)*, ed. by Sarga Moussa (Paris: L'Harmattan, 2003), pp. 385–407 (p. 404)).

[80] *Dictionnaire des idées reçues*, p. 369, p. 338.

The Arnoux couple's nanny then disappears from the narrative. Was she dismissed in their gradual financial decline? Is she still present but not discussed, as if her racial difference had dissolved into the neutrality of a generic servant-figure? Much later, at their final meeting in 1867, Frédéric remembers Mme Arnoux's 'négresse' with nostalgia, but we never learn of the servant's destiny. In her one appearance she is given so little depth that she can barely be called a secondary character. She is, rather, a signifier, but a signifier with no signified. *L'Éducation sentimentale* does, however, offer us a teasing echo of the missing maidservant. Much later in the novel she resurfaces in a different form, once again standing in lieu of Mme Arnoux herself.

By now the Arnoux marriage has deteriorated following Marie's discovery of her husband's infidelity. Frédéric, again in pursuit of Mme Arnoux, makes his way with difficulty to visit the factory on the outskirts of Paris where Arnoux is making another attempt at fortune in the shape of mass-produced crockery. One of the workers is impertinent to the supervisor (Sénécal) but apparently she has the special protection of M. Arnoux himself. She is noticeable because she is wearing 'un madras et de longues boucles d'oreilles. Tout à la fois mince et potelée, elle avait de gros yeux noirs et les lèvres charnues d'une négresse' (259).[81] The more neutral 'foulard' of the maidservant on the ship has reverted to the 'madras' which, along with her earrings, suggests the worker's Creole origins. The slippage between the earlier maidservant and the Creole factory worker is moreover suggested by the fact that in some scenarios Arnoux's mistress was going to be *either* a worker or a maid, 'petite ouvrière ou femme de chambre'.[82] So the black maid who stood metonymically as a red herring for Marie Arnoux's supposed exoticism in the opening scene has disappeared, but she is replaced by her husband's Creole, mixed-blood mistress. The woman is known as 'la Bordelaise', and Bordeaux had been France's second most important port in the slave trade, which makes it more likely that she is of mixed origin. 'Bordelaise' also resonates with 'bordel' or bordello, and more specifically with the infamous 'maison basse' (65) 'au bord de l'eau' (509), the brothel run by the enigmatically named 'Zoraïde Turc' that is evoked elliptically in the second chapter of the novel, to be explained more fully in the closing chapter.[83] Framing the novel, the exotic 'bordel' is another red herring, pointing to an erotic satisfaction that never takes place.[84] Arnoux is extravagant on behalf of his mistress (342) and later, despite his own family's bankruptcy, we learn that he has set her up

---

[81] The draft reads: 'Toutes femmes—une ouvrière, boucles d'oreilles, <type des bordelaises à coiffure des> en madras'; she has '[les] lèvres charnues bras nus le coude appuyé sur une planche d'ardoise[?]—air boudeur et rêveur' (N.A.F. 17604, fol. 88 V). It is likely that 'coiffure des...' was going to be completed 'îles'.

[82] Scenario XXIV, fol. 33, Williams, ed., p. 254. See also scenario VIII, fol. 35, and scenario XXV, fol. 36, p. 256.

[83] Knight suggests an alternative motivation for the Bordelaise origins of the woman in Flaubert's 1840 travel notes, the *Voyage aux Pyrénées et en Corse* ('Object Choices', pp. 212–13).

[84] Lowe cites this as one of the most crucial of a 'series of linguistic and social postures of incompletion' (*Critical Terrains*, pp. 97–8; see also pp. 99–100 for a discussion of the brothel belonging to 'la Turque').

running a 'magasin de blanc' (430), or linen shop.[85] 'Magasin de blanc' was also slang for a brothel[86] and, in a further irony, appears to suggest that the daughter of black slaves is trading in white. The sexual suggestiveness of blackness as a myth returns, and with it the echo of slavery or oppression: in her husband's factory Mme Arnoux herself disapproves of the harshness of the supervisor, Sénécal, towards the Bordelaise, and identifies with her rather than simply seeing her as a rival.[87] From a mere metonymy of her mistress, and a misleading one at that, the black woman has been substituted for her as a mistress-servant, but can still stand for her symbolically.

African servants appear elsewhere in Flaubert's *œuvre*. Both Kuchouk-Hanem and Salammbô have black maids.[88] And Flaubert was equally fascinated by the black manservant, as a figure of abjection with whom he identifies. In the 1845 *Éducation sentimentale* this figure also reflects a de-Orientalizing stance: Jules's fantasy of complete gratification involves the imagined possession of an athletic black manservant 'en jaquette de soie rouge à fermoir d'argent, nu-bras, nu-jambes, à formes magnifiques et à allure puissante' on a black stallion with a gold rope in its mouth (I: 956). In desultory reality, on the ship that takes Henry to America this fantasy figure morphs into the African Itatoè, whose life is an abject version of the sentimental education.[89] Itatoè 's'en retournait dans son pays après avoir été domestique en France'. The fantasized exotic jacket is replaced by ragged livery, the phallic 'formes magnifiques' by dusty, bleeding feet wrapped in rags, and the equally suggestive air of energetic potency by complete exhaustion: 'il dormait comme un mort' (I: 975). We are given his life story in indirect free discourse, and although the account is brief, it is a rare example of the perspective of the subaltern in nineteenth-century French fiction:

> Son père l'avait vendu pour un paquet de clous; il était venu en France comme domes-tique. Il avait volé un foulard pour une femme de chambre qu'il aimait—on l'avait mis cinq ans aux galères.—Il était revenue de Toulon au Havre à pied pour revoir sa maîtresse; il ne l'avait pas retrouvée.—Il s'en retournait maintenant au pays des Noirs. (I: 978)

Even without the key Flaubertian reference to the scarf of the beloved woman, in this case stolen as an offering to her, it is clear that Flaubert puts much of himself into Itatoè. This is a portrait of the self as abject other, a third auto-fictional portrayal set alongside the two protagonists, Jules and Henry: 'Celui-là aussi', we are told, 'avait fait son éducation sentimentale' (I: 978). Like Flaubert, Itatoè amuses himself (and his audience) by reproducing clichés, using his penknife to carve 'le

---

[85] As early as Carnet 19 Arnoux sets up his mistresses with 'des fonds de lingerie' (Carnet 19, fol. 37Vº E, Williams, ed., p. 330).

[86] See Alfred Delvau's invaluable *Dictionnaire érotique moderne* (Paris: Éditions 1900, 1990 [1864]), p. 194: 'MAGASIN DE BLANC. —Bordel—où l'on dépose en effet des quantités considérables de sperme'.

[87] Peter M. Wetherill notes Sénécal's inhumane indifference in this scene ('L'Histoire dans le texte', *Zeitschrift für Französische Sprache und Literatur*, 95:2 (1985), 163–74 (p. 167). See also Knight, 'Object choices', p. 212.

[88] Kuchouk's servant is a 'négresse', 'une esclave d'Abyssinie' (*Voyage en Orient*, II: 663). On parallels between Mme Arnoux, Kuchouk-Hanem and Salammbô, see my article 'Like an apparition'.

[89] In earlier editions the name was spelt 'Statoë'.

portrait de l'Empereur sur des calebasses de coco' (I: 977).[90] Disillusioned, he sleeps as much as possible; his eyes gleam, but he seems sad. In contrast, the ship's captain reminds us of society's smiling hypocrisy: Maître Nicole, who likes coloured women, 'était un excellent homme' (itself a cliché, in indirect free discourse, that reflects the judgement of the European travellers) who is nostalgic for the slave trade and the extra money it used to provide (I: 977). Itatoè, like the stray dog that later haunts Jules (I: 1025–31), is weary, limping, and sad. As in the case of the dog's scabies, or the blind beggar in *Madame Bovary*, Itatoè's physical suffering and broken, oozing skin mark the eruption of the abject into the everyday. Unlike Zola's sinister, filthy Antonia, Flaubert's abject African is a figure of suffering (with Christ-like undertones suggested by his bleeding feet and the fact that he was sold for a bag of nails). Already, in a short story he wrote at the age of sixteen, 'Quidquid volueris', Flaubert put much of himself into the protagonist Djalioh, son of a black slave and an orang-utan. More sensitive than the 'civilized' man who is his callous father-figure, the mute Djalioh is a Romantic embodiment of the alienated self as identified with the wretched of the earth.[91]

Such identification with the racial other is absent from Flaubert's mature works, but a parallel with the black maidservant as red herring is to be found in the elliptical, enigmatic presence of the black servant in 'Un cœur simple'. He is the means by which Félicité acquires her beloved parrot and so is linked to a chain of lost love objects, a chain whose links are only apparently random. Félicité's love is at one point focused on her nephew Victor, who leaves for Havana where she imagines him 'parmi des nègres dans un nuage de tabac' (60). After the July Revolution Pont-l'Évêque gets a new sub-prefect who has been consul in America so that his nieces 'possédaient un nègre et un perroquet' (65), and when the family leaves they send the 'nègre' to give the parrot to Félicité's mistress. In case we missed the metonymic chain linking the parrot to the African-American slave, the future Loulou is handed over 'dans sa cage, avec le bâton, la chaîne et le cadenas' (67). The parrot, indeed, has long exercised Félicité's imagination, 'car il venait d'Amérique, et ce mot lui rappelait Victor, si bien qu'elle s'en informait auprès du nègre' (67).[92] It has been

---

[90] One wonders whether these alliterative 'calebasses de coco' are the ancestors of the 'quatre coquetiers en coco', mentioned in Chapter 1, that are offered for sale to Emma Bovary (III: 240). In both cases Flaubert clearly liked the sound rather than any real object, since a 'calebasse' is not the fruit of the coconut palm, and it is not clear how an eggcup could be made from a coconut shell.

[91] As Anne Green has shown, in his youth and early writings up to about 1850, Flaubert repeatedly identified himself with figures of the 'barbarian', who he associated with energy, passion, and poetry; later he was less optimistic about the capacity of 'barbarian' energy to resist westernization ('Flaubert's myth', p. 219). Green sees Flaubert's identification with the 'barbare' as strongest in the 1840s, when the first *Éducation sentimentale* was written. See also Sucheta Kapoor, 'Silence as Alterity: the Portrait of Djalioh in *Quidquid volueris*', *Dix-Neuf*, 15:1 (2011), 140–6.

[92] It is no doubt because of the 'nègre' of 'Un cœur simple' that Proust, in his pastiche of Flaubert, includes a 'nègre' who pulls an orange out of his pocket, and a lady with a parrot on her hat. His pastiche of Sainte-Beuve in turn is a spoof critique of the spoof Flaubert passage: 'Voyageur! [...] comme on vous reconnaît vite, ne serait-ce qu'à ce nègre, à cette orange, tout à l'heure à ce perroquet, fraîchement débarqués avec vous, à tous ces accessoires rapportés que vous vous dépêchez bien vite de venir plaquer sur votre esquisse...' (Marcel Proust, *Pastiches*, in *Contre Sainte-Beuve précédé de Pastiches et mélanges et suivi de Essais et articles*, ed. by Pierre Clarac (Paris: Gallimard 'Pléiade', 1971), pp. 5–59 (p. 18)). Proust's fictive Sainte-Beuve clearly had not understood the metonymic role of Flaubert's Africans.

suggested that the inclusion of a rare date—1819—for Victor's departure from Le Havre for Cuba may be a clue that it is in fact a slave ship, since the trade had been theoretically banned the year before, which drove up prices. The black 'tache' made by Victor's ship thus 'takes on a moral aspect'.[93] The parrot, meanwhile, is a substitution for Victor in an associative chain of love objects that also includes Virginie, Mme Aubain's short-lived daughter; but it is simultaneously part of a metonymic chain that links Félicité herself to slavery. Indeed, the intertextual reference to Bernardin de Saint-Pierre's novel *Paul et Virginie* places Félicité in the role of the devoted black servant Domingue, who saves Paul and Virginie when they are in danger just as she does. Félicité is Flaubert's ultimate black maid.

So Flaubert's early black men are sometimes figures of abject ugliness (Djalioh) and suffering (Itatoè) in whom the alienated self is embodied, but in his mature works the black maid and manservant serve rather as misleading markers that only acquire signification through the (mis)interpretations of the protagonists. His sensitivity to the subaltern remains, however, not far beneath the surface.

BLACKNESS BETWEEN MYTH AND HISTORY

Both Flaubert and Manet situate the black woman less as myth than as a specifically contemporary figure. Flaubert also exposes Frédéric's misinterpretation of her significance, and makes the racial origins of Mme Arnoux's maid a red herring. When the black maidservants in *Olympia* and *L'Éducation sentimentale* evoke fantasies of an erotic/exotic 'elsewhere' situated outside history, it is in order to undermine these *idées reçues*. The black maidservant helps 'stage' her mistress as a 'belle des îles' through the association of the erotic and the exotic, but both maid and mistress are in fact situated in the reality of contemporary Paris. Zola, responding to both Manet and Flaubert, does something rather different. He calls on the mythic resonance of the racializing imagination, rather than situating race within history. While Flaubert and Manet use racial blackness as a slippery signifier that serves to make whiteness less white, as an art critic Zola read Manet's *Olympia* in terms of binary contrast of tone, and he uses this contrastive pairing of black and white in *Son Excellence Eugène Rougon*. Nevertheless, he too uses metonymy both as contrast and as analogy.

The metonymical function of the black maidservant makes her a perfect example of Macherey's assertion that it is what the text does not say—or cannot say—that is important.[94] The nature of this unspoken content differs, however. Zola's Antonia is a way of saying the unspeakable, that is, the bodily nature of female sexuality. In the hands of Flaubert and Manet the discourse of sexuality works alongside that other unspoken truth which is the imbrication of metropolitan and world history, whereby the maid is situated within the new urban proletariat as well as having her origins in colonial slavery. A study of servants in the English novel argues that the domestic servant is necessarily a non-representative figure whose presence 'signifies

---

[93] Reed, p. 219.　　　[94] *Pour une théorie*, p. 107.

the absence of the people'; servants are 'signs of the unrepresented'.[95] This is doubly the case with literary black servants, a non-representative representation of both the proletariat and the African or Creole experience. And yet we have seen that in Flaubert's hands the black servant is not so very distant from the proletarian factory worker or the subaltern migrant.

[95] Robbins, *The Servant's Hand*, pp. 26–7.

6

The Primitive Within

In the literature of the nineteenth century, racial difference and colonial contacts are used to evoke a range of ill-defined threats within the rapidly changing society of metropolitan France itself. At times race is invoked as an analogy to help justify a 'scientific' vision of class difference or uncontained sexuality. Elsewhere, brief embedded narratives establish colonial contagion as a threat to the equilibrium of metropolitan society. The term 'race' was much bandied about during the nineteenth century (and indeed until 1945), but it was a shifting, not a stable category. I shall maintain the scare quotes around it when discussing the term itself and allow them to lapse otherwise. Indeed, I shall often be using 'racialize' as a verb, for what I am interested in here is not race itself so much as a process by which paradigms of race are used to situate anxieties about class conflict, social mobility, and gender. Moreover, in the novels considered here, although Balzac, Zola, and Maupassant do register these racialist paradigms, they keep them at a distance through historicist context, or the ambivalence and fluctuation of what, elsewhere, are treated as fixed categories.[1]

The deployment of theories of racial difference to understand human society was not new, but the tendency gained wider currency, and a more extensive pseudo-scientific apparatus, as the nineteenth century wore on. Naturalists, from the mid eighteenth century onwards, had sought to define differences between human groups in dominantly biological terms, focusing on the divisions of humanity into three, or sometimes five, human 'races' or 'varieties' or even 'species' that were fixed (rather than subject to fluctuations due to climate as in older theories), and located in a hierarchy of value. This increasing emphasis on biological difference came to be applied in the social sciences too. The 1820s, in particular, saw a strengthening of the 'belief in the racial determination of the phenomena of material and symbolic civilization'[2] and the idea that race was the motor of history.[3] And race was used to define identity *within* nations as well as between them. Since the seventeenth

---

[1] On the mobile nature of racial physiognomy in the colonial novel, see the sub-section 'L'Altérité atténuée ou la biologie instable' in my book *Clichés de la femme exotique: un regard sur la littérature coloniale française entre 1871 et 1914* (Paris: L'Harmattan, 2000), pp. 93–107.

[2] Claude Blanckaert, 'On the Origins of French Ethnology: William Edwards and the Doctrine of Race', in *Bones, Bodies, Behaviour: Essays in Biological Anthropology*, ed. by George W. Stocking (Madison: University of Wisconsin Press, 1988), pp. 18–55 (p. 18). See also his chapter 'Les conditions d'émergence de la science des races au début du XIXe siècle', in *L'Idée de 'race' dans les sciences humaines et la littérature (XVIIIᵉ et XIXᵉ siècles)*, ed. by Sarga Moussa (Paris: L'Harmattan, 2003), pp. 133–49.

[3] The racial conception of history was popularized in France by Augustin and Amédée Thierry (see, among others, Blanckaert, 'On the Origins', 20–6). On the relationship between literature and the use of race in writing history, see Saminadayar-Perrin, 'Antiquité des races'.

century class difference had been understood in terms of the presence, within the
nation, of two historically and biologically distinct races (Gauls and Franks in the
case of France).[4] The historian Amédée Thierry took up this theory of the 'two
races', which was combined with naturalists' anatomical theories in a very influential publication by William Frédéric Edwards in 1829.[5] Edwards asserted the racial
basis of class divisions within a given population, a subject of urgent concern in the
face of social unrest.

As Louis Chevalier has shown, the rapid urbanization of the French population
created such pressure on the accepted norms of society that the new Parisian proletariat came to be understood in racial terms as defined by a permanently different
physiology, and compared to culturally foreign groups such as 'sauvages', 'nomades',
or 'barbares'.[6] The ethnography of the late eighteenth and early nineteenth century
already reflected a convergence of concepts, with both the savage and the European
'common man' increasingly represented through 'images of bestiality'.[7] Building
on this foundation, the 1820s and the 1840s saw the emergence of studies charting
'the phenomenon of crime in the cities', and the multiplication of literary portrayals
of 'dangerous classes and dangerous races', as Daniel Pick notes. Theories of degeneration, he argues, were used not only in anthropological studies of non-European
peoples, 'but also to pose a vision of internal dangers and crises within Europe',
and to explain a perceived social decline that saw the emergence of new metropolitan races 'so miserable, inferior and bastardised that they may be classed as below
the most inferior savage races, for their inferiority is sometimes beyond cure'.[8] The
threat of revolutionary violence from within French society added to the conceptual
immediacy of such theories in the 1830s and 1840s, but a parallel movement
towards the racialization of class can be observed in Britain,[9] and it continued in
France towards the end of the century.[10]

[4] See the influential study by Léon Poliakov, *Le Mythe aryen: Essai sur les sources du racisme et des
nationalismes* (Brussels: Éditions complexe, 1987 [1971]), pp. 29–48, and Pierre Michel, *Un mythe
romantique: Les Barbares 1789–1848* (Lyon: Presses Universitaires de Lyon, 1981).

[5] William Frédéric Edwards, *Des caractères physiologiques des races humaines considérés dans leurs
rapports avec l'histoire: Lettre à M. Amédée Thierry, auteur de l'histoire des Gaulois* (1829). On the long-
term influence of this famous 'Lettre', see Blanckaert, 'On the origins'.

[6] Louis Chevalier, *Classes laborieuses et classes dangereuses à Paris pendant la première moitié du XIXe
siècle* (Paris: Plon, 1958), pp. 451–62. The 'barbare' within French society, and the various political
applications of the term, are also studied by Michel (*Un mythe romantique*).

[7] Ter Ellingson, *The Myth of the Noble Savage* (Oakland, CA: University of California Press, 2001),
p. 126.

[8] Daniel Pick, *Faces of Degeneration: A European Disorder, c.1848–c.1918* (Cambridge: Cambridge
University Press, 1989), p. 21 and p. 60, quoting Buchez (1857). Pick criticizes Johannes Fabian—
and to some extent Said—as flattening out differences *within* Western society (pp. 37–9). Pick himself
has however been criticized for a view of degeneracy theory that is too exclusively European (see Ann
Laura Stoler, *Race and the Education of Desire: Foucault's 'History of Sexuality' and the Colonial Order of
Things* (Durham: Duke University Press, 1995), p. 31, p. 32).

[9] On the racialization of class in British literature, see the survey article by Moore, 'Colonialism
in Victorian Fiction'. On British Gothic literature's absorption of racial imagery in order to depict the
concept of a savage underclass, particularly following fears of violence after the French Revolution, see
Howard L. Malchow, *Gothic Images of Race in Nineteenth-Century Britain* (Redwood, CA: Stanford
University Press, 1996), p. 61 and ch. 2.

[10] One of the most influential uses of race to understand class dates to 1894, by the sociologist
Gustave Le Bon, for whom the lowest classes within European societies were the equivalent of

For the bourgeois writer, venturing onto the terrain of the working classes was like exploring a distant territory inhabited by savages. Eugène Sue set out to write *Les Mystères de Paris* much as Fenimore Cooper described the American Indians, and Balzac too draws frequent comparisons between contemporary Paris and Cooper's wild American forests.[11] Edmond de Goncourt later explained his choice of working-class subjects by the contrast with his own social standing: 'le peuple, la canaille si vous le voulez, a pour moi l'attrait de populations inconnues et non découvertes, quelque chose de l'*exotique*, que les voyageurs vont chercher avec mille souffrances dans les pays lointains'.[12] But the concept of race is not merely a *metaphor*: it is, according to Laura Doyle, the conceptual basis of class difference.[13]

In the novels studied here, it is not only in descriptions of the working classes that ideas of racial difference are to be found. Rather, such imagery is used to embody an ill-defined threat whose origins are not entirely 'other', and yet not comfortably to be accepted as 'self'. Such a category has been memorably discussed by Julia Kristeva as the 'abject': abjection, she argues, confronts us with the precarious borderline state where 'l'homme erre dans les territoires de l'*animal*'.[14] In the nineteenth-century novel this threatened proximity of the animal draws on imagery of primitive or prehistoric man, imagery that is in turn influenced by the conceptions of racial inequality that were dominant at the time.

My reading of the role played by racial tropes in the construction of class and sexuality owes much to Ann Laura Stoler's invaluable work applying Michel Foucault's theories, which concentrate on discourses of sexuality, to concepts of race. Stoler situates in the early nineteenth century the emergence of the bourgeois use of 'race and sexuality as ordering mechanisms', but argues that 'a repertoire of racial and imperial metaphors were deployed to clarify class distinctions in Europe' from a much earlier date. '[E]xternal colonisation', she claims, provided a metaphorical framework for understanding Europe itself, 'a template for conceptualizing social inequalities in Europe and not solely the other way around'.[15] Following Stoler, I understand the analogy as operating in both directions: class difference was exported to the colonies as a conceptual framework on which to base imperial

'primitives', incapable of civilization, and time alone would be sufficient to make them as separate from the upper class as blacks from whites (*Les Lois psychologiques de l'évolution des peuples*; see Todorov, *Nous et les Autres*, p. 161). See also Carole Reynaud-Paligot, *La République raciale: paradigme racial et idéologie républicaine 1860–1930* (Paris: Presses Universitaires de France, 2006), pp. 11–31.

[11] On Balzac's widespread references to Cooper's Mohican stories, see Prendergast, *Order of Mimesis*, p. 222 and *Balzac: Fiction and Melodrama*, p. 88; Brooks, *Realist Vision*, p. 22; Macherey, *Pour une théorie*, pp. 314–16; Vanoncini, 'Le sauvage', *passim*. Chevalier, too, sees Balzac as blurring the distinction between the working classes and Fenimore Cooper's 'savages' (pp. 494–5).

[12] *Journal*, vol. 2, p. 476 (3 December 1871), his emphasis. On the Goncourts' self-ascribed role as anthropologists examining the exotic customs of the popular classes, see Pierre Dufief, 'Les Goncourt et la race: Au carrefour de la prosopographie et de l'idéologie', *Excavatio*, 16:1–2 (2002), 35–45.

[13] See Doyle, *Freedom's Empire*.   [14] *Pouvoirs de l'horreur*, p. 20, her emphasis.

[15] *Race and the Education*, p. 9; p. 123; p. 75. See also Ann Laura Stoler, 'State Racism and the Education of Desires: A Colonial Reading of Foucault', in *Deep HiStories: Gender and Colonialism in Southern Africa*, ed. by Wendy Woodward, Patricia Hayes, and Gary Minkley (Amsterdam: Rodopi, 2002), 3–26 (p. 18): 'imperial images of the colonized and eroticized native American, African and Asian savage/barbarian saturated the discourses of class'.

power, but at the same time the model of racial difference was imported from the colonial encounter as a means of containing new anxieties about metropolitan society. The framework of colonial imagery is not only applied to the threat presented by the working classes. French *women*, and more specifically the threat of uncontrolled sexuality, are frequently assimilated with other races. This was formalized in the closing decades of the century in craniological studies cited by Gustave Le Bon to support his opinion that women—even Parisian women—were beings on a par with the so-called 'lower' races.[16] Prostitutes in particular embodied 'atavistic sexuality' and revealed the '"primitive" hidden beneath the surface'.[17] And the common trait of the racialist paradigms that we shall consider is their emphatically sexual nature, though this includes predatory sexuality exercised against women. Naturally this does not preclude a grounding in class conflict. As McClintock puts it, 'race, gender and class are not distinct realms of experience, existing in splendid isolation from each other [...] Rather, they come into existence *in and through* relation to each other—if in contradictory and conflictual ways'.[18] This triangulation is also analysed by Stoler who asserts that sexual urges, as well as class difference, were understood through a racial paradigm. 'To be truly European was to cultivate a bourgeois self in which [...] sex was held in check [...] by parcelling out demonstrations of excess to different social groups'; the 'respectable sexuality' of the middle class was 'a defence against an internal and external other that was at once essentially different but uncomfortably the same'.[19] One can set this in the context of Robert Young's argument that nineteenth-century theories of race are 'covert theories of desire'.[20] This covert desire, coupled with less covert fear, produces a recurrent pattern in which violence, of a more or less explicitly sexual nature, is understood through links to racial or colonial contexts. Discourses of race were used in consolidating, and policing, emerging bourgeois sexual norms.

Since racializing metaphors and colonial contact are used to evoke both class difference and sexual menace, I find it hard to follow Jameson when he asserts that the 'prototypical paradigm of the Other in the late nineteenth century', the terrifying ogre and threat of the archaic 'wild man', comes from the 'other imperial nation state'—notably, for the French after 1870, from Germany. He also argues that it is only in the 'non-canonical adventure literature of imperialism' that one finds the representation of 'the more radical otherness of colonized, non-Western peoples'.[21] As I shall now show, the indirect imprint of such representation is in fact to be found at the heart of the realist and naturalist canon.

---

[16] See Todorov, *Nous et les Autres*, pp. 161–2.
[17] See Gilman, *Difference and Pathology*, p. 104.   [18] *Imperial Leather*, p. 5, her emphasis.
[19] *Race and the Education*, pp. 182–3, p. 193. See also Jean Borie, *Mythologies de l'hérédité au XIXᵉ siècle* (Paris: Galilée, 1981), p. 14, on the new industrial proletariat, and contact with colonial populations, as both inspiring fear of proliferating degeneration and social pathology; and p. 102 on the policing of bourgeois bodily purity in opposition to the animality of the worker.
[20] *Colonial Desire*, p. 9; he argues that the question of whether or not humans are a single species was the central issue of anthropological, cultural, and scientific debates in the nineteenth century.
[21] Jameson, 'Modernism and Imperialism', p. 10.

BALZAC: *LA COUSINE BETTE* AND THE NEW
URBAN PROLETARIAT

Balzac's *La Cousine Bette* (1846) combines this yoking of discourses of class and race with the foregrounding of gender. The premise of Balzac's masterpiece is the hidden menace presented by the eponymous Bette, whose status is at once financially and sexually marginal within the bourgeois family, since she is both a poor relative and a spinster. Bette is also located within the new urban proletariat, and racial paradigms are used to affirm this class difference. Now the idea of racial difference situated *within* the family may seem contradictory, but this can be understood in the context of the mobile and historically determined nature of class in *La Comédie humaine*. Both the upper and working classes are mobile categories. The Hulot family is a remnant of the Napoleonic aristocracy, on the wane since the Restoration, so that Adeline Hulot is no longer the brilliant star of First-Empire society that she became through marriage to the Baron Hulot. Peasant origins preceded her meteoric rise, and they remain visible in the shape of her cousin, Lisbeth Fischer or Bette. Bette is a 'Paysanne des Vosges, dans toute l'extension du mot' (VII: 80); she has worked in the fields, and reached adulthood illiterate. In Prendergast's words, she represents the 'endemic primitive wildness of the peasant mentality'.[22] Yet Lisbeth too has changed class, 'devenue *ouvrière* en passementerie d'or et d'argent' (my emphasis, VII: 81) in the workshop of a skilled artisan, and she has taught herself to read and write. In other words she has joined the new urban working class whose explosive growth was transforming Paris. For she is not alone: 'Son intelligence paysanne avait d'ailleurs acquis, dans les causeries de l'atelier, par la fréquentation des ouvriers et des ouvrières, une dose du mordant parisien' (VII: 82). Where the published version of her first appearance reads 'un étranger aurait hésité à saluer la cousine Bette comme une parente de la maison, car elle ressemblait tout à fait à une couturière en journée' (VII: 57), Balzac's manuscript repeats the more politically marked reference to her status as a worker: 'elle ressemblait tout à fait à une *ouvrière*' (MS Lov. A 48, fol. 2, my emphasis).

The class of displaced peasants who were swelling the ranks of the urban proletariat represented a new threat within the fabric of Parisian society and, as Stoler observes, the working-class woman in particular was often seen as a 'primitive relic' of the wild woman.[23] This helps us to understand how Bette's secret savagery in the heart of a respectable Parisian family fits with the description of the area where she lives, the sinister *quartier du Doyenné* (VII: 99–101), where the seedy side of Paris juxtaposes the palace of the king. The Louvre seems to call out for such 'verrues' to be removed from its face (VII: 100), in an echo of Bette's own warts (VII: 80). Peter Hulme offers a compelling analysis of *La Cousine Bette* in terms of anxiety about the 1840s urbanization of the population, evoked by the slum quarter and its inhabitants. Following Macherey he sees the text's unconscious anxiety—'the threat to order'—as displaced from the margins onto 'the *narrative* centre (Bette)' who reveals what Macherey calls the 'determinate absence' of the novel, that is,

---

[22] *Balzac*, p. 107.   [23] *Race and the Education*, p. 128.

history itself. This anxiety is not, Hulme emphasizes, simply a response to the proletariat.[24] Rather, the threat of violence or disorder embodied in Bette is over-determined in ways that remind us of the necessity of linking psychological and political/historical analysis: the feminine/familial jealousy of the ugly spinster for her beautiful cousin underlies the resentment of the have-nots for the bourgeoisie. As a child, Bette attacked Adeline and would have killed her, and even as an adult, '[c]ette fille qui, bien observée, eût présenté le côté féroce de la classe paysanne, était toujours l'enfant qui voulait arracher le nez de sa cousine' (VII: 85). Bette's urge to destroy the Hulot family is a contained, adult version of her childhood violence: she will bite Adeline in the new ways she has learned along with the 'mordant parisien' (VII: 82). Thanks to her Parisian experience 'des lois et du monde', she has managed to tame the savage urge that once led her straight from feeling to action (VII: 86), so that she can conceal her violent instincts and channel them in devious ways, notably through an unholy alliance with that most Parisian of all women, Valérie Marneffe.[25] Even Bette's work—sewing decorations for military uniforms—reiterates her situation *within* the masculine power-structures that once rested so securely on the broad shoulders of Hulot. The fact that the threat to the bourgeois patriarchal order comes from inside the family helps us to under-stand why it so often takes the form of a sexual menace. Bette is both insider and outsider, the undetected stranger within the family. Her difference is not that of an absolute other but of the abject. Here we have, as Hulme puts it, 'social anxiety figured as a family romance'.[26] Within the newly urbanized working classes, Bette retains her peasant savagery and her treacherous nature, a characteristic commonly found in 'le peuple' and which 'peut en expliquer la conduite pendant les révolutions' (VII: 86). The beast within the family embodies the threat of revolution.

Social anxiety is also figured through race or, rather, through racializing metaphors. Bette's social separation from her beautiful blonde cousin is evoked in markedly physical terms, as a contrast of darkness and whiteness, from the *second* description of her onwards (I shall come back to the first description in a moment). Her ugli-ness is both emphatically dark and linked to her lack of education: 'cette fille aux yeux noirs, aux sourcils charbonnés, et qui ne savait ni lire ni écrire' (VII: 81). The opposition is between golden hair, gentleness, and bourgeois status on the one hand, and darkness, repressed violence, and the physical labour of 'la terre' or the workshop, on the other. This supports Stoler's argument that 'nineteenth-century bourgeois sexuality' emerged in the context of 'an imperial landscape where the cultural accoutrements of bourgeois distinction were partially shaped through contrasts forged in the politics and language of race', and that an 'implicit racial grammar' underwrites bourgeois sexual norms.[27] This 'implicit racial grammar'

---

[24] Peter Hulme, 'Balzac's Parisian Mystery: *La Cousine Bette* and the Writing of Historical Criticism', *Literature and History*, 11:1 (1985), 47–64 (p. 53, p. 55).

[25] André Vanoncini sees this taming of her violent instincts as limiting, rather than channeling, her savagery ('Le sauvage dans "La Comédie humaine"', *L'Année balzacienne* (2000), 231–47 (p. 238)), but this would suggest that urban life reduces, rather than increases, the likelihood of revolution, which contradicts the evidence of history.

[26] 'Balzac's Parisian Mystery', p. 60.   [27] *Race and the Education*, p. 5, p. 12.

drives the depictions of Bette, who is 'brune, les cheveux d'un noir luisant, les sourcils épais et réunis par un bouquet, les bras longs et forts, les pieds épais, quelques verrues dans sa face longue et *simiesque*' (Balzac's emphasis, VII: 80). Sometimes 'elle ressemblait aux singes habillés en femmes, promenés par les petits Savoyards' (VII: 86). Repeated again and again with the definite article, her nickname 'la Bette' (VII: 82, 85, 94, 98), also reminds us of this presence of the beast within the family.

The physical descriptions that underlie Bette's position at the margins of the Hulots' bourgeois nuclear family suggest a parallel with *Jane Eyre* as analysed by Spivak in one of the foundational essays of postcolonial studies.[28] In her reading, Rochester's mad wife Bertha Mason, 'the white Jamaican Creole', is used to render 'the human/animal frontier as acceptably indeterminate', and it is the 'active ideology of imperialism' that allows Jane to move from the marginal 'counter-family', constituted by the governess or poor relative, to the 'closed circle of the nuclear family'. Such a move, Spivak claims, is the greatest project conceived of by 'nineteenth-century feminist individualism'.[29] The crucial difference is that whereas *Jane Eyre* splits the primitive/colonial 'other' (Bertha) away from the aspiring female subject (Jane), *La Cousine Bette* combines them. As a result, the dynamics of imperialism do not propel Bette into the hallowed family core. Now to see Balzac as motivated by feminist individualism would require considerable critical gymnastics,[30] but Balzacian characters have minds of their own: Bette herself has rejected proposals of marriage and chosen spinsterhood in order to keep her independence, and she forms a passionate attachment based on female solidarity. In the eyes of her creator, however, this self-determinism is not incompatible with a primitive or animalistic nature.

The proximity of the animal is no surprise in *La Comédie humaine*, given Balzac's explicit assertion of the equivalence between the human and animal kingdoms in the 1842 'Avant-Propos'. More striking here is the mapping of the comparison with an ape or monkey onto the markers that reiterate Bette's membership of the newly-urbanized working classes. To what extent, in this pre-Darwinian world, should one take comparisons with long-armed apes to reflect racial categories? In fact by the 1830s and 1840s such categories had already gained currency. The comparison of so-called 'lower' races with great apes was a common feature of naturalist debates, reaching a low point (in terms of the abuse of an individual's human rights and dignity) in 1815 with the infamous exhibition and scientific examination of the 'Vénus Hottentote' Sarah Baartman, a Khoisan woman actually named Saartjie or Sawtche who was notably examined (alive) by Geoffroy Saint-Hilaire and (dead) by Georges Cuvier.[31] Balzac, great admirer of both

[28] Gayatri Chakravorty Spivak, 'Three Women's Texts and a Critique of Imperialism' [1985], in *'Race', Writing, and Difference*, ed. by Henry Louis Gates, Jr (Chicago/London: University of Chicago Press, 1986), pp. 262–80.

[29] Spivak, 'Three Women's Texts', pp. 266–7. For an overview of the critical response to Spivak's article, see Loomba, pp. 73–4.

[30] Though it has been attempted: see Nathalie Aubert, 'En Attendant les barbares: *La Cousine Bette*, le moment populaire et féminin de *La Comédie humaine*', *Women in French Studies*, 8 (2000), 129–37.

[31] See, among many other studies, Gilman, *Difference and Pathology*, pp. 84–91.

these naturalists, borrows from their language. It is hard to account for Bette's malignancy without registering the role of racialization in the construction of her character.[32]

Nevertheless, Balzac's use of race does not reflect the rigid categories that would come into currency in the second half of the century, when the emergent discipline of physical anthropology developed systematic racialist comparatism. Indeed, the contrast he establishes between the two cousins Bette and Adeline stems largely from the Romantic opposition of *la brune et la blonde*, itself derived from an older scientific theory in which climate was a determinate influence. Contrasts between 'Nordic' and 'Meridional' types recur throughout *La Comédie humaine*, and Bette herself is compared to a Calabrian or Corsican peasant. This reflects a transitional phase in French imaginary geography, which was shifting from a dominantly North–South axis (as popularized by Mme de Staël) to a newer East–West axis.[33] The Romantic figure of the Meridional brunette as passionate, and passionately resentful, is given a more sexually enticing form in *Le Contrat de mariage* (1835), but even in *La Cousine Bette* the descriptions that emphasize Bette's ugliness and spinsterhood are balanced by Balzac's almost regretful observation that she could have made more of her 'chevelure noire' and her 'beaux yeux durs' (VII: 86). In her heyday she was 'la brune piquante de l'ancien roman français', with all the attractions of a 'regard perçant, son teint olivâtre, sa taille de roseau' (VII: 83). The Nordic/Meridional contrast is not gender-neutral: in *Le Contrat de mariage* it indicates the danger posed by the wrong kind of woman, specifically the predatory nature of a mother and daughter of Creole origin. In *La Cousine Bette*, too, Valérie Marneffe, though of purely French origins (she is the illegitimate daughter of an aristocrat and a Parisian courtesan), shares some of Bette's darkness, being described as a 'vraie créole de Paris', with 'la redoutable intelligence de la créole parisienne' (VII: 150; 151).[34]

Just as the descriptions of Bette waver between the new racial model and an older, pre-racial imaginary, so too the term 'sauvage', often applied to her, does not denote a fixed category—nor is it an entirely negative attribute. On the one hand it is to be understood as part of a reaction to Enlightenment ideas of the noble savage: nineteenth-century references are often to an 'ignoble' savage. On the other hand, the Balzacian savage has a certain primitive energy. Her (or his) mind is capable of a single obsession at a time: 'le Sauvage n'admet qu'une idée à la fois' (VII: 86), and Bette shows 'cette singularité [dans les idées] qu'on remarque chez

---

[32] The point is made convincingly by Scott McCracken in his critique of Jameson's overtly Freudian reading of the novel ('Cousin Bette: Balzac and the Historiography of Difference', *Essays and Studies*, 44 (1991), 88–104 (p. 100).

[33] The Romantic binary opposition of *la brune et la blonde* retains some currency even later in the century. Zola, for example, draws on it in *La Faute de l'abbé Mouret* when he contrasts the blonde Albine who conjoins spiritual and sensual love, with the dark Désirée, in whom the flesh dominates and whose sexuality is expressed in animal terms.

[34] Jameson sees her as 'a kind of *emanation* of Bette' ('*La Cousine Bette* and Allegorical Realism', p. 247, his emphasis).

les Sauvages qui pensent beaucoup et parlent peu'.[35] She has a male counterpart in the Brazilian Baron Montès de Montéjanos, whose 'caractère quasi sauvage [...] se rapprochait beaucoup de celui de Lisbeth' (VII: 397), but he is emphatically neither a woman nor working-class. The *implicitly* racial resentment and destructive power of the urban proletariat are in the end neutralized by the *explicitly* colonial (and ultra-masculine) violence epitomized in the autocratic figure of the Baron. The 'savage', Othello-like baron is needed to undo the 'savage' Bette and her Parisian/creole avatar, Valérie. In their obsessive passion, both Montéjanos and Bette have some of the characteristics of that quintessentially Balzacian figure, the monomaniac, who is also driven by one dominant idea. As Anne-Marie Baron puts it, Balzac's great monomaniacs are 'des sauvages': 'Puissance concentrée, maîtrise stoïque de soi, énergie et intuition sont leurs atouts maîtres.' She argues that the word 'sauvage', which occurs so frequently in the *Comédie humaine*, must be seen as 'une pierre angulaire du système balzacien' perhaps reflecting the 'nostalgie d'un âge d' or'.[36] Balzac's monomaniacs are possessed by a single idea at the expense of their moral and personal duties—the obsessive womanizing of Adeline's husband Baron Hulot is what makes the Hulot family vulnerable—but among them one must also count the creative geniuses who are closest to the obsessive, driven creator of the *Comédie humaine* himself.[37]

There is, moreover, an important reason *not* to read Bette's character as defined solely through a racial conception of biological determinism. Balzac's novels shift between physiological and social determinisms; identity is mobile rather than given. Thus the first description of Bette gives us details only of her clothes (VII: 57), in an exclusively, even emphatically *non*-physiological approach. Her identity is subject to her own whim, and thus to something like individual agency. Her darkness both is and is not overdetermined: 'Bette's "primitive" nature [... is] not fully reified into an ideology of racial or sexual inferiority'.[38] In *La Comédie humaine* a world of fixed types—in which the centre is menaced by threatening sexual, or racialized 'others'—co-exists with a conception of class as historically mobile. And the ignoble savage, the wild other, is situated within the family itself.[39]

---

[35] This comparison with 'sauvages' was added as an afterthought in Balzac's manuscript, in a passage whose original emphasis was on 'les ouvriers' (MS Lov. A 48, fol. 17).

[36] Anne-Marie Baron, *Balzac, ou les hiéroglyphes de l'imaginaire* (Paris: Honoré Champion, 2002), pp. 22–4. In the late nineteenth century, too, the figure of the 'primitive', though marked by inferiority, is identified as a source of energy (see Citti, pp. 248–9). See also Vanoncini, 'Le sauvage', on some of the positive aspects of the term.

[37] And Balzac identified himself with the 'savage', for example in a letter to Victor Ratier of 21 July 1830 (*Correspondance*, vol. 1, pp. 303–04).

[38] McCracken, 'Cousin Bette', p. 102.

[39] On the progressive internalization of the 'Wild Man' lurking within us all (though in Bette's case it is of course a Wild Woman), see Hayden White, 'The Forms of Wildness: Archaeology of an Idea', in *The Wild Man Within: An Image in Western Thought from the Renaissance to Romanticism*, ed. by Edward Dudley and Maximillian E. Novak (Pittsburgh, PA: University of Pittsburgh Press, 1972), pp. 3–38 (p. 7).

THE COLONIAL ORIGINS OF METROPOLITAN VIOLENCE: EMBEDDED NARRATIVES IN BALZAC, MAUPASSANT, AND ZOLA

The threat posed to the family and to metropolitan society was embodied in Bette in terms that skirt around racial difference, but return to it obsessively. I shall turn now to another threat situated within the family but this time originating outside it, in the colonial heterotopia. Colonial experience is often found in embedded narratives, though in conformity with the tendency for such experience to remain firmly offstage these are usually 'minimal' embedded narratives without a clearly distinguished narrative situation.[40] Our first example, that of Philippe Bridau in *La Rabouilleuse*—one of Balzac's most sinister creations—has already been discussed in relation to fraud in Chapter 3. Unwilling to join the Bourbons after the fall of Napoleon, Philippe rejects an initial colonial plan, the suggestion that he should serve in a foreign army in the East.[41] Instead he embarks on the attempt at colonization in Texas by ex-officers of the Napoleonic old-guard, the 'Champ d'Asile'. The project fails, and at great cost to his family Philippe returns via New York. The embedded narrative of his experiences begins when 'Le paquebot arriva par une belle matinée du mois d'octobre 1819' in Le Havre, so that the traveller enters the precise spatio-temporal world of the realist novel only at the moment of his *return* to France (IV: 303). The account is concerned not with the events themselves but with their effects on his character: 'Ses malheurs au Texas, son séjour à New York, pays où la spéculation et l'individualisme sont portés au plus haut degré, où la brutalité des intérêts arrive au cynisme [...] enfin, les moindres événements de ce voyage avaient développé chez Philippe les mauvais penchants du soudard: il était devenu brutal, fumeur, personnel, impoli; la misère et les souffrances physiques l'avaient dépravé.' Like Charles Grandet after his experience of the slave trade, Bridau has lost 'les moindres scrupules en fait de moralité' (IV: 303). Once again Balzac's use of a colonial embedded narrative, however minimal, introduces a spatio-temporal hiatus that brings together the two different chronotopes that Bakhtin calls 'adventure-time' and 'everyday time'.[42] The meeting of these two chronotopes leads to a narrative of metamorphosis, through a *transforming* or more often *disfiguring* impact on the character.[43] In *La Rabouilleuse* the threat of social disruption and violence is again internal to the respectable family: just as *La Cousine Bette*

---

[40] Minimal embedded narratives are discussed briefly by Bal (*Narratology*, p. 60). They are characterized by their brevity, lack of a narrator distinct from the primary narrator, and relatively seamless integration into the main flow of the narration. The narrative situation of these embedded narratives is usually what Genette calls 'extradiégétique-hétérodiégétique', that is, where a first-degree narrator tells a story from which he is absent (*Figures III*, p. 255).

[41] That is, 'dans l'Orient, aux Indes'; but the Bonapartiste Philippe does not want to serve under a foreign flag. As his witty younger brother, the artist Joseph, puts it, 'le Français est trop fier de sa Colonne pour aller s'encolonner ailleurs' (IV: 300).

[42] *The Dialogic Imagination*, p. 111. Bakhtin sees such sequences of 'adventure-folktale' time, which are ruled by chance, as subordinate to the laws governing the primary sequence, which are those of individual guilt and responsibility (pp. 118–19).

[43] The term is used by Hamon in relation to Zola, whose characters undergo a process of 'défiguration' (*Le Personnel du roman*, p. 162).

situated the fault line between cousins, here it divides two brothers, the gentle genius Joseph and his feral brother Philippe. Primitive violence emerges from within society, but at the same time it presents the characteristics of alterity. Unlike Bette, however, Philippe Bridau is not marked by signs of pseudo-racial difference:[44] instead, he is transformed by his colonial experience.

Philippe's second colonial adventure is narrated not in terms of effects but of events, in one rapid paragraph covering the years 1834–9 which he spends fighting in Algeria, until he is abandoned by his men, decapitated, and hacked to pieces on the battlefield (IV: 540). This is poetic justice, a symmetrical answer to his initial apprenticeship in random violence and rampant individualism in the Far West. In somewhat teleological terms, Jameson sees Philippe's death as 'prophetic', considering that 'this ultimate anti-climactic episode of the Napoleonic soldier overwhelmed by the Berbers stands as a first distorted and nightmarish apprehension of the negation of our society by a Third World it has summoned into being against itself'.[45] Philippe Bridau's violence, Jameson writes elsewhere, prefigures a 'Victorian fantasy-image of the lumpen-proletarian at his most threatening'; in other words he sees colonial experience as standing in lieu of class difference (to which one might object that in the course of his adventures Philippe, son of a high-ranking civil servant, becomes a count and, albeit briefly, a millionaire). As discussed in Chapter 3, Jameson offers two distinct and 'mutually exclusive' diagnoses for the 'principle of disorder and violence' thus revealed: one is historical, the other psychological. The historicist diagnosis emphasizes Philippe's inability to fit himself for the new society that has followed the fall of Napoleon, so that he is consigned to 'the very boundary of "civilized society"', where, in the campaign to seize Algeria from the Bey, like Tête d'Or arriving at the limits of empire only to confront the faceless but absolute Otherness of an alien horde, he is overwhelmed by the earliest Third World guerrillas represented in modern literature'.[46] As already noted, Jameson himself argues for a critical 'two-way street' that would combine this historical/political account with a psychological/individual approach, but— constrained perhaps by his own view of the new colonial world order as beginning only at the very end of the nineteenth century—he seems to give more weight to the latter. This psychological approach sees Philippe's violence as arising from maternal indulgence in the absence of an adequate father-figure. After the fall of the *ancien régime* and the decapitation of the king, followed by the fall and exile of Napoleon, this is however both a personal and a political predicament. Philippe's first colonial foray is an attempt to find a new Napeolonic order among his fellow officers in the Texan colony, and his death in Algeria results from the failure of true paternal authority that unleashes an exacerbated, castrating masculinity. As an element incapable of social assimilation under the Restoration, Philippe's destiny—refused once, aborted at a second attempt, and conclusive in the third instance—is to be expelled from the modern metropolitan system into the colonial heterotopia.

[44] Philippe, blond and blue-eyed, takes after his beautiful mother (IV: 287).

[45] 'Imaginary and Symbolic', p. 65. On Algeria as attracting and exposing 'an atavistic Napoleonic element' that Balzac condemns, see Bell, 'Balzac's Algeria', p. 40.

[46] *Political Unconscious*, pp. 158–9.

As French colonialism becomes more solidly entrenched, novels increasingly return to the incursion into the metropolis of violence brought back from the colonies. As remarked in Chapter 1, Algeria in the 1830s and 1840s proved a training ground in the kind of violence against civilians that has been called 'total war'.[47] While the novelistic chronotope of adventure still holds out more possibilities than the chronotope of the everyday, these are less openings for self-realization than a process of decivilization that threatens the civic peace of the metropolis. This reverses two (contrasting) narratives inherited from the Enlightenment. The narrative of *Robinson Crusoe*, in which savage nature is conquered by civilized man, is inverted, particularly by naturalism.[48] And the pre-sexual exotic idyll of *Paul et Virginie*, where it is the *metropolis* that triggers the advent of socio-sexual awareness, is inverted by realist colonial heterotopias that tend to associate the *colonial* space with contagious sexuality. These narratives cannot, however, be understood simply as a racist attribution of violence to non-European origins, for the colonial heterotopia is also the site of violence exercised by the colonist.

The stark realities of colonial rule are a training ground for violence in Maupassant's *Bel-Ami*. It is in Algeria that Georges Duroy has learned the complete lack of principles that enables him to conquer metropolitan society. In the early scenes the protagonist's imagination transposes the colonial possibilities of boundless violence onto the smug metropolitan crowd: 'il se rappelait ses deux années d'Afrique, la façon dont il rançonnait les Arabes dans les petits postes du Sud. Et un sourire cruel et gai passa sur ses lèvres au souvenir d'une escapade qui avait coûté la vie à trois hommes de la tribu des Ouled-Alane et qui leur avait valu, à ses camarades et à lui, vingt poules, deux moutons et de l'or, et de quoi rire pendant six mois' (199). His experience in the army removes his sense of shared humanity: 'Il avait été soldat, il avait tiré sur des Arabes, sans grand danger pour lui, d'ailleurs, un peu comme on tire sur un sanglier, à la chasse' (313). This has been read in Darwinian terms: for Susan Barrow, Georges Duroy returns from his service in Algeria stripped of 'the restraints of conventional morality; accustomed to living by his base instincts, he has regressed to the primal state of Elemental Man'. There is some danger, however, that such emphasis on Duroy '"becom[ing]" Africa by internalizing the code of the wild' might depoliticize Maupassant's novel. It is not *African* violence that Duroy brings back with him, but the violence of the colonial State; so although, as Barrow puts it, the novel does indeed illustrate 'how French society has been irreversibly altered by the experience of colonialism', Maupassant makes it quite clear that Duroy's violence was not learnt *from* Arabs but perpetrated by French soldiers *against* them.[49] Giacchetti phrases it more carefully: in her terms, Algeria and Morocco are mimetic models for Duroy, for whom colonial domination and exploitation offer a 'modèle actantiel' to be reproduced in the metropolis.[50]

---

[47] The term is used in pioneering work on the history of colonial violence by Olivier Le Cour Grandmaison (see Gallois, *History of Violence*, pp. 14–16).

[48] See Françoise Gaillard, 'Le Soi et l'Autre: le retour de la bête humaine', in *Du visible à l'invisible: pour Max Milner*, ed. by Stéphane Michaud (Paris: José Corti, 1988), pp. 97–110 (p. 107).

[49] Barrow, pp. 317–18, p. 326. On 'Darwinisme littéraire' in *Bel-Ami*, see also Vial, 277–8.

[50] Maupassant, *Espaces du roman*, p. 129.

Bel-Ami displays a new anxiety about the effects of colonialism on the colonizing culture. I began this chapter by tracing the association of the working classes with so-called 'primitive' races. *Bel-Ami*, however, does not use racial imagery to describe the working classes: it uses colonial violence as a metonym for the driving force behind the new dominant class, the rising bourgeoisie. Duroy's origins are humble—the first chapter of the novel insists on his initial state of poverty, and a visit to his parents shows us his peasant origins—but he embodies the unchecked social mobility of the parvenu. As Stoler argues, 'Colonialism was not a secure bourgeois project. It was not only about the importation of middle-class sensibilities to the colonies, but about the *making* of them.'[51] In *Bel-Ami* social rapacity is not understood through the metaphor of racial difference but through the metonym of colonial violence; at the same time, the latter is more than a mere metonym since it works through contagion to have a relation of cause and effect. One remembers Césaire's denunciation of the boomerang effect of imperialism, with its '*ensauvagement*' of Europe itself: the practice of treating the colonized as an animal transforms the colonizer himself 'en bête'.[52] In terms borrowed from Althusser, we could say that Duroy conquers power by transforming state-sanctioned colonial violence into domination of the ideological apparatus—that is, the press—and thus achieving recognition by the central metropolitan State itself. The novel ends with the protagonist's marriage in the Madeleine church whose architecture mirrors that of the *Assemblée nationale* that stands facing it on the other bank of the Seine. The place and the ceremony mark Duroy's official entry into France's ruling elite. No less a figure than the Bishop of Tangiers officiates, reminding us of the colonial basis of his meteoric rise. Duroy's Algerian pillaging is thus the seedy underside of the new bourgeois State itself.

Two years after *Bel-Ami*, Zola also used a colonial minimal embedded narrative, in this case to show an apprenticeship in State violence and sexual predation in the peasantry. In *La Terre* (1887), the ne'er-do-well nicknamed 'Jésus-Christ' is a peasant rendered inapt for work, 'un paresseux et un ivrogne', by his years as a conscript putting down the recent revolts in Algeria; he now lives 'de braconnage et de maraude, comme s'il eût rançonné encore un peuple tremblant de Bédouins' (IV: 380).[53] He amuses his peers with tales of 'des oreilles de Bédouins coupées et enfilées en chapelet, des Bédouines à la peau frottée d'huile, pincées derrière les haies et tamponnées dans tous les trous. Jésus-Christ surtout répétait une histoire qui enflait de rires énormes les ventres des paysans: une grande cavale de femme, jaune comme un citron, qu'on avait fait courir toute nue, avec une pipe dans le derrière' (IV: 425–6). Here, as in *Bel-Ami*, women are the objects of predatory sexuality, but in Jésus-Christ's case it is explicitly the sexuality of a colonial rapist, 'violeur de filles et détrousseur de grandes routes' (IV: 380). The novel, however, does not make him fully responsible: 'au fond de ses beaux yeux noyés, il y avait de la goguenardise

---

[51] *Race and the Education*, p. 99, her emphasis.
[52] Aimé Césaire, *Discours sur le colonialisme* (Paris/Dakar: Présence africaine, 1955), p. 11, p. 18.
[53] In contrast with *Bel-Ami*, which reverses the general trajectory of the Naturalist novel into the story of a vertiginous rise, this subplot of *La Terre* (like *La Terre* as a whole) repeats Zola's preferred plot curve of decline.

pas méchante, le cœur ouvert d'une bonne crapule' (IV: 380). Zola's point is to show the effects of conscription on the peasantry, those who are unable to pay for substitutes when their number comes up for military service. *La Terre*, like *Bel-Ami*, offers an implicit critique of the dehumanizing experience of service in the colonial army. Like the penal colony of *Le Ventre de Paris*, this is one of the spaces of State violence. In Foucault's terminology it is a heterotopia of deviation into which elements that do not conform to the norm are expelled; but the expulsion is ineffective, and the deviance is only deepened by it.

In two of Zola's novels of the 1860s, written before the Rougon-Macquart series, contact with colonial lands also degrades the metropolitan character. I shall discuss the more famous *Thérèse Raquin* (1867) separately, below. In *Madeleine Férat* (1868) a minimal colonial embedded narrative sees the secondary character Jacques Berthier depart to become a military doctor in Cochinchina (today south Vietnam). He is mistakenly thought to have been killed in a shipwreck at the Cape of Good Hope, but remains present as an invisible third party in the marriage between his ex-mistress Madeleine and the protégé of his schooldays, Guillaume; his unexpected return causes their marriage to crumble.[54] Jacques's role as *tiers*, and his virility compared to Guillaume, make him a father-figure whose presence, in classic Œdipal terms, destroys the relationship of the son with his proxy mother, Madeleine.[55] But reading the novel in a narrowly Freudian light risks reducing it to the stark simplic-ity of Zola's 1865 play *Madeleine*, in which only the kernel of the novel's plot is present.[56] The novel itself introduces a colonial embedded narrative that triggers a significant transformation in Jacques, the process that Hamon calls 'défiguration'[57] and of which we have seen variants in the cases of Charles Grandet, Philippe Bridau, Georges Duroy, and 'Jésus-Christ'. Before his colonial experience Jacques was 'bon enfant', light-hearted and devoted (87). Now, '[s]on visage s'était comme épaissi et durci; les vents de la mer, le grand soleil l'avaient couvert d'un hâle couleur de brique [...] Il paraissait avoir grandi, être devenu plus gros; ses épaules carrées, sa poitrine large, ses membres solides en faisaient une sorte de lutteur, aux poings énormes, à la tête bestiale. Il revenait légèrement brute [...] il avait [...] si bien vécu de la vie animale [...] qu'il n'éprouvait plus de besoins de cœur, et qu'il lui suffisait de contenter sa chair' (183). Zola's embedding of distant colonial space is, however, all the more striking when one thinks of the claustrophobic space that is more typical of his early novels.[58] Transformation occurs through a kind of colonial

---

[54] The prolonged absence, and subsequent return, of a man who is then the third party to a couple that believed him dead, also provides the plot of *Le Ventre de Paris* (1873) and the short story 'Jacques Damour' (1883), as discussed in Chapter 4. References to *Madeleine Férat*, included in the text, are to the edition by Henri Mitterand (Paris: Mémoire du livre, 1999).

[55] Borie, *Zola et les mythes*, pp. 53–9.

[56] *Madeleine*, a play in three acts, written in 1865, was rejected by two different theatres in 1866. Zola enriched his material considerably to turn it into a novel two years later. The play itself was not performed until 1889, when it was a great success.

[57] *Le Personnel du roman*, p. 162.

[58] Chantal Bertrand-Jennings demonstrates that the second half of *Madeleine Férat* returns to the setting of the first half in reverse order, and indeed she argues that most of Zola's early novels reflect the same spatial structure of 'enfermement' and abortive attempts at escape ('*Madeleine Férat* ou les lieux ennemis', *Revue de l'Université d'Ottawa*, 48:4 (1978), 407–14 (p. 412)). Zola uses distant space

contagion, though in a gesture towards the stereotypes of the exotic novel, we are told that Jacques was in no hurry to return because 'il était alors l'amant d'une femme indigène dont l'étrange beauté le charmait' (181). Contagion rather than inheritance is the mode of transmission in this early novel because Zola is interested in acquired characteristics rather than inherited traits: Jacques is *marked* by his colonial experience in parallel with the indelible marking or influence that he, as Madeleine's first lover, has left on her womb. Following the theory of impregnation that Zola had learnt from Michelet and Prosper Lucas, a woman will throughout her life 'belong' to the man who has first 'possessed' her sexually.[59]

Critics have tended to ignore the colonial trigger that provokes Jacques's *défiguration*.[60] The embedded colonial narrative serves as a metaphor for physiological determinism. It figures the return of the repressed (Madeleine's early illicit sexuality) in terms of bestial male sexuality emerging in the colonial heterotopia. It is thus hard to agree entirely with Borie's claim that 'la colonie offre un espace vierge où l'on peut enfin bâtir—et se bâtir—sans avoir à détruire pour cela une présence antérieure [...] l'angoissante présence ancestrale'.[61] On the contrary, in Zola's works of the 1860s the colonial other comes to stand for the terrifying ancestral presence within the metropolis itself. And this colonial alibi for a return to 'la vie animale' offers a precedent for Zola's later use of racial motifs to emphasize *inherited* determinism.

THÉRÈSE RAQUIN: COLONIAL INHERITANCE
BEFORE HEREDITY

Published a year before *Madeleine Férat*, *Thérèse Raquin* is much more often read and studied, both in its own right and as a precursor to the twenty-novel Rougon-Macquart series (1871–93). It too foregrounds physical determinism, but through fixed rather than acquired traits. In this, Zola is fully in tune with the 'mythe héréditaire' that dominated medical and naturalist thought in the second half

---

in contrast to this enclosed metropolitan space. Thus *Madeleine Férat* also incorporates elements of the Far West or colonial escape fantasy, when Guillaume daydreams: 'Nous quitterions la France [...] Personne ne nous connaîtrait' (248), but in typically realist style this is an escapist daydream, in marked contrast to the real, though undescribed, colonial space from which the virile Jacques returns; Guillaume's daydream projects the fantasy landscapes of childhood onto a 'real' outside world (250–2).

[59] Michelet's *L'Amour* (1858) and *La Femme* (1859) repeat the thesis of impregnation developed in Prosper Lucas's *Traité philosophique et physiologique de l'hérédité naturelle dans les états de santé et de maladie du système nerveux* (1847–50).

[60] John Lapp has Jacques leave simply for a 'post abroad' (*Zola Before the Rougon-Macquart* (Toronto: University of Toronto Press, 1964), p. 122). In Borie's Freudian reading Jacques as a character is 'anodin' and 'sans mystère', only taking on meaning insofar as he stands for the father (*Zola et les mythes*, p. 63). In another Freudian reading of the novel, Anthony John Evenhuis emphasizes the determining role of (Œdipal) 'ineffaceable guilt' or 'unpardonable sin', but claims at the same time that sin is 'brought about by the return of Jacques' ('Zola and the Unpardonable Sin: A Psychoanalytical Study of *Madeleine Férat*', *Excavatio*, 9 (1997), 122–35 (p. 122, p. 134)).

[61] *Zola et les mythes*, pp. 181–2. Borie also says that 'pour Zola, le vrai bâtisseur ne peut être qu'un colonisateur'. He is basing these claims primarily on his reading of the much later *Fécondité*.

of the century: intellectual and moral, as well as physical characteristics, were increasingly understood as being biologically transmitted from one generation to the next. By the end of the century, Levin notes, the novel too 'was more concerned with man's place in nature than with man's place in history'.[62] Naturalism places less emphasis on history and mobile class identity than we saw in the cases of Philippe Bridau and Bette. But within the work of Zola himself it is possible to observe a shift from the early novels of the 1860s, which include references to the experience or inheritance of colonialism, to a more biological viewpoint in which, by 1890, history becomes pre-history and 'racial' difference is internalized.

The mark of heredity appears in Thérèse's repressed passionate nature and sensuality, which are explained by her Algerian ancestry. We learn, very briefly, how she arrived in the household of her aunt, Mme Raquin: 'Un jour, seize années auparavant [...] son frère, le capitaine Degans, lui apporta une petite fille dans les bras. Il arrivait d'Algérie' (71).[63] The girl's father is killed in Africa some years later, after legally recognizing her as his own. Her aunt brings her up alongside her own son Camille, later Thérèse's husband: 'Elle sut vaguement que la chère petite était née à Oran et qu'elle avait pour mère une femme indigène d'une grande beauté' (72). Like the reference in *Madeleine Férat*, this minimal embedded narrative could be the summary of an 'exotic' novel such as those made popular by Pierre Loti, which seem in other ways the antithesis of the Zolian novel. In Zola's hands, however, the function of the exotic embedded narrative is to stand for inherited characteristics: it rehearses his later, more developed portrayal of atavism *within* European ancestry.

Thérèse's exotic origins are reflected in her feline energy, a metaphor familiar to us from Balzac's semi-oriental heroines Paquita and Esther and the entirely oriental and extremely feminine panther Mignonne of 'Une passion dans le désert'. Indeed, Thérèse's sexual intensity is itself an Orientalist cliché, though Zola includes more specifically (North) African references.[64] Terrifying even her lover, her sexuality is inherited from her mother: 'le sang de sa mère, ce sang africain qui brûlait ses veines, se mit à couler, à battre furieusement dans son corps maigre' (93). Thérèse's mother was 'fille d'un chef de tribu, en Afrique', and she yearns for an outdoor, nomadic life (94), often takes a squatting position (72; 91; 94), is

<hr/>

[62] *Gates of Horn*, p. 59. Levin ascribes this largely to the impact of Darwin, but the emphasis on physical determinism in France pre-dates Darwin's influence.

[63] References, included in the text, are to Émile Zola, *Thérèse Raquin* [1867], ed. by Henri Mitterand (Paris: 'GF' Flammarion, 1970).

[64] 'Thérèse [...] has a mixed Algerian-European parentage; in Orientalist fashion this presumably explains her latent seething passion' (Ross Shideler, *Questioning the Father: From Darwin to Zola, Ibsen, Strindberg, and Hardy* (Redwood, CA: Stanford University Press, 1999), p. 38). On Thérèse's animal nature and feline qualities, see Susan Harrow, '*Thérèse Raquin*: animal passion and the brutality of reading', in *The Cambridge Companion to Émile Zola*, ed. by Brian Nelson (Cambridge: Cambridge University Press, 2007), pp. 105–20 (p. 111). So too, in Balzac's short story 'Le Succube' (1833) a 'Morisque' describes herself as 'une paouvre fille africquaine, en laquelle Dieu avoyt miz ung sang tres chauld' [*sic*] in *Les Cent Contes drolatiques, Œuvres diverses* vol. 1, 251–99 (p. 278). The multiple frames around this description suggest however that we are not to take it at face value (it is presented as a Renaissance story modernising a thirteenth-century written account of an oral trial). 'Le Succube' is the only finished version of Balzac's planned novel *La Morisque*.

compared to an animal or a savage, and alternates between passion and fatalistic immobility (77; 78).

It has been suggested that Zola plays down any potential Arab identity and describes Thérèse as half African: 'for Zola, she is pure, uncompromisingly black. Africa is perceived as dark, black. Blackness signifies, among other things, perverse sexuality and animality.'[65] Zola certainly emphasizes blackness in describing Thérèse—her eyes in particular are constantly described as black, 'un abîme sombre où l'on ne voyait que de la nuit' (115)—but he does not invoke the more common (and more racist) paradigms through which black Africans were almost invariably described during the nineteenth century. Indeed, Thérèse's physiognomy is essentially European, and the emphasis on her white skin, thin lips, black eyes and thin muscular body are partly to be explained by the influence of Manet's painting *Olympia* (1863), discussed in Chapter 5.[66] Like the descriptions of Manet's painting in his art criticism, Zola's word portrait of Thérèse dwells on the abstract contrast of dark and light, and the 'primitive within' is condensed into blackness itself. Africa, however, is not forgotten. As in *Madeleine Férat*, the wide colonial space offstage is contrasted with the claustrophobic space of the Raquins' dark shop, itself enclosed within an arcade. The boating outing on the Seine, which culminates in the murder of Thérèse's husband by her lover Laurent, is imagined as a return to her original milieu: she enjoys dirtying her dress on the pebbles and in the mud; they walk towards the river on a blindingly white, dust-covered road; the sky is blue, the air burning hot, and the sun bites Laurent's neck in a foreshadowing of the bite Camille will inflict before he drowns. This being Zola, the African analogy is made explicit: 'Ils étaient au désert' (114).

In his study of French colonial novels set in Africa, Seillan sees Zola as sending Thérèse's father to Africa 'à seule fin de donner à celle-ci la sauvagerie atavique exigée par la thèse du roman'.[67] It is however striking, when one returns to *Thérèse Raquin* from a reading of the Rougon-Macquart series, that in 1867 Zola felt that atavistic savagery *needed* to be linked explicitly to Africa, just as in *Madeleine Férat* he felt that Jacques Berthier's exaggerated virility should develop through colonial experience. Both are figured as 'returns': Jacques returns from Cochinchina, while Thérèse's sexuality is a return of her mother's 'African' sensuality and her father's fatal exotic passion. In Jacques's animal brutality one can read the resurgence of a primeval forefather whose imprint is, through the ancient theory of impregnation, left in the womb of the woman he has been first to possess; the weaker, effeminate or degenerate Guillaume cannot defeat his influence. So too the sickly Camille cannot satisfy, or withstand, the animal force of Thérèse's primitive instincts. Before being stories of the 'return' of guilt or of ghosts, these novels tell a story about the

---

[65] Sharpley-Whiting, *Black Venus*, p. 81; she adds that Thérèse is 'sex in motion, as passionate and exotic feline', and her adultery reveals her fully sexual, African nature (p. 83).

[66] See Mitterand, Introduction to *Thérèse Raquin*, pp. 32–3; Lethbridge, 'Zola, Manet and *Thérèse Raquin*', pp. 286–9; and Sharpley-Whiting, p. 80.

[67] *Aux sources*, p. 11. For Seillan, the absence of Africa from the Rougon-Macquart series can be explained by Zola's 'double théorie des milieux sociologiques et de l'hérédité familiale' which militated in favour of a narrow geographical focus (p. 357); he does not consider the possible action of the colonies as a repressed presence within that narrow metropolitan geography.

'return' of a sexual intensity that is in excess of modern metropolitan norms. Once again, the colonial heterotopia gives rise to what has been called a 'menacing racialised figure'.[68]

In *Thérèse Raquin* Zola explores theories of determinism influential in the 1850s and 1860s, most explicitly ancient theories of temperament, but also Taine's theory of the influence of 'race', milieu, and moment. Taine's use of the term 'race' to indicate heredity, from the 1860s onwards, focuses on the transmission of inherited traits. Ideas concerning the biological transmission of human characteristics were very much present in progressive intellectual circles *before* the influence of Darwin's theories was widely felt in France. Critics have long assumed that Zola too had read Darwin and was directly influenced by him, but David Baguley has persuasively argued that Zola's emphasis on heredity and biological determinism is probably independent of any direct Darwinian influence.[69] Certainly, his novels of the 1860s, and his first plans for the Rougon-Macquart series, were essentially pre-Darwinian. Nor had Zola yet read the theories of physiology developed by Charles Letourneau, a philosopher of sociology who pioneered the field of ethno-psychology, Prosper Lucas (from whose *Traité philosophique de l'hérédité* he would take extensive notes in preparation for the Rougon-Macquart series, immediately *following* the writing of *Thérèse Raquin*, in 1868–89[70]) or Cesare Lombroso and other exponents of the new physical anthropology. And yet it seems necessary to qualify Henri Mitterand's assertion that, in the 1867 novel, Zola 'n'avait pas prétendu rapporter la conduite de Thérèse et Laurent à une fatalité héréditaire'.[71] While Zola was not yet in possession of the theoretical model that would supply him with a coherent framework for hereditary determinism, we do see such determinism at work in *Thérèse Raquin* where it is linked to an ill-defined colonial transmission. In the Rougon-Macquart series, however, the theoretical model supplied by Zola's additional scientific reading was to provide new physiological markers of the primitive that no longer needed a colonial alibi.

[68] See Kaplan, 'Imagining empire', p. 208. Such figures are more often female than male in British fiction, where Kaplan observes 'the invasive and disturbing presence of a woman of African or partly African descent on English soil' in terms that resonate interestingly with *Thérèse Raquin*.

[69] David Baguley, 'Zola and Darwin: A Reassessment', in *The Evolution of Literature: Legacies of Darwin in European Cultures*, ed. by Nicholas Saul and Simon J. James (Amsterdam: Rodopi, 2011), pp. 201–12. Although *The Origin of Species* was first translated in 1862, it did not have a widespread impact in France until the 1880s, and even then was often misunderstood. Earlier critics tended to read Zola through a Darwinian lens: in 1986, for example, Brian Nelson asserted that all Zola's novels 'may in fact be read as an attempt to reconcile the themes of Darwinism and social responsibility' ('Zola's Ideology', p. 165). More recently *Thérèse Raquin* has been seen as reflecting Zola's inaccurate understanding of the 'post-Darwinian laws of nature' (Shideler, p. 35).

[70] Zola's notes on Lucas, and Charles Letourneau's *Physiologie des passions* (1868), are reproduced in the appendix of Mitterand's Pléiade edition of the Rougon-Macquart (V: 1677–91 and 1692–1728). From Lucas he noted down racial characteristics among other atavistic traits: an example of 'hérédité en retour' or 'loi de l'intermittence' is a 'Mère produisant un nègre, parce qu'un de ses aïeux était nègre' (1706), and he repeats the point in his summary (1725). See David Baguley, 'Darwin, Zola, and Dr Prosper Lucas's *Treatise on Natural Heredity*', in *The Literary and Cultural Reception of Charles Darwin in Europe*, ed. by Thomas F. Glick and Elinor Shaffer, 4 vols (London: Bloomsbury, 2014), vol. 4, pp. 416–30.

[71] In his otherwise invaluable study of *La Bête humaine*, IV: 1705–58 (p. 1710).

THE RACIAL OTHER GOES UNDERGROUND: *LA BÊTE HUMAINE* AND THE BORN CRIMINAL

In 1868, in preparation for his multi-volume 'Histoire d'une famille', Zola looked back at his achievements in both *Madeleine Férat* and *Thérèse Raquin* and noted aspects that he should retain and others to eliminate. Much later, beginning to map out his novel about criminality, he noted his intention to return to 'quelque chose de pareil à *Thérèse Raquin*'; 'quelque chose d'hallucinant, d'effroyable come Madame Raquin, qui reste à jamais dans la mémoire, qui fasse un cauchemar à toute la France' (MS 10274, fols 338 and 352). As we have seen, it is also in 1868 that Zola undertook much more extensive scientific reading on which to base the organizational principle of the hereditary flaw or 'fêlure' that was to link the novels.

His original plan for a series of ten books already included a novel about 'le monde judiciaire', which would eventually become *La Bête humaine* (1890). It famously portrays a compulsive serial killer driven to murder women as soon as he experiences sexual desire for them. Post-Freudian studies of the novel, not least by Gilles Deleuze,[72] have emphasized Zola's central interest in the unconscious, which was much debated in the last decades of the century. Indeed, it is possible to read Zola's novel—with its determinist rail networks, trains entering the gaping mouth of a tunnel, objects ill-concealed in holes and obsessive patterning of red and black—as a pre-psychoanalytical map of the unconscious. Borie offers a resounding analysis of the figure of the *bête humaine* within what he calls Zola's 'anthropologie mythique' as a 'régression sadique-anale'.[73] I would suggest however that pursuing a Freudian reading might lead us to neglect the implications of Borie's own apt choice of words: the signs of the unconscious are indeed overdetermined by the new *anthropological* imaginary. Derived from Zola's readings in the emergent fields of criminology and physical anthropology, this anthropological vision transforms and displaces the colonial contagion that we saw in his earlier work.

La Bête humaine examines several murderers, and different motivations for murder. The idea of a rational murder is dismissed: 'Est-ce qu'on tue par raisonnement! On ne tue que sous l'impulsion du sang et des nerfs, un reste des anciennes luttes, la nécessité de vivre et la joie d'être fort' (IV: 1299). Jacques himself proffers various conflicting hypotheses to explain his murderous urges towards women. These reflect hesitation between the two main contemporary theories of criminal heredity. The first, derived from the degeneration theory of Bénédict-Augustin Morel,[74] saw acquired characteristics as passed down to ill effect in future generations,

---

[72] Gilles Deleuze, 'Zola et la fêlure' [1969], reprinted in Zola, *La Bête humaine*, ed. by Henri Mitterand (Paris: Gallimard 'Folio', 1977), pp. 7–24. For further discussion of Zola's use of theories of the unconscious activities of the human mind, see Rae Beth Gordon, '*La Bête humaine*: Zola and the poetics of the unconscious', in *The Cambridge Companion to Émile Zola*, ed. by Brian Nelson (Cambridge: Cambridge University Press, 2007), pp. 152–68; for a recent psychoanalytical approach, see Andrew Counter, 'The Legacy of the Beast: Patrilinearity and Rupture in Zola's *La Bête humaine* and Freud's *Totem and Taboo*', *French Studies*, 62:1 (2008), 26–38.

[73] *Zola et les mythes*, p. 63; on *La Bête humaine*, see pp. 43–124.

[74] Bénédict-Augustin Morel, *Traité des dégénérescences physiques, intellectuelles et morales de l'espèce humaine et des causes qui produisent ces variétés maladives* (1857).

reversing evolution: Jacques's murderous urges may arise because his mother had him too young or his ancestors drank too much (IV: 1042–3). The second theory was influenced by what we now call palaeoanthropology, a growing field following a series of discoveries (notably of Neanderthals in 1856) that was popularized by works such as Louis Figuier's *L'Homme primitif* (1870). More specifically, distant primitive traits were thought to reappear through atavism, according to the new Italian school of criminology that followed Cesare Lombroso, whose book *L'Homme criminel* was published in French in 1887.[75] Zola was clearly fascinated by the theories of Lombroso, though he imagines them in narrative terms so that Jacques's urge to murder women may well be 'une soif toujours renaissante de venger des offenses très anciennes' that comes from the ancient 'rancune amassée de mâle en mâle' following the first infidelity committed by women, 'la première tromperie au fond des cavernes' (IV: 1044, repeated 1297). This negative conception of the 'primitive' marks a divergence from Morel's theory of degeneration, which implied both decline from a more perfect earlier state and the impact of social or acquired factors rather than pure heredity.[76] For Lombroso, on the other hand, 'primitive' referred to 'savage' traits that had not been perfected by the process of civilization.[77]

We saw that sexual excess was associated with the colonies in Zola's novels of the 1860s. A rather different version of the racial other reappears in his use of Lombroso. Lombroso's theory of criminality drew on the new science of physical anthropology, which aimed to establish objective, quantitative criteria on which to base the division of humanity into separate races, hierarchically ordered. He posited the existence of a 'born criminal', an evolutionary throwback to a more primitive type of man whose traits were also conserved in the 'lower' races. The skulls of criminals, Lombroso claims, are closer to those of 'savages' or prehistoric men than to madmen.[78] They suffer momentary states of alienation during which 'ils ne s'appartiennent plus', and this phenomenon is to be observed among animals and 'peuplades sauvages' too.[79] Such moments of alienation are dramatically depicted in *La Bête humaine*, when Jacques murders Séverine under the influence of 'une clameur de foule, dans son crâne' and 'des morsures de feu [...] le chassaient de son propre corps, sous le galop de l'autre, la bête envahissante' (IV: 1296). Lombroso concludes his study of criminal man by asserting that it is possible to

---

[75] Cesare Lombroso, *L'Homme criminel* [1876], trans. by MM. Régnier and Bournet (Paris: Félix Alcan, 1887). On Zola's reading of Lombroso, see Colette Becker, 'Zola et Lombroso: à propos de la Bête Humaine', *Les Cahiers naturalistes*, 80 (2006), 37–49. On debates in France over Lombroso's theories, see Robert Nye, *Crime, Madness, and Politics in Modern France: the Medical Concept of National Decline* (Princeton, NJ: Princeton University Press, 1984), ch. 4.

[76] Jacques Hochmann, 'La théorie de la dégénérescence de B.-A. Morel, ses origines et son évolution', in *Darwinisme et Société*, ed. by Patrick Tort (Paris: Presses Universitaires de France, 1992), pp. 402–12 (p. 407). Hochmann stresses Morel's rejection of racist applications of his thesis of degeneration.

[77] The split between Jacques's two hypotheses has also been described by Deleuze as a contrast of 'petite hérédité', or the individual's inheritance of recent acquired characteristics, and 'grande hérédité', or the atavistic inheritance of the species from the deep past ('Zola et la fêlure', p. 11).

[78] *L'Homme criminel*, pp. 134–5; p. 145; p. 147.   [79] *L'Homme criminel*, pp. 276–7; p. 271.

'voir dans le criminel l'homme sauvage' and that 'la différence est bien petite, quelquefois nulle, entre le criminel, l'homme du people sans éducation et le sauvage'.[80] Influenced by Lombroso (though he was later to express doubts about the importance of inherited criminal tendencies), the French criminologist Alexandre Lacassagne also points out scientifically significant parallels between criminals, primitive man, and contemporary 'hommes sauvages' encountered by travellers in, for example, West Africa.[81]

The working-class male characters of *La Bête humaine* all show atavistic signs of the human beast within them. Two of the traits that Zola reiterates concern the shape of the skull, a favourite focus of the new craniometry and racial comparatism in the hands of Paul Broca in the 1860s and 1870s. The first is the low forehead and 'flat' head which characterize the secondary characters Roubaud ('sa tête un peu plate, au front bas, à la nuque épaisse', IV: 1000), Pecqueux the train driver ('le front bas', IV: 1060), and Cabuche ('La face massive, le front bas disaient la violence de l'être borné', IV: 1098). The second trait is the protruding lower jaw that so strikingly contrasts with Jacques Lantier's otherwise gentlemanly appearance: Jacques is 'très brun, beau garçon au visage rond et régulier, mais que gâtaient des mâchoires trop fortes' (IV: 1026); Pecqueux too has '[l]a bouche large dans une mâchoire saillante' (IV: 1060). In the preparatory character sketch Jacques is repeatedly described as 'beau', but when revising his notes Zola added above the line: 'Plus mâchoires trop fortes' (MS 10274, fol. 539). This emphasis on the character's protruding lower jaw, or 'prognathism', draws on Lombroso's assertion that the lower jaw is more developed in the criminal type than in normal men. It reflects the continued influence of the theory of the facial angle, invented by Petrus Camper (1722–89), which played a considerable role in physical anthropology and racial theory, though after 1875 it began to be replaced by the measurement of the dimensions and form of the skull, or craniometry.[82] The facial angle, although initially developed as a means of portraying Africans convincingly in art, was widely used in a racialist way to classify the principal human races according to a scale of judgement that situated Europeans at the top with wide facial angles, and Africans closer to the great apes with narrow angles; the angle corresponded to a relative measure of intelligence according to both Cuvier and Geoffroy Saint-Hilaire.[83]

---

[80] *L'Homme criminel*, p. 454; p. 463; on parallels with the 'sauvages', see also p. 456, pp. 461–2.

[81] Alexandre Lacassagne, 'L'homme criminel comparé à l'homme primitif', *Lyon médical*, 39 (1882) Part 1, pp. 210–17, and Part 2, pp. 244–55 (particularly p. 211, p. 215, p. 252).

[82] Claude Blanckaert, '"Les vicissitudes de l'angle facial" et les débuts de la craniométrie (1765–1875)', *Revue de synthèse*, 4:3–4 (1987), 417–53 (p. 420). Derived from Camper's theory, the distinction between prognathous and orthognathous types was widely used in racialist classifications—among European races as well as to distinguish broader human groupings—from the 1840s to the 1940s. In the mid nineteenth century the most ancient human skeletons were also described as brachycephalous, that is, having a 'short' rather than a 'long' skull (see Claude Blanckaert, 'L'Indice céphalique et l'ethnogénie européenne: A. Retzius, P. Broca, F. Pruner-Bey (1840–1870)', *Bulletins et mémoires de la société d'anthropologie de Paris*, 1:3–4 (1989), 165–202 (p. 166, p. 170, p. 183)). Jacques Lantier, with his round head and protruding jaw, is a 'brachycéphale prognathe', combining traits of 'primitive' man and 'lower' races.

[83] Blanckaert, 'Les vicissitudes', p. 427, p. 434.

Lombroso's born criminal also has thick dark hair, generally curly or frizzy ('frisés'), but is beardless (in contrast, as he puts it, with novelists' clichés). Stressing the paradox, he also emphasizes the pallor of the criminal, which can make us mistakenly interpret criminals' physiognomy as being 'plus délicate et plus gentille qu'elle ne l'est en réalité'.[84] The 'cheveux frisés' are shared by Roubaud (IV: 1000) and Jacques; Cabuche has only a thin (curly) beard (IV: 1098). The description of Jacques superficially follows the Lombrosian recipe to the letter: 'Ses cheveux, plantés drus, frisaient, ainsi que ses moustaches, si épaisses, si noires, qu'elles augmentaient la pâleur de son teint' (IV: 1026). In Zola's preparatory notes these traits are already emphasized: 'Très brun de cheveux. Il a les cheveux frisés, en touffe, très drus, et il les porte demi ras. Il n'a que les moustaches épaisses et noires [...] le menton nu' (MS 10274, fol. 540).[85] Jacques's strikingly pale face may also be an indication that Zola read Lombroso while in the process of developing his characters: when the homicidal character, then still called Étienne, was first sketched, he was 'un peu noir de peau, les cheveux demi courts et frisant naturellement' (MS 10308, fol. 7). The influence of Lombroso probably also triggered a change in the hair colour of the character who was to become Séverine: in the outline she was first blonde, then 'rousse', 'avec des yeux noirs'; she acquired dark hair and blue eyes later on (MS 10274, fol. 376). Her momentary stint as a redhead harks back to Zola's most infamous woman of sin, Nana, who was blonde with red body hair: 'Nana était toute velue, un duvet de rousse faisant de son corps un velours; tandis que, dans sa croupe et ses cuisses de cavale [...] il y avait de la bête' (II: 1271).[86] *Nana* (1880), like the first sketch of Séverine, clearly predates Zola's reading of Lombroso, who exonerates redheads from innate criminal tendencies; for him, criminal women have abundant but dark hair.[87] The thick dark hair Séverine eventually acquires marks a return to the reiterated darkness of Thérèse, with whom she shares many traits. Zola was from the outset intent on evoking 'la bête', but he modified its outside appearance after reading Lombroso.

Zola did not, however, accept the racialist and positivist ideas of the Italian school of criminology without question, and he engages in a hidden polemic with Lombroso.[88] Zola having explicitly declared that he had drawn on Lombroso's work for *La Bête humaine*, the Italian criminologist responded with courteous

---

[84] *L'Homme criminel*, p. 195, p. 180.

[85] Jack the Ripper, one of the sources for Zola's Jacques, was also identified by some as a man of 'foreign appearance' (see Lisa Downing, *The Subject of Murder: Gender, Exceptionality, and the Modern Killer* (Chicago, IL: University of Chicago Press, 2013), p. 73).

[86] On *Nana*, see Gilman, 'Black Bodies, White Bodies', pp. 253–6.

[87] On born criminals not being redheads, see *L'Homme criminel*, p. 183; on their dark hair, pp. 190–1. Lombroso, in collaboration with Guglielmo Ferrero, was to develop his discussion of female criminals, a category in which he included prostitutes, in 1893 in *La Donna delinquente: la prostituta et la donna normale* (translated into French in 1896 as *La Femme criminelle et la prostituée*). Lombroso's association of criminality in women with African traits has been studied in some detail by Sander Gilman. For Lombroso, Gilman points out, even supposed genital anomalies among prostitutes were 'atavistic throwbacks to the Hottentot, if not the chimpanzee' ('Black Bodies, White Bodies', p. 245).

[88] Bakhtin discusses the 'hidden polemic', in which discourse is 'directed toward an ordinary referential object' but simultaneously strikes 'a blow' at another person's discourse in *Problems of Dostoevsky's Poetics*, ed. and trans. by Caryl Emerson (Minneapolis/London: University of Minnesota Press, 1984), pp. 195–9. Critics have tended to play down Zola's inclusion of hesitation in relation to Lombroso's

acknowledgement, but also criticized the novel. He found the characters of Roubaud and Jacques too ambiguous. Jacques's polite and civilized traits do not square with the nature of the born criminal, he should not be able to have a temporarily normal sexual relationship with Séverine, and his physiology is too mixed.[89] Jacques's dual nature is however carefully and deliberately established by Zola. He is a member of the newly skilled working classes, a product of the industrial age, master of the new technologies of steam and iron; he is handsome and even refined. In other words, Zola deliberately chose to embody atavistic primitive urges in what might seem an unlikely subject. As if to underline this choice, he *does* include the likely subject, that is, Cabuche, a character who fulfils all of Lombroso's requirements for the born criminal... except that he is not in fact the killer. That Zola was thinking of Lombroso's criminal typology, but at the same time aiming to diverge from it, is clear from the *dossier préparatoire*: deliberately opting to make Jacques handsome, he nevertheless adds or underlines notes to himself not to forget the traits of the 'criminel-né'; 'Il faudrait garder le type physique du criminel-né et l'embellir. À voir' (MS 10274, fols 540–1, also 539).

In fact, Jacques is constantly described in terms of a dynamic, shifting hybrid physiology that reflects his double nature. As Hamon puts it, many of Zola's characters combine 'des traits antithétiques', and their nature shifts from one pole to the other through a process of transformation focused on their faces—this can be a positive 'transfiguration' but is more often the negative 'défiguration' already discussed. Hamon also suggests that for Zola protruding jaws are a conventional means of signalling animality because 'c'est la partie du visage la plus tournée vers la terre' and also that by association they indicate the 'dévoreurs' of the Rougon-Macquart.[90] This dualism of high and low belongs to a conception of the face that is given explicit form in Hegel's *Æsthetics*, where the upper part of the face expresses human spirituality, while the lower part, and particularly the jaw, reflects bestiality.[91] In 1890, when writing *La Bête humaine*, Zola drew insistently on this venerable symbolism as well as on new positivist theories, but his characters' dualism is dynamic. Shortly before killing Séverine, feeling the impulse to murder, Jacques still has 'sa tête ronde de beau garçon, ses cheveux frisés, ses moustaches très noires, ses yeux bruns diamantés d'or, mais sa mâchoire inférieure avançait tellement, dans une sorte de coup de gueule, qu'il s'en trouvait défiguré' (IV: 1294). Séverine herself shows similar if less dramatic dualism in the reiterated contrast of (black) fringe

theories; Downing, for example, sees *La Bête humaine* as 'adher[ing] rigidly to a model of predetermination and the belief in inherited moral, criminal, and sexual traits' (*The Subject of Murder*, p. 75).

[89] Cesare Lombroso, 'La Bête humaine et l'anthropologie criminelle', *La Revue des revues*, 4–5 (1892), reprinted in Zola, *Les Rougon-Macquart*, 5 vols (Paris: Robert Laffont, 2002), vol. 5, pp. 1410–15 (p. 1412). Lombroso also protests against the novelist's repeated use of the same weapons, and the concentration of so many murders in one space.

[90] Hamon, *Le Personnel du roman*, p. 162, p. 170, p. 171; see also p. 175.

[91] Gabriel Tarde mocked the influence of Hegel's theory on Lombroso (*La Criminalité comparée*, 2nd edition (Paris: Félix Alcan, 1890 [1886]), p. 15). In Zola's novel *L'Œuvre* (1886) a similar facial dualism characterizes Christine, whose calm and gentle forehead belies her prominent jaw and excessively full lips. See Hamon, *Le Personnel du roman*, p. 170. Dualism also characterizes Madeleine Férat, but with an inversion of the usual high-low contrast: the upper part of her face is masculine, the lower half delicately feminine (33).

190 *The Colonial Comedy*

versus (blue) eyes: 'elle séduisait par le charme, l'étrangeté de ses larges yeux bleus, sous son épaisse chevelure noire' despite the less attractive traits of 'la face longue, la bouche forte, éclairée de dents admirables' (IV: 1001).[92] Again, the contrast is dynamic: as she remembers her childhood sexual abuse by Grandmorin, and her husband presses his unwanted desires on her, the dark side comes to the fore: 'Le noir reflet de sa chevelure assombrissait ses calmes yeux de pervenche, sa bouche forte saignait dans le doux ovale de son visage' (IV: 1011).

Now unity and consistency of character are often seen as a central trait of Realism, but Zola works very hard precisely to contradict the idea that human identity is single and consistent. It seems that the 'incoherence of the self was accepted by realistic novelists long before it was "discovered" by political philosophers [...] and radical literary critics'.[93] Hamon, as we have seen, points out the dualism of Zola's characters. He does not connect it to racial imagery, but for Lombroso the parallel between criminals within European races and so-called 'primitive' races was evident. To understand the process of 'défiguration' described by Hamon it is useful to turn back to Robert Young, who suggests that racism does not operate only through binaries of self–other and black–white but on 'the computation of normalities and degrees of deviance from the white norm.'[94] Along with the work of Stoler and McClintock, Young's approach helps us to understand this 'deviance from the white norm' as part of a policing of socio-sexual borders. For Zola does not use Lombroso's parallels between the born criminal and present-day 'lower races' in order to characterize the working classes. Indeed, in his 'working-class' novels—*Germinal, L'Assommoir, La Terre*—the stereotype that associates working-class identity with racial otherness is remarkable for its absence.[95] In *Pot-Bouille*, too, the slatternly housemaid Adèle, a Breton peasant, is depicted without any racializing or primitivist imagery of her abject, suffering body. Any initial association of the working classes with primitive atavism may well have been lost as Zola moved towards a more favourable judgement of working-class struggle, notably while researching *Germinal* (1885). The homicidal protagonist of Zola's judicial novel was originally to have been Étienne Lantier, hero of *Germinal*, who was also to have appeared in a novel on the Paris Commune.[96] Étienne's emerging

[92] This dualism is discussed by Hamon, *Le Personnel du roman*, p. 171. With her long skull, Séverine is probably a 'dolichocéphale' (see Blanckaert, 'L'Indice céphalique', p. 170).

[93] Raymond Tallis, *In Defence of Realism* (London: Edward Arnold, 1988), pp. 67–8, and p. 71.

[94] *Colonial Desire*, p. 180.

[95] As Marin observes, in *La Bête humaine* 'le primitivisme est repéré notamment à travers les singularités anatomiques et psychologiques de l'être originaire', but 'dans la triade ouvrière' Zola does not adopt 'ces stéréotypes populaires' (*Le Livre enterré*, p. 18).

[96] Zola's 1868 list of the novels planned for his series included one on the 'monde judiciaire' whose main character would be Étienne 'un de ces cas étranges de criminel par hérédité qui, sans être fou, tue un jour dans une crise morbide, poussés par un instinct de bête' ('1er plan remis à Lacroix', fol. 63, in appendix, V: 1776). In 1874 Étienne and Jacques are still a single character, and Zola notes 'Un homme qui a besoin de tuer (mon roman judiciaire. Forçat)' (MS 10294, fol. 141). In this manuscript use of the word 'forçat' we may have a clue to the eventual fate of Étienne, who loses his homicidal nature but ends up deported to a penal colony. Étienne was still the main character of *La Bête humaine* when Zola began work on the novel. For details of the character's development, see Colette Becker, 'Du meurtrier par hérédité au héros révolutionnaire. Étienne Lantier dans le dossier préparatoire de *Germinal*', *Cahiers de l'UER Froissart*, 5 (1980), 99–111. Becker sees the moment when Zola adds a

identity as a working-class hero would have limited the narrative possibilities of the 'homicide' novel, so when preparing *La Bête humaine* Zola decided to opt for the invention of a new brother, and gave Claude and Étienne Lantier a younger sibling, Jacques.[97] The splitting of Étienne and Jacques marks Zola's distancing of himself from the equation of working-class identity with the primitive within.

DUALISM: ZOLA'S FERAL VICTOR AND HIS BOURGEOIS FATHER

Before returning to Zola's ambivalent use of racialization in *La Bête humaine* I shall look at a similar phenomenon in the novel on which Zola began work immediately afterwards, *L'Argent* (1891).[98] Here the split between the civilized modern subject and the primitive atavistic throwback does, superficially, appear to fall along class lines, opposing bourgeois creative energies with sub-proletarian mindless violence. The borderline between classes acts however as a mirror rather than a real line of demarcation. The 'human beast' is within all of us—and, as in the case of cousin Bette and Philippe Bridau, it is very much within the family.

Since *L'Argent* most obviously explores financial speculation and whether or not it can play a role in furthering human progress (as we saw in Chapter 3), the sub-plot involving Saccard's son Victor might seem at odds with the logic of the novel as a whole. Critics have sometimes seen it as an extraneous narrative addition, or simply emphasized the terrifying narrative loose end posed by Victor's disappearance.[99] And yet the plot strand involving the scandalous existence of Saccard's son is carefully woven into the fabric of the novel, and Zola deliberately keeps its dramatic dénouement for the closing chapter.[100]

Saccard never acknowledges his illegitimate son. Confronted by the evidence, he welcomes the boy's existence in theory, but in practice he never makes the time to

new brother—Jacques Lantier—as the point at which he distances himself from the 'affirmations de Lombroso et d'autres criminalistes sur la possibilité de reconnaître physiquement les criminels et de protéger, par là, la société' ('Zola et Lombroso', p. 42).

[97] The choice of the name 'Jacques' is curiously overdetermined: the Jacques of *Madeleine Férat* may himself be a recollection of a murderer called Jacques in Zola's 1866 short story, 'Un mariage d'amour', which shares its main plot ingredients with *Thérèse Raquin*. And yet, in deciding to name the protagonist of *La Bête humaine* 'Jacques', Zola was no doubt thinking of Jack the Ripper, whose crimes fascinated Paris as well as London from September 1888. Strangely, in 1891—a year after the publication of *La Bête humaine*—Zola gave the name 'Jacques' to his son by Jeanne Rozerot. Lapp suggests that Zola associated the name with father-figures, but this does not fit all of these cases. He is also puzzled to find no resemblance between the Jacques of *Madeleine Férat* and the Jacques of *La Bête humaine* apart from the name, since he does not observe the pattern of 'défiguration' and primitive traits that we have seen in both cases (*Zola before the Rougon-Macquart*, p. 138, p. 147). The short story 'Jacques Damour' (1883) also has links to a penal colony.

[98] See Baguley, *Naturalist Fiction*, p. 216, on the proximity of the two novels and their contrasting treatment of Darwinian themes.

[99] See Saminadayar-Perrin, 'Fictions de la bourse', p. 59; Lukács, 'Narrate or Describe', p. 123; Becker, 'Zola et Lombroso', p. 49.

[100] In his detailed plan Zola noted 'Je vois que je garderai le viol et tout le drame pour le chap. XII' (MS 10268, fol. 213).

meet his youthful progeny since the appearance of 'Victor', although at a moment when Saccard 'restât victorieux' (V: 293), corresponds with the rumblings that signal the imminent collapse of his investment bank. Though his son's name appears to suggest victory, it marks the triumph of bestial energy within humanity, not a rational investment of the creative energy produced by speculation. Victor's very existence reminds us of the dangers presented by Saccard's uncontrolled urges, for he is the product of a rape committed when Saccard first came to Paris, a rape so violent that it left its victim handicapped and unable to work, pushing her from the working classes into the sub-proletariat. Reflecting the theory that the moment of conception exercises an influence on physical inheritance, the child thus conceived in violence has 'l'œil en dessous, avec sa joue gauche plus forte que la droite, tirant la bouche dans une moue de férocité goguenarde' (V: 362; see also 151; 365). In insisting on the asymmetry of Victor's cheek, Zola is once again following Lombroso.[101] Zola's fascination with criminal children is already apparent in *Germinal* (1885), which predates his reading of Lombroso. Here, however, the description of Jeanlin Maheud is very different: the child is thin, blond and green-eyed, with protruding ears and an agile frame. His increasing criminality—moving from minor thefts to full banditry and a random murder—embodies the threat of a working-class reversion to savagery, but it is not described in terms of primitive physiognomy.[102] Victor, on the other hand, can be seen as the Rougon-Macquart's prime illustration of the late nine-teenth-century recapitulation theory that saw individual development as passing through less evolved forms, reflecting the evolution of the species. As Dorian Bell puts it, he 'epitomizes in his disproportioned body the three-fold parallelism of child, primitive ancestor and inferior present-day adult'.[103]

Victor has been raised in the disease-ridden shantytown to the North of Paris as a member of the sub-proletariat. The area is also described in the Goncourts' 1865 novel *Germinie Lacerteux*, where the workers in the new Northern suburbs live in 'ces huttes, tenant de la cabane et du terrier' that terrify even Germinie; the language conflates 'primitive' and animal dwellings.[104] The middle-class Mme Caroline

---

[101] 'Une asymétrie, joue plus forte que l'autre' (MS 10268, fol. 294). Facial asymmetry is mentioned by Lombroso as an acquired (rather than atavistic) characteristic, in his preface to the fourth edition of *L'Homme criminel*, on which the 1887 French translation was based, p. 24; he also notes that facial asymmetry, frequent among delinquent children, is one of the traits of the criminal type along with a low forehead and prominent jaws (pp. 114–15).

[102] A comparison between Jeanlin in *Germinal* and Victor in *L'Argent* is briefly evoked by Diane Smith ('The Evolution of the Working Class Novel in Europe: Darwinian Science and Literary Naturalism', *Excavatio*, 8 (1996), 72–85 (p. 78)). She sees Zola's use of animal metaphors as merely depicting 'the dehumanizing effects of poverty' (p. 76).

[103] Dorian Bell, 'Cavemen Among Us: Genealogies of Atavism from Zola's *La Bête humaine* to Chabrol's *Le Boucher*', *French Studies*, 62:1 (2008), 39–52 (pp. 44–5). The association of criminality, and primitive characteristics, with illegitimate and abandoned children is made explicitly by Lacassagne, p. 211.

[104] Goncourt, *Germinie*, p. 116. McClintock studies middle-class ventures into the slums, suggesting they were seen, like colonial spaces, as 'anachronistic worlds of deprivation and unreality'; this 'collapse of history' into prehistory is the sign of a middle-class 'failure of representation, disavowed and projected onto the underclasses as a condition of their racial atavism'. She sees this as a specifically male, scopic venture (*Imperial Leather*, p. 121). Interestingly, Zola's middle-class explorer is Caroline Hamelin, who though a woman is the rationalist, secular avatar of the author.

Hamelin finds him there in a stinking hole behind a barricade of refuse, where he lives in symbolic incest with a woman old enough to be his mother.[105] At the dramatic end of the novel Victor perpetuates the violence of his conception by raping the pallid aristocratic virgin Alice de Beauvilliers and leaving her half-strangled. The act reveals his animality, 'la brusque faim du monstre pour cette chair frêle' triggering 'le saut du mâle' (V: 364). Violent rape thus sees the atavistic beast within modern man destroy the degenerate descendant of a fading aristocratic family. 'Avait-elle donc un sens, cette rencontre imbécile et abominable? Pourquoi avoir brisé ceci contre cela?' asks Caroline (V: 365). The 'sens', we may infer, lies in the meeting of Lombroso and Morel, or the theories of primitive atavism and degeneration. As is very often the case, Zola puts into play more than one theory and asks (in this case explicitly) the reader to interpret them.[106]

Victor's crime is committed in an enclosed space, and he escapes over the rooftops without leaving a trace by a route so dangerous that 'beaucoup se refusaient à croire qu'un être humain avait pu le suivre' (V: 365). This may be an echo of Lombroso, for whom criminals show 'une agilité particulière, souvent simiesque'.[107] But Zola is also drawing on Edgar Allan Poe's *Murders in the rue Morgue*, in which the mysterious murderer must have escaped by an apparently impossible route out of the window.[108] Poe has his visionary amateur sleuth Dupin consider, and then reject, the idea that the murder was committed by a human of Asiatic or African origins, and logically deduce that the culprit who has displayed such superhuman agility was, in fact, an equally foreign orang-utan. Zola's Victor, aged only fifteen, is 'trapu [...] déjà poilu, ainsi qu'une bête précoce', 'velu comme un homme' (V: 151, 364).[109] In the preparatory notes he was even more reminiscent of an orang-utan, with 'Les yeux jaunes enfoncés sous des arcades sourcilières

---

[105] The woman is even called 'la mère Eulalie'. The abjection of maternal incest is underlined in true Zolian fashion by the abscess on her thigh, and she lives half naked, sagging and wrinkled like 'une outré à moitié vide'; the stinking hole they share is half rotten, slimy with humidity; rain comes in through a 'crevasse, une fente verte' (V: 150). This upbringing enveloped in the slime of abject femininity seems to stand for the absence of paternal discipline, which lends itself to a reading as political allegory commenting on the Second Empire. As in the case of Philippe Bridau, maternal influence alone is powerless to channel and control violent urges within the male.

[106] Zola insistently portrays the Beauvilliers family as degenerate. Alice's brother dies young (V: 366), and the family's decline and defeat seem inevitable (V: 372). Moreover, when the engineer Hamelin talks of regenerating the Orient his windows overlook the garden of the Beauvilliers' house, so that the 'antique société tombant en poudre' of which he speaks seems to be the French aristocracy as well as the Orient (V: 60–1).

[107] *L'Homme criminel*, p. 455.

[108] Zola probably read Poe in Baudelaire's 1856 translation. Like Poe, Zola emphasizes the mystery concerning the circumstances of the rape, which happened in a room closed from the inside: 'Mais que de points obscurs, que de questions stupéfiantes et insolubles! Comment n'avait-on rien entendu, pas un bruit de lutte, pas une plainte? Comment de si effroyables choses s'étaient-elles passées si vite, dix minutes à peine? Surtout, comment Victor avait-il pu se sauver, s'évaporer pour ainsi dire, sans laisser de trace?' (V: 364–5). On the menace posed to enclosed domestic spaces by the crazed 'gallop' of (highly sexualized) human violence, see Borie, pp. 151–6. The mother and daughter victims of Poe's story, Mme and Mlle Camille l'Espanaye, may also have influenced Zola's double portrait of the Countess de Beauvilliers and her daughter Alice. Incidentally, Poe's fictive rue Morgue was situated in the sinister quartier du Doyenné where Bette lived.

[109] Precocity is one of the characteristics of childhood obscenity cited by Lombroso (*L'Homme criminel*, p. 111). Dualism also characterizes Victor, who as a child has the fine, pure skin of a girl

profondes, les lèvres épaisses' and '[des c]heveux roux, frisés' (MS 10268, fol. 294). The deep orbits were another sign of Lombroso's born criminal, but as we have seen he specifically excludes red hair from the tell-tale characteristics, which may be why the 'cheveux roux' disappear from the published novel. Red hair was, however, attributed to primitive man by some contemporaries,[110] and it is also reminiscent of the non-human 'poils fauves' found clutched in the hands of the murdered Mme l'Espanaye in Poe's story, as translated by Baudelaire. Where Poe's orang-utan strangled the younger woman, Victor leaves his victim half-strangled and rapes her, so that the ill-defined threat of Poe's Gothic tale becomes explicitly sexual, in a nightmare of rape and random violence that once again reflects European fears of an abject, racialized other.

In his own variants on the detective story in *L'Argent* and in *La Bête humaine*, Zola displaces the mystery from the question of *who* did it to that of *what* did it: what, within modern society, is responsible for apparently inexplicable crime? And behind the question of '*What*...?' lies the implicit question of '*Whence*...?': whence comes the threat that is simultaneously inside and outside society? The 'lingering and more dangerous enemy turns out to be the beast lurking within civilized society itself.'[111] Prendergast, following Ginzburg, sees the detective novel as the apt symbolic representation of the extension of the 'basic tracking model' of the hunt (the 'cynegetic paradigm') to 'whole sections of the population [...] the "deviant" and "criminal" classes'. In the late nineteenth century, when this tracking or hunting paradigm takes on a new pre-eminence, the detective story introduces elements derived from the emerging science of criminology into what is in effect a much older pattern.[112] Zola leaves Victor's destiny unresolved so that the inner beast remains an ongoing threat, and Caroline asks herself: 'ce monstre, lâché par le monde, errant et traqué, quelle hérédité du mal allait-il assouvir au travers des foules, comme un loup dévorateur ?' (V: 373). Unlike Jacques in *La Bête humaine*, Victor remains at large within the apparently civilized, explicitly urban world, and Caroline imagines him 'rôdant un soir de noir dégel, affamé, un couteau au poing' (V: 375); 'Victor, déjà, était loin, galopait là-bas, par la ville, au fond de l'effrayant inconnu' (V: 376). The new wilderness, the terrain in which the detective novel (whose form is sketched out in this subplot) stages the modern hunt, is the anonymous urban jungle.

The hunt is unsuccessful, and the threat of the savage cannot be eliminated, because the savage who is lost in the modern city is in fact part of us. Victor bears a striking resemblance to his respectable bourgeois father ('Victor est tout son portrait', V: 39; also 144, 151, and Zola's notes too stress the character's 'ressemblance frappante avec Saccard', MS 10268, fol. 294). Saccard has '[la] peau brune,

---

(V: 151; see also Zola's notes on 'les traits délicats, le teint de fille', MS 10268, fol. 294). Lombroso's born criminal, as we have seen, had a curiously delicate complexion.

[110] Quatrefages, according to Tarde, p. 15, n. 1.

[111] Ellingson, *Myth of the Noble Savage*, p. 126. See also Kristeva on the ambivalent spatial situation, and porous borders, that characterize the abject (*Pouvoirs de l'horreur*, pp. 15–16).

[112] Prendergast, *Order of Mimesis*, pp. 222–3, and Carlo Ginzburg, 'Morelli, Freud and Sherlock Holmes: Clues and Scientific Method', *History Workshop*, 9 (1980), 5–36.

envahie avec l'âge d'un poil de bête' (V: 211). For Victor *is* Saccard: just as his stooge Sabatani takes on the unacceptably seedy attributes of the bourgeois speculator, Victor embodies the animal urges that drive him (including his irrational lust for victory and money). The family flaw is not only in the working-class Macquart inheritance, but in the bourgeois Rougon side too. The unspeakable, concealed answer to the classic question posed by the detective story—Who did it?—is: Saccard himself; the bourgeois respectable individual; us. The simian Victor provides a racialist embodiment of the primitive within us all.

As well as embodying the dark, irrational energies unleashed within the metropolitan world, Victor is part of yet another Zolian thought-experiment. Fished out of his slum, he is recuperated by *L'Œuvre du Travail*, an orphanage funded by the charitable Princess d'Orviedo, which seeks to regenerate the disinherited children of Parisian crime (V: 53). Once again his name is particularly revelatory, for 'Victor' was the name given to the 'Wild Boy of Aveyron' found in 1797, who had apparently lived through most of his childhood without human contact; like Zola's Victor he was discovered in his early teens.[113] Victor de l'Aveyron was the subject of considerable learned interest, since he seemed an illustration of the Enlightenment principle that it is education that makes us human. He was initially studied in Paris by a specialist in the education of deaf-mutes, the abbé Roch-Ambroise Cucurron *Sicard* (my emphasis); Sicard proved unable to educate him, and entrusted his care to a medical student (Jean Marc Gaspard Itard) who was marginally more successful. Like Victor de l'Aveyron, Victor *Saccard* (to give him his father's name, though at the time of conception Saccard was using the false name *Sicardot*[114]) is an experimental subject that allows the novel to test the ability of education to transform the human savage into a civilized citizen—the fundamental premise of the charitable orphanage. Of course, Victor de l'Aveyron is the child of 'nature', while Victor Saccard is the child of the urban slum: but in both cases recuperation by education fails. And yet Zola seems to hesitate in adopting this position, which would contradict his desire for social reform.[115] The novel also contrasts the illegitimate Victor with his half-brother Maxime Rougon, and we are encouraged to compare them because Caroline pays them successive visits. Zola's notes make clear that the contrast is allegorical: 'Victor, c'est le vice et le crime faute d'argent, opposé à Maxime' (MS 10268, fol. 217). Caroline wonders whether civilization is situated in the superficial superiority conferred by money—which corresponds to the views put forward by the French sociological school of criminology, notably by Gabriel

[113] The 'Wild Boy of Aveyron' died in 1828. On the use of colonial terminology in the pedagogical discussions of idiocy in relation to his case, and parallels drawn with the new world savage, see Murray K. Simpson, 'From Savage to Citizen: Education, Colonialism and Idiocy', *British Journal of Sociology of Education*, 28:5 (2007), 561–74. For a brief but useful discussion of the links between Victor de l'Aveyron and Zola's Victor, see Andrew McQueen, 'The Wild Child in Zola's *L'Argent*', *Excavatio*, 12 (1999), 53–9.

[114] The name 'Sicardot' was used by Zola in the first volume of the Rougon-Macquart cycle, *La Fortune des Rougon*, so the echo of the Abbé Sicard's name may be a simple coincidence.

[115] Nelson sees *L'Argent* as part of Zola's attempt 'to reconcile his Darwinian view of life with a need for responsible social leadership' ('Zola's Ideology', p. 165). In the 1880s and early 1890s the tendency in France was towards social rehabilitation of criminals, but after around 1895 a more pessimistic view, with less emphasis on sociology and free will, came to dominate (see Nye, pp. 98–9).

Tarde, who criticized Lombroso's explanation of criminal behaviour through atavism or biology—but she observes in truly Zolian fashion that 'la même boue humaine restait dessous' (V: 154).

ZOLA, THE EXPERIMENTAL NOVEL, AND EPISTEMOLOGICAL DOUBT

We saw that Balzac gives us a non-physiological description of cousin Bette followed by a racialized portrayal of her dark, simian characteristics, but that she also has some of the traits of the Romantic brunette. Balzacian racialization is held in balance with competing explanations, not presented as a complete totalizing formula. In Zola's novels this balance of competing theories is more deliberately maintained. He deploys a set of ideas derived from race, but at the same time establishes critical distance from them. The relationship between the indices of primitive origin and criminal behaviour is not as clear-cut as might be thought. This uncertainty must be understood in the context of Zola's frequently derided idea of the novel as experiment. I suggest that his work can be understood in terms of a tension between the novel as *thesis* (the *roman à thèse*) and the novel as *experiment*. In the former, a single theory about the world is demonstrated to the reader; in the latter, although there is no truly open experiment, conflicting theories are explored and events favour one or the other. The novels where experimentation takes a lead role are still characterized by what Hamon calls a 'volonté décryptive', in which Zola is intent on decoding or unveiling the truth about his characters, but they offer more than one possible interpretation of that truth. This limits the 'lisibilité' that Hamon sees as central to Zola's work, or rather offers us two conflicting but equally 'lisible' interpretative modes.[116] So *L'Argent* shows financial speculation to be either the fecundating energy necessary for world progress, *or* an amoral primitive drive. The fact that Saccard's illegitimate son Victor is not redeemed by the orphanage's best efforts could indicate the dominance of hereditary determinism over social determinism, *or* it could indicate the failure of late education to modify early social influence (the dark 'trou' of the slum). Different models of heredity could explain Jacques Lantier's homicidal urges; and Cabuche both is, and is not, the type of the born criminal.

Following the publication of *La Bête humaine*, Zola was accused of inconsistency for having depicted four different criminal types and drawn on conflicting theories of degeneration and atavism. A contemporary criminologist defended him, arguing that *La Bête humaine* showed competing explanations employed by a science in the process of discovering itself, and moreover the two theories might be reconciled if one understood degeneration as the loss, in later generations, of the recently acquired veneer of civilization.[117] Zola certainly shows an ambivalent attitude to

---

[116] Hamon, *Le Personnel du roman*, pp. 35–6, p. 38.

[117] Jules Héricourt, '*La Bête humaine* de M. Zola et la physiologie du criminel', *Revue Bleue* (7 June 1890), 710–18 (p. 711, p. 712).

the models of physiological determinism that he adopts. As early as *Thérèse Raquin*, Camille purchases the works of the natural historian Buffon in what has been qualified as 'une ironique mise en abyme'.[118] The irony is double: Buffon's work is out of date when Camille attempts to better himself by aiming to study it, so his pretentions are misplaced from the start; and Buffon was one of the great pioneers of the theory of degeneration under the influence of climate or milieu, of which Camille himself is a superb example.[119] So too, in *Germinal*, Étienne Lantier reads, and half understands, fragments and summaries of Darwin in a cheap edition (III: 1524). Zola made a habit of including such self-reflexive intertextual references as a way of keeping some distance from currents of thought with which he might otherwise be too directly identified.[120]

The inclusion of Buffon in *Thérèse Raquin* hints at an ironic reflection on natural history, and crime in the novel goes undetected and unpunished by the institutions of justice. So too, twenty years later in *La Bête humaine* Zola ironically undermines rigorous classification and moral judgement based on physiognomy, even as he appears on the surface to be following their dictates. The dualism of Zola's characters, which Lombroso saw as mere inconsistency, is a means of incorporating doubt about the latest scientific theories. The figure of Denizet, the examining magistrate who is in charge of the case, shows how Zola undermines any simple equation between physiognomy and guilt. Denizet misinterprets both the murders of the novel and condemns the wrong men. Like the police in Poe's *Murders in the Rue Morgue*, Denizet looks for a rational, financial motive, and thus sees Roubaud as guilty of the murder of Séverine. They fail to identify the irrational act of the orang-utan or the compulsive homicide, Jacques. And Denizet sees the innocent Cabuche as guilty of the earlier murder that was in fact committed by Roubaud, mainly on the grounds of his physique which presents all the traits of Lombroso's born criminal. This Lombrosian stance is, according to Becker, contested by Zola 'avec une ironie amère'.[121] Or as Pick puts it, in Zola's novel 'the physical index of crime is neither infallible nor adequate'.[122] Judicial error was part of Zola's plan for *La Bête humaine* from early on, when he sought an ironic take on the perceptive judge of Dostoyevsky's *Crime and Punishment* 'et tant d'autres romans'.[123] The name of Zola's judge Denizet itself suggests that the man is too clever by half, *déniaisé*, and not prepared to grasp the obvious. And he is indeed led astray by his desire for

[118] François-Marie Mourad, '*Thérèse Raquin*, roman expérimental', *Les Cahiers naturalistes*, 84 (2010), 157–64 (p. 157).

[119] On Buffon and degeneration theory, see Blanckaert, 'Les conditions d'émergence'. It has also been suggested that the inclusion is ironic because Buffon was an opponent of the physiognomical theories that Zola adopted (E. Paul Gauthier, 'New Light on Zola and physiognomy', *Publications of the Modern Language Association of America*, 75 (1960), 297–308 (p. 305)).

[120] Pick suggests that *Le Docteur Pascal* dramatizes 'the contradictions, indeed even the disintegration, of the positivism which had hitherto partially structured Zola's own project', and emphasizes the growing contradiction between theories of degeneration and the scientist as a detached, 'perfectly unified thinking subject' (p. 4, p. 42).

[121] 'Zola et Lombroso', p. 44.   [122] *Faces of Degeneration*, p. 85.

[123] On Zola's reading of Dostoyevsky's *Crime and Punishment*, published in French in 1884, see Henri Mitterand IV: 1715. Zola did not accept Dostoyevsky's view of remorse or of rational murder, seeing crime as an act of hereditary madness.

complex, rational theories, by 'trop de finesse, par ses habitudes de métier, son idée fixe du crime, son abandon professionnel de la simplicité': the truth is too simple for him to see (MS 10274, fols 358 and 383). The novel repeatedly refers to him being blinded by 'trop de finesse' (IV: 1084; also 1102; 1312), a trait that is ironically echoed in his own physiognomy through a play on words: he is 'fin' or astute (IV: 1115, 1116), and his lips are 'fines' or thin (IV: 1100). His 'lèvres mobiles s'amincissaient' even more as he makes a final error (IV: 1312). These thin lips are very much a trait of the middle class in contrast to the wide-mouthed lower-class characters who abound in the novel, as well as being a European trait. It is this 'finesse' that leads him to apply theories about the physiological make-up of the born criminal that turn out to be merely confirmation of stereotypes held by the population in general.[124] The association of 'primitive' traits with crime, and white European traits with rational knowledge, is thus simultaneously adopted and undermined by Zola.

Zola may have been encouraged to keep his distance from Lombroso by the critical reception of the biologically determinist Italian school of criminology among French sociologists and magistrates.[125] Tarde, among others, argued for criminality to be treated as the product of social factors and mocked Lombroso's frequent comparisons of the criminal 'type' with that of the 'sauvage', in part by referring to the observations of contemporary anthropologists.[126] Zola does at times deploy Lombrosian paradigms of criminality in ways that seem entirely non-ironic, but at times he also frames them in such a way as to set them at a distance. As we saw, the most explicit linking of Jacques's homicidal urges to primitive atavism is voiced by Jacques himself, as one hypothesis among others. The idea horrifies him: when Séverine proposes that they murder her husband naked, to avoid having tell-tale stains on their clothes, he is horrified: 'Non, non!…comme des sauvages, alors. Pourquoi pas lui manger le cœur?' (IV: 1292). Zola leads us to doubt the adequacy of a straightforward racialist sign-system. And despite his own tendency to adopt formulaic slogans in his critical writing, his novels undermine any idea of a single uncontested means of interpreting the world. It is of course tempting to think that this includes an ironic conception of his own practice as novelist. In his notes on Denizet he drew a parallel between the magistrate and the novelist: 'la justice continue son roman, et frappe à tort à travers' (MS 10274, fol. 358).

Zola also likes to leave hostages to fortune, open ends to counteract what might otherwise be the excessive closure of his narrative dénouements. As we have seen, *L'Argent*'s final chapter offers us not only the positive image of Mme Caroline's resilience and the hope of real progress in the Middle East, but also the escape of

[124] Roubaud himself draws on these stereotypes in describing an imaginary assassin who turns out to resemble Cabuche; and later Cabuche is 'bien tel qu'on se l'imaginait […] le type même de l'assassin, des poings énormes, des mâchoires de carnassier' (IV: 1320).

[125] See Nye, ch. 4.

[126] Tarde published his criticism of Lombroso based on the Italian edition a year before the publication of the French translation (Gabriel Tarde, *La Criminalité comparée*, 1886). Zola's notes do not mention Tarde but Mitterand argues in favour of Zola being influenced by him (IV: 1715–16).

the feral Victor, knife in hand, while his father Saccard too is alive and rebuilding his lost fortune in Holland. In *Le Docteur Pascal* we learn that both these narrative strands are still open in the early years of the Third Republic (V: 1016). Zola also uses departure to America, where Lazare goes to seek his fortune at the end of *La Joie de vivre* (V: 1017). Deportation to the penal colonies is another form of imperfect narrative closure. Florent is deported, not killed, at the end of *Le Ventre de Paris*. Jacques Lantier dies, but his brother Étienne is deported to New Caledonia after his involvement in the Commune (V: 1017). The 1893 version of the family tree, which represents the notes made by Dr Pascal on his family in the final novel of the series, tells us that Étienne Lantier the miner 'Vit encore, à Nouméa, déporté. Marié là-bas, dit-on, et a des enfants, peut-être, qu'on ne peut classer.'[127] Dr Pascal's information is incomplete and uncertain: 'on disait même qu'il s'y était tout de suite marié et qu'il avait un enfant, sans qu'on sût au juste le sexe' (V: 1017). As Geoff Woollen suggests, this 'indication télégrammatique' is sufficient to open up 'la perspective crédible qu'un transporté joue un rôle civilisateur' and may become 'un utile acteur dans la mise en valeur d'un territoire d'outre-mer, à la sexualité non réprimée mais procréatrice'.[128] In other words, the open-ended narrative strand represented by Étienne's destiny may already point towards Zola's turn to utopianism. By the end of the Rougon-Macquart series the colonies are liberated from the threat of the primitive, leaving them free to offer the promise of a colonialist utopia in the startlingly unpopulated Sudan evoked in *Fécondité*.[129] Earlier, however, off-stage colonial heterotopias and racialist metaphors are incorporated with more ambivalence, as though they tested the boundaries of the naturalist gaze. Dr Pascal does not actually *know* what becomes of Étienne after his deportation to New Caledonia, and it is this gap in the character's biography that leaves space for hope, just as Zola is careful to introduce epistemological gaps between possible theories. As Tallis puts it in his defence of Realism, there is 'no obligation upon the realistic novelist [...] to resolve all conflicts in a harmonious closure', nor to 'subsume all the voices and viewpoints of the characters under an over-riding voice', despite what anti-realist critics have tended to assert.[130]

---

[127] The 1893 family tree was included as part of *Le Docteur Pascal*. In the 1878 version the name of the homicidal character was still 'Étienne Lantier' (see annex to Pléiade V).

[128] Geoff Woollen, 'Les transportés dans l'œuvre de Zola', *Les Cahiers naturalistes*, 72 (1998), 317–33 (p. 328).

[129] On Zola's deliberate misuse of his source material in order to depict Sudan as deserted before the arrival of the Froment family to colonize it, see Seillan, 'L'Afrique utopique de *Fécondité*', p. 194.

[130] Tallis, *In Defence*, p. 57.

Conclusion
Colonialism, Postcolonialism, and the Realist Mode

As we have seen, nineteenth-century narrative fiction in the realist mode portrayed the wider colonial sphere indirectly through metonymy and offstage spaces. Extra-metropolitan themes are one of the means by which the realist mode incorporates ethical and epistemological doubt, and questions the validity of the referential knowledge it displays. In this Conclusion I shall begin by looking at the heritage of late Realism, or Naturalism, in the colonial novel, focusing on the reification of doubt into the recurrent stereotype of the 'unknowable other'. Whereas Realism might on the surface appear to be predicated on the possibility of knowing the real and conveying that knowledge through language, the 'unknowable other' theme focuses on the failure of objective knowledge to deal with racial and cultural difference. This topos of epistemological failure is accompanied by anxiety about the identity of the colonizer himself. Now, it has long been argued that doubt concerning the referential function of language, and colonial anxiety, are central to modernism. We shall see here that they come to the fore within realist aesthetics, and that they have even older origins. The final part of this Conclusion will go on to examine the debates that pitted Realism against modernism in the twentieth century, and question the relevance of such a polarity to postcolonial writing. It will summarize recent calls to re-assess the contributions of the realist mode to postcolonial literature. In this context, *The Colonial Comedy*'s argument that we also need to re-assess the links between colonialism and so-called 'Classic Realism' appears particularly timely.

* * *

The realist mode was the main literary response to direct experience of the French colonies for a host of minor writers of the new 'littérature coloniale' from the 1880s to the 1930s. Naturalism, in particular, provided a model for colonial writers such as Louis Bertrand, Marius-Ary Leblond, and Robert Randau. They situated themselves in opposition to the 'exotic' novel, associated with the works of Pierre Loti whose penchant for dreamlike, melancholic subjectivity symbolized all that the colonial novel sought to repudiate.[1] As discussed in the Introduction

---

[1] According to Peter Dunwoodie, Louis Bertrand was the key figure in this disdainful rejection of exoticism and adoption of 'aggressive realism' (*Writing French Algeria* (Oxford: Clarendon Press, 1998), p. 93). As late as the 1920s the new colonial literature was explicitly claiming its models to be the metropolitan novels of Balzac and Zola (Marius-Ary Leblond, *Après l'exotisme de Loti: le roman colonial* (Paris: Vald. Rasmussen, 1926), p. 8).

to this volume, the rejection of this late-Romantic exoticism was a key strategy adopted by many of the writers and theorists of the new colonial literature. We have seen, however, that Realism moved beyond Romanticism by devouring or incorporating it; the same is true for colonial literature, which expends a great deal of energy denouncing exoticism precisely because it is so close to it.

It is in terms of this contrast with exoticism that contemporary theorists of the 'school' of colonial literature tended to stake out its claims to documentary precision and objectivity.[2] So too, many colonial writers imitated Zola by including claims to scientific objectivity in the paratextual apparatus—prefaces, articles, and even book-length studies—published alongside their fiction. In the preface to one of his novels, Louis Bertrand claimed that the novel must represent reality by relying on the 'progrès des sciences biologiques', adhering to 'la méthode strictement impersonnelle qu'inaugurèrent les maîtres du roman vers la seconde moitié du XIXᵉ siècle, et qui consiste uniquement à représenter'[3]. The prefaces of novels by the colonial naval doctor Paul Vigné d'Octon follow Zola still more closely in evoking the methods of experimental medicine: in his novels, it is claimed, 'l'âme des exotiques [...] est disséquée ainsi qu'un cadavre à l'amphithéâtre, et la chair, toute la chair humaine exposée et décrite fibre à fibre avec [...] exactitude'.[4] Vigné d'Octon adopts the scientific terminology Zola had himself learnt from Taine and Claude Bernard, but also relies on his own training in medicine and biology to apply la 'méthode évolutionniste'.[5]

These claims to apply the methods of the biological sciences should however— as in the case of Zola himself—be taken with a grain of salt. Although much of the paratextual apparatus of colonial literature makes claims to objectivity, a reading of the novels themselves often demands a significant modification of any triumphalist vision of all-conquering Western knowledge.

THE 'UNKNOWABLE OTHER', OR THE PROBLEM WITH(IN) REALISM

As we have seen, French colonial literature until 1890 often reflected doubt and apprehension. Even later colonial literature, contemporary with a newly assertive rhetoric concerning France's *mission civilisatrice* and the energizing potential of the colonial experience for the French themselves, was frequently beset by doubt. Hesitation concerning colonial policy, epistemological uncertainty, and a feeling of besieged identity are not to be mistaken for a postcolonial attitude—indeed, in

---

[2] Pierre Jourda, for example, saw colonial literature as true Realism that rejected sensibility, entertainment, and local colour. 'On transporte à la colonie les méthodes naturalistes: le livre colonial devient objectif et documentaire; l'observation exacte l'emporte sur l'analyse sentimentale' (*L'Exotisme dans la littérature française depuis Chateaubriand: t. 2, du romantisme à 1939* (Paris: Presses Universitaires de France, 1956), p. 222 (the volume was written in 1939, but its publication was delayed by the war)).

[3] Louis Bertrand, *La Cina* (Paris: Paul Ollendorff, 1901), Preface, p. ix.

[4] Preface by Paul Cladel to Vigné d'Octon's novel *Chair noire* (Paris: Lemerre, 1889), p. x.

[5] Preface to his novel *Fauves amours* (Paris: Lemerre, 1892), p. ii. *Fauves amours* was dedicated to Zola.

some cases they are founded on racialist presumptions—but their very existence disturbs reductive views of the nature of Realism and of colonial discourse. In particular, it would be misleading to think of colonial literature as predicated on the knowability of the other. In fact, one of its recurrent stereotypes assumes precisely the opposite: that racial difference created an insurmountable obstacle for Western knowledge. This idea of the impenetrability of different races is an anti-realist trope insofar as it challenges assumptions that it is possible to know, analyse, and describe phenomena objectively. Colonial fiction takes this uncertainty to its heart.

Despite colonial literature's claims to break with exoticism, the idea of the 'unknowable other'[6] is essentially Romantic, born out of the nineteenth century's new emphasis on cultural relativism and the idea that there were fundamental differences between peoples.[7] For Mario Praz the ineffable (so frequently associated with exoticism) was the very essence of Romanticism, which came 'to consist in that which cannot be described'.[8] Colonial fiction counts among its Romantic roots the exotic imagery used to embody a forbidden truth that must not, or cannot, be exposed: the veiled figure of Isis inspires a doomed Promethean striving to unveil her.[9] In the English tradition this is associated with the Gothic mode, which seems on the surface to be completely distinct from Realism's focus on typical events functioning in a normal environment: 'The antithesis of the real in this sense is the unimaginable, the incomprehensible, the Gothic.'[10]

But novels in the realist mode *do* seek to speak of the incomprehensible, and the topos of the impossibility of ever truly knowing the other is passed down from Romanticism and becomes a way for Realism to examine its own limits. There are of course differences between the Romantic and Realist versions of the 'unknowable'. The Romantic use of exoticism, and in particular the veil, suggests a mystical truth about humanity itself that is beyond words, and its radical relativism stresses 'essences' of different peoples that are not primarily biological. The Oriental woman, in particular, often embodies the 'unknowable' feminine, like the Arab

---

[6] I presented some thoughts concerning the 'unknowable other' theme at the conference of the Société Internationale d'Étude des Littératures de l'Ère Coloniale ('Frontières du monde/Frontières du moi', Montpellier, 2010), under the title 'Le naturalisme aux colonies: échec du savoir, faillite du moi rationnel'. The lively discussion that ensued taught me that many people still attribute great value to the documentary veracity of colonial discourse.

[7] Todorov denounces this victory of relativism in the nineteenth century as a rejection of the ideal of equality, and points to the danger of obscurantism in the idea of the incommunicability of different cultures (*Nous et les autres*, part 1, and p. 125).

[8] Mario Praz, *The Romantic Agony*, trans. by Angus Davidson (Oxford: Oxford University Press, 1970 [1933]), p. 14.

[9] See Friedrich von Schiller's famous poem on an unwary youth who unveils the statue of Isis to seek the 'truth' ('The Veiled Statue at Sais', 1795). Exotic lands, and in particular Egypt, are the site of Romantic terror aroused by longing to transgress divine or natural boundaries. The rarely-acknowledged continuity of Romanticism in naturalism—albeit in a 'scientific' form—is apparent in Zola's essay 'L'Égypte il y a trois mille ans': the thought of ancient Egypt arouses his 'désirs de science sans jamais les satisfaire'; Egypt 'reste voilée, immobile, souriant mystérieusement, un doigt sur la bouche' (in *Mes Haines, Œuvres complètes*, ed. by Henri Mitterand, 15 vols (Paris: Cercle du livre précieux, 1962–9), vol. 10, pp. 93–8 (p. 93)).

[10] Brown, 'Logic of Realism', p. 228.

'fille du désert' who figures at the close of Balzac's *Physiologie du mariage* (XI: 1203).[11] Naturalist Realism, on the other hand, approaches difference in biological terms; but it too emphasizes the limitations of rational enquiry and the threat of epistemological stalemate, frequently embodied in a female figure.

The continuity of Romantic exoticism within colonial discourse also appears in the association of forbidden knowledge with blindness, particularly in relation to the 'darkness' of Africa. Victor Hugo declared, 'Il semble que voir l'Afrique, ce soit être aveuglé.'[12] Miller shows that Africanist discourse produces Africa as a blank, associated with sleep, darkness, and absence, and thus with the unknowable. Examples of this discourse share 'the same will-to-knowledge seen in Orientalism but find their will and desire pitted against an otherness that appears to have no "actual identity," that refuses to be acquired and domesticated.' He sees Africanist discourse as 'an unhappy Orientalism, a discourse of desire unfulfilled and unfulfillable'.[13] Bernard Mouralis also links Africa to the frustration of the European will-to-knowledge, and thus with a form of madness. He highlights a double movement that asserts the absolute alterity of Africa and of Africans, but at the same time expresses the conviction that it is possible and necessary to take them as the object of scientific study, creating a fundamental epistemological problem at the heart of the Western 'mission' for rational knowledge.[14]

This well-known theme of the 'unknowable other' has sometimes been seen as a wilful avoidance strategy that characterizes exotic, rather than colonial, writing.[15] Loti is held up as an example of this obscurantism, and used as a foil whose influence the writers of 'littérature coloniale' struggled to shake off; and Loti of course reiterated

[11] Owen Heathcote suggests that this character conflates stereotypes by showing the limitations of the Western philosopher whose wisdom does not go beyond his own book ('Gérer l'altérité? Le travail du corps dans les *Études analytiques*', in *Balzac, l'aventure analytique*, ed. by Claire Barel-Moisan and Christèle Couleau (Saint-Cyr-sur-Loire: Éditions Christian Pirot, 2009), pp. 215–27 (p. 216)).

[12] Victor Hugo, 'Discours sur l'Afrique' [1879], in *Œuvres complètes*, ed. by Jean Massin, 18 vols (Paris: Club français du livre, 1967–70), vol. 15, pp. 1450–4 (p. 1451).

[13] Christopher L. Miller, *Blank Darkness: Africanist Discourse in French* (Chicago: University of Chicago Press, 1985), p. 23. 'Even in the presence of empirical knowledge', Miller claims, 'Africa and things African are a privileged locus of lags, breaches, delays, and failures in understanding and knowledge. The perception of the continent remains "dark".' 'From the earliest times, Black Africa was experienced as the literal end of European knowledge', as one sees in the use of the label 'terra incognita' on ancient maps (p. 20, pp. 22–3).

[14] Bernard Mouralis, 'L'Afrique comme figure de la folie', *Cahiers CRLH-CIRAOI*, 5 (1988), 45–59 (pp. 45–6).

[15] Denise Brahimi, notably, writes 'Voulant tirer le plus de substance possible de son impossibilité à comprendre l'objet exotique, le sujet européen orchestre le thème de l'inconnaissable par l'affirmation qu'il n'y a rien à connaître, ou qu'il y a mensonge et fuite de l'autre, ou qu'il est racialement (parce que racialement) incompréhensible' ('Enjeux et risques du roman exotique français', *Cahiers CRLH. CIRAOI*, 5 (1988), 11–18 (p. 14)). Brahimi follows Jourda, who also held up Fromentin, in contrast to Loti, as a 'realist' because of his supposed use of pure observation (*Exotisme dans la littérature française*, vol. 2, pp. 69–75). Kapor also suggests that the 'indicible' is an exotic rather than colonial topos (*Pour une poétique*, p. 45). Jean-François Durand finds the 'unknowable other' theme within both exoticism and colonial literature except where the latter adopts what he calls an 'esprit pionnier' ('Littératures coloniales, littératures d'Empire ?', *Romantisme*, 139:1 (2008), 47–58 (p. 51)). There is certainly a subsection of colonial literature that declares the mystery to be solved: 'Les races ont été pénétrées et décrites, le mystère est éclairci sur leur compte [...] La Mission a soulevé l'un des derniers voiles de ténèbres qui recouvraient encore ces régions du Continent noir' (Durand, p. 57, quoting Lenfant writing in 1909).

the unknowable nature of exotic cultures and peoples. The colonial writer Pierre Mille mocked the formulaic nature of the exotic novel: 'Une âme impénétrable, plus trois cent pages.'[16] And yet many of the colonial writers who rejected Loti's exoticism followed him in reiterating the fundamental impossibility of truly knowing the other. Even an author such as Vigné d'Octon, held up by Roland Lebel as a paragon of good colonial *realist* literature—in contrast to Loti-style exoticism[17]— revisits the Romantic truism of the unknowable nature of the other, adding Gothic flourishes of vampirism and disease for good measure.

The theme of the 'unknowable other' sits ill at ease with the reductive view of Realism as based on a denial 'that there was a reality of essences or forms which was not accessible to ordinary sense perception, insisting instead that reality be viewed as something immediately to hand, common to ordinary human experience, and open to observation'.[18] In fact writers working within the realist mode do not hesitate to assert the limitations of human understanding. The 'unknowable other' stereotype flourished alongside its opposite—the ideal of positive and comprehensive knowledge— and it is arguably a way of recuperating the apparently 'unrepresentable' within representation: as Prendergast points out, when the notions of 'the "beyond" [and] the "unrepresentable" are articulated in or as language, they are perforce inscribed in, and hence negated by, the very logic of representation they seek to exceed'.[19] The 'unknowable other' topos is thus a means to recuperate or contain difference, pre-empting the failure of Western rationalism. Nevertheless, a certain type of colonial literature tirelessly reiterates that very failure.

Although Vigné d'Octon's prefaces declared the supremacy of scientific knowledge, his novels tell the opposite story. In one emblematic novel, his hero is a doctor who attempts to understand African 'types' through anthropological study but whose rational mind is overwhelmed by irresistible and 'inexplicable' sexual drives.[20] This shift in the 'unknowable other' theme reflects the new importance ascribed, by the end of the century, to the role of the unconscious, with its drives that exceed the capacities of objective knowledge. Nor is colonial anxiety of this kind limited to literature: Vigné d'Octon, after his career as a doctor in the colonial army with a sideline as a colonial novelist, became a virulently anticolonial politician.

---

[16] This was Mille's response to a survey by *La Dépêche coloniale* (1 October 1909), quoted by Citti, who notes that this formula produced a rich supply of narratives because 'une âme impénétrable provoque à la percer': it allowed the creation of love stories in which either 'l'obstacle des races et des civilisations rehausse la force de la passion' or 'on pénètre un peu dans ces âmes et on n'y trouve rien' (*Contre la décadence*, pp. 247–8).

[17] Roland Lebel repeatedly asserts that Vigné d'Octon portrayed the reality of Senegal, and its women in particular (p. 192; p. 200), claiming that '[e]xotisme s'oppose à colonialisme comme romantisme s'oppose à naturisme', *L'Afrique occidentale dans la littérature française depuis 1870* (Paris: Larose, 1925), p. 229.

[18] George J. Becker, 'Introduction' in *Documents of Modern Literary Realism* (Princeton, NJ: Princeton University Press, 1963), pp. 3–38 (p. 6).

[19] *Order of Mimesis*, p. 17.

[20] *Chair noire*; for 'inexplicable', see p. 160, p. xvi. For more detail, including a discussion of Vigné d'Octon's other works, see my article 'Malaria and the Femme Fatale: Sex and Death in French Colonial Africa', *Literature and Medicine*, 21:2 (2002), 201–15.

By the end of the nineteenth century, the impossibility of understanding foreigners had become a truism of the growing travel literature.[21] The view that non-Europeans are resistant to objective knowledge is far from being a sign of respect. Indeed Simone de Beauvoir compares it to the 'mysterious' nature of Woman: there is 'un mystère du Noir, du Jaune, en tant qu'ils sont considérés absolument comme l'Autre inessentiel'; 'le Mystère est propriété de l'esclave'.[22] Albert Memmi denounces this as one of the classic mechanisms of the colonial relationship, which remove the humanity of the colonized in the eyes of the colonizer: 'l'humanité du colonisé, refusée par le colonisateur, lui devient en effet opaque. Il est vain, prétend-il, de chercher à prévoir les conduites du colonisé ("Ils sont imprévisibles!"... "Avec eux, on ne sait jamais !"). [...] il faut penser que le colonisateur a de fortes raisons de tenir à cette illisibilité.'[23]

In its most common form, then, the idea that it is impossible to know the colonized tips rapidly into colonial stereotype. In using that term, what I seek to highlight is the *naturalization* of a concept. To say that one does not understand something is not a stereotype, but to assert that it is in the (biological, non-historical) nature of that thing to be unknowable *is*. The stereotype of the 'unknowable other' relies on an assumption that different peoples have completely separate and incommunicable essences or natures ('l'âme des races'). Writing in the realist mode, however, alternates between two different forms of lack of knowledge—this essentialist version, and a specific, historically grounded one. For example, in Maupassant's North African short story 'Allouma' one finds traces of the points made in his journalism concerning French ignorance of their colonized subjects: 'Jamais peut-être un peuple conquis par la force n'a su échapper aussi complètement à la domination réelle, à l'influence morale, et à l'investigation acharnée, mais inutile du vainqueur.' According to this analysis, the eponymous heroine's resistance to rational knowledge, her status as 'être de fuite', is a deliberate act of subversion by her as a member of a population living under violent repression. But the narrator rapidly goes on to *naturalize* his own ignorance in terms of the insurmountable difference between races, which he then uses as an analogy for the incomprehensible 'nature' of women in general.[24]

This naturalized view of the colonized as inherently unknowable is a form of commodification, but it nevertheless suggests that we should treat with caution assertions that 'colonial discourse produces the colonized as a social reality which is at once an "other" and yet entirely knowable and visible'.[25] The tendency to see

---

[21] Indeed, Lisa Lowe suggests that the 'description of the foreign people as incomprehensible' was a 'requisite', among the 'generic and rhetorical features of travel literature' well into the twentieth century (*Critical Terrains*, p. 188).

[22] Simone de Beauvoir, *Le Deuxième sexe*, 2 vols (Paris: Gallimard, 1976 [1949]), vol. 1, p. 403.

[23] Albert Memmi, *Portrait du colonisé précédé de Portrait du colonisateur* (Paris: Gallimard, 1985 [1957]), p. 106.

[24] Maupassant, *Contes et nouvelles* II, pp. 1095–117 (p. 1104).

[25] Bhabha, *Location of Culture*, pp. 70–1. Following Said, Bhabha adds that colonial discourse 'employs a system of representation, a regime of truth, that is structurally similar to realism', by which he appears to mean Realism in the pejorative sense of naïve belief in objective, transparent portrayal. He does, of course, analyse the anxiety and ambivalence of the colonial stereotype, but via a psychoanalytic approach to colonial fantasy and fetishism (see his chapter 'The Other Question: stereotype,

colonial discourse, at least on the conscious level, as a process of 'making plain' derives from the influence of Said, for whom the Orientalist 'makes the Orient speak, describes the Orient, renders its mysteries plain for and to the West', while latent Orientalism is understood as a form of 'untouchable [...] positivity' that is unanimous, stable, and durable.[26] Even in his later work, Said asserts that: 'such domestic cultural enterprises as narrative fiction and history (once again I empha-size the narrative component) are premised on the recording, ordering, observing powers of the central authorizing subject, or ego'.[27] Let us look more closely at the nature of this central ego and its power to observe, order, and record.

ANXIETY AND THE DISSOLUTION OF THE SELF

Since the 1990s studies of British colonialism, such as Sara Suleri's work on English India, have identified the recurrent theme of epistemological failure as one of the 'narratives of anxiety' in which 'aggression functions as a symptom of terror'. Such terror typically translates into the ostensible unreadability of the subcontinent, a 'discursive fear' that fetishizes its own cultural ignorance. For Suleri, it is Romantic narrative conventions that allow colonial literature 'to posit the fiction that the national realities of the subcontinent lie beyond the pale of representation'.[28]

In French colonial literature too one finds such narratives of anxiety, no doubt in part resulting from the diminution of spatial barriers following imperialist expansion and the development of faster and cheaper transport. But the dual struc-ture of imperialist power itself led to a new anxiety about the colonizer's own identity, expressed in terms that foreshadow—though in a more egotistical way—Césaire's analysis, at the moment of decolonization, of the *'ensauvagement'* of Europe by its own colonial violence.[29] The anxiety of empire focused on the iden-tity of the colonizer himself.

There was, of course, an important strand of colonial literature that sought to use the colonial experience as an 'école de virilité' that would strengthen an identity weakened by the decadence of metropolitan culture.[30] But many colonial novels appear to demonstrate entirely the opposite theory: that the colonial experience threatens the moral identity of troubled or anti-heroic European protagonists.[31] Many men who were drawn to colonial careers were in fact misfits or dropouts in their own society. Living outside the everyday routine of European 'behavioural

discrimination and the discourse of colonialism', from 1983, reprinted in *Location of Culture*, pp. 66–84).

[26] *Orientalism*, pp. 20–1, p. 206.   [27] *Culture and Imperialism*, p. 95.
[28] Sara Suleri, *The Rhetoric of English India* (Chicago: University of Chicago Press, 1992) p. 6, p. 11.
[29] *Discours sur le colonialisme*, p. 11. We discussed the contagion of colonial violence within France itself in Chapter 6 of this volume.
[30] Ernest Psichari is a notable example, as Alec Hargreaves shows ('European Identity and the Colonial Frontier', *Journal of European Studies*, 12:47 (1982), 166–79). For the overall context of this struggle against a perceived European decadence, see Citti, *Contre la décadence*.
[31] Astier Loutfi, p. 26; she also points out the themes of sickness and suffering in the colonies, as well as the 'risques de corruption morale'; characters are 'menacés de déchéance' (p. 34).

norms' meant that 'white men were liable to find their defences lowered against all kinds of psychological impulses normally repressed at home' and 'in addition they were exposed to the dangers of what became known as "going native"'.[32] Whereas the adventure novel thrived on happy endings and success, novels inspired by naturalism tended to be pessimistic and focus on anti-heroes or 'vies manquées',[33] presenting its readers with the defeat of the Western individual in the colonies.

This anti-heroic colonial protagonist does not disappear after the 1890s, despite the rise of a more assertive colonial ideology. In Claude Farrère's Goncourt-winning *Les Civilisés* (1905) the meeting of different cultures in the colonial sphere leads to corruption and moral relativism, associated with opium and absinthe: like the Balzacian theme of the hardening experience of the slave trade that we saw in Chapter 2, opium gives a momentary clairvoyance, a kind of second sight, but ends in degradation. Balzac's treatment of the loss of moral compass is specific to the 'commerce d'hommes', whereas in the colonial novel there is a more diffuse threat to identity that fits within naturalism's entropic vision.[34] The risk that the colonizer would lose his French identity by 'going native' is evoked through a variety of terms by writers at the time ('encongayement', 'décivilisation', etc.) and by recent critics ('indifférenciation' or 'mêmification'[35]).

Said had described Orientalism in terms that place the Western subject rather differently: 'In a quite constant way, Orientalism depends for its strategy on this flexible positional superiority, which puts the Westerner in a whole series of possible relationships with the Orient without ever losing him the relative upper hand.'[36] Later critics, informed by gender theory, encourage us to see the 'Westerner' as less monolithically in control of the colonized and of himself—*him*self being particularly appropriate since masculinity is one of the traits that is endangered by the colonial encounter. Eve Kosofsky Sedgwick points to a threat of contagion or 'going native' that is derived from the English Gothic tradition, just as I have suggested the French version has its roots in Romanticism and parallels in the fantastic. Colonial loss of identity is an apparently objective way to approach older fears, giving rational form to the 'mechanisms of psychological dividedness, always important in the Gothic'. She adds that 'a partly Gothic-derived paranoid racist thematics of male penetration and undermining by subject peoples became a prominent feature of national ideology in western Europe. Its culmination is an image of male rape.'[37] In French colonial and exotic fiction the threat is more

[32] Hargreaves, 'European Identity', pp. 171–4.   [33] See Seillan, *Aux sources*, p. 187.
[34] See Baguley, *Naturalist Fiction: the Entropic Vision*.
[35] 'Comment ne pas remarquer l'insistance de ce désir d'indifférenciation qui saisit inéluctablement l'Occidental aux colonies [...]?', asks Alain Buisine. What he calls 'indifférenciation' is 'un insurmontable désir d'osmose, de fusion et de confusion qui iront jusqu'à la perte d'identité et à la totale déperdition du sujet'. He links this process of 'mêmification' to the death drive and a return to the Mother. Interestingly, his analysis includes Psichari, one of the main writers to claim that the colonies were an antidote to metropolitan decadence. Alain Buisine, *L'Orient voilé* (Paris: Zulma, 1993), p. 215, p. 220.
[36] *Orientalism*, p. 7.
[37] Eve Kosofsky Sedgwick, *Between Men: English Literature and Male Homosocial Desire* (New York: Columbia University Press, 1985), p. 182; see also p. 183. Buisine also discusses the passivity to which colonial novels progressively reduce the colonial adventurer, p. 223.

often evoked in terms of a dissolution of the self associated with sex, fever, and miscegenation (Vigné d'Octon and Loti), or isolation and heat (Bonnetain).[38]

FROM COLONIAL NATURALISM TO MODERNISM

Despite the continuing attraction of the naturalist model, by the 1890s sophisticated Parisian literary circles saw it as somewhat outdated.[39] The aesthetics of colonial literature relied in particular on two central realist tenets: contemporary subject matter and verisimilitude. In contrast, the deliberate questioning of naturalism by some of Zola's own disciples was often marked by the use of non-colonial exoticism; this is notably the case in Huysmans's *À rebours* (1884), as well as Octave Mirbeau's *Le Jardin des supplices* (1899). Here, exoticism is used to challenge assumptions of direct mimeticism in novels that otherwise share many traits of Realism. Nevertheless, there are precursors to modernism within the colonial novel itself, and a suggestive case is that of Bonnetain, once a disciple of Zola, but later one of the signatories of the *Manifeste des cinq* that broke with the master. He sought new subjects for naturalism in colonial Indochina and Africa, and also used some of the formal traits that would come to be associated with modernism, such as a fragmented narrative style and a first-person narrator.

Although there are of course differences in formal approach, any clear-cut opposition between naturalist and modernist approaches to colonialism tends to break down once one looks at the topoi of the 'unknowable other' and the dissolution of the self. Although Said's discussions of modernist literary formal experimentation tended to emphasize its underlying assumption of domination,[40] others have followed Jameson in focusing on the breakdown of identity within modernism. For Elleke Boehmer, the representation of empire at its height incorporated modernist 'expressions of cognitive failure—the failure to see fully, to know completely'. Modernist art forms arguably 'derive their energy from their diagnosis of the failure of the imperial enterprise'.[41] The colonial anxiety that we have seen as a recurrent theme of colonial literature thus re-emerges in modernism, which itself functions as 'the sign not of imperial power or confidence, but precisely the loss of that confidence'.[42]

---

[38] Notably Paul Vigné d'Octon, *Chair noire* (1889), Pierre Loti, *Le Roman d'un spahi* (1881), Paul Bonnetain, *Dans la brousse (Sensations du Soudan)* (1895). On the threat to identity posed by miscegenation, see Jennifer Yee, 'Neither Flesh Nor Fowl: "Métissage" in fin-de-siècle French Colonial Fiction', *L'Esprit créateur*, 37:1 (1998), 46–56.

[39] Colonial literature's adherence to 'the naturalist aesthetic [...] was out of step with the literary climate in mainland France' (Dunwoodie, p. 138; see also p. 134 on the influence of naturalism on Algerian colonial writing in particular). As we have seen, Zola and Balzac remained important literary models in the 1920s (Dunwoodie, p. 132, Leblond, p. 8).

[40] See comments by Chrisman, *Postcolonial Contraventions*, p. 55.

[41] Elleke Boehmer, *Empire, the National, and the Postcolonial 1890–1920: Resistance in Interaction* (Oxford: Oxford University Press, 2002), p. 172, p. 173.

[42] See Patrick Williams, '"Simultaneous uncontemporaneities": theorising modernism and empire', in *Modernism and Empire*, ed. by Howard J. Booth and Nigel Rigby (Manchester: Manchester University Press, 2000), pp. 13–38 (p. 17).

Joseph Conrad's *Heart of Darkness* (1899) is the modernist text that most famously stages the dissolution of the Western self in contact with alterity. Here we find both the ineffable nature of the other and the threat to the identity of the European self, themes familiar from French colonial literature. As discussed in Chapter 4, postcolonial approaches to Conrad's short novel have been polarized following Chinua Achebe's denunciation of its Eurocentrism. Achebe observes Conrad's insistent use of adjectives denoting the incomprehensibility and mystery of Africa, and sees this as Conrad simply purveying 'comforting myths'.[43] Miller, in contrast, argues that *Heart of Darkness* subverts Africanist discourse from within.[44] Others have interpreted it as a universalizing portrait of the inner emptiness of humanity or the failure of language to register meaning.[45] Whether it is universal, or specifically colonial, Conrad's 'the horror!' points towards the tipping point between language and non-language in the same way as the 'ou-boum' which confronts Adela Quested in the Marabar caves of E.M. Forster's *Passage to India* (1924). And another immediate inheritor of the topos of the 'unknowable other' is Victor Segalen's modernist conception of a true exoticism that would not be 'la compréhension parfaite d'un hors soi-même qu'on étreindrait en soi, mais la perception aiguë et immédiate d'une incompréhensibilité éternelle', an 'aveu d'impénétrabilité'.[46] Indeed, Segalen's attempt to invent a new form of exoticism relies on the intensity of the experience of incomprehension, though it strives to avoid the complacent acceptance of defeat which the 'unknowable other' stereotype so often entails. The major reversal of the topos is that for Segalen the threat to the identity of the self arises from the *loss* of difference, not the confrontation with it: he takes up the old theme of the encounter with the incomprehensible 'other' and gives it a newly positive and productive turn.

Modernist foregrounding of the failure of rational knowledge and language itself was part of its own self-declared rejection of Realism. Now that we have some critical distance from the claims of modernism, it is however possible to situate this topos within a much longer tradition. Modernism's much-vaunted rejection of what came before can be thought of in terms of modification (or incorporation) rather than complete reversal. The Gothic or Romantic emphasis on ineffable mystery is handed down to Realism and its derivative naturalism, acquiring a new emphasis first on fraud or erroneous perceptions (as we saw in Chapters 3 and 4), and then on biologically defined boundaries. In the last third of the century the *indicible* is increasingly refigured in psychological terms, and associated with the

---

[43] Achebe, p. 253.
[44] According to Miller, it is in *Heart of Darkness* that, for the first time, the feeling of Africanist writers that they were 'cut off from comprehension in some way' becomes 'an epistemological perception, where it is not so much the African object as the Africanist subject—the explorer, the writer—who is called into question' (*Blank Darkness*, p. 170). He also points out that there are '[d]ozens of colonial novels in French and English' whose common theme is a European who goes 'native', with a resulting 'voyage into the incomprehensible depths of Africa' (p. 183).
[45] For example Brooks, *Reading for the Plot*, p. 250. Tzvetan Todorov, in his chapter on *Heart of Darkness*, also reads it in universal terms (*Poétique de la prose, suivi de Nouvelles recherches sur le récit* (Paris: Seuil, 1978 [1971]), pp.161–73).
[46] Victor Segalen, *Essai sur l'exotisme*, in *Œuvres complètes*, ed. by Henry Bouillier, 2 vols (Paris: Robert Laffont, 1995), vol. 1, pp. 745–81 (p. 751).

'other within' through a new fascination with primitivism and the unconscious. But modernism itself does not arise from nowhere, or by destroying what preceded it.

Is it time, then, to re-assess the modernist denunciation of Realism, reiterated in the mid twentieth century by cultural theorists of the age of suspicion? And what, if anything, can Realism's focus on contemporary sociopolitical detail contribute to our understanding of the more recent postcolonial novel?

THE REALIST/MODERNIST DEBATE AND POSTCOLONIAL FICTION

Critics who view cultural history within an ideology of progress are naturally inclined to see modernism as uniquely capable of admitting ironic self-awareness and plurality. This has encouraged a tendency to read realist works with a preconceived idea of the absence of such traits. The grounds for the modernist attack on Realism are partly based on a resulting accusation of epistemological naïvety. They are also ideological: Realism is frequently seen as either inherently politically conservative, or totalitarian in the socialist sense. The apparent contradictions of this double ideological identification are best understood by situating the debate in its historical contexts. Firstly, for the generations that were writing at the turn of the nineteenth and twentieth centuries, Realism represented the formal choices of the immediate past and was thus associated with backward-looking politics. Later, in the mid twentieth century, critical approaches were informed by the Cold War ideology that contrasted Western avant-garde stylistic experimentation with Soviet Realism.[47] In this context, the 1930s and 1940s saw left-leaning or communist critics defending certain traits of Realism—unobtrusive style; evocation of contemporary social and political circumstances—as not only non-conservative, but perhaps even inherently revolutionary. In the 1940s Sartre, notably, argued for stylistic clarity in the service of a *littérature engagée*.[48] In 1943, during the Occupation, the underground journal *Confluences* devoted a special issue to the novel, valorizing Realism because of its political and social significance. And yet Realism, and the realist use of description in particular, were widely criticized as conservative, notably by the surrealists and later by the *nouveaux romanciers*.[49]

The question of whether or not Realism is inherently politically conservative could be called the 'Lukács versus Adorno' debate. Taking a Marxist perspective, Lukács saw Realism—particularly as used by Balzac—as a tool of political critique. He emphasized Balzac's theory of types and the sense of underlying historical forces and political change within his novels. On the other hand, for Adorno and other critical theorists of the Frankfurt school, modernist experimental style was

[47] Cleary offers a succinct overview of the history of these debates ('Realism after Modernism', pp. 262–3).

[48] *Qu'est-ce que la littérature?*, p. 30.

[49] See Moura, *Littérature des lointains*, pp. 170–1. Robbe-Grillet, for example, rejects politically committed literature alongside socialist Realism, on the grounds that they cannot be revolutionary since form and content are indivisible (*Pour un nouveau roman* (Paris: Minuit, 1963), pp. 35–44).

the means by which the work of literature resists recuperation by the culture industry that commodifies pleasure. From this perspective, 'Realism' was necessarily a term of opprobrium. One could give a slightly simplistic introduction to the 'Lukács versus Adorno' debate by asking whether art is subversive when it reflects directly on the sociopolitical system through mimesis, or, on the contrary, when it exposes representation and language themselves as constructs, through experimental style.[50] To be entirely fair to Lukács it is necessary to point out that he in fact excluded naturalism from his praise of Realism, a distinction that there is no space to examine fully here.[51]

In the mid-twentieth-century debate, Adorno's was the winning side. The conflict tended however to minimize both the modernism within Realism, and the realist elements within modernism. The critical victory of modernism was soon nuanced, for example by Fredric Jameson, who agrees with Adorno that the *forms* of nineteenth-century literature are part of its ideology, but defends modernism against accusations that it is apolitical.[52] He rejects the idea of a complete volte-face from a mimetic mode focused on contemporary non-literary realities to an apolitical modernism devoted to autonomous Art. Jameson claims that one can identify, within modernism, the 'informing presence of the extraliterary, of the political and the economic'. He also argues that there is a link between 'the emergence of a properly modernist "style" and the representational dilemmas of the new imperial world system'.[53] In other words, it is the ongoing presence of Realism *within* modernism that makes it political, and Jameson emphasizes modernism's 'repressed space of a world of work and history and of protopolitical conflict which may in this respect be seen as the trace and the remnant of the content of an older realism, now displaced and effectively marginalized by the emergent modernist discourse'. History (which was foregrounded by Realism) is what is unsuccessfully repressed by high modernism so that the political, no longer visible, 'has at last become a genuine Unconscious'.[54]

In the 1980s Jameson's Marxist historicist perspective did encourage him to situate Realism as a response to the classic phase of capitalism: logically, therefore,

[50] Rajeev S. Patke discusses the 'Lukács and Adorno' debate in *Modernist Literature and Postcolonial Studies* (Edinburgh: Edinburgh University Press, 2013), pp. 49–54. A variant on this debate is discussed by Jameson in his chapter 'Reflections on the Brecht-Lukács Debate' [1977], in *Ideologies of Theory*, pp. 434–50; on Adorno and the Cold War context, see p. 444. For a recent discussion of the Adorno–Lukács debate and its limitations, see WReC, pp. 57–80.

[51] Lukács reproached Naturalism for fetishizing hereditary factors and focusing on aberrant individuals or surface phenomena rather than exposing deep historical movements and representative types. See for example *Studies in European Realism*, and 'Realism in the balance' [1938] trans. by Rodney Livingstone, in *Aesthetics and Politics*, by Ernst Bloch, Georg Lukács, Bertolt Brecht, Walter Benjamin, Theodor Adorno (London/Brooklyn, New York: Verso 1980 [1977]), pp. 28–59 (p. 39).

[52] In particular in *Marxism and Form* (Princeton, NJ: Princeton University Press, 1971); see also 'Modernism and Imperialism', p. 7, p. 15. He takes, however, an equivocal position on Realism in 'Beyond the Cave: Demystifying the Ideology of Modernism' [1975], republished in *Ideologies of Theory*, pp. 415–33.

[53] Jameson, 'Modernism and Imperialism', p. 7, p. 19.

[54] *The Political Unconscious*, p. 195, p. 270. He also writes that 'all modernistic works are essentially simply cancelled realistic ones' ('Beyond the Cave', in *Ideologies of Theory*, p. 429; see also p. 72).

Realism is now cancelled out, and no longer directly relevant today.[55] Of course, if one adopts a philosophical definition of 'Realism' rather than a historicist approach, one runs the opposite risk, since in this sense it can be found everywhere. Raymond Tallis, notably, argues that it is nigh impossible to find literature that is *not* in fact realist, at least to some extent.[56] If instead one adopts, in lieu of a hard and fast definition, the loose series of pragmatically defined characteristics that I gave for the realist mode in the Introduction, it is hard to see it as dead after 1857, or even after 1945. And the pitfalls of using a reductive definition of Realism apply when looking backwards to the 1830s, as well as forwards to modernism. Prendergast, as we saw earlier, warns that clear-cut naïvely realist novels are hard to find, because nineteenth-century narrative is in fact aware of the limits of its own representational strategies.[57] And as Jameson admits, the tendency to define Realism historically, as 'that which modernism has had to break, that norm from which modernism is the deviation', means that whenever you search for 'pure' Realism it vanishes. If you look closer at so-called traditional 'realistic novels' they are 'transformed' 'as though by magic' into modernists or precursors of the modern.[58]

What, then, of the view that the realist novel is a vehicle for hegemony, repeating the dominant ideology beneath apparent neutrality? Critics inspired by Althusser have seen literature in general, and Realism in particular, as Ideological State Apparatuses.[59] Although Realism includes contradictory attitudes and incompatible points of view, it can never, according to this view, acknowledge contradiction as inevitable and central: its function is to gather up these apparent conflicts into a homogeneous discursive space that reflects the single point of view of the privileged classes. And yet even in the 1960s—the heyday of pro-modernist criticism—there were voices calling for a less negative understanding of literary Realism. Among them, perhaps surprisingly, was Georges Perec, who defines Realism as a way of giving form to the movement and history of the world. For him, 'Toute littérature réaliste est révolutionnaire, toute littérature révolutionnaire est réaliste.'[60] More recently, Tallis argues resoundingly that: 'There is of course no reason whatsoever why realistic fiction should not "foreground contradiction". Nor is there any reason why it should not unmask the workings of ideology by which "Nature is passed off as History" and the mystification which "transforms petit-bourgeois culture into a universal nature".'[61]

[55] Jameson does not really assess the potential of the realist mode after the mid nineteenth century, when he sees it as dying in France. Henry James, although he can hardly be described as a Marxist, also claimed that 'realism seems to us with *Madame Bovary* to have said its last word', which Levin suggests may be 'somewhat premature' (*Gates of Horn*, p. 249).
[56] *In Defence*, pp. 96–118.
[57] *Order of Mimesis*, p. 15.   [58] Jameson, *Ideologies of Theory*, p. 61.
[59] For a polemical discussion of this tendency, see Tallis, *In Defence*, pp. 43–90.
[60] Perec writes of Realism as 'ce dévoilement, cette mise en ordre du monde'; for him, 'le réalisme est description de la réalité, mais décrire la réalité c'est plonger en elle et lui donner forme, c'est mettre à jour l'essence du monde: son mouvement, son histoire' ('Pour une littérature réaliste' [1962], in Georges Perec, *L.G.: Une aventure des années soixante* (Paris: Seuil, 1992), pp. 47–66 (pp. 51–2)).
[61] *In Defence*, p. 56. For other arguments against the use of 'naïve realism' as a critical scapegoat, see Bruce Robbins, 'Modernism and Literary Realism: Response', in *Realism and Representation: Essays*

Emerging in the 1980s and 1990s, however, Anglo-American postcolonial criticism as a whole adopted the modernist view of Realism as the height of ideological blindness and imperialist discursive practice.[62] Recently the denunciation of Realism has even been used in order to salvage the reputations of Enlightenment literature or Romanticism.[63] This view of Realism as an ideological blind spot sees 'resistance narrative' as necessarily characterized by polyphony and formal experimentation.[64] Recent calls for a return to the literary within postcolonial studies often mean a return to a knowing literariness, including those key modernist values of 'indeterminacy' and 'distancing'.[65] Modernist aesthetic experimentation has long been associated with a rejection of imperialist ideology. Parry, for example, follows Said in seeing imperialism as inseparably linked to the nineteenth- and early twentieth-century realist novel form. In this view, moving away from the narrative authority that is assumed in the realist mode is a necessary step in order 'to include the difference and *agency* of colonial worlds'. And yet she strikes a note of caution, warning 'that modernism's stylistic ambiguity and irony do not in themselves constitute a negative critique of imperialism or act to disempower its ideology'.[66]

The anti-realist tendency of postcolonial theory is encouraged by the issue of how literary form relates to cultural identity. The origins of the novel as we know it today correspond with a specific historical moment in a specific culture—the rise of the Western European bourgeoisie in the eighteenth and nineteenth centuries. Do the formal traits that characterize the realist mode also reflect the attitude of Western Europe in the nineteenth century, and does this make its use in other cultural contexts problematic? Moretti describes the novel in cultures on the periphery of the literary system as a 'compromise between foreign form and local materials'.[67] This suggests a need to read the postcolonial novel dialogically, though

---

on the Problem of Realism in Relation to Science, Literature and Culture, ed. by George Levine (Madison: Wisconsin University Press, 1993), pp. 225–31 (p. 227).

[62] Emily Apter, for example, focuses specifically on colonial literature as the point where Realism becomes most blind to its own ideological assumptions: 'As a repository of racial, ethnic, and gender caricatures and exoticist cartoons of landscape and local color, colonial realism often functioned as the handmaiden to colonial ideology, offering literary stereotypes as the *Stoff* of national character.' Colonial Realism is thus a meeting of 'tourist narrative and realist Orientalism (as featured in Balzac's *La Fille aux yeux d'or* or *La Peau de chagrin*)', interpellating 'the subject at the blindest spot of his or her identity in national space', *Continental Drift*, p. x, p. 167.

[63] See Aravamudan, *Enlightenment Orientalism*, for example p. 3, p. 6, as discussed in the Introduction. Makdisi, meanwhile, sees Romanticism as a precursor to modernist opposition to imperialism. He explicitly excludes the realist novel that comes in between: 'modernist literary experiments, arising partly out of the perceived exhaustion of the realist novel and especially the Bildungsroman by the early twentieth century, would return to and elaborate an earlier romantic obsession with fractured, disjointed, and disruptive temporalities, both in poetry and in prose', *Romantic Imperialism*, p. 9.

[64] Barbara Harlow, *Resistance Literature* (New York/London: Methuen, 1987), pp. 95–8.

[65] Nicholas Harrison, for example, inclines towards the idea that the 'most literary' texts are the 'most political', and follows Derrida in using 'indeterminacy' or 'distancing' to determine what makes the literary. 'Who Needs an Idea of the Literary?' *Paragraph*, 28:2 (2005), 1–17 (p. 13, p. 14). In Chapter 4 we saw that indeterminacy and distancing are in fact often present in realist narratives, though often in forms such as parody, double focalization and narrative embedding.

[66] Parry, *Postcolonial Studies*, p. 116, p. 118.

[67] Franco Moretti, 'Conjectures on World Literature', in *Debating World Literature*, ed. by Christopher Prendergast (London: Verso, 2004), pp. 148–62 (p. 154).

it does implicitly assume that the form itself belongs inevitably to the cultural context of its origins.[68]

There has however been a recent move towards questioning the set of underlying aesthetic values, tacit within postcolonial theory, that reject Realism and valorize modernism as the formula for political radicalism.[69] Neil Lazarus, notably, has argued that postcolonial critics' assumptions have 'fairly systematically' mystified their putative object. More specifically, following Raymond Williams's critique of the politics of literary modernism, he looks at how, in the postcolonial criticism of the 1980s and 1990s, anxiety about representing others 'gave way to the struggle *against representation* itself'.[70] Along similar lines, but with a more specific focus on literary Realism, Sorenson criticizes the 'modernist ethos' that relies on a 'fetishiza-tion of characteristically modernist literary techniques', in an 'uncritical "leap"' that simplifies the possible relationships of the literary and the political. This modernist ethos canonizes texts that conform to certain Western criteria, such as experimental style, irony, resistance to closure, and self-consciousness. Theory's anti-realist posi-tion tends to employ a 'homogenised conception of realism' which can then be rejected as part of 'the identity-construction of postcolonial studies as a radical discipline'.[71] The overturning of the straw-man of Realism is, then, a founding act for postcolonial theory just as it was for modernism.

Jameson's own more recent approaches to the realist novel continue to view it as structurally and inherently conservative, since he sees it as resisting any possibility of a radically different future.[72] He does, however, expose its internal 'antinomies' and, as we saw in the Introduction, asks whether one might not redefine realist literature to foreground its self-questioning nature, so that 'realism would then name any narrative that is organized [...] around the very interrogation of realism and the realistic itself'.[73] Recently he has contributed to a movement that seeks to reclaim the realist mode as having a powerful political and representational role to play in the postcolonial novel, under the aegis of the term 'Peripheral Realisms'.[74] This was the topic of a special issue of the *Modern Language Quarterly* in 2012,

---

[68] One might of course argue that the novel, a notoriously slippery and flexible genre, is not to be limited to its original cultural context. Cultures are constantly moving and shifting, and they adopt different cultural forms as they do different technological innovations. The car, which by most accounts was invented in Germany, is no longer considered 'foreign' in other cultural contexts—or if it is, it is because those contexts are being reified and defined by their immobility.

[69] This is not to say that there were no earlier calls to revalue the referential function as a 'crucial strategy for survival in marginalized social groups' (see Stephen Slemon, 'Modernism's last post', in *Past the Last Post: Theorizing Post-Colonialism and Post-Modernism*, ed. by Ian Adam and Helen Tiffin (New York/London: Harvester and Wheatsheaf, 1991), pp. 1–11 (p. 5)).

[70] Neil Lazarus, *The Postcolonial Unconscious* (Cambridge: Cambridge University Press, 2011), pp. 16–17, p. 19 (his emphasis). Chapter 3 of *The Postcolonial Unconscious* offers a more developed critique of postcolonial theorists' suspicion of representation itself (pp. 114–60).

[71] Sorenson, pp. 7–8, pp. 30–1, pp. 41–3, p. 140, p. 154 n. 33. Of course, as we have seen, the realist mode itself often employs irony and self-consciousness.

[72] *Antinomies*, p. 215.   [73] 'Antinomies of the Realism-Modernism Debate', pp. 478–9.

[74] The term was modelled on Benita Parry's use of 'Peripheral Modernisms' ('Aspects of Peripheral Modernisms', *Ariel: A Review of International English Literature*, 40:1 (2009), 27–55), which itself took inspiration from Harry Harootunian's use of the term 'peripheral modernities' (quoted by Parry, p. 28).

edited by Jed Esty and Colleen Lye. They argue that various Realisms—in the plural—are present in much recent postcolonial writing under the 'crust of global modernist discourse', and claim that postcolonial theory is taking 'a new realist turn'. This return to Realism is effected in part via a re-reading of Lukács, following whom Esty and Lye argue that 'a realistic mode of representation is meant not to reproduce reality but to interrupt the quasi-natural perception of reality as a mere given',[75] a view that fits in well with my examination of 'Critical Orientalism' in Chapter 4. Of course, Esty and Lye do—somewhat tentatively—attempt to distinguish these new 'Peripheral Realisms' from the old 'Classic Realism'. But there is a new desire to recognize that both forms of Realism 'invite their publics to grasp the world-system, via its local appearances or epiphenomenal effects, and not to imagine it as a foreclosed or fully narrativized entity'.[76]

In his contribution to the 'Peripheral Realisms' issue, Joe Cleary reminds us of the dangers of applying limiting judgments based on an opposition between modernism (good) and Realism (bad) to postcolonial literary production, since it leads critics to marginalize certain writers: 'postcolonial studies has privileged modernist-associated terms such as hybridity, polyphony, pastiche, irony, and defamiliarization rather than realist-associated conceptual categories such as historical transition, class consciousness, and totality'.[77] Certainly, Realism is rejected by postcolonial *theory*, rather than by *fiction* itself, and many postcolonial writers employ the Realist mode. Tallis—who sees Realism as open, forward-looking, and capable of changing over time—asserts that it 'may be expropriated by the oppressed on behalf of the oppressed [...] to express the reality that faces them'.[78] Certain traits of Realism have indeed been adopted—and adapted—by many postcolonial writers, though others have made very different formal choices. In the international frame, writers such as Naguib Mahfouz, Pramoedya Ananta Toer, Rohinton Mistry, Ngugi wa Thiong'o, and Amitav Ghosh can be said to work in a primarily realist mode, and a valorization of modernist experimental form at all costs tends to marginalize such writers.[79]

In the Francophone postcolonial novel, a conjunction of literary and political history has encouraged a divergent geographical distribution for realist writing on the one hand, and modernist-experimental writing on the other. Among the most vocal critics of Realism was the Martinican theorist, novelist, and poet Édouard Glissant. He sees its apparent claims to objectivity as inadequate for representing the Caribbean experience. In his theoretical writing he rejects clarity of meaning and linear narratives, as well as the aspiration of Realism to a 'total' reproduction of the world, in favour of a poetics of opacity that resists reductionism, a 'bienheureuse

---

[75] Esty and Lye, pp. 276–7.   [76] Esty and Lye, p. 285.
[77] Cleary, 'Realism after Modernism', p. 265.   [78] *In Defence*, p. 57.
[79] According to Lazarus, this is the reason for the restricted corpus of canonical postcolonial literature, with its repetitive valorization of Salman Rushdie (*Postcolonial Unconscious*, p. 22). Interestingly, in a much earlier article he rejects Realism, but this is primarily in order to argue against Lukács's dismissal of naturalism, which Lazarus argues has an important role to play in African writing (see 'Realism and Naturalism in African Fiction' [1987], in *African Literature: An Anthology of Criticism and Theory*, ed. by Tejumola Olaniyan and Ato Quayson (Oxford: Blackwell, 2007), pp. 340–4).

opacité, par quoi l'autre m'échappe'.[80] Dorothy Blair, in her early history of African literature in French, argues that this emphasis on experimentation, part of the inheritance of *Négritude*, is a primarily Caribbean movement. In contrast, the insistence on collective commitment that characterized *African* fiction in French in the period of decolonization meant that it tended to take the form of 'the political or social realist novel', though Blair sees much of this literature as excessively didactic.[81] Realism was also credited with a crucial role in African literature by Mongo Beti in his 1955 manifesto 'Afrique noire, littérature rose', which denounced art for art's sake, the picturesque, and non-realist representational strategies in favour of an anticolonial stance grounded firmly in literary Realism. For Beti, the colonial establishment was trying to crush African realist literature precisely because the reality that it sought to depict was colonization and its disastrous effects; in such circumstances the picturesque, and along with it the 'fantastique' of modernism (of which even Faulkner is an example), amount to mere political conformism.[82] Indeed, it is sometimes claimed that literary Realism flourished in two main periods and places: in Europe and America in the nineteenth century, and in Sub-Saharan Africa in the mid twentieth century.[83] Nevertheless, Blair's neat distinction between African literature (realist) and Caribbean literature (modernist/experimental) is far too dogmatic, and the rich, diverse literary production of the last few decades testifies to the impossibility of establishing such strict critical categories along geographical lines.

   Novels by the Senegalese author Ousmane Sembène provide a striking example of the use of social Realism around the period of decolonization. In *Les Bouts de bois de Dieu* (1960), a socially committed novel that recounts a workers' strike against white managers during the construction of the railway, Sembène uses elements of African oral tradition integrated within a form reminiscent of Zola's novels *Germinal* and *La Bête humaine*.[84] An essentialist literary history might lead one to see this as an inappropriate importation of a novelistic form into a context to which it is alien. But the Senegalese society portrayed in *Les Bouts de bois de Dieu* is one of political and economic change and instability, where international capitalism and local African traditions meet. Like capitalism or technology, the novel itself—and the realist mode in particular—are imports that become local. After decolonization Francophone African novels dealt with a greater variety of subjects and adopted more varied formal approaches (Ahmadou Kourouma's writing is a striking example of both). But for Blair, writing in the 1970s, the 'most

---

[80] Édouard Glissant, *Le Discours antillais* (Paris: Gallimard, 'Folio', 1997 [1981]), p. 474. Naturally Glissant's celebration of stylistic or *formal* opacity is not to be equated with the *theme* of opacity I described earlier with the 'unknowable other' topos.

[81] Dorothy Blair, *African Literature in French: A History of Creative Writing in French from West and Equatorial Africa* (Cambridge: Cambridge University Press, 1976), pp. 317–18.

[82] Mongo Beti, 'Afrique noire, littérature rose', *Présence africaine*, 1–2 (1955), 133–45 (pp. 137–9).

[83] David Chioni Moore, 'Ousmane Sembène, *Les Bouts de bois de dieu* and the Question of Literary Realism—African, European or Otherwise', *Genre*, 28 (1995), 67–94 (p. 71).

[84] See Moore, 'Ousmane Sembène', and Gilbert Darbouze, '*Les Bouts de bois de Dieu* d'Ousmane Sembène: L'esthétique naturaliste d'Émile Zola dans un roman sénégalais', *Excavatio*, 11 (1998), 182–7. Blair also compares Sembène's *Les Bouts de bois de Dieu* to *Germinal* (*African Literature in French*, p. 233); on Sembène's *Xala* and naturalist aesthetics, see also Sorensen, pp. 75–95.

outstanding of the novels are still in the tradition of nineteenth-century realism or naturalism, inspired by Balzac, Flaubert, Zola'.[85]

Mongo Beti's polemical rejection of anything but Realism, and the purist modernist praise of experimental form at all costs, are equally in danger of dictating a single form for the postcolonial novel, and denying writers access to the full range, and the potential hybridity, of forms that are available to the novel as a genre. Patrick Williams reminds us of the importance of keeping in mind 'the extent to which the adoption of realism or modernism remains a matter of choice and not simply an automatic reaction'; in certain circumstances modernism will take the back foot because of a 'perceived political and cultural need for realism as a more appropriate means of responding to the situation at that time'.[86] According to Chris Bongie, postcolonial theory has too often been 'informed by a surreptitiously elitist (and modernist) perspective' with 'homogenizing imperatives' towards experimental fiction.[87] There is always a danger of reifying postcolonial fiction, and thus denying the plurality of styles, subjects, and orientations included in that category. Jameson himself risked doing so in his much-derided claims concerning the incompatibility of 'third-world' political engagement and formalist experimentation: 'All third-world texts are to be read [...] as national allegories' and not as individual stories; they remind us (the Western reader) 'of outmoded stages of our own first-world cultural development' so that we experience 'a popular or socially realistic third-world novel [...] as though already-read'.[88] This infamous dismissal of any literary-formalist pretentions of the 'third-world' (that is, postcolonial) novel relegated it to mere Realism and allegory, or even Realism *as* allegory. If one makes abstraction of Jameson's unwary use of absolute truths ('all'), one might however read this article as a defence of the idea that the realist mode might be a useful tool for some postcolonial writers, for the purposes of comment on broader national issues rather than individual experience—and that therefore it is not really outmoded after all.

* * *

As we have seen, voices from within postcolonial literary criticism are calling for a re-examination of Realism as it is used by postcolonial writers, and questioning the preconceived idea of the superiority of modernist experimental form.[89] *The Colonial Comedy* has argued that we also need to review reductive conceptions of 'Classic' (or nineteenth-century) Realism, and, at the same time, that the apparent absence of the wider colonial sphere in nineteenth-century French Realism is deceptive. Certainly, there were generic reasons for metropolitan Realism to be ill at ease when dealing with colonial space. As we have seen, however, nineteenth-century

[85] *African Literature in French*, p. 320.   [86] Williams, pp. 32–3.

[87] Chris Bongie, 'Belated Liaisons: Writing Between the Margins of Literary and Cultural Studies', *Francophone Postcolonial Studies*, 1:2 (2003), 11–24 (p. 14, p. 15).

[88] Fredric Jameson, 'Third-World Literature in the Era of Multinational Corporations', *Social Text*, 15 (1986), 65–88 (p. 73).

[89] In Lazarus's words, writing in 2011: 'my conviction [is] that we ought, today, to begin to redress a long-standing imbalance in postcolonial literary studies by focusing anew on realist writing' (*Postcolonial Unconscious*, p. 82).

writers working within the Realist mode use this unease precisely in order to destabilize Realism's own claims to mimeticism, objectivity, and transparency. Acknowledging the realist novel's dialogical basis allows us to recognize its divided and self-questioning nature. As *The Colonial Comedy* has shown, the realist mode engages in polemic with earlier attitudes, such as Romantic Orientalism, and with other genres, such as the travel narrative. Colonial mimesis is capable of reflecting unease, internal polemic, failures, fraud—in other words flaws within the *doxa* or received opinion. Even the later, more directly 'colonial' literature reiterates stereotypes that are revelatory of anxiety and splitting in the colonial culture rather than merely serving the purposes of colonial propaganda. We have seen, too, that the realist mode is capable of metatextual or epistemological self-awareness. This does not mean that the referential function itself should be rejected as mere naïvety: mimesis remains relevant because it 'provides forms for engaging with what remains the order of the day'.[90] Realism's manifest aim to incorporate history and the political-material realities of the present do not make it inherently monological; quite the contrary. And metonymy itself, that fundamental prop of mimesis and verisimilitude, is, as we have seen, one means of bringing into the metropolitan novel glimpses of the global world-system.

[90] Prendergast, *Order of Mimesis*, p. 253.

Bibliography

EDITIONS OF PRIMARY TEXTS AND CORRESPONDENCE OF MAIN AUTHORS STUDIED

Honoré de Balzac
La Comédie humaine, ed. by Pierre-Georges Castex, 12 vols (Paris: Gallimard 'Pléiade', 1976–81)
Œuvres complètes, ed. by La Société d'Études Balzaciennes, 28 vols (Paris: Guy Le Prat/Club de l'honnête homme, 1956–63)
Œuvres diverses, ed. by Pierre-Georges Castex, 2 vols (Paris: Gallimard, 'Pléiade', 1990–6)
Premiers romans, 1822–1825, ed. by André Lorant, 2 vols (Paris: Robert Laffont, 1999)
Correspondance, ed. by Roger Pierrot, 5 vols (Paris: Garnier, 1960–9)
Lettres à Madame Hanska, ed. by Roger Pierrot, 2 vols (Paris: Robert Laffont, 1990)

Alphonse Daudet
Œuvres, ed. by Roger Ripoll, 3 vols (Paris: Gallimard 'Pléiade', 1986–94)

Gustave Flaubert
Bouvard et Pécuchet, ed. by Jacques Suffel (Paris: Flammarion 'GF', 1966)
L'Éducation sentimentale, ed. by Claudine Gothot-Mersch (Paris: Flammarion 'GF', 1985)
Œuvres complètes, ed. by Claudine Gothot-Mersch, 3 vols to date (Paris: Gallimard 'Pléiade', 2001–13)
Trois contes, ed. by Pierre-Marc de Biasi (Paris: Flammarion 'GF', 1986)
Correspondance, ed. by Jean Bruneau and Yvan Leclerc, 5 vols (Paris: Gallimard 'Pléiade', 1973–2007)

Guy de Maupassant
Chroniques, ed. by Hubert Juin, 3 vols (Paris: Union générale des éditions '10/18', 1980)
Contes et nouvelles, ed. by Louis Forestier, 2 vols (Paris: Gallimard 'Pléiade', 1974, 1979)
Romans, ed. by Louis Forestier (Paris: Gallimard 'Pléiade', 1987)

Émile Zola
Fécondité (Paris: Fasquelle, 1957)
Madeleine Férat, ed. by Henri Mitterand (Paris: Mémoire du livre, 1999)
Œuvres complètes, ed. by Henri Mitterand, 15 vols (Paris: Cercle du livre précieux, 1962–9)
Paris, ed. by Jacques Noiray (Paris: Gallimard 'Folio', 2002)
Les Rougon-Macquart: Histoire naturelle et sociale d'une famille sous le second empire, ed. by Armand Lanoux and Henri Mitterand, 5 vols (Paris: Gallimard 'Pléiade', 1960–7)
Thérèse Raquin, ed. by Henri Mitterand (Paris: Flammarion 'GF', 1970)

MANUSCRIPT SOURCES AND EARLIER VERSIONS CONSULTED

Honoré de Balzac

La Cousine Bette, Bibliothèque de l'Institut, MS Lov. A 48

Gobseck, earlier versions: under the title 'Les dangers de l'inconduite' in *Scènes de la vie privée*, vol. 1 (Paris: Mame-Delaunay et Vallée, 1832 [1830]; under the title 'Le Papa Gobseck', in *Scènes de la vie parisienne*, vol. 9 (Paris: Madame Charles-Béchet, 1835)

Modeste Mignon, Bibliothèque de l'Institut, MS Lov. A 150; corrected printer's typeset Lov. A 151 and 151 bis

Gustave Flaubert

Carnets de travail, ed. by Pierre-Marc de Biasi (Paris: Balland, 1988)

L'Éducation sentimentale, Appendice, in *Œuvres complètes*, ed. by the Société d'Études Littéraires Françaises (Paris: Club de l'honnête homme, 1971), vol. 12

L'Éducation sentimentale: les scénarios, ed. by Tony Williams (Paris: José Corti, 1992)

L'Éducation sentimentale, Bibliothèque Nationale de France, nouvelles acquisitions françaises (N.A.F.) MS 17599–17611

Madame Bovary, Bibliothèque de Rouen, MS gg 9, g 221, g 222 and g 223 see http://www.bovary.fr

Émile Zola

L'Argent, dossier préparatoire, Bibliothèque Nationale de France, nouvelles acquisitions françaises (N.A.F.) MS 10268, 10269

La Bête humaine, dossier préparatoire, Bibliothèque Nationale de France, nouvelles acquisitions françaises (N.A.F.) 10274

Carnets d'enquêtes: une ethnographie inédite de la France, par Émile Zola, ed. by Henri Mitterand (Paris: Plon 'Terre humaine', 2005 [1986])

La Fabrique des Rougon-Macquart: édition des dossiers préparatoires, ed. by Colette Becker and Véronique Lavielle, 6 vols to date (Paris: Honoré Champion, 2003–13)

SECONDARY WORKS

Abbott, Elizabeth, *Sugar: A Bittersweet History* (London/New York: Duckworth, 2009)

Achebe, Chinua, 'An Image of Africa: Racism in Conrad's *Heart of Darkness*' [1977], reprinted in *Heart of Darkness*, Joseph Conrad, ed. by Robert Kimbrough (New York/London: W.W. Norton & Company, 1988) pp. 251–62

Ahmad, Aijaz, *In Theory: Classes, Nations, Literatures* (London: Verso, 1992)

Alcorn, Clayton, 'The Domestic Servant in Zola's Novels', *L'Esprit Créateur*, 11:4 (1971), 21–35

Anderson, Benedict, *Imagined Communities: Reflections on the Origin and Spread of Nationalism* (London/New York: Verso, 1991 [1983])

Apter, Emily, 'Fétichisme et domesticité: Freud, Mirbeau, Buñuel', *Poétique*, 70 (1987), 143–66

Apter, Emily, *Feminizing the Fetish: Psychoanalysis and Narrative Obsession in Turn-of-the-Century France* (Ithaca, NY: Cornell University Press, 1991)

Apter, Emily, *Continental Drift: From National Characters to Virtual Subjects* (Chicago, IL: University of Chicago Press, 1999)

Apter, Emily, 'Speculation and Economic Xenophobia as Literary World Systems: The Nineteenth-Century Business Novel', in *French Global: A New Approach to Literary*

History, ed. by Christie McDonald and Susan Rubin Suleiman (New York: Columbia University Press, 2010), pp. 388–403

Aravamudan, Srinivas, 'Introduction', in *Slavery, Abolition and Emancipation: Writings in the British Romantic Period*, ed. by Peter J. Kitson and Debbie Lee, 8 vols (London: Pickering and Chatto, 1999), vol. 6, pp. vii–xxii

Aravamudan, Srinivas, *Tropicopolitans: Colonialism and Agency 1688–1804* (Durham, NC: Duke University Press, 1999)

Aravamudan, Srinivas, *Enlightenment Orientalism: Resisting the Rise of the Novel* (Chicago, IL: University of Chicago Press, 2011)

Aravamudan, Srinivas, 'Response: Exoticism beyond Cosmopolitanism?', *Eighteenth-Century Fiction*, 25:1 (2012), 227–42

Arzalier, Francis, 'Les mutations de l'idéologie coloniale en France avant 1848', in *Les Abolitions de l'esclavage*, ed. by M. Dorigny and B. Gainot (Paris: Éditions UNESCO, 1995), pp. 301–08

Astier Loutfi, Martine, *Littérature et colonialisme: l'expansion coloniale vue dans la littérature romanesque française 1871–1914* (Paris/La Haye: Mouton, 1971)

Aubert, Nathalie, 'En Attendant les barbares: *La Cousine Bette*, le moment populaire et féminin de *La Comédie humaine*', *Women in French Studies*, 8 (2000), 129–37

Auriant [pseudonym], *François Bravay ou le 'Nabab'* (Paris: Mercure de France, 1943)

Azim, Firdous, *The Colonial Rise of the Novel* (London/New York: Routledge, 1993)

Baguley, David, 'Le supplice de Florent: à propos du *Ventre de Paris*', *Europe*, 468–9 (1968), 91–6

Baguley, David, *Fécondité d'Émile Zola: roman à thèse, évangile, mythe* (Toronto: University of Toronto Press, 1973)

Baguley, David, 'Du récit polémique au discours utopique; l'Évangile républicain de Zola', *Les Cahiers naturalistes*, 54 (1980), 106–21

Baguley, David, *Naturalist Fiction: the Entropic Vision* (Cambridge: Cambridge University Press, 1990)

Baguley, David, *Zola et les genres* (Glasgow: University of Glasgow French and German Publications, 1993)

Baguley, David, 'Le Capital de Zola: Le Fétichisme de la monnaie dans *L'Argent*', in *Currencies: Fiscal Fortunes and Cultural Capital in Nineteenth-Century France*, ed. by Sarah Capitanio, et al. (Bern: Peter Lang, 2005), pp. 31–42

Baguley, David, 'Zola and Darwin: A Reassessment', in *The Evolution of Literature: Legacies of Darwin in European Cultures*, ed. by Nicholas Saul and Simon J. James (Amsterdam: Rodopi, 2011), pp. 201–12

Baguley, David, 'Darwin, Zola, and Dr Prosper Lucas's Treatise on Natural Heredity', in *The Literary and Cultural Reception of Charles Darwin in Europe*, ed. by Thomas F. Glick and Elinor Schaffer, 4 vols (London, Bloomsbury Press, 2014), vol. 4, pp. 416–30

Baker, Geoffrey, 'Empiricism and Empire: Orientalist Antiquing in Balzac's *Peau De Chagrin*', *Yearbook of Comparative and General Literature*, 51 (2003–4), 167–74

Baker, Geoffrey, *Realism's Empire: Empiricism and Enchantment in the Nineteenth-Century Novel* (Columbus, OH: Ohio State University Press, 2009)

Bakhtin, Mikhail, *The Dialogic Imagination: Four Essays*, ed. by Michael Holquist, trans. by Caryl Emerson and Michael Holquist (Austin: University of Texas Press, 1981)

Bakhtin, Mikhail, *Problems of Dostoevsky's Poetics*, ed. and trans. by Caryl Emerson (Minneapolis/London: University of Minnesota Press, 1984)

Bal, Mieke, *Narratology: Introduction to the Theory of Narrative* (Toronto: University of Toronto Press, 2009 [1985])

Baldensperger, Fernand, *L'Appel de la fiction orientale chez Honoré de Balzac*, 'The Zaharoff Lecture' (Oxford: Clarendon Press, 1927)

Baldensperger, Fernand, *Orientations étrangères chez Honoré de Balzac* (Paris: Champion, 1927)

Bancquart, Marie-Claire, 'Maupassant, la guerre, la politique', *Magazine littéraire*, 156 (1980), 18–21

Bannerjee, Rohini, 'Hors du mythe exotique: *Thérèse Raquin* et ses tactiques', *Excavatio*, 16:1–2 (2002), 100–11

Barbéris, Pierre, *Le Monde de Balzac* (Paris: Arthaud, 1973)

Baron, Anne-Marie, *Balzac, ou les hiéroglyphes de l'imaginaire* (Paris: Honoré Champion, 2002)

Barrow, Susan, 'East/West: Appropriation of Aspects of the Orient in Maupassant's Bel-Ami', *Nineteenth-Century French Studies*, 30:3–4 (2002), 315–28

Barthes, Roland, *Œuvres complètes*, ed. by Éric Marty, 3 vols (Paris: Seuil, 1993)

Baudrillard, Jean, *Le Système des objets* (Paris: Gallimard, 1968)

Beauvoir, Simone de, *Le Deuxième sexe*, 2 vols (Paris: Gallimard, 1976 [1949])

Beauvois, Frédérique, 'L'indemnité de Saint-Domingue: "Dette d'indépendance" ou "rançon de l'esclavage"?', *French Colonial History*, 10 (2009), 109–24

Becker, Colette, 'Du meurtrier par hérédité au héros révolutionnaire: Étienne Lantier dans le dossier préparatoire de *Germinal*', *Cahiers de l'UER Froissart*, 5 (1980), 99–111

Becker, Colette, '*Thérèse Raquin*: La Science comme projet, le fantasme comme aveu', *Excavatio*, 1 (1992), 1–10

Becker, Colette, *Zola: le saut dans les étoiles* (Paris: Presses Universitaires de la Sorbonne Nouvelle, 2002)

Becker, Colette, 'Zola et Lombroso: à propos de *la Bête Humaine*', *Les Cahiers naturalistes*, 80 (2006), 37–49

Becker, George J., 'Introduction', in *Documents of Modern Literary Realism*, ed. by George J. Becker (Princeton, NJ: Princeton University Press, 1963), pp. 3–38

Béguin, Albert, *Balzac lu et relu* (Paris: Seuil, 1965)

Behdad, Ali, *Belated Travelers: Orientalism in the Age of Colonial Dissolution* (Cork: Cork University Press, 1994)

Beizer, Janet L., *Family Plots: Balzac's Narrative Generations* (New Haven/London: Yale University Press, 1986)

Bell, David F., 'Genealogies and Simulacra in Zola's *Son Excellence Eugène Rougon*', *Modern Language Notes*, 97:4 (1982), 810–26

Bell, David F., *Models of Power: Politics and Economics in Zola's Rougon-Macquart* (Lincoln, NE: University of Nebraska Press, 1988)

Bell, Dorian, 'Cavemen Among Us: Genealogies of Atavism from Zola's *La Bête humaine* to Chabrol's *Le Boucher*', *French Studies*, 62:1 (2008), 39–52

Bell, Dorian, 'Beyond the Bourse: Zola, Empire, and the Jews', *Romanic Review*, 102: 3–4 (2011), 485–501

Bell, Dorian, 'Balzac's Algeria: Realism and the Colonial', *Nineteenth-Century French Studies*, 40:1–2 (2011–12), 35–56

Bellet, Roger, 'La Bourse et la littérature dans la seconde moitié du XIXe siècle', *Romantisme*, 40 (1983), 53–64

Bem, Jeanne, *Clefs pour l'Éducation sentimentale* (Tübingen/Paris: Gunter Narr/Jean-Michel Place, 1981)

Bem, Jeanne, 'L'Orient ironique de Flaubert', in Jeanne Bem, *Le Texte traversé* (Paris: Champion, 1991), pp. 131–41

Benjamin, Walter, *The Arcades Project*, trans. by Howard Eiland and Kevin McLaughlin (Cambridge, MA: Belknap Press/Harvard University Press, 2003 [1999])

Bernheimer, Charles, *Figures of Ill Repute: Representing Prostitution in Nineteenth-Century France* (Durham, NC: Duke University Press, 1997 [1989])

Bersani, Leo, *A Future for Astyanax: Character and Desire in Literature* (Boston/Toronto: Little, Brown and Company, 1969)

Bertrand, Louis, *Gustave Flaubert* (Paris: Mercure de France, 1912)

Bertrand-Jennings, Chantal, *L'Éros et la femme chez Zola: de la chute au paradis retrouvé* (Paris: Klincksieck, 1977)

Bertrand-Jennings, Chantal, 'Madeleine Férat ou les lieux ennemis', *Revue de l'Université d'Ottawa/University of Ottawa Quarterly*, 48:4 (1978), 407–14

Bertrand-Jennings, Chantal, *Espaces romanesques: Zola* (Sherbrooke, Québec: Éditions Naaman, 1987)

Besson, Mme A., 'Le séjour de Flaubert en Algérie', *Amis de Flaubert* (1968), 4–52

Beti, Mongo, 'Afrique noire, littérature rose', *Présence africaine*, 1955 (1–2), 133–45

Bhabha, Homi K., 'Representation and the Colonial Text: A Critical Exploration of Some Forms of Mimeticism', in *The Theory of Reading*, ed. by Frank Gloversmith (Totowa, NJ: Barnes and Noble, 1984), pp. 93–122

Bhabha, Homi K., *The Location of Culture* (London/New York: Routledge, 1994)

Biasi, Pierre-Marc de, *Gustave Flaubert: Une manière spéciale de vivre* (Paris: Grasset, 2009)

Birch, Edmund, 'Maupassant's *Bel-Ami* and the Secrets of *Actualité*', *The Modern Language Review*, 109:4 (2014), 996–1012

Blair, Dorothy S., *African Literature in French: A History of Creative Writing in French from West and Equatorial Africa* (Cambridge: Cambridge University Press, 1976)

Blanckaert, Claude, '"Les vicissitudes de l'angle facial" et les débuts de la craniométrie (1765–1875)', *Revue de synthèse*, 4:3–4 (1987), 417–53

Blanckaert, Claude, 'On the Origins of French Ethnology: William Edwards and the Doctrine of Race', in *Bones, Bodies, Behavior: Essays in Biological Anthropology*, ed. by George W. Stocking (Madison, WI: University of Wisconsin Press, 1988), pp. 18–55

Blanckaert, Claude, 'L'Indice céphalique et l'ethnogénie européenne: A. Retzius, P. Broca, F. Pruner-Bey (1840–1870)', *Bulletins et mémoires de la société d'anthropologie de Paris*, 1:3–4 (1989), 165–202

Blanckaert, Claude, 'Les conditions d'émergence de la science des races au début du XIXe siècle', in *L'Idée de 'race' dans les sciences humaines et la littérature (XVIIIe et XIXe siècles)*, ed. by Sarga Moussa (Paris: L'Harmattan, 2003), pp. 133–49

Blancpain, François, 'L'Ordonnance de 1823 et la question de l'indemnité', in *Rétablissement de l'esclavage dans les colonies françaises, 1802: Ruptures et continuités de la politique coloniale française (1800–1830)*, ed. by Yves Bénot and Marcel Dorigny (Paris: Maisonneuve et Larose, 2003), pp. 221–9

Boehmer, Elleke, *Empire, the National, and the Postcolonial 1890–1920: Resistance in Interaction* (Oxford: Oxford University Press, 2002)

Bonaccorso, Giovanni, *L'Oriente nella narrativa di Gustave Flaubert*, 2 vols (Messina: Edizioni Dott. Antonino Sfameni, 1979–81)

Bongie, Chris, *Exotic Memories: Literature, Colonialism, and the Fin de Siècle* (Redwood, CA: Stanford University Press, 1991)

Bongie, Chris 'Belated Liaisons: Writing Between the Margins of Literary and Cultural Studies', *Francophone Postcolonial Studies*, 1:2 (2003), 11–24

Bonnetain, Paul, *Dans la brousse (Sensations du Soudan)* (Paris: Lemerre, 1895)

Bonnetain, Paul, *Au Tonkin*, ed. by Frédéric Da Silva (Paris: L'Harmattan, 2010 [1884])

Booker, John T., 'Starting at the End in *Eugénie Grandet*', *L'Esprit créateur*, 31:3 (1991), 38–48

Booth, Howard J. and Rigby, Nigel, eds, *Modernism and Empire* (Manchester: Manchester University Press, 2000)

Bordas, Eric, 'L'Orient balzacien ou l'impossible narratif d'un possible romanesque— l'exemple de "La Fille aux yeux d'or"', *Studi francesi*, 122 (1997), 322–30

Borie, Jean, *Zola et les mythes ou de la nausée au salut* (Paris: Seuil, 1971)

Borie, Jean, *Mythologies de l'hérédité au XIXe siècle* (Paris: Galilée, 1981)

Bornecque, Jacques-Henri, *Les Années d'apprentissage d'Alphonse Daudet* (Paris: Nizet, 1951)

Bornecque, Jacques-Henri, ed., *Aventures prodigieuses de Tartarin de Tarascon* (Paris: Garnier 1968), 'Introduction', pp. iii–lxxiii

Bourdieu, Pierre, *Les Règles de l'art: genèse et structure du champ littéraire* (Paris: Seuil, 1992)

Bouvier, Jean, '*L'Argent*: roman et réalité', *Europe*, 468–9 (1968), 54–64

Brahimi, Denise 'Enjeux et risques du roman exotique français', *Cahiers CRLH–CIRAOI*, 5 (1988), 11–18

Brantlinger, Patrick, *Rule of Darkness: British Literature and Imperialism, 1830–1914* (Ithaca, NY: Cornell University Press, 1988)

Brantlinger, Patrick, 'Nations and Novels: Disraeli, George Eliot, and Orientalism', *Victorian Studies: A Journal of the Humanities, Arts and Sciences*, 35:3 (1992), 255–75

Bredin, Hugh, 'Metonymy', *Poetics Today*, 5:1 (1984), 45–58

Brocheux, Pierre and Hémery, Daniel, *Indochine: la colonisation ambiguë 1858–1954* (Paris: Éditions de la découverte, 2001)

Brodeur, Pierre-Olivier, 'Pourquoi l'anti-roman?', *French Studies Bulletin*, 119 (2011), 28–31

Brody, Jennifer DeVere, 'Black Cat Fever: Manifestations of Manet's *Olympia*', *Theatre Journal*, 53 (2001), 95–118

Brombert, Victor, *The Novels of Flaubert: A Study of Themes and Techniques* (Princeton, NJ: Princeton University Press, 1966)

Brooks, Peter, *Reading for the Plot: Design and Intention in Narrative* (Cambridge, MA: Harvard University Press, 1984)

Brooks, Peter, *Realist Vision* (New Haven, CT: Yale University Press, 2005)

Brown, Bill, 'Thing Theory', *Critical Inquiry*, 28:1 (2001), 1–16, Special issue later published as *Things*, ed. by Bill Brown (Chicago, IL: University of Chicago Press, 2004)

Brown, Bill, *A Sense of Things: The Object Matter of American Literature* (Chicago, IL: University of Chicago Press, 2003)

Brown, Marshall, 'The Logic of Realism: A Hegelian Approach', *Publications of the Modern Language Association of America*, 96:2 (1981), 224–41

Bruegel, Martin, 'A Bourgeois Good? Sugar, Norms of Consumption and the Labouring Classes in Nineteenth-Century France', in *Food, Drink and Identity: Cooking, Eating and Drinking in Europe since the Middle Ages*, ed. by Peter Scholliers (Oxford/New York: Berg, 2001), pp. 99–118

Brunschwig, Henri, *Mythes et réalités de l'impérialisme colonial français, 1871–1915* (Paris: Armand Colin, 1960)

Bui, Véronique, 'D'Issoudun à Java ou l'Inde en Indre-et-Loire', in *Balzac voyageur: parcours, déplacements, mutations*, ed. by Nicole Mozet and Paul Petitier (Tours: Publications de l'Université François Rabelais, 2004), pp. 259–75

Buisine, Alain, *L'Orient voilé* (Paris: Zulma, 1993)

Cannadine, David, *Ornamentalism: How the British Saw their Empire* (London: Allen Lane, 2001)

Cario, Louis, and Régismanset, Charles, *L'Exotisme: la littérature coloniale* (Paris: Mercure de France, 1911)

Carles, Patricia and Desgranges, Béatrice, 'Son Excellence Eugène Rougon ou la métairie des Beaux-Arts', *Nineteenth-Century French Studies*, 21:1–2 (1992–3), 114–29

Caws, Mary Ann, *Reading Frames in Modern Fiction* (Princeton, NJ: Princeton University Press, 1985)

Célestin, Roger, *From Cannibals to Radicals: Figures and Limits of Exoticism* (Minneapolis/London: University of Minnesota Press, 1995)

Césaire, Aimé, *Discours sur le colonialisme* (Paris/Dakar: Présence africaine, 1955)

Champion, Catherine, '*Fortunio*, un rêve romantique indien dans le Paris d'Haussmann', *Corps Écrit*, 34 (1990), 57–64

Chateaubriand, François-René de, *Essai sur les Révolutions/Génie du christianisme*, ed. by Maurice Regard (Paris: Gallimard 'Pléiade', 1978)

Chevalier, Louis, *Classes laborieuses et classes dangereuses à Paris pendant la première moitié du XIXe siècle* (Paris: Plon, 1958)

Chrisman, Laura, 'The Imperial Unconscious? Representations of Imperial Discourse', *Critical Quarterly*, 32:3 (1990), 38–58

Chrisman, Laura, 'Rethinking the Imperial Metropolis of Heart of Darkness', in *Conrad at the Millennium: Modernism, Postmodernism, Postcolonialism*, ed. by Gail Fincham, Atti De Lange, and Wieslaw Krajka (Boulder, CO: Social Science Monographs, 2001), pp. 399–426

Chrisman, Laura, *Postcolonial Contraventions: Cultural Readings of Race, Imperialism and Transnationalism* (Manchester: Manchester University Press, 2003)

Citron, Pierre, 'Sur deux zones obscures de la psychologie de Balzac', *L'Année balzacienne* (1967), 3–27

Citron, Pierre, 'Le Rêve asiatique de Balzac', *L'Année balzacienne* (1968), 303–36

Citti, Pierre, *Contre la décadence* (Paris: Presses Universitaires de France, 1987)

Clark, T.J., *The Painting of Modern Life: Paris in the Art of Manet and his Followers* (London: Thames & Hudson, 1984)

Clayton, Alcorn, 'The Domestic Servant in Zola's Novels', *L'Esprit Créateur*, 11:4 (1971), 21–35

Cleary, Joe, 'Realism after Modernism and the Literary World-System', *Modern Language Quarterly*, Prologue to the special issue 'Peripheral Realisms', 73:3 (2012), 255–68

Cohen, Margaret, *The Sentimental Education of the Novel* (Princeton, NJ: Princeton University Press, 1999)

Colatrella, Carol, 'The Significant Silence of Race: La Cousine Bette and "Benito Cereno"', *Comparative Literature*, 46:3 (1994), 240–66

Constable, Elizabeth Louise, 'Critical Departures: *Salammbô*'s Orientalism', *Modern Language Notes*, 111:4 (1996), 625–46

Counter, Andrew, 'The Epistemology of the Mantelpiece: Subversive Ornaments in the Novels of Guy de Maupassant', *Modern Languages Review*, 103 (2008), 682–96

Counter, Andrew, 'The Legacy of the Beast: Patrilinearity and Rupture in Zola's *La Bête humaine* and Freud's *Totem and Taboo*', *French Studies*, 62:1 (2008), 26–38

Court-Pérez, Françoise, 'Figures de l'ironie chez Daudet', *Écritures XIX/La Revue des Lettres modernes*, 1 (2003) '*Alphonse Daudet, pluriel et singulier*', 67–81

Courteix, René-Alexandre, *Balzac et la révolution française: aspects idéologiques et politiques* (Paris: Presses Universitaires de France, 1997)

Crouzet, Michel, 'Passion et politique dans *L'Éducation sentimentale*', in *Flaubert, la femme, la ville*, ed. by Marie-Claire Bancquart (Paris: Presses Universitaires de France, 1982), pp. 39–71

Culler, Jonathan, *Flaubert, the Uses of Uncertainty* (London: Elek, 1974)

Czyba, Lucette, *Mythes et idéologie de la femme dans les romans de Flaubert* (Lyon: Presses Universitaires de Lyon, 1983)

Da Silva, Frédéric, 'Introduction: Paul Bonnetain, le chercheur d'inconnu', *Les Cahiers naturalistes*, 85 (Special issue on Paul Bonnetain) (2011), 4–14

Da Silva, Frédéric, 'Pour un naturalisme exotique: *L'Opium* et sa préface inédite', *Les Cahiers naturalistes*, 85 (Special issue on Paul Bonnetain) (2011), 67–75

Dallal, Jenine Abboushi, 'French Cultural Imperialism and the Aesthetics of Extinction', *The Yale Journal of Criticism*, 13:2 (2000), 229–57

Dällenbach, Lucien, *Le Récit spéculaire: essai sur la* mise en abyme (Paris: Seuil, 1977)

Danger, Pierre, *Sensations et objets dans le roman de Flaubert* (Paris: Armand Colin, 1973)

Darbouze, Gilbert, '*Les Bouts de bois de Dieu* d'Ousmane Sembène: L'esthétique naturaliste d'Émile Zola dans un roman sénégalais', *Excavatio*, 11 (1998), 182–7

Darmon, Pierre, *Un siècle de passions algériennes: une histoire de l'Algérie coloniale 1830–1940* (Paris: Fayard, 2009)

Davis, Lennard J., *Factual Fictions: the Origins of the English Novel* (New York: Columbia University Press, 1983)

Degoumois, Léon, *L'Algérie d'Alphonse Daudet d'après Tartarin de Tarascon et divers fragments des autres œuvres: essai sur les sources et les procédés d'imitation d'Alphonse Daudet, suivi de la première version de Tartarin* (Geneva: Éditions Sonor, 1922)

Delaisement, Gérard, *Maupassant journaliste et chroniqueur* (Paris: Albin Michel, 1956)

Delaisement, Gérard, 'Les chroniques coloniales de Maupassant', in *Maupassant et l'écriture*, ed. by Louis Forestier (Paris: Nathan, 1993), pp. 53–9

Deleuze, Gilles, 'Zola et la fêlure' [1969], reprinted in Zola, *La Bête humaine*, ed. by Henri Mitterand (Paris: Gallimard 'Folio', 1977), pp. 7–24

Delvau, Alfred, *Dictionnaire érotique moderne* (Paris: Éditions 1900, 1990 [1864])

Demont, Bernard, *Représentations spatiales et narration dans les contes et nouvelles de Guy de Maupassant: Une rhétorique de l'espace géographique* (Paris: Champion, 2005)

Déruelle, Aude, '"L'Égypte, c'est tout sables": Balzac et le récit de voyage', in *Voyager en France au temps du romantisme: poétique, esthétique, idéologie*, ed. by Alain Guyot and Chantal Massot (Grenoble: ELLUG, 2003), pp. 325–41

Dezalay, Auguste, 'Les mystères de Zola', *Revue des Sciences Humaines*, 160 (1975), 475–87

Dezalay, Auguste, *L'Opéra des Rougon-Macquart: Essai de rythmologie romanesque* (Paris: Klincksieck, 1983)

Diamond, Marie Josephine, 'Flaubert's "Quidquid Volueris": The Colonial Father and the Poetics of Hysteria', *Sub-Stance*, 27:1 (1998), 71–88

Dignan, Don, 'Europe's Melting Pot: A Century of Large-Scale Immigration into France', *Ethnic and Racial Studies*, 4:2 (1981), 137–52

Dionne, Ugo, and Gingras, Francis, 'Présentation: l'usure originelle du roman: roman et antiroman du Moyen Âge à la Révolution', *Études françaises*, 42:1 (2006), 5–21

Donnard, Jean-Hervé, *Balzac: Les réalités économiques et sociales dans* La Comédie Humaine (Paris: Armand Colin, 1961)

Dord-Crouslé, Stéphanie, 'Le darwinisme de Flaubert', in *L'Idée de 'race' dans les sciences humaines et la littérature*, ed. by Sarga Moussa (Paris: L'Harmattan, 2003), pp. 283–97

Doueihi, Milad, 'Flaubert's Costumes', *Modern Language Notes*, 101:5 (1986), 1086–109

Downing, Lisa, *The Subject of Murder: Gender, Exceptionality, and the Modern Killer* (Chicago, IL: University of Chicago Press, 2013)

Doyle, Laura, *Freedom's Empire: Race and the Rise of the Novel in Atlantic Modernity, 1640–1940* (Durham, NC: Duke University Press, 2008)

Du Camp, Maxime, *Souvenirs littéraires* [1892] ed. by Daniel Oster (Paris: Aubier, 1994)

Duchet, Claude, 'Romans et objets: L'exemple de *Madame Bovary*', *Europe*, 485–7 (1969), 172–201

Dufief, Anne-Simone, *Alphonse Daudet romancier* (Paris: Champion, 1997)

Dufief, Anne-Simone, 'Tartarin, les avatars d'un disciple de Saint Hubert', *Romantisme*, 129 (2005), 61–78

Dufief, Anne-Simone, 'Voyages et rêverie dans l'œuvre de Daudet', in *Apprendre à porter sa vue au loin: Hommage à Michèle Duchet*, ed. by Sylviane Albertan-Coppola (Lyon: ENS Éditions, 2009), pp. 331–42

Dufief, Pierre, 'Les Goncourt et la race: Au carrefour de la prosopographie et de l'idéologie', *Excavatio*, 16:1–2 (2002), 35–45

Dufour, Philippe, *Flaubert ou la prose du silence* (Paris: Nathan, 1997)

Dunwoodie, Peter, *Writing French Algeria* (Oxford: Clarendon Press, 1998)

Dupuy, Aimé, 'Balzac colonial', *Revue d'histoire littéraire de la France*, 50:3 (1950), 257–79

Dupuy, Aimé, 'L'Algérie dans l'œuvre de Maupassant', *Documents algériens*, Série culturelle, 51 (26 December 1950), no page numbers

Dupuy, Aimé, 'Balzac et l'Algérie', *Documents algériens*, *Série culturelle*, 52 (1 March 1951), no page numbers

Durand, Jean-François, 'Littératures coloniales, littératures d'Empire?', *Romantisme*, 139 (2008), 47–58

Durry, Marie-Jeanne, *Flaubert et ses projets inédits* (Paris: Nizet, 1950)

Dutton, Michael and Williams, Peter, 'Translating Theories: Edward Said on Orientalism, Imperialism and Alterity', *Southern Review*, 26:3 (1993), 314–57

Ellingson, Ter, *The Myth of the Noble Savage* (Oakland, CA: University of California Press, 2001)

Esty, Jed and Lye, Colleen, 'Peripheral Realisms Now', *Modern Language Quarterly*, Introduction to the special issue 'Peripheral Realisms', 73:3 (2012), 269–88

Evenhuis, Anthony John, 'Zola and the Unpardonable Sin: A Psychoanalytical Study of *Madeleine Férat*', *Excavatio*, 9 (1997), 122–35

Fabian, Johannes, *Time and the Other: How Anthropology makes its Object* (New York: Columbia University Press, 2002 [1983])

Fairlie, Alison, 'La quête de la femme à travers la ville dans quelques œuvres de Flaubert', in *Flaubert, la femme, la ville*, ed. by Marie-Claire Bancquart (Paris: Presses Universitaires de France, 1983), pp. 77–87

Fanoudh-Siefer, Léon, *Le Mythe du nègre et de l'Afrique noire dans la littérature française (de 1800 à la 2e Guerre mondiale)* (Paris: Klincksieck, 1968)

Fargeaud, Madeleine and Pierrot, Roger, 'Henry le trop aimé', *L'Année balzacienne* (1961), 29–66

Farrant, Tim, *Balzac's Shorter Fictions: Genesis and Genre* (Oxford: Oxford University Press, 2002)

Ferreras, Daniel F., 'Amour noir et mort blanche: "Boitelle" de Maupassant, ou le naturalisme contre le racisme', *Excavatio*, 8 (1996), 185–93

Finch, Alison, 'The Stylistic Achievements of Flaubert's Fiction', in *The Cambridge Companion to Flaubert*, ed. by Timothy Unwin (Cambridge: Cambridge University Press, 2004), pp. 145–64

Foucault, Michel, 'Des espaces autres' [lecture 1967, published 1984] in *Dits et Écrits*, ed. by Daniel Defert and François Ewald, 4 vols (Paris: Gallimard, 1994), vol. 4, pp. 752–62

Franklin, Michael J., ed., *Romantic Representations of British India* (London: Routledge, 2006)

Freedgood, Elaine, *The Ideas in Things: Fugitive Meaning in the Victorian Novel* (Chicago, IL: University of Chicago Press, 2006)

Freud, Sigmund, 'Fetishism' [1927] in *On Sexuality*, trans. by James Strachey, ed. by Angela Richards (London: Penguin, 1977)

Fulford, Tim and Kitson, Peter J., eds, *Romanticism and Colonialism: Writing and Empire, 1780–1830* (Cambridge: Cambridge University Press, 1998)

Gaillard, Françoise, 'Le Soi et l'Autre: le retour de la bête humaine', in *Du visible à l'invisible: pour Max Milner*, ed. by Stéphane Michaud (Paris: José Corti, 1988), pp. 97–110

Gaillard-Pourchet, Gusti Klara, 'Aspects politiques et commerciaux de l'indemnisation haïtienne', in *Rétablissement de l'esclavage dans les colonies françaises, 1802: Ruptures et continuités de la politique coloniale française (1800–1830)*, ed. by Yves Bénot and Marcel Dorigny (Paris: Maisonneuve et Larose, 2003), pp. 231–7

Gallois, William, *Zola: the History of Capitalism* (Bern: Peter Lang, 2000)

Gallois, William, 'Genocide in nineteenth-century Algeria', *Journal of Genocide Research*, 15:1 (2013) 591–610

Gallois, William, *A History of Violence in the Early Algerian Colony* (Basingstoke: Palgrave Macmillan, 2013)

Gantrel, Martine, 'Homeless Women: Maidservants in Fiction', in *Home and its Dislocations in Nineteenth-Century France*, ed. by Suzanne Nash (New York: State University of New York Press, 1993), pp. 247–64

Gaultier, Jules de, *Le Bovarysme: essai sur le pouvoir d'imaginer* (Paris: Société du Mercure de France, 1903 [first published as *Le Bovarysme*, 1902])

Gaultier, Jules de, *Le Bovarysme: La Psychologie dans l'œuvre de Flaubert*, ed. by Didier Philippot (Paris: Éditions du Sandre, 2008 [1892])

Gauthier, E. Paul, 'New Light on Zola and physiognomy', *Publications of the Modern Language Association of America*, 75 (1960), 297–308

Gautier, Théophile, 'Le Pied de momie', in *Contes fantastiques* (Paris: José Corti, 1986 [1962]), pp. 149–63

Geggus, David Patrick and Fiering, Norman, eds, *The World of the Haitian Revolution* (Bloomington, IN: Indiana University Press, 2009)

Genette, Gérard, *Figures II* (Paris, Seuil: 1969)

Genette, Gérard, *Figures III* (Paris: Seuil, 1972)

Genette, Gérard, *Nouveau discours du récit* (Paris: Seuil, 1983)

Genette, Gérard, *Palimpsestes: La littérature au second degré* (Paris: Seuil, 1982)

Giacchetti, Claudine, *Maupassant: Espaces du roman* (Geneva: Droz, 1993)

Gilman, Sander L., 'Black Bodies, White Bodies: Toward an Iconography of Female Sexuality in Late Nineteenth-Century Art, Medicine, and Literature', in *Race, Writing, Difference*, ed. by Henry Louis Gates (Chicago, IL: University of Chicago Press, 1985), pp. 223–61

Gilman, Sander L., *Difference and Pathology: Stereotypes of Sexuality, Race, and Madness* (Ithaca, NY: Cornell University Press, 1985)

Ginzburg, Carlo, 'Morelli, Freud and Sherlock Holmes: Clues and Scientific Method', *History Workshop*, 9 (1980), 5–36

Ginzburg, Carlo, *Wooden Eyes: Nine Reflections on Distance*, trans. by Martin Ryle and Kate Soper (New York: Columbia University Press, 2001)

Girardet, Raoul, *L'Idée coloniale en France de 1871 à 1962* (Paris: La Table ronde, 1972)

Giraud, Raymond, *The Unheroic Hero in the Novels of Stendhal, Balzac and Flaubert* (Rutgers University Press, 1957)

Glissant, Édouard, *Le Discours antillais* (Paris: Gallimard, 'Folio', 1997 [1981])

Gomart, Hélène, *Les Opérations financières dans le roman réaliste: Lectures de Balzac et de Zola* (Paris: Champion, 2004)

Goncourt, Edmond and Jules de, *Journal*, ed. by Robert Ricattte and Robert Kopp (Paris: Robert Laffont, 1989), 3 vols

Goncourt, Edmond and Jules de, *Germinie Lacerteux* [1865], ed. by Nadine Satiat (Paris: Flammarion 'GF', 1990)

Goodlad, Lauren M.E. 'The Trollopian Geopolitical Aesthetic', *Literature Compass*, 7–9 (2010), 867–75

Gordon, Rae Beth, '*La Bête humaine*: Zola and the poetics of the unconscious', in *The Cambridge Companion to Émile Zola*, ed. by Brian Nelson (Cambridge: Cambridge University Press, 2007), pp. 152–68

Gouaux-Coutrix, Mireille, '*Au Soleil* de Guy de Maupassant ou un romancier face à la colonisation', in *Actes du Colloque international 'Entre l'Occident et l'Orient'*, ed. by the Laboratoire d'Histoire Quantitative (Nice: Université de Nice, 1983), pp. 271–84

Goyet, Florence, 'L'Exotisme du quotidien: Maupassant et la presse', in *Maupassant multiple*, ed. by Yves Reboul (Toulouse: Presses Universitaires du Mirail, 1995), pp. 17–28

Grant, Richard B., 'The Jewish Question in Zola's *L'Argent*', *Publications of the Modern Language Association of America*, 70:5 (1955), 955–67

Grant, Richard B., *Zola's Son Excellence Eugène Rougon* (Durham, NC: Duke University Press, 1960)

Grauby, Françoise, 'Corps privé et vêtement public: les jeux et les enjeux du costume féminin dans *L'Éducation sentimentale* de Flaubert', *New Zealand Journal of French Studies*, 18:1 (1997), 5–19

Green, Anne, 'Flaubert: Paris, Elsewhere', *Romance Studies*, 22 (1993), 7–15

Green, Anne, 'Flaubert's myth of civilisation and the Orient', in *Romantic Geographies*, ed. by Colin Smethurst (Glasgow: University of Glasgow French and German Publications, 1996), pp. 215–25

Green, Martin, *Dreams of Adventure, Deeds of Empire* (London: Routledge, 1980)

Greene, John P., 'Cosmetics and Conflicting Fictions in Balzac's *César Birotteau*', *Neophilologus*, 83:2 (1999), 197–208

Gregorio, Laurence A., *Maupassant's Fiction and the Darwinian View of Life* (Bern: Peter Lang, 2005)

Groot, Joanna de, '"Sex" and "Race": the Construction of Language and Image in the Nineteenth Century', in *Sexuality and Subordination*, ed. by Susan Mendus and Jane Renall (London: Routledge, 1989), pp. 89–128

Groot, Joanna de, 'Metropolitan desires and colonial connections: reflections on consumption and empire', in *At Home with the Empire: Metropolitan Culture and the Imperial World*, ed. by Catherine Hall and Sonya O. Rose (Cambridge: Cambridge University Press, 2006), pp. 166–90

Guégan, Stéphane, 'Le moment Baudelaire', in *Manet, inventeur du moderne*, ed. by Stéphane Guégan (Paris: Gallimard/Musée d'Orsay, 2011), pp. 135–57

Haddad, Emily A. *Orientalist Poetics: The Islamic Middle East in Nineteenth-Century English and French Poetry* (Aldershot: Ashgate, 2002)

Haig, Stirling, *Flaubert and the Gift of Speech: Dialogue and Discourse in Four 'Modern' Novels* (Cambridge: Cambridge University Press, 1986)

Hall, Catherine, ed., *Cultures of Empire: Colonisers in Britain and the Empire in the Nineteenth and Twentieth Centuries* (Manchester: Manchester University Press, 2000)

Hall, Catherine and Rose, Sonya O., eds, *At Home with the Empire: Metropolitan Culture and the Imperial World* (Cambridge: Cambridge University Press, 2006)

Hall, Stuart, 'When was "the post-colonial"? thinking at the limit', in *The Post-Colonial Question*, ed. by Iain Chambers and Lidia Curti (London: Routledge, 1996), pp. 242–60

Hamon, Philippe, 'Le savoir dans le texte', *Revue des Sciences humaines*, 4 (1975), 489–99

Hamon, Philippe, *Le Personnel du roman: le système des personnages dans les Rougon-Macquart d'Émile Zola* (Genève: Droz, 1983)

Hamon, Philippe, *Texte et idéologie* (Paris: Presses Universitaires de France, 1984)

Hamon, Philippe, *La Bête humaine d'Émile Zola* (Paris: Gallimard, 1994)

Hargreaves, Alec, 'European Identity and the Colonial Frontier', *Journal of European Studies*, 12:47 (1982), 166–79

Harlow, Barbara, *Resistance Literature* (New York/London: Methuen, 1987)

Harrison, Nicolas, *Postcolonial Criticism: History, Theory and the Work of Fiction*, (Cambridge: Polity, 2003)

Harrison, Nicholas, 'Who Needs an Idea of the Literary?', *Paragraph*, 28:2 (2005), 1–17

Harrow, Susan, '*Thérèse Raquin*: animal passion and the brutality of reading', in *The Cambridge Companion to Émile Zola*, ed. by Brian Nelson (Cambridge: Cambridge University Press, 2007), pp. 105–20

Harrow, Susan, *Zola: The Body Modern: Pressures and Prospects of Representation* (Oxford: Legenda, 2010)

Hayes, Jared, *Queer Nations: Marginal Sexualities in the Maghreb* (Chicago, IL: University of Chicago Press, 2000)

Hayward, Susan, *French Costume Drama of the 1950s: Fashioning Politics in Film* (Bristol: Intellect, 2010)

Heathcote, Owen, 'From Cannibal to Carnival: Orality and Violence in Balzac's Gobseck', *The Modern Language Review*, 91:1 (1996), 53–64

Heathcote, Owen, 'Verbal Hygiene for Oscar: The Expression and Containment of Violence in Balzac's *Un début dans la vie*', in *Confrontations: Politics and Aesthetics in Nineteenth-Century France*, ed. by Kathryn M. Grossman, Michael E. Lane, Bénédicte Monicat, and Willa Z. Silverman (Amsterdam: Rodopi, 2001), pp. 107–30

Heathcote, Owen, 'Gérer l'altérité? Le travail du corps dans les *Études analytiques*', in *Balzac, l'aventure analytique*, ed. by Claire Barel-Moisan and Christèle Couleau (Saint-Cyr-sur-Loire: Éditions Christian Pirot, 2009), pp. 215–27

Hemmings, F.W.J., 'Zola and *L'Éducation sentimentale*', *The Romanic Review*, 50:1 (1959), 35–40

Hemmings, F.W.J., ed. and main author, *The Age of Realism* (London: Penguin, 1974)

Hennessy, Susie, '(Re)producing Death in Emile Zola's Rougon-Macquart', in *Aimer et Mourir: Love, Death, and Women's Lives in Texts of French Expression*, ed. by Eilene Hoft-March and Judith Holland Sarnecki (Newcastle upon Tyne: Cambridge Scholars, 2009), pp. 48–63

Hentsch, Thierry, *L'Orient imaginaire: La vision politique occidentale de l'Est méditerranéen* (Paris: Éditions de Minuit, 1988)

Héricourt, Jules, '*La Bête humaine* de M. Zola et la physiologie du criminel', *Revue Bleue* (7 June 1890), 710–18

Hiner, Susan, 'Lust for luxe: "Cashmere fever" in Nineteenth-Century France', *The Journal for Early Modern Cultural Studies*, 5:1 (2005), 76–98

Hiner, Susan, *Accessories to Modernity: Fashion and the Feminine in Nineteenth-Century France* (Philadelphia, PA: University of Pennsylvania Press, 2010)

Hochmann, Jacques, 'La théorie de la dégénérescence de B.-A. Morel, ses origines et son évolution', in *Darwinisme et Société*, ed. by Patrick Tort (Paris: Presses Universitaires de France, 1992), pp. 402–12

Hoffmann, Léon-François, 'Balzac et les noirs', *L'Année balzacienne* (1966), 297–308

Hoffmann, Léon-François, *Le Nègre romantique* (Paris: Payot, 1973)

Hoffmann, Léon-François, 'Le Nègre romantique', *Notre Librairie*, 90 (1987), 34–9

Hoffmann, Léon-François, 'Representations of the Haitian Revolution in French Literature', in *The World of the Haitian Revolution*, ed. by David Patrick Geggus and Norman Fiering (Bloomington, IN: Indiana University Press, 2009), pp. 339–51

Huggan, Graham, '(Not)Reading *Orientalism*', *Research in African Literatures*, 36:3 (2005), 124–36

Hugo, Victor, 'Discours sur l'Afrique' [1879], in *Œuvres complètes*, ed. by Jean Massin, 18 vols (Paris: Club français du livre, 1967–70), vol. 15, pp. 1450–4

Hulme, Peter, 'Balzac's Parisian Mystery: *La Cousine Bette* and the Writing of Historical Criticism', *Literature and History*, 11:1 (1985), 47–64

Hurlburt, Sarah, 'Educating Emma: A Genetic Analysis of Reading in *Madame Bovary*', *Nineteenth-Century French Studies*, 40:1–2 (2011–12), 81–95

Ippolito, Christophe, *Narrative Memory in Flaubert's Works* (Bern: Peter Lang, 2001)

Israel-Pelletier, Aimée, 'Flaubert and the Visual', in *The Cambridge Companion to Flaubert*, ed. by Timothy Unwin (Cambridge: Cambridge University Press, 2004), pp. 180–95

Jakobson, Roman, *Language in Literature*, ed. by Krystyna Pomorska and Stephen Rudy (Cambridge, MA: Harvard University Press, 1987)

James, Harold, 'The Literary Financier', *The American Scholar*, 60:2 (1991) 251–7

James, Henry, 'Translator's Preface', *Port-Tarascon*, *Harper's New Monthly Magazine*, 81 (June 1890)

Jameson, Fredric, '*La Cousine Bette* and Allegorical Realism', *Publications of the Modern Language Association of America*, 86:2 (1971), 241–54

Jameson, Fredric, 'Imaginary and Symbolic in *La Rabouilleuse*', *Social Science Information*, 16:59 (1977), 59–81

Jameson, Fredric, *The Political Unconscious: Narrative as a Socially Symbolic Act* (London/New York: Routledge, 1981)

Jameson, Fredric, 'Third-World Literature in the Era of Multinational Capitalism', *Social Text*, 15 (1986), 65–88

Jameson, Fredric, 'Modernism and Imperialism', *Nationalism, Colonialism and Literature: A Field Day Pamphlet*, 14 (Derry: Field Day Theatre Co., 1988), 5–23

Jameson, Fredric, *The Ideologies of Theory* (London: Verso, 2008)

Jameson, Fredric, 'Antinomies of the Realism-Modernism Debate', *Modern Language Quarterly*, Afterword to the special issue 'Peripheral Realisms', 73:3 (2012), 475–85

Jameson, Fredric, *The Antinomies of Realism* (London: Verso, 2013)

Jameson, Maureen, 'Métonymie et trahison dans *L'Éducation sentimentale*', *Nineteenth-Century French Studies*, 19:4 (1991), 566–82

JanMohamed, Abdul, 'The Economy of Manichean Allegory: The Function of Racial Difference in Colonialist Literature', in *'Race', Writing, and Difference*, ed. by Henry Louis Gates Jr (Chicago, IL: University of Chicago Press, 1986 [1985]), pp. 78–106

Jefferson, Ann, 'Realism Reconsidered: Bakhtin's Dialogism and the "Will to Reference"', *Australian Journal of French Studies*, 23:2 (1986), 169–84

Jennings, Lawrence C., *French Anti-Slavery: the Movement for the Abolition of Slavery in France, 1802–1848* (Cambridge: Cambridge University Press, 2000)

Jenson, Deborah, 'Bovarysm and Exoticism', in *The Columbia History of Twentieth-Century French Thought*, ed. by Lawrence D. Kritzman and Brian J. Reilly (New York: Columbia University Press, 2006), pp. 167–70

Joachim, Benoît, 'L'indemnité coloniale de Saint-Domingue et la question des rapatriés', *Revue Historique*, 246:2 (1971), 359–76

Joachim, Benoît, 'La reconnaissance d'Haïti par la France (1825): Naissance d'un nouveau type de rapports internationaux', *Revue d'histoire moderne et contemporaine*, 22:3 (1975), 369–96

Jourda, Pierre, *L'Exotisme dans la littérature française depuis Chateaubriand: t. 2, du romantisme à 1939* (Paris: Presses Universitaires de France/Slatkine Reprints, 1970 [1956; written 1939])

Julien, Charles-André, *Histoire de l'Afrique du Nord: Tunisie, Algérie, Maroc* (Paris: Payot, 1951–2)

Julien, Charles-André, *Histoire de l'Algérie contemporaine, vol. 1 La conquête et les débuts de la colonisation (1827–1871)* (Paris: Presses Universitaires de France, 1964)

Julien, Charles-André, *L'Affaire tunisienne 1878–1881* (Tunis: Dar el-Amal, 1981)

Kaminskas, Jurate D., '*Thérèse Raquin*: Les Couleurs de l'abîme', *Les Cahiers naturalistes*, 58 (1985), 23–31

Kaminskas, Jurate D., 'De la séduction et du pouvoir: *Son Excellence Eugène Rougon*', *Excavatio*, 15:3–4 (2001), 92–106

Kaplan, Cora, '"Like a Housemaid's Fancies": The Representation of Working-Class Women in Nineteenth-Century Writing', in *Grafts: Feminist Cultural Criticism*, ed. by Susan Sheridan (London: Verso, 1988), pp. 55–76

Kaplan, Cora, 'Imagining empire: history, fantasy and literature', in *At Home with the Empire: Metropolitan Culture and the Imperial World*, ed. by Catherine Hall and Sonya O. Rose (Cambridge: Cambridge University Press, 2006), pp. 191–211

Kapoor, Ilan, 'Hyper-Self-Reflexive Development? Spivak on Representing the Third World', *Third World Quarterly*, 25:4 (2004), 627–47

Kapoor, Sucheta, 'Silence as Alterity: the Portrait of Djalioh in *Quidquid volueris*', *Dix-Neuf*, 15:1 (2011), 140–6

Kapor, Vladimir, *Pour une poétique de l'écriture exotique: les stratégies de l'écriture exotique dans les lettres françaises aux alentours de 1850* (Paris: L'Harmattan, 2007)

Keates, Laurence W., 'Mysterious Miraculous Mandarin: Origins, Literary Paternity, Implications in Ethics', *Revue de littérature comparée*, 40:4 (1966), 497–525

Kelly, Dorothy, 'Experimenting on Women: Zola's Theory and Practice of the Experimental Novel', in *Spectacles of Realism: Gender, Body, Genre*, ed. by Margaret Cohen and Christopher Prendergast (Minneapolis, MN: University of Minnesota Press, 1995), pp. 231–46

Knellwolf, Christa and Iain McCalman, 'Introduction', in *Eighteenth-Century Life*, special issue on 'Exoticism and the Culture of Exploration', 26:3 (2002), 1–9

Knight, Diana, 'Object Choices: Taste and Fetishism in Flaubert's *L'Éducation sentimentale*', in *French Literature, Thought and Culture in the Nineteenth Century*, ed. by Brian Rigby (London: Macmillan, 1993), pp. 198–217

Knight, Diana, 'From Gobseck's Chamber to Derville's Chambers: Retention in Balzac's *Gobseck*', *Nineteenth-Century French Studies*, 33:3–4 (2005), 243–57

Krell, Alan, *Manet and the Painters of Everyday Life* (London: Thames & Hudson, 1996)

Kristeva, Julia, *Pouvoirs de l'horreur* (Paris: Seuil, 1980)

Lacassagne, Alexandre, 'L'homme criminel comparé à l'homme primitif', *Lyon médical*, 39 (1882) Part 1, 210–17, and Part 2, 244–55

Lacoste, Francis, 'L'Orient de Flaubert', *Romantisme*, 119 (2003), 73–84

Laforgue, Pierre, *1830: romantisme et histoire* (Paris: Eurédit, 2001)

Lalande, Bernard, 'Les États successifs d'une nouvelle de Balzac: *Gobseck*', *Revue d'Histoire Littéraire de la France*, 46 (1939), 180–200 and 47 (1947), 69–89

Lambart, Michel, 'Maupassant et la politique coloniale ou Maupassant le pacifique', *Bulletin Flaubert-Maupassant*, 21 (2007), 41–51

Lanoux, Armand, *Maupassant, le 'Bel-Ami'* (Paris, Fayard: 1967)

Lapp, John, *Zola Before the Rougon-Macquart* (Toronto: University of Toronto Press, 1964)

Lavielle, Véronique, 'Le cycle des Rougon-Macquart, la science et l'imaginaire', *Les Cahiers naturalistes*, 68 (1994), 23–7

Lazarus, Neil, 'Realism and Naturalism in African Fiction' [1987], in *African Literature: An Anthology of Criticism and Theory*, ed. by Tejumola Olaniyan and Ato Quayson (Oxford: Blackwell, 2007), pp. 340–4

Lazarus, Neil, *The Postcolonial Unconscious* (Cambridge: Cambridge University Press, 2011)

Le Calvez, Éric, 'Gobseck and Grandet: Semes, Themes, Intertext,' *Romance Studies*, 23 (1994), 43–60

Le Huenen, Roland, 'Dans le sillage de Sterne et Nodier: le *Voyage de Paris à Java* de Balzac et l'écriture du supplément', in *Apprendre à porter sa vue au loin: Hommage à Michèle Duchet*, ed. by Sylviane Albertan-Coppola (Lyon: ENS Éditions, 2009), pp. 311–29

Le Yaouanc, Moïse, 'Échanges romantiques: Balzac et "Gamiani", Balzac et "Fortunio"', *L'Année balzacienne* (1976), 71–86

Leask, Nigel, *British Romantic Writers and the East: Anxieties of Empire* (Cambridge: Cambridge University Press, 1992)

Leask, Nigel, '"Wandering through Eblis": absorption and containment in Romantic exoticism', in *Romanticism and Colonialism: Writing and Empire, 1780–1830*, ed. by Tim Fulford and Peter J. Kitson (Cambridge: Cambridge University Press, 1998), pp. 165–88

Lebègue, Raymond 'Notes sur le personnage de la servante', *Revue d'histoire littéraire de la France*, 83:1 (1983), 3–14

Lebel, Roland, *L'Afrique occidentale dans la littérature française depuis 1870* (Paris: Larose, 1925)

Lebel, Roland, *Histoire de la littérature coloniale en France* (Paris: Larose, 1931)

Leblond, Marius-Ary, *Après l'exotisme de Loti: le roman colonial* (Paris: Vald. Rasmussen, 1926)

Lebron, Monica, 'Madame Caroline: Expéditions discursives dans *L'Argent*', *Les Cahiers naturalistes*, 73 (1999), 217–25

Lethbridge, Robert, 'Zola, Manet and *Thérèse Raquin*', *French Studies*, 34:3 (1980), 278–99

Lethbridge, Robert, 'Zola et la fiction du pouvoir: *Son Excellence Eugène Rougon*', *Les Cahiers naturalistes*, 44 (1998), 291–304

Lethbridge, Robert, 'Zola and Contemporary Painting', in *The Cambridge Companion to Emile Zola*, ed. by Brian Nelson (Cambridge: Cambridge University Press, 2007), pp. 67–85

Levin, Harry, *The Gates of Horn: A Study of Five French Realists* (Oxford: Oxford University Press, 1963)

Liauzu, Claude, *Histoire de l'anticolonialisme en France, du XVIe siècle à nos jours* (Paris: Armand Colin, 2007)

Lilley, E.D., 'Two Notes on Manet', *The Burlington Magazine*, 132 (1990), 266–9

Little, Roger, ' "Tiens, Forestier!": Maupassant et la colonisation', Plaisance: rivista di letter-
      atura francese moderna e contemporanea, 3:8 (2006) 75–87
Lombroso, Cesare, L'Homme criminel [1876], trans. by M. Régnier and M. Bournet (Paris:
      Félix Alcan, 1887)
Lombroso, Cesare, 'La Bête humaine et l'anthropologie criminelle', La Revue des revues, 5
      (1892), reprinted in Émile Zola, Les Rougon-Macquart, 5 vols (Paris: Robert Laffont,
      2002), vol. 5, pp. 1410–15
Loomba, Ania, Colonialism/Postcolonialism (London/New York: Routledge, 2005 [1998])
Lörinszky, Ildiko, L'Orient de Flaubert. Des écrits de jeunesse à Salammbô: la construction
      d'un imaginaire mythique (Paris: L'Harmattan, 2003)
Lowe, Lisa, Critical Terrains: French and British Orientalisms (Ithaca, NY: Cornell University
      Press, 1991)
Lowe, Lisa, 'Nationalism and Exoticism: Nineteenth-Century Others in Flaubert's
      Salammbô and L'Éducation sentimentale', in Macropolitics of Nineteenth-Century
      Literature: Nationalism, Exoticism, Imperialism, ed. by Jonathan Arac and Harriet Ritvo
      (Philadelphia, PA: University of Pennsylvania Press, 1991), pp. 213–42
Lucey, Michael, 'Legal Melancholy: Balzac's "Eugénie Grandet" and the Napoleonic Code',
      Representations, 76 (2001), 1–26
Lukács, Georg, The Theory of the Novel [1920], trans. by Anna Bostock (London: Merlin
      Press, 1971)
Lukács, Georg, 'Narrate or Describe?' [1936] in Writer and Critic, trans. by Arthur Kahn
      (London: Merlin Press, 1978), pp. 110–48
Lukács, Georg, 'Realism in the balance' [1938] trans. by Rodney Livingstone, in Aesthetics
      and Politics, by Ernst Bloch, Georg Lukács, Bertolt Brecht, Walter Benjamin, Theodor
      Adorno (London/Brooklyn, New York: Verso, 1980 [1977]), pp. 28–59
Lukács, Georg, Studies in European Realism, trans. by Edith Bone (London: Merlin Press,
      1989 [1950])
Lumbroso, Olivier, Zola, la plume et le compas: la construction de l'espace dans Les Rougon-
      Macquart d'Émile Zola (Paris: Champion, 2004)
Macherey, Pierre, Pour une théorie de la production littéraire (Paris: François Maspero, 1974
      [1966])
Makdisi, Saree, Romantic Imperialism: Universal Empire and the Culture of Modernity
      (Cambridge: Cambridge University Press, 1998)
Malchow, Howard L., Gothic Images of Race in Nineteenth-Century Britain (Redwood, CA:
      Stanford University Press, 1996)
Manet, Édouard, Lettres de jeunesse, 1848–1849: Voyage à Rio (Paris: Louis Rouart, 1928)
Marchetti, Adriano, 'La tentazione esotica nel romanzo filosofico di Alphonse Daudet',
      Questione Romantica: Rivista Interdisciplinare di Studi Romantici, 12–13 (2002),
      129–40
Marin, Mihaela, Le Livre enterré: Zola et la hantise de l'archaïque (Grenoble: ELLUG, 2007)
Martin, Morag, Selling Beauty: Cosmetics, Commerce, and French Society, 1750–1830
      (Baltimore, MD: Johns Hopkins University Press, 2009)
Martin-Fugier, Anne, La Place des bonnes: la domesticité féminine à Paris en 1900 (Paris:
      Grasset, 1979)
Marx, Karl, Capital: A Critique of Political Economy, trans. by Ben Fowkes, 3 vols (London:
      Penguin, 1990 [1976]), vol. 1
Mayer-Robin, Carmen, 'Justice, Zola's Global Utopian Gospel', Nineteenth-Century French
      Studies, 36:1–2 (2007), 135–49

McClintock, Anne, *Imperial Leather: Race, Gender and Sexuality in the Colonial Context* (New York/London: Routledge, 1995)

McCracken, Scott, 'Cousin Bette: Balzac and the Historiography of Difference', *Essays and Studies*, 44 (1991), 88–104

McDonald, Christie and Suleiman, Susan Rubin, *French Global: A New Approach to Literary History* (New York: Columbia University Press, 2010)

McQueen, Andrew, 'The Wild Child in Zola's *L'Argent*', *Excavatio*, 12 (1999), 53–9

Memmi, Albert, *Portrait du colonisé précédé de Portrait du colonisateur* (Paris: Gallimard, 1985 [1957])

Ménard, Sophie, *Émile Zola et les aveux du corps: les savoirs du roman naturaliste* (Paris: Garnier, 2014)

Meyer, Jean et al., *Histoire de la France coloniale. I: La Conquête, des origines à 1870* (Paris: Armand Colin, 1991)

Meyer, Susan, *Imperialism at Home: Race and Victorian Women's Fiction* (Ithaca, NY: Cornell University Press, 1996)

Meynier, Gilbert and Thobie, Jacques, *Histoire de la France coloniale. II: L'Apogée, 1871–1931* (Paris: Armand Colin, 1991)

Michel, Pierre, *Un mythe romantique: Les Barbares 1789–1848* (Lyon: Presses Universitaires de Lyon, 1981)

Miller, Christopher L. *Blank Darkness: Africanist Discourse in French* (Chicago, IL: University of Chicago Press, 1985)

Miller, Christopher L., *The French Atlantic Triangle: Literature and Culture of the Slave Trade* (Durham, NC: Duke University Press, 2008)

Mitterand, Henri, 'Pour une poétique de l'espace romanesque: l'exemple de Zola', in *Zola and the Craft of Fiction*, ed. by Robert Lethbridge and Terry Keefe (Leicester: Leicester University Press, 1990), pp. 80–8

Mitterand, Henri, *L'Illusion réaliste de Balzac à Aragon* (Paris: Presses Universitaires de France, 1994)

Moore, David Chioni, 'Ousmane Sembène, *Les Bouts de bois de dieu* and the Question of Literary Realism—African, European or Otherwise', *Genre*, 28 (1995), 67–94

Moore, Grace, 'Colonialism in Victorian Fiction: Recent Studies', *Dickens Studies Annual: Essays on Victorian Fiction*, 37 (2006), 251–86

Moore-Gilbert, Bart, 'Beyond Orientalism? Culture, Imperialism and Humanism', *Wasafiri*, 23 (1996), 8–13

Moretti, Franco, *Atlas of the European Novel 1800–1900* (London: Verso, 1998 [1997])

Moretti, Franco, 'Conjectures on World Literature', in *Debating World Literature*, ed. by Christopher Prendergast (London: Verso, 2004), pp. 148–62

Moretti, Franco *Graphs, Maps, Trees: Abstract Models for a Literary History* (London: Verso, 2005)

Morris, Pam, *Realism* (London/New York: Routledge 'New Critical Idiom', 2003)

Morrison, Toni, *Playing in the Dark: Whiteness and the Literary Imagination* (New York: Vintage, 1993 [1992])

Morton, Timothy, 'Blood Sugar' in *Romanticism and Colonialism: Writing and Empire, 1780–1830*, ed. by Tim Fulford and Peter J. Kitson (Cambridge, Cambridge University Press, 1998), pp. 87–106

Mossman, Carol, 'Sotto voce-Opera in the Novel: The Case of *Le Père Goriot*', *The French Review*, 69:3 (1996), 387–93

Moura, Jean-Marc, *La Littérature des lointains: histoire de l'exotisme européen au XXᵉ siècle* (Paris: Champion, 1998)

Moura, Jean-Marc, 'Littérature coloniale et exotisme: examen d'une opposition de la théorie littéraire coloniale', in *Regards sur les littératures coloniales, t. 1, Afrique franco-phone: découvertes*, ed. by Jean-François Durand (Paris: L'Harmattan, 2000), pp. 21–39

Mourad, François-Marie, ' *Thérèse Raquin*, roman expérimental', *Les Cahiers naturalistes*, 84 (2010), 157–64

Mouralis, Bernard, *Les Contre-Littératures* (Paris: Presses Universitaires de France, 1975)

Mouralis, Bernard, 'L'Afrique comme figure de la folie', *Cahiers CRLH-CIRAOI*, 5 (1988), 45–59

Mozet, Nicole, *La Ville de province dans l'œuvre de Balzac. L'espace romanesque: fantasme et idéologie* (Paris: SEDES, 1982)

Mozet, Nicole, 'Yvetot vaut Constantinople. Littérature et géographie en France au XIXème siècle', *Romantisme*, 35 (1982), 91–114

Mozet, Nicole, *Balzac au pluriel* (Paris: Presses Universitaires de France, 1990)

Mozet, Nicole, 'De sel et d'or: *Eugénie Grandet*, une histoire sans Histoire', in *Corps/décors: Femmes, orgie, parodie*, ed. by Catherine Nesci (Amsterdam: Rodopi, 1999), pp. 203–20

Naturel, Mireille, 'Proust et Flaubert: réalité coloniale et phantasmes d'Orient', *Bulletin Marcel Proust*, 49 (1999), 55–69

Neefs, Jacques, 'Le Parcours du zaïmph', in *La Production du sens chez Flaubert*, ed. by Claudine Gothot-Mersch (Paris: Union générale des éditions, 1975), pp. 227–42

Nelson, Brian, 'Energy and Order in Zola's *L'Argent*', *Australian Journal of French Studies*, 17:3 (1980), 275–300

Nelson, Brian, 'Zola's Ideology: The Road to Utopia', in *Critical Essays on Emile Zola*, ed. by David Baguley (Boston, MA: G.K. Hall and Co., 1986), pp. 161–72

Nesbitt, Nick, 'The Idea of 1804', *Yale French Studies*, 107 (2005, 'The Haiti Issue'), 6–38

Nesci, Catherine, '"Le Succube" ou l'itinéraire de Tours en Orient: Essai sur les lieux du poétique balzacien', *L'Année balzacienne*, 5 (1985), 263–95

Nochlin, Linda, *The Politics of Vision: Essays on Nineteenth-Century Art and Society* (London: Thames & Hudson, 1991 [1989])

Nye, Robert, *Crime, Madness, and Politics in Modern France: the Medical Concept of National Decline* (Princeton, NJ: Princeton University Press, 1984)

O'Connell, David, 'The Black Hero in French Romantic Fiction', *Studies in Romanticism*, 12:2 (1973), 516–29

O'Gorman, Francis, *Victorian Literature and Finance* (Oxford: Oxford University Press, 2007)

O'Grady, Lorraine, 'Olympia's Maid: Reclaiming Black Female Subjectivity', in *The Feminism and Visual Culture Reader*, ed. by Amelia Jones (London: Routledge, 2003), pp. 174–87

Olds, Marshall C., 'Globalisation and "la pièce de cent sous": Balzac's nation-state', in *Currencies: Fiscal Fortunes and Cultural Capital in Nineteenth-Century France*, ed. by Sarah Capitanio, Lisa Downing, Paul Rowe, and Nicholas White (Bern: Peter Lang, 2005), pp. 175–91

Parry, Benita, *Postcolonial Studies: A Materialist Critique* (London/New York: Routledge, 2004)

Parry, Benita, 'Aspects of Peripheral Modernisms', *Ariel: A Review of International English Literature*, 40:1 (2009), 27–55

Patke, Rajeev S., *Modernist Literature and Postcolonial Studies* (Edinburgh: Edinburgh University Press, 2013)

Patterson, Orlando, *Slavery and Social Death: A Comparative Study* (Cambridge, MA: Harvard University Press, 1982)

Pelletier, Jacques, 'Le Peuple-femme: La "Marque fatale du sexe"', *Études Françaises*, 39:2 (2003), 47–61

Perec, Georges, 'Pour une littérature réaliste' [1962], in Georges Perec, *L.G.: Une aventure des années soixante* (Paris: Seuil, 1992), pp. 47–66

Perrottet, Samuel, 'Souvenirs d'un voyage autour du monde: Île de Java' *Revue des Deux Mondes* (October–November 1830), 21–56

Pétré-Grenouilleau, Olivier, *Les Traites négrières: essai d'histoire globale* (Paris: Gallimard, 2004)

Petrey, Sandy, *In the Court of the Pear King: French Culture and the Rise of Realism* (Ithaca, NY: Cornell University Press, 2005)

Pick, Daniel, *Faces of Degeneration: A European Disorder, c.1848–c.1918* (Cambridge: Cambridge University Press, 1989)

Pinson, Guillaume, *L'Imaginaire médiatique: histoire et fiction du journal au XIXe siècle* (Paris: Garnier, 2012)

Poliakov, Léon, *Le Mythe aryen: essai sur les sources du racisme et des nationalismes* (Brussels: Éditions complexe, 1987 [1971])

Pollock, Griselda, *Differencing the Canon: Feminist Desire and the Writing of Art's Histories* (London: Routledge, 1999)

Pommier, Jean and Digeon, Claude, 'Du nouveau sur Flaubert et son œuvre', *Mercure de France*, 315 (1952), 37–55

Porter, Dennis, '*Orientalism* and its Problems', in *The Politics of Theory*, ed. by Francis Barker (Colchester: University of Essex Press, 1983), pp. 179–93

Prasad, Pratima, *Colonialism, Race, and the French Romantic Imagination* (London/New York: Routledge, 2009)

Praz, Mario, *The Romantic Agony*, trans. by Angus Davidson (Oxford: Oxford University Press, 1970 [1933])

Prendergast, Christopher, *Balzac: Fiction and Melodrama* (Edward Arnold, 1978)

Prendergast, Christopher, *The Order of Mimesis: Balzac, Stendhal, Nerval, Flaubert* (Cambridge: Cambridge University Press, 1986)

Prendergast, Christopher, 'Le Panorama, la peinture et la faim: Le Début du *Ventre de Paris*', *Les Cahiers naturalistes*, 67 (1993), 65–71

Prendergast, Christopher, *Paris and the Nineteenth Century* (Oxford: Blackwell, 1995 [1992])

Prince, Gerald, 'Introduction à l'etude du narrataire', *Poétique*, 14 (1973), 178–96

Prince, Gerald, '*Bel-Ami* and Narrative as Antagonist', *French Forum*, 11:2 (1986), 217–26

Proust, Marcel, *Pastiches*, in *Contre Sainte-Beuve précédé de Pastiches et mélanges et suivi de Essais et articles*, ed. by Pierre Clarac (Paris: Gallimard 'Pléiade', 1971), pp. 5–59

Raimond, Michel, 'Le corps féminin dans *L'Éducation sentimentale*', in *Flaubert, la femme, la ville*, ed. by Marie-Claire Bancquart (Paris: Presses Universitaires de France, 1983), pp. 23–31

Raitt, Alan, 'La Décomposition des personnages dans *L'Éducation sentimentale*', in *Flaubert, la dimension du texte*, ed. by P.M.Wetherill (Manchester: Manchester University Press, 1982), pp. 157–74

Reed, Arden, *Manet, Flaubert, and the Emergence of Modernism: Blurring Genre Boundaries* (Cambridge: Cambridge University Press, 2003)

Reff, Theodore, 'Manet's Portrait of Zola', *The Burlington Magazine*, 117 (1975), 35–44

Reff, Theodore, *Manet: Olympia* (London, Penguin: 1976)

Reffait, Christophe, *La Bourse dans le roman du second XIXe siècle: discours romanesque et imaginaire social de la spéculation* (Paris: Champion, 2007)

Reverzy, Éléonore, *La Chair de l'idée: poétique de l'allégorie dans Les Rougon-Macquart* (Geneva: Droz, 2007)

Reynaud-Paligot, Carole, *La République raciale: paradigme racial et idéologie républicaine 1860–1930* (Paris: Presses Universitaires de France, 2006)

Richard, Jean-Pierre, *Littérature et sensation* (Paris: Seuil, 1954)

Richard, Jean-Pierre, *Études sur le romantisme* (Paris: Seuil, 1970)

Ripoll, Roger, *Réalité et mythe chez Zola* (Paris: Champion, 1981)

Rivet, Daniel, *Le Maghreb à l'épreuve de la colonisation* (Paris: Hachette, 2002)

Robb, Graham, *Balzac: A Biography* (London: Picador, 1994)

Robbe-Grillet, Alain, *Pour un nouveau roman* (Paris: Minuit, 1963)

Robbins, Bruce, *The Servant's Hand: English Fiction from Below* (NY: Columbia University Press, 1986)

Robbins, Bruce, 'Modernism and Literary Realism: Response', in *Realism and Representation: Essays on the Problem of Realism in Relation to Science, Literature and Culture*, ed. by George Levine (Madison, WI: Wisconsin University Press, 1993), pp. 225–31

Ronai, Paul, 'Tuer le mandarin', *Revue de littérature comparée*, 10 (1930), 520–3

Rudich, L. and N., 'Eugénie Grandet, martyre du capitalisme', *Revue de l'institut de sociologie*, 3–4 (1973), 651–69

Ruscio, Alain, 'Littérature, Chansons et colonies', in *Culture coloniale: la France conquise par son Empire*, ed. by Pascal Blanchard and Sandrine Lemaire (Paris: Autrement, 2003), pp. 67–80

Sachs, Murray, *The Career of Alphonse Daudet: A Critical Study* (Cambridge, MA: Harvard University Press, 1965)

Said, Edward, *Orientalism: Western Conceptions of the Orient* (London: Penguin, 1991 [1978])

Said, Edward, *Culture and Imperialism* (London: Chatto & Windus, 1993)

Saisselin, Rémy G., *The Bourgeois and the Bibelot* (New Brunswick, NJ: Rutgers University Press, 1985)

Salinas, Michèle, ed., *Guy de Maupassant, Lettres d'Afrique (Algérie, Tunisie)* (Paris: La Boîte à documents, 1990)

Saminadayar-Perrin, Corinne, 'Antiquité des races et naissance des nations: modèles scientifiques et logiques discursives', in *L'Idée de 'race' dans les sciences humaines et la littérature (XVIIIᵉ et XIXᵉ siècles)*, ed. by Sarga Moussa (Paris: L'Harmattan, 2003), pp. 385–407

Saminadayar-Perrin, Corinne, 'Fictions de la Bourse', *Les Cahiers naturalistes*, 78 (2004), 41–62

Saminadayar-Perrin, Corinne, ' D'impossibles nouveaux mondes: Zola, *L'Argent / Fécondité*', *Cahiers naturalistes*, 88 (2014), 27–44

Sartre, Jean-Paul, *Qu'est-ce que la littérature?* (Paris: Gallimard, 1948)

Sartre, Jean-Paul, 'Le colonialisme est un système' [1956], in Jean-Paul Sartre, *Situations, V, Colonialisme et néo-colonialisme* (Paris: Gallimard, 1964), pp. 25–48

Schapira, Marie-Claude, 'Guy de Maupassant en Algérie: critique du fait colonial et portrait du colonisé', in *L'Idée de 'race' dans les sciences humaines et la littérature (XVIIIe et XIXe siècles)*, ed. by Sarga Moussa (Paris: L'Harmattan, 2003), pp. 329–41

Schehr, Lawrence, '*Salammbô* as the Novel of Alterity', *Nineteenth-Century French Studies*, 17:3–4 (1989), 326–41

Schehr, Lawrence R., *Figures of Alterity: French Realism and its Others* (Redwood, CA: Stanford University Press, 2003)

Schehr, Lawrence R., *Subversions of Verisimilitude: Reading Narrative from Balzac to Sartre* (New York: Fordham University Press, 2009)

Schor, Naomi, 'Le Sourire du sphinx: Zola et l'énigme de la féminité', *Romantisme*, 6 (1976), 183–96

Schor, Naomi, *Zola's Crowds* (Baltimore, MD: Johns Hopkins University Press, 1978)

Schor, Naomi, *Breaking the Chain: Women, Theory, and French Realist Fiction* (New York: Columbia University Press, 1985)

Schor, Naomi, 'Fetishism and its Ironies', *Nineteenth-Century French Studies*, 17 (1988–9), 89–97

Schor, Naomi, *Reading in Detail: Aesthetics and the Feminine* (London/New York: Routledge, 2007)

Schuerewegen, Franc, *Balzac contre Balzac: les cartes du lecteur* (Toronto: Paratexte, 1990)

Schwab, Raymond, *La Renaissance orientale* (Paris: Payot, 1950)

Sedgwick, Eve Kosofsky, *Between Men: English Literature and Male Homosocial Desire* (New York: Columbia University Press, 1985)

Segalen, Victor, *Essai sur l'exotisme*, in *Œuvres complètes*, ed. by Henry Bouillier, 2 vols (Paris: Robert Laffont, 1995), vol. 1, pp. 745–81

Séginger, Gisèle, 'La Tunisie dans l'imaginaire politique de Flaubert', *Nineteenth-Century French Studies*, 32:1–2 (2003–4), 41–57

Seillan, Jean-Marie, 'L'Afrique utopique de *Fécondité*', *Les Cahiers naturalistes*, 75, (2001), 183–202

Seillan, Jean-Marie, *Aux sources du roman colonial: L'Afrique à la fin du XIXᵉ siècle* (Paris: Karthala, 2006)

Seillan, Jean-Marie, 'La (para)littérature (pré)coloniale à la fin du XIXᵉ siècle', *Romantisme*, 139 (2008), 33–45

Seillan, Jean-Marie, 'Littératures coloniales et contraintes génériques', *Les Cahiers de la S.I.E.L.E.C.*, 6 (2010), 28–50

Seillan, Jean-Marie, 'Zola et le fait colonial', *Cahiers naturalistes*, 88 (2014), 13–26

Sessions, Jennifer, *By Sword and Plough: France and the Conquest of Algeria* (Ithaca, NY: Cornell University Press, 2011)

Sharafuddin, Mohammed, *Islam and Romantic Orientalism: Literary Encounters with the Orient* (London: Tauris, 1994)

Sharpley-Whiting, Tracy Denean, *Black Venus: Sexualized Savages, Primal Fears, and Primitive Narratives in French* (Durham, NC: Duke University Press, 1999)

Sherrington, R.J., *Three Novels by Flaubert: A Study of Techniques* (Oxford: Clarendon Press, 1970)

Shideler, Ross, *Questioning the Father: From Darwin to Zola, Ibsen, Strindberg, and Hardy* (Redwood, CA: Stanford University Press, 1999)

Silvestre de Sacy, Samuel, 'Balzac et le mythe de l'aventurier', *Mercure de France* (1 January 1950), 115–28

Simpson, Murray K., 'From Savage to Citizen: Education, Colonialism, and Idiocy', *British Journal of Sociology of Education*, 28:5 (2007), 561–74

Slemon, Stephen, 'Modernism's last post', in *Past the Last Post: Theorizing Post-Colonialism and Post-Modernism*, ed. by Ian Adam and Helen Tiffin (New York/London, Harvester and Wheatsheaf, 1991), pp. 1–11

Smethurst, Colin, 'De Java à Kiew: Le moi du voyageur', *L'Année balzacienne*, 3 (2002), 269–78

Smith, Diane, 'The Evolution of the Working Class Novel in Europe: Darwinian Science and Literary Naturalism', *Excavatio*, 8 (1996), 72–85

Sorensen, Eli Park, *Postcolonial Studies and the Literary: Theory, Interpretation and the Novel* (Basingstoke/New York: Palgrave Macmillan, 2010)

Sorlin, Pierre, *L'Art sans règles: Manet contre Flaubert* (Paris: Presses Universitaires de Vincennes, 1995)

Soubias, Pierre, 'La Place de l'Afrique dans l'imaginaire de Maupassant: Une Lecture des nouvelles africaines', in *Maupassant multiple*, ed. by Yves Reboul (Toulouse: Presses Universitaires du Mirail, 1995), pp. 29–39

Spivak, Gayatri Chakravorty, 'Three Women's Texts and a Critique of Imperialism' [1985], reprinted in *'Race', Writing, and Difference*, ed. by Henry Louis Gates, Jr (Chicago, IL: University of Chicago Press, 1986), pp. 262–80

Spivak, Gayatri Chakravorty, 'Can the subaltern speak?', in *Marxism and the Interpretation of Culture*, ed. by Cary Nelson and Lawrence Grossberg (Chicago, IL: University of Illinois Press, 1988), pp. 271–313

Steins, Martin, 'L'épisode africain de *Fécondité*', *Les Cahiers naturalistes*, 48 (1974), 164–81

Steins, Martin, 'Zola colonialiste', *Revue des langues vivantes*, 41:1 (1975), 15–30

Stoler, Ann Laura, *Race and the Education of Desire: Foucault's 'History of Sexuality' and the Colonial Order of Things* (Durham, NC: Duke University Press, 1995)

Stoler, Ann Laura, 'State Racism and the Education of Desires: A Colonial Reading of Foucault', in *Deep HiStories: Gender and Colonialism in Southern Africa*, ed. by Wendy Woodward, Patricia Hayes, and Gary Minkley (Amsterdam: Rodopi, 2002), pp. 3–26

Suleri, Sara, *The Rhetoric of English India* (Chicago, IL: University of Chicago Press, 1992)

Sullivan, Antony Thrall, *Thomas-Robert Bugeaud, France and Algeria, 1784–1849: Politics, Power, and the Good Society* (Hamden, CT: Archon Books, 1983)

Tadiar, Neferti Xina M., 'The Dream-Work of Modernity: The Sentimental Education of Imperial France', *boundary 2*, 22:1 (1995), 143–83

Tallis, Raymond, *In Defence of Realism* (London: Edward Arnold, 1988)

Tarde, Gabriel, *La Criminalité comparée*, 2nd edition (Paris: Félix Alcan, 1890 [1886])

Terdiman, Richard, *Discourse/Counter-Discourse: The Theory and Practice of Symbolic Resistance in Nineteenth-Century France* (Ithaca, NY: Cornell University Press, 1985)

Thompson, C.W., *French Romantic Travel Writing: Chateaubriand to Nerval* (Oxford: Oxford University Press, 2012)

Todorov, Tzvetan, *Introduction à la littérature fantastique* (Paris: Seuil, 1970)

Todorov, Tzvetan, *Poétique de la prose, suivi de Nouvelles recherches sur le récit* (Paris: Seuil [1971], 1978)

Todorov, Tzvetan, *Nous et les autres: La réflexion française sur la diversité humaine* (Paris: Seuil, 1989)

Tooke, Adrianne, 'Flaubert's travel writings', in *The Cambridge Companion to Flaubert*, ed. by Timothy Unwin (Cambridge: Cambridge University Press, 2004), pp. 51–66

Trotter, David, 'Modernity and Its Discontents: Manet, Flaubert, Cézanne, Zola', *Paragraph: A Journal of Modern Critical Theory*, 19:3 (1996), 251–71

Trouillot, Michel-Rolph, *Silencing the Past: Power and the Production of History* (Boston, MA: Beacon Press, 1995)

Unwin, Timothy, *Textes réfléchissants: réalisme et réflexivité au dix-neuvième siècle* (Bern: Peter Lang, 2000)

Vanoncini, André, 'Le sauvage dans "La Comédie humaine"', *L'Année balzacienne*, 1 (2000), 231–47

Vanoncini, André, 'Le Pacte: Structures et évolutions d'un motif balzacien', *L'Année balzacienne*, 3 (2002), 279–92

Vial, André, 'Flaubert émule et disciple émancipé de Balzac', *Revue d'Histoire littéraire de la France*, 48:3 (1948), 233–63

Vial, André, *Guy de Maupassant et l'art du roman* (Paris: Nizet, 1954)

Watt, Ian, *The Rise of the Novel: Studies in Defoe, Richardson and Fielding* (London: Pimlico, 2000 [1957])

Watts, Andrew, *Preserving the Provinces: Small Town and Countryside in the Work of Honoré de Balzac* (Bern: Peter Lang, 2007)

Weber, Jacques, ed., *Littérature et histoire coloniale: Actes du colloque de Nantes, 6 décembre 2003* (Paris: Les Indes savantes, 2005)

Wetherill, Peter M., 'L'Histoire dans le texte', *Zeitschrift für Französische Sprache und Literatur*, 95:2 (1985), 163–74

Wettlaufer, Alexandra K., 'Metaphors of Power and the Power of Metaphor: Zola, Manet and the Art of Portraiture', *Nineteenth-Century Contexts*, 21:3 (1999), 437–63

Whelpton, R. Anthony, 'L'Atmosphère étrangère de *Modeste Mignon*', *L'Année balzacienne* (1967), 373–5

White, Hayden, 'The Forms of Wildness: Archaeology of an Idea', in *The Wild Man Within: An Image in Western Thought from the Renaissance to Romanticism*, ed. by Edward Dudley and Maximillian E. Novak (Pittsburgh, PA: University of Pittsburgh Press, 1972), pp. 3–38

White, Hayden, 'The Noble Savage Theme as Fetish', in *First Images of America: The Impact of the New World on the Old*, ed. by Fredi Chiappelli, 2 vols (Berkeley, CA: University of California Press, 1976), vol. 1, pp. 121–35

Wilde, Oscar, 'The Decay of Lying' [1891], in Oscar Wilde, *De Profundis and Other Writings* (London: Penguin, 1987), pp. 57–87

Williams, D.A., 'Sacred and Profane in "L'Education sentimentale"', *The Modern Language Review*, 73:4 (1978), 786–98

Williams, D.A., *The Hidden Life at its Source: A Study of Flaubert's* L'Éducation sentimentale (Hull: Hull University Press, 1987)

Williams, Patrick, '"Simultaneous uncontemporaneities": theorising modernism and empire', in *Modernism and Empire*, ed. by Howard J. Booth and Nigel Rigby (Manchester: Manchester University Press, 2000), pp. 13–38

Williams, Raymond, *The Long Revolution* (London: Chatto & Windus, 1961)

Woestelandt, Evelyne, 'Système de la mode dans *L'Éducation sentimentale*', *The French Review*, 58:2 (1984), 244–54

Woollen, Geoff, 'Le darwinisme chez Zola: réflexe ou réflexion?', *Cahiers de l'U.E.R. Froissart*, 5 (1980), 27–36

Woollen, Geoff, 'Des brutes humaines dans *La Bête humaine*', in *Zola: La Bête humaine: Colloque du centenaire à Glasgow*, ed. by Geoff Woollen (Glasgow: Glasgow University Press, 1990), pp. 149–75

Woollen, Geoff, 'Les transportés dans l'œuvre de Zola', *Les Cahiers naturalistes*, 72 (1998), 317–33

WReC (Warwick Research Collective), *Combined and Uneven Development: Towards a New Theory of World-Literature* (Liverpool: Liverpool University Press, 2015)

Wrona, Adeline, 'Mots à crédit: *L'Argent* de Zola, ou la presse au cœur du marché de la confiance', *Romantisme*, 151 (2011), 67–79

Yates, Susan, *Maid and Mistress: Feminine Solidarity and Class Difference in Five Nineteenth-Century French Texts* (Bern: Peter Lang, 1991)

Yee, Jennifer, 'Neither Flesh Nor Fowl: "Métissage" in fin-de-siècle French Colonial Fiction', *L'Esprit créateur*, 37:1 (1998), 46–56

Yee, Jennifer, *Clichés de la femme exotique: un regard sur la littérature coloniale française entre 1871 et 1914* (Paris: L'Harmattan, 2000)

242   *Bibliography*

Yee, Jennifer, 'Malaria and the Femme Fatale: Sex and Death in French Colonial Africa', *Literature and Medicine*, 21:2 (2002), 201–15

Yee, Jennifer, 'Undermining Exoticism: Flaubert's use of antithesis in *L'Éducation sentimentale*', *Dix-Neuf*, 15:1 (2011), 26–36

Yee, Jennifer, ' "Like an apparition": Oriental ghosting in Flaubert's *Éducation sentimentale*', *French Studies*, 67:3 (2013), 340–54

Young, Robert J.C., *Colonial Desire: Hybridity in Theory, Culture and Race* (London/New York: Routledge, 1995)

Young, Robert J.C., *Postcolonialism: An Historical Introduction* (Oxford: Blackwell, 2001)

Zürcher, Erik J., *Turkey: A Modern History* (London/New York: I.B. Tauris, 1993)

Index